MANAGING PEOPLE AT WORK

Julian Randall and Allan J. Sim

LONDON AND NEW YORK

First published 2014
by Routledge
2 Park Square, Milton Park, Abingdon, Oxon OX14 4RN

and by Routledge
711 Third Avenue, New York, NY 10017

Routledge is an imprint of the Taylor & Francis Group, an informa business

British Library Cataloguing in Publication Data
A catalogue record for this book is available from the British Library

Library of Congress Cataloging in Publication Data
Randall, Julian
Managing people at work / Julian Randall and Allan Sim.
pages cm
Includes bibliographical references and index.
1. Personnel management. I. Sim, Allan. II. Title.
HF5549.R334 2013
658.3–dc23
2013016392

ISBN: 978-0-415-53438-3 (hbk)
ISBN: 978-0-415-53439-0 (pbk)
ISBN: 978-1-315-88326-7 (ebk)

Typeset in Bembo
by GreenGate Publishing Services, Tonbridge, Kent

MIX
Paper from
responsible sources
FSC
www.fsc.org   FSC® C013056

Printed and bound in Great Britain by
TJ International Ltd, Padstow, Cornwall

To all our past students whose enthusiasm and commitment over our years of teaching them have kept alive our interest in developing the subject and inspired this text. To all our future students who we hope will continue to kindle the flame of learning.

MANAGING PEOPLE AT WORK

This book arises from the need of students who have little or no threshold knowledge of human resource management (HRM) but who need to link it to their studies in other subjects. *Managing People at Work* encourages readers to examine the underlying concepts that reach out beyond discrete disciplinary boundaries and require connection with theories from different disciplines and their common practice wherever it applies to people within a company. The book also addresses the need to understand and contribute to the strategic discussions that are expected in senior management forums.

The book describes the links between company strategy, human resource (HR) planning and implementation using cost–benefit analysis to illustrate the hard and soft approaches to HRM. It also looks at evaluating the results of HR in terms of both efficiency and effectiveness in the main management interventions that lie within the human resource development activities. Students are aided with their understanding by activities that lie at the end of each chapter. These exercises can be done individually or in tutor-led groups.

This book makes clear the links between HRM, organizational behaviour and strategy, and the theory of HRM is linked to its claimed HR outcomes, sometimes referred to as:

- strategic integration
- commitment
- quality
- flexibility.

This book helps to provide MBA and Masters postgraduate students and those on management trainee programmes to accelerated promotion career paths with a more detailed understanding of these theories and how they drive the organization's strategy and decisions about its people at work.

Julian Randall is Senior Lecturer at the University of Aberdeen Business School. He began his career as a graduate management trainee at GEC, eventually setting up his own management consultancy company. He completed his MSc (HRM) at the University of Stirling and his PhD in Perceptions of the Management of Change at the University of St Andrews. He currently teaches Managing Consultancy and Change and Managing People at Work.

Allan J. Sim is a graduate of the University of Aberdeen with an MA in Sociology and Social Anthropology and a PhD in Social Anthropology. He has worked in the oil industry, managed a bookstore and run his own research and training company. He is currently Senior Teaching Fellow at the University of Aberdeen Business School where he teaches on both undergrad   is co-author on developing gradual

CONTENTS

List of figures   *viii*
List of tables   *ix*
List of abbreviations   *x*

1 Introduction to HRM   1

2 Strategy and strategic integration   31

3 The business environment and human resource management   64

4 Human resource management in an organizational context   95

5 Managing change/changing managers   134

6 Employee resourcing   167

7 Developing your people   200

8 Performance management   242

9 Rewarding people at work   273

10 Employee relations: equality and diversity   309

11 Disciplinary, grievance and sick absence   339

12 IHRM, review, critique and developments   366

Index   *398*

FIGURES

1.1	The traditional bureaucratic layers	12
1.2	The Shamrock organization	17
1.3	Managing consultants	20
2.1	Outside-in (market-led) approach	32
2.2	Inside-out (resource-led) approach	34
2.3	The traditional bureaucratic layers	40
2.4	Managing consultants	52
2.5	Management cycle	58
3.1	Traditional bureaucratic layers and functions	71
3.2	Matrix organization and flexible teams	73
4.1	Force-field analysis	106
4.2	Managing consultants	118
5.1	Three levels of culture	135
5.2	Segments of the Shamrock organization	141
5.3	Steps in the Total Quality Management cycle	146
6.1	Growth in job demands in the first few months	169
7.1	Systematic training cycle	207
9.1	Elements in reward assessment	288
10.1	Learning cycle	329
10.2	Evaluational cycle	330
10.3	Management cycle	330
11.1	Segments of the Shamrock organization	355

TABLES

1.1	Overview of links in human resource management theory	6
1.2	Graduate attributes, University of Aberdeen	25
2.1	Overview of links in human resource management theory	32
3.1	Shift in occupational levels in the UK, 1951–1999	77
3.2	Shift in occupational levels in the UK, 2001–2011	77
4.1	Overview of links in human resource management theory	115
5.1	Overview of links in human resource management theory	140
5.2	Different test: validity and reliability	165
7.1	NVQ SVQ frameworks	205
7.2	Training evaluation levels	210
7.3	Behavioural terms	226
7.4	Correctly/incorrectly worded	227
7.5	Group and team characteristics	230
9.1	Skills self-assessment questionnaire	302
10.1	Trade union membership UK, 1990–2011	311
11.1	Overview of links in human resource management theory	354
12.1	Overview of links in human resource management theory	385

ABBREVIATIONS

ACAS	Advisory, Conciliation and Arbitration Service
BATNA	best alternative to a negotiated agreement
BPR	business process re-engineering
CIPD	Chartered Institute of Personnel Development
CPD	continuing professional development
DALD	Department of Agriculture: Learning and Development
DoA	Department of Agriculture
EI	employment involvement
HCN	home country national
HR	human resource
HRD	human resource development
HRM	human resource management
IiP	Investors in People
L&D	learning and development
MBWA	management by walking about
MNC	multinational company
NLP	neuro-linguistic programming
OD	organization development
PBR	Personal Bill of Rights
PCN	parent country national
PRP	performance related pay
PRP	profit related pay
SHRM	strategic human resource management
TCN	third country national
TQM	Total Quality Management
USP	unique selling proposition

1

INTRODUCTION TO HRM

Learning objectives

- from personnel to HRM
- human resource policies and organizational outcomes
- organizational change and human resource management
- knowledge work and the knowledge worker.

Introduction

For many younger workers the rise of human resource management (HRM) is something that they will not have lived through. We are referring to events that took place nearly 30 years ago. So, they may not have been around when personnel departments changed their name to human resources. Nor will they have been privy to discussions on hard or soft HRM as different approaches that HR departments might adopt. But that debate remains alive and there are researchers who have sought to test whether the claims made for HRM as a theory are supported by the evidence over those ensuing years or not. Organizational commitment, one of the outcomes by which the theory placed great store, has been influenced by many factors, not all of them positive. In this chapter we will look at some of the influences that may have made it difficult for HRM theory and practice to realize its promises.

It would be unfair to suggest that HRM is without precedent in its interest in gaining the commitment of workers. The early proponents of looking after all aspects of workers' lives can be found in the nineteenth century with examples such as the Rowntree Foundation, which built a dedicated town for its workers, Bourneville. Its founders believed that looking after workers was not only a religious duty, but also a benefit in that workers arrived at work well motivated, and therefore prepared to work for a company that took the trouble to look after them. For workers who were not in receipt of such benefits, the rights had to be more closely fought for through political action, and the rise of trade unions galvanised action into political initiatives to enshrine their employment rights into law.

After the First World War what would become the Institute of Personnel Management was set up specifically to address welfare at work for all workers. Looking after people seemed a more sensible personnel strategy than treating them as 'the hands' whose only purpose was to fulfil their working functions efficiently, as had been the philosophy at Ford through the work of F.W. Taylor. This movement to pay more attention to workers' motivation was reinforced by the findings of the Hawthorne experiments in which researchers found that when changes were made to the working conditions of factory workers, such as changes in heating and lighting, productivity went up as people responded to the concern shown for their welfare by members of the management (Mayo, 1933; Roethlisberger and Dickson, 1939; Gillespie, 1991).

Involving workers more proactively in changes to their working conditions was pioneered in the USA by Lewin (1947) after the Second World War. He advocated working with small groups of workers using sensitivity or T-groups in which individuals were encouraged to speak about their experiences of work and their feelings about their job. This first phase in his three-step approach he called 'unfreezing'. We could argue that this was an early example of emergent change in that what he attempted to achieve in this first phase encouraged workers to be frank about their beliefs and expectations of their jobs and allowed the change agent to hear at first hand what were taken-for-granted assumptions or beliefs that might be difficult for managers or change agents to challenge without generating resistance from the workforce. Following the second phase involving the change itself, Lewin saw the third phase as being 'refreezing' workers' attitudes and practices around the new work regime. His work was influential both at the time and later and it is no mischance that Argyris, Schein and McGregor, who were all early collaborators with Lewin in his work, went on to develop their own approaches to developing people in organizations through such change interventions.

In the UK the human relations movements in the 1950s pursued similar initiatives to involve workers in changing their working conditions or solving problems whose solutions were not immediately apparent to the organization or its managers. The solution might be much more obvious to the workers themselves (Trist and Bamforth, 1951). A sympathetic listener, facilitator or change agent might well uncover such solutions listening to the workers discussing the options they perceived for making effective changes. In a similar tradition, Action Learning found a very supportive and active proponent in Reg Revans (2011), whose work as Director of Education in the coal industry enabled him to develop the concept and share his experiences in getting workers more proactively involved in managing their own working environment, solving problems and implementing solutions to secure their jobs and the industry itself.

The personnel function

This interest in workers' welfare and their ideas found its focus in the work of the personnel department. Henry Ford is alleged to have said that all you needed was a girl and a filing cabinet, but most large companies included a dedicated team whose responsibilities might cover traditional personnel functions for all departments in their day-to-day dealings with individuals. One of the most important would be recruitment and selection procedures, dealing with job applications, sifting through applications, arranging interviews, drawing up job contracts and keeping up-to-date files on all individuals in the company. So, too, induction training might be part of the remit of the personnel department and there might be a dedicated training manager, particularly for the more general aspects of induction training in company policy, procedures and practices, and health and safety at work.

For many companies, too, the work of pay and pensions took up a significant amount of time and might similarly be delegated to the personnel department. Pay itself was often governed by annual incremental pay awards, so keeping abreast with promotions and taking part in union negotiations to secure pay differentials between grades could well be an important part of personnel's work.

In the public sector, there was a strong tradition of personnel as a counselling provider and mediator where misunderstandings occurring between individuals at work could be discussed and resolved. In this respect personnel could provide advice on personal or work concerns when they arose, though personnel were rarely involved with strategic decisions made by the senior managers. So, in that sense personnel's work was reactive to demands from requests for help and support from individuals inside the company, or to outside change affecting employment law and its implementation in company policy and procedures.

In this respect, however, there were significant changes in the legal constraints on employment in the 1970s with the Health and Safety at Work Act in 1974 and a series of acts intended to curb discrimination of all kinds in all workplaces. In the 1980s there was further legislation intended to curb militant union action and in all these respects personnel was responsible for ensuring the company's policy, procedure and practices were brought in line with current legislation and suitable training given to staff involved in applying that new legislation with their own staff.

The birth of Human Resource Management

Interest in more proactive approaches to managing people at work found a voice in a popular book entitled *In Search of Excellence* by Peters and Waterman (1982). They drew up eight factors that they saw as characterizing excellent companies:

1   a bias for action, active decision making – 'getting on with it'. Facilitating quick decision making and problem solving tends to avoid bureaucratic control;

2   being close to the customer – learning from the people served by the business;

3   autonomy and entrepreneurship – fostering innovation and nurturing 'champions';
4   productivity through people – treating rank and file employees as a source of quality;
5   being hands-on, value-driven – management philosophy that guides everyday practice – management showing its commitment;
6   sticking to the knitting – staying with the business that you know;
7   simple form, lean staff – some of the best companies have minimal HQ staff;
8   simultaneous loose–tight properties – autonomy in shop-floor activities plus centralized values.

It should be said that the context in which they wrote had more corporate organizations that might encompass many different businesses and the authors believed that this detracted from the single-minded approach needed to run a business successfully. At the time, the book triggered much debate among managers seeking to build up an excellent company. It also attracted attention from academics, who were on the whole more sceptical of the validity of the claims made by its authors. In the context of the time, however, Peters and Waterman did stimulate a significant debate among managers and, as proof of a more general interest in the issues they raised, the book sold more copies than any previous book on management. The fact that 75 per cent of companies they cited as being excellent went out of business within five years made no difference to those who wanted to improve their business effectiveness using the principles outlined.

Shortly after this came the advent of HRM, whose roots may be found in the Michigan model of HRM (Fombrun *et al.*, 1984).

Basically, the model shows how the *recruitment and selection* process leads into the *performance* that can be achieved and this performance is regularly *appraised* leading to *reward* and *development*. Thus, engaging staff in a more consistently linked career path feeds back to *continuing performance development* and *career opportunities*.

These links indicate that joined-up personnel should be a more dynamic and deliberate process that is managed to ensure that there is a constant review of the factors that can be traced between the people who work in the organization, their performance, the appraisal of their performance and the outcome in terms of reward and development – leading once more to enhanced performance. The review also includes reinforcing continuing development and drawing attention to the implications for the profile of people the business needs in the future.

In a sense what we see here is an attempt to connect the management interventions with individual workers to reinforce the links between what will become the stages of a human resource development (HRD) list which would include:

• recruitment and selection
• induction training
• supervision
• management

- review
- appraisal
- reward
- development
- structure
- communication.

Linking these in the way the Michigan model suggests makes sense because it becomes a virtuous circle that governs the working life of everyone working in the company. The best outcome is that *communication* then becomes the sum of all the experiences that people have with the company in the management interventions that have taken place in their working life from the time that they joined the company through to their leaving.

But HRM's proponents also extended their attention to different groups that lie outside the company. These aspects are laid out in the Harvard model of HRM (Beer *et al.*, 1984). In this example the *context* of the company, referred to by the authors as *situational influences* links with the *stakeholders* (includes shareholders but not just them exclusively) and these include the government, the unions and the local community. These together lead to what the authors describe as *HR policy factors* (going back to the content of the way in which people are managed). This in turn drives the *HR outcomes* which include commitment, competence, congruence and cost-effectiveness. This leads to *long-term consequences* for the individual, the organization and society. Once again these factors feed back into benefits for the *situational influences* and the *stakeholders*.

One of the important aspects of the second diagram is its focus on the external groups crucial to the company's planning. These are often external to the company – its *context* (what goes on outside it, which is not always either accessible or controllable by managers). This compares with its *content* (what goes on inside the company and therefore ought to be both more accessible and controllable by managers). HRM likes to be viewed as an approach to management that considers people 'as our most important resource'. This compares starkly to early models such as scientific managerialism in which workers were sometimes referred to as 'the hands' (Taylor, 1911). Their only contribution was to work at their tasks but they were never consulted about their working conditions or the strategic direction of the company in the future. By way of contrast, critical to the theory of HRM is the individual worker internalizing the company's objectives – something referred to as *strategic integration*. That being the case, it is important to communicate well with employees, involve them in what is going on in the company's plans in order to foster their *commitment* to and engagement with the organization. In fact, *organizational commitment* is central to the four HR outcomes that HRM theory supported. So, a strategic approach to the acquisition, management and motivation of people is heavily emphasised in the early writing of the proponents of HRM.

Testing the theory

Not everyone agreed that the outcomes suggested by HRM theorists were as easy to achieve as was suggested by the original writers. Indeed, in 1992 an edited volume was published by Blyton and Turnbull entitled *Reassessing Human Resource Management*. In it, Noon, for example, asks whether HRM is a theory, a model or a map. In other words, does HRM theory connect in practice in the ways suggested by its proponents or not? David Guest offers a diagram in the volume (p. 21) which his subsequent research sought to test out in organizations with which he worked.

The left-hand column in Table 1.1 is a summary of factors that appear on the HRD list. Getting those right should link with the HR outcomes listed in the second column, with the final column offering the outcomes that ought to be apparent in the organization. We will consider their implications in the context of HRM theory:

Strategic integration

This HR outcome is focused on the plan that the organization or company has defined as its business targets. In one sense there is nothing new here in that the steps for bringing organizational objectives down to the functional end of the business have been part of management practice for a long time and are therefore well established in management theory and practice. Drucker (1954) suggested three levels that needed to be linked:

- organizational objectives (which need to be broken down into)
- departmental goals (which in turn need to be broken down into)
- individual key tasks.

TABLE 1.1 Overview of links in human resource management theory

HRM policies	Human resource outcomes	Organizational outcomes
Organization objectives Management of change	Strategic integration	High problem solving/change
Recruitment/selection/ socialization	Commitment	Innovation and creativity
Appraisal, training and development	Flexibility/adaptability	High cost-effectiveness
Communication of standards and targets	Quality	Fewer customer complaints Low turnover/absence/ grievance

Source: Adapted from Guest (1989) in Blyton and Turnbull (1992: 21).

So, a target to increase the company's profitability by 5 per cent would need to be split up into different departmental goals. Sales would need different targets than production, for example, as the contribution of sales to the bottom line of the company depends on the margins achieved on different products. Production targets would need to be reset to allow for less to be sold than is held in stock. Finally, sales targets for individual salespeople will vary according to the potential of the sales territories and the aptitude of the individual salespeople who work in them.

But there is something more than that involved with *strategic integration* in the context of HRM: while traditional firms would have changed the sales targets of individual salespeople, they might not have made them aware of the margins on products and services and their contribution to company profit. That in-depth knowledge is now a prerequisite of *strategic integration*. Failure to inform individuals of their role in achieving the organizational objectives would be to diminish their ability to make the decisions necessary to achieve those targets.

Commitment

This leads us to the second intended outcome of good HRM practice which is *organizational commitment*. In simple terms: workers should be so committed to the company that they would not seek to work anywhere else. It is worth noting here that commitment as a concept can be considered at different levels:

- *job* commitment (which it is suggested is formed between four and 11 months into a job);
- *work* commitment (an interest beyond the job – encouraged by job or work rotation);
- *career* commitment (associated with professional qualifications or apprenticeships – where leaving can be costly to the individual in many respects);
- *organizational* commitment (that final belief that there is a job for life in the organization).

It should be noted that in the 1950s the majority of UK workers stayed with one company from the time of leaving full-time education until their retirement (in those days 65 for males and 60 for females). Joining the railway on leaving school meant a career whose stages would lead from engine cleaner to top-link driver by the age of 60 with the final five years as an express passenger train driver with a gold watch and pension to follow on retirement at 65. That figure is now 11 per cent and falling in the workforce and is likely to apply to those coming to the end of their full-time economically active life. This suggests that *organization commitment* may be more difficult to sustain under present conditions and we will examine why this may have occurred in subsequent chapters.

Flexibility

The search for flexibility has been constant in organizational change programmes. Inflexibility was the undoing of organizations that needed to embrace different working practices in order to respond quickly to perceived market needs. But, it is worth mentioning that *flexibility* itself can be subdivided into four different factors:

- *time* (note that in the retail sector part-time workers can be as high a percentage of the staffing as 80 per cent);
- *number* (flexible working can allow employers to organize staffing levels to coincide with customer flows in the transport sector leading to split shifts that coincide with morning and evening rush hours);
- *cost* (there can be variation in pay depending on working shifts or unsocial hours undertaken);
- *functional* (where one individual is trained to do more than one job – the basis, for example, of quality circles).

It should be mentioned that *functional flexibility* was the desired goal during the 1980s. It was one way of overcoming the inflexibility of union working, which had previously carefully guarded members' jobs from infringement by others undertaking to do their work. One well-known example of circumventing such inflexibility would be to close a brownfield site and open up a greenfield site. One well-known example was Nissan where 2,000 jobs were offered to competent and experienced workers who were prepared to work outside the union framework (Wickens, 1987). There were claims later that this strategy had yielded the highest productivity in the company worldwide. A similar example of radical change can be found in British Airways by Georgiades (1990), who was part of the HR team that implemented the change programme for all staff (50,000 at that time), seeking to bring about a privatized mindset in those who were used to working for what had up to then been a public-owned airline. Working for maximum profitability requires the engagement of workers and change in their mindset to ensure that their efforts are applied efficiently to achieving the organizational objectives without inflexible working practices obstructing their ability to respond to customer need.

Quality

This is a consistent theme throughout HRM theory, reinforced by such initiatives as Total Quality Management (TQM) and similar movements to bring about consistency of performance. It focuses on optimizing efficiency/productivity factors, which is sometimes referred to as managerialism or performativity (Rowlinson and Hassard, 2011). It means that managers focus on the productivity factors within the organization's processes. These factors are often listed as:

- time
- quality
- quantity
- cost.

As we said earlier, this is, or should be, the *content* of an organization's managerial life. However, we also need to evaluate the *effectiveness* of our efforts as well and this is dependent on two factors:

- the customers
- the competition.

As we shall see, markets do not stand still, which means that customer expectancy is always on the move, driven by the latest edition of whatever interests them. Steve Jobs of Apple knew this very well and always pushed to extend the limits of what technology could support in his latest products. Apple's competition struggled to keep up and he enjoyed a significant advantage of being first in the market with new technology applied to day-to-day applications for his customers. In return he generated significant customer loyalty and commitment.

Finally, measuring the success of HRM's application is to be found in the third column in Table 1.1: *Organizational outcomes*. As we can see, these include measuring both positive and negative factors for the organization. In short, if we succeed in linking the activities in the HRD list to the *strategic objectives* of the company, through the HR outcomes, we can guarantee that the benefits, such as innovation and high cost-effectiveness, are achieved and the disadvantages, such as staff turnover and absenteeism, are obviated or avoided. As we will see, measuring is one important function, but evaluation can be more difficult, as it depends on customer perception.

Hard and soft HRM

This brings us to the distinction between hard and soft HRM (Legge, 1995). Hard HRM seeks to calculate how much HRD intervention in the workforce costs – for example costly training events: what are their benefits, and can a cost–benefit analysis be made to illustrate this? One simple example might be staff turnover, which as we have remarked can vary in cost from checkout staff (£1,500 per leaver according to some in the sector) to graduate management trainees (£10,000 according to some blue-chip companies). Now we know that the turnover of graduate management trainees can be as high as 30 per cent within the first six months of joining the company. So, in both cases we might seek to assess whether, say, the serious interference costs of staff turnover can be alleviated by appropriate training or development initiatives.

Soft HRM, by comparison, focuses on the human issues arising from working conditions. We have seen recently much more interest in work–life balance, for example (Wheatley, 2012), and programmes to help the avoidance of stress at work (Mulholland, 2004). The armed services take more seriously their duty to provide counselling for those affected by post-traumatic stress disorder – something that would have been unthinkable to previous generations of war victims. And now mentors, personal coaches and shadowing are all ways of supporting and developing people at work, particularly in the early stages of their job or project.

It is important not to make this distinction between hard and soft HRM exclusive. Both approaches have their place in the company's HR strategy and in later chapters we will look at examples of both hard and soft approaches and the contexts in which their implementation might be important. In fact when we think about the problems attached to managing people in difficult circumstances, we may well need to address both the hard and soft sides of HRM practice. Our questions would be:

- What is the problem?
- What are we going to do about it?
- What will it cost us to take action?
- What will it cost us if we take no action?

So, for example, the solution may be a soft approach and the cost of implementing the strategy must be weighed against the cost of inaction, or as Drucker once said: 'If you think training's expensive, try ignorance.'

Personnel or HRM – what's the difference?

The question remains whether there is a difference between personnel and HRM? And there are lists that seek to summarize the differences (Storey, 1992: 38). Interestingly, while many companies changed the name on the door and people's titles in the personnel function from personnel to HR department, Marks & Spencer refused to change their titles internally and retained the personnel title they had always used. Most people would think that their personnel practices were exemplary in the retail sector. Looking after their people and encouraging them to stay with the company was an essential part of their success strategy with their people long before HRM theory was developed.

So, what we can say is that the theorists of HRM would see it as vitally important that the HR function is fully involved in the formulation of strategy. That would mean that it would be reasonable for their senior HR manager to be on the Board of Directors. Overall, the number of Boards that include the HR manager has remained steady at about 6 per cent (CIPD figures). There is a debate to be had as to whether, for example, involvement in discussions over redundancies would then find the HR manager compromised, as they attempted to implement the policy they had been party to. However, the fact remains that *strategic integration* lies at the heart of successful HRM implementation. Without full knowledge of the company's strategy and its implications for everyone working in the company, it is difficult to see how the theory can work out in practice when HR is excluded from key strategic discussions that relate to the workforce.

For the HR department itself, awareness of the company's strategic objectives allows a more focused approach to how they implement HRD interventions. Who the company employs, for example, depends on what the company is trying to achieve and every subsequent management intervention must be designed to reinforce those employment objectives as they apply to the different personnel on whom the company's success depends.

The movement of personnel duties to line managers

Another important initiative included in the theory of HRM was the movement of personnel responsibilities to the *line managers*. The HRD list should be part of the manager's responsibility for the team of workers he/she manages. That does not mean that HR will not be involved in giving advice and support to managers on their duties and responsibilities and ensuring that they are trained to undertake those roles professionally. Indeed, HR may well offer to sit in on important interviews to ensure that the legal requirements are fulfilled. It is clear that managers who conduct key interviews infrequently will be much less practised in the skills and knowledge required to accomplish the required outcomes. Those whose working lives in HR involve practising the skills day to day are in an ideal position to offer such support to the managers.

One other aspect of HR theory includes the *evaluation* of the company's personnel activities. Monitoring how successful the company is at keeping its people is a necessary prerequisite of responsible management. But how effective we are needs more work and brings us back to the ideas of the Harvard model above. There are other stakeholders outside the company – they may be customers, investors or wider society. How we influence them should also be evaluated. No company gets everything right all of the time. Managers and workers make mistakes and the temptation to cover up can become significant (as we notice with whistle blowers in the Health Service). Involvement in disciplinaries and grievance interviews, for example, may be the first indicator that all is not well in the company at a deeper level than appears at first sight. HR is often the first receiver of such messages. It needs to voice its concerns within the company at a senior level to see that their reasons are examined and resolved.

Organizational change and HRM

It would be strange if the present day were still able to offer the same context for HR as was apparent when it was first proposed in 1984. So, it may be worthwhile taking time to consider what changes have taken place to organizations and how those changes have affected HR practices. If we go back to the beginning and consider the traditional organization, a traditional pyramid diagram, as in Figure 1.1, expresses it well.

FIGURE 1.1 The traditional bureaucratic layers.

The span of control required in managing a large group of people has generally been considered to be 1:8 – in other words eight functional workers at what might be referred to as the bottom of the organization, would need one supervisor. If we go up to that next level of what are sometimes referred to as first-line managers, then eight front-line managers would need a manager themselves. It becomes apparent then that as the number of people at the bottom of the organization increases, the number of levels of management required above them increases too (Weber, 1947).

Functional workers

Traditionally, functional workers have required induction training to bring them up to speed with company practices, health and safety rules and the other factors that affect their day-to-day working lives. Sometimes this knowledge is referred to as know-how – we might also say that there is an element of know-what, too. Some writers referred to this as single loop learning (Argyris and Schon, 1974). *Functional workers* needed to be efficient and work well in a team to make sure that they were up to speed and able to produce to the targets set by the company. So, for example, in the retail sector, there is often a target for checkout operatives to scan a certain number of items per minute – in one case 14 items/minute if the checkout operative was packing or 22/minute if they were not packing. Obviously, the checkout equipment can monitor the speeds of different operatives and compare the results with the target set.

In some production companies, workers in teams can see the number of items they have produced on a board above their heads. They can also see the results of the teams working around them. Informal breaks are not encouraged and are carefully monitored to ensure that full advantage is taken of the available time to work towards the targets required.

All of this suggests that the workers have little or no autonomy to alter the working conditions imposed on them. Their lives are circumscribed by predictive rules and targets and there is little room for manoeuvre, adjustment or discretion allowed to them without prior permission from members of management.

Supervisors/first-line managers

Traditionally, supervisors have been drawn from the ranks of functional workers. It made sense that those who monitored what others were supposed to be doing should know the job very well themselves. This gave them the advantage of learning the job so that they could support workers who might be struggling with problems; they knew the system and why it worked in the way that it did. But, perhaps most importantly, they could explain the system to others – whether staff or customers. Furthermore, retail companies that wanted to ensure that staff were quickly supported through a problem and customers more quickly satisfied would alter the span of control by appointing more supervisors. So, in the case of Marks & Spencer, the span of control was 1:4 to ensure that queries and problems were responded to and supported more quickly.

Obviously, more training and development was required for undertaking this role – not just the knowledge of what we do and how the system works, but also, in order to explain it to others, why the system works in the way that it does. We might describe this as know-why as it requires extra knowledge as well as skill in applying the knowledge and putting it across to others. So, for example, in pilot training the skills of handling an aircraft are complemented by knowledge about engines; airframes; different control systems, such as pressurization and the systems supporting it; meteorology; air law; signalling; emergency systems; navigation; communication systems and so on. Such knowledge is intended not only to make the pilot more knowledgeable but also to enable the pilot to respond to emergencies proactively with a greater chance of successfully diagnosing and overcoming any problems as they arise.

Argyris (1976) refers to this as double loop learning. Knowing how a system works offers a greater chance of intervening successfully should the system fail or break down. The rest is down to experience and accounts for why less experienced fliers operate with a more senior colleague who can both give the opportunity for hands-on experience and comment on responses to unexpected events and how to deal with them. In a similar way, in the bus industry, inspectors would have been expected to pass through the earlier jobs of conductor and driver so that they would both know the skills and knowledge required in the jobs they were supervising and also some of the shortcuts that crews might seek to use (such as buses travelling in threes so that the first bus is picking up most of the passengers and the third bus is picking up no one – thus giving the crew an easier time).

Executives

Strictly speaking, the term suggests a decision-making function within the business. Given that investment is usually required to run any business, the question of what is in the budget and how it is to be spent, together with monitoring whether the planned budget is being exceeded or not, is crucial to the life of any executive. But more is required of the senior executive: systems do not remain effective for ever. What once served the company well may be superseded by competitive pressures or technological advances that require decisions about change. It includes both single and double loop learning but also involves a third loop which questions the whole rationale of what has previously been done and the reasons that we did them. Its authors describe it thus:

> Circular design precepts appear to provide a structural facilitation of single and double loop learning. In this respect, the circular design tends to act as a facilitating infrastructure for triple loop learning, that is, exploring the structural opportunities and key competences people need to participate in making well-informed choices about policies, objectives and other issues.
>
> (Romme *et al.*, 1999)

Executives have traditionally been protective of their rights and responsibilities around such decision making and have not always welcomed participation or involvement from those lower down the organization. In some countries in Europe industrial democracy has advanced to the stage where a worker representative is included on the Board of Directors. Such openness has always been stoutly resisted in the UK by senior managers, perhaps to avoid workers knowing too much about the detail of how the company operates. But nonetheless its absence could be detrimental to the achievement of *organizational commitment* and *strategic integration*.

Changing the traditional triangle

Multilayered organizations have traditionally presented their own problems of adapting quickly to market changes. Decisions may take time to get through from the top decision makers and even when decisions are made, they have a tendency to take a while to filter down to those who need to know at the end-user or front-facing team.

There were a number of influences that affected the traditional organizational structure as described above:

1   the Japanese approach to car making in the UK and elsewhere;
2   the movement to delayer the organization;
3   the movement to unbundle different parts of the business and allow them more freedom to adapt to changing customer requirements closer to the front line;
4   the quality circles movement that lay at the heart of TQM.

The hierarchical approach to managing workers has in many countries involved different social levels between the bottom and top of the company. For example, in many companies functional workers might have a canteen, while managers had a dining room and directors a totally separate provision away from other workers. Separation in this way seems traditionally to have been part of the hierarchical view of ranking and control of others.

Symbolic changes

A similar example would be parking at work. In the past directors could expect a named parking space, usually near the front door. Even if they were away, others were not authorized to park in these named spots. Those with lesser status were further away from the door, perhaps on a first-come, first-served basis.

The Japanese changed such practices very simply by setting up one catering facility, which everyone was expected to go to. They abandoned all named parking spaces, so that the first to come, be they cleaner or janitor, got the space close to the door. In some manufacturing plants everyone, including the directors, was expected to wear the company uniform and take part in any company exercises at the beginning of the day.

Delayering

In one car company in the UK there were 120 levels between functional workers and the managing director. Within those levels there were approaching 500 different grades. Personnel spent much of its time negotiating pay increases year by year with the unions and care had to be taken to ensure that pay differentials between grades were maintained. Peter Drucker always maintained that this was the reason that senior executives were paid extortionately large amounts of money. It had nothing to do with the value-added they offered to the company. It was the result of their being at the top of multi-layered grades each of which had to have an enhanced pay grade. The more layers, the higher the emoluments paid to the CEO.

So, for Japanese factories the layers between the functional end of the business and the senior executive have been reduced to five or six levels. It makes decision making more immediate and means that pay differentials are less of a problem in inflated wages at the senior level. Interestingly, the Sheehy Report (Leishman *et al.*, 1995) suggested among other things that the police reduce their ranks from 12 to 5/6. Needless to say, the Police Federation and the Association of Chief Police Officers evaded or resisted implementing such recommendations. The effect on policing makes a ranked organization more expensive to run – especially in small forces – and less responsive in terms of responding with resources at the functional end of the service. Interestingly, Scotland has now decided to move to a single Police Force and there are similar discussions taking place in England and Wales. The government's austerity drive has been a trigger to focus the minds of managers in all public services to look at economies of scale linked to the continued search for effectiveness that governs the success of all organizations without artificially inflated on-costs born of organizational structuring.

Unbundling

A further movement that companies have taken advantage of is unbundling. corporate behemoths such as the British Motor Corporation, originally an agglomeration of small independent car-making companies put together to achieve economies of scale and a more dominant presence in the market. What happened was that individual marques which customers valued and paid for ceased to have the distinctiveness that customers had always valued. Decision making took longer and eventually a break-up of the businesses was needed to re-establish the value-added and distinctiveness that the market wanted as the original marques were sold off again.

Smaller businesses have a dynamic of their own that can become lost in the larger corporate environment. Responsiveness to customers is one aspect that unbundling is intended to bring about. The other is responsiveness to the competition. Reporting lines should be shorter and the expertise of the unit is consolidated rather than dispersed through a larger organization.

An example of this can be found in Storey (1992) regarding Jaguar's release from the corporate ownership and management of BMC (the British Motor Corporation) by John Egan who managed it with considerable success, restoring the car to its supremacy in the US market. However, even he managed to persuade only 45 per cent of his workers to adopt working in quality circles. This would seem to reinforce the belief that brownfield sites may often need a fresh start on a greenfield site in order to achieve radical change to working practices.

All of this leads us to a well-known model that offers an explanation of the changes that took place to traditionally structured organizations in the 1980s.

The Shamrock organization

Charles Handy wrote *Understanding Organizations* in 1985. Having completed his PhD, which few people read, he decided to devote his time and effort to writing books that managers and readers would read and understand. One such book contained what he called the Shamrock organization (Figure 1.2). In this book he looked forward to the future and predicted what he thought might be an enduring trend in organizational development.

In a sense we can see the emerging trends already referred to both in delayering the pyramidal organization of its restrictive and expensive levels within the hierarchy, and by unbundling elements of the business that it does not need to manage directly itself.

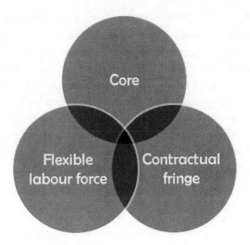

FIGURE 1.2 The Shamrock organization.

Source: Adapted from Handy (1989).

So *core workers*, as their name suggests, work on a traditional employment contract and carry out the functions that are key to the organization's core business. However, it is clear that there are functions within the organization that do not need to be undertaken by core staff and these functions can be subcontracted to those who specialize in that area. *Subcontractors* may take over such duties as cleaning, security and catering. For aircraft companies baggage handling, ticket desks and reception centres/lounges can similarly be undertaken by subcontracted staff. The advantage means that little or no core management time is spent supervising and managing such staff. It also means that the contract can be put out to further competitive tendering at the end of the contract term, thereby keeping contractors on their toes.

For professional services, such as legal, financial and IT services, it may be possible to hire experts on an ad hoc, *consultancy* basis. Daily fees for such professionals are high. But using them only when necessary means that cost flexibility can be achieved rather than keeping them on a permanent contract. Such arrangements are not always without challenges and Robertson and Swan (2003) describe the tensions that can arise between dedicated professionals who value their autonomy with their clients and the business targets required by senior managers in the core business.

As we have seen, the airline industry has proceeded some way down this road. Were the industry not closely regulated, it is possible that they would already have moved to fewer cabin staff and even, perhaps, one pilot. Certainly the statements of Michael O'Leary, CEO of Ryanair, would suggest that such economies are his ultimate aim in running the company. Even so, the difference in reward for crews in the traditional flag-flying carriers and their cheaper rivals is now significant with fewer of the costs, such as medicals and licence renewal, being picked up for individual fliers by their low-cost employers, which the more traditional carriers would have paid.

In his book *The Age of Unreason* (1989) Handy originally suggested that the age range for core workers would be from 27 to 45 years of age. This later entry into the workplace would, he suggested, allow individuals to acquire a business qualification, specialist qualification and languages, to enable the core worker to be fully equipped to undertake a full range of roles within the organization. In a later book, *The Empty Raincoat* (1994), he admitted that he had been wrong about the top age of core employment which he now saw evidence of reducing to nearer 35. That would suggest that significant career change comes earlier in a career than he had thought in his original book.

Implications for HRM

In some ways the impact on the work of HR departments now becomes more complex. Keeping track of temporary employment contracts across the organization can be demanding and time consuming. Self-employed consultants, for example, have traditionally been allowed to spend only 75 per cent of their available time with one organization before they lose their self-employed status. Subcontractors have to renegotiate each year and the tendering process will need to be arranged. Such complexity in the privatized railway industry defies easy description and has led on one occasion to legal challenge and the collapse of the franchise offer. What looks a system that supports time, number and cost flexibilities for the organization and its use of labour, can be more complex for the HR function to organize and monitor.

It is clear that the benefits of such a flexible organization should mean that the HRD list is reduced for both subcontractors and consultancy staff. Subcontractors are responsible for hiring and training their own staff, paying them, monitoring their performance and investing in their development. Similarly, consultants come already qualified, responsible for their own continuous professional development requirements and usually aware of comparative rewards within their sector and confident to negotiate their rates.

However, the company is still responsible for their performance on behalf of the firm. Accidents, health and safety violations, cases of discrimination, failure to perform to contract or grievance still fall within the responsibility of the company and HR is the agent for ensuring that company policy, procedure and practice is adhered to. All such cases must be investigated and appropriate action taken by HR. So, there is a cost to administering the Shamrock organization, much of it borne by the HR department. If we return to the HR outcomes which Guest shows in the second column of Table 1.1, we will need to ask whether they are more or less likely to be achieved in this fragmented organization, or whether the search for economies of scale can put at risk the *quality* sought after.

Strategic integration may be more difficult to achieve with staff who, in the case of consultants, are probably working for two or more organizations. Subcontractors, too, are less likely to feel involved in the company's strategic objectives, particularly as their contract is regularly up for renewal with no guarantee of renewal at the end of the term.

Commitment may be more difficult to achieve, particularly if we are looking for *organizational* commitment, which the proponents of HRM originally envisaged. *Career* commitment is likely to exist among consultants. But, it will be seen in the context of a portfolio career (Iles, 1997), in which the present experience is valued for the enhanced knowledge, skill and experience it offers – thereby making the consultant more employable in view of increased competence and experience. For the subcontractors there is job commitment, which enables them to fulfil the contract on behalf of their employer. But their organizational commitment will be given to the subcontractor who employs them.

Flexibility: It is clear that all sides benefit from time, number and cost flexibility. For consultants, there is the opportunity of working with other organizations and, provided the subcontractor is successful, there can be opportunities for job and work rotation between contracts. What is less likely to be apparent is functional flexibility – the opportunity to learn more than one job. The openings for such flexibility are likely to be reduced in the Shamrock organization as peripheral functions are outsourced (Knox and Walsh, 2005).

Quality: If everyone is working to the contracted standards then it should not matter what the employment status of the individual is within the organization: subcontract or consultancy, it should make no difference. However, management requires monitoring and that aspect of checking will be as necessary for subcontractors and consultants as it is for core staff. And where its consistency is lacking, HR need to initiate remedial action with line managers to remedy the situation. As the recent problem of horse meat entering the food chain under the guise of beef, the links in the supply chain owe it to their customers to check the quality of their supplies. This responsibility cannot be delegated without serious consequences occurring.

The rise of the knowledge worker

There has been an increasing focus in recent years on the rise in the numbers of knowledge workers. There are those who would say that jobs have always required knowledge to be conducted effectively. But we can probably accept that more jobs require knowledge, skill and experience prior to engaging with the work required and that though there are training paths initially for most occupations, for knowledge workers their expertise has often been developed through experience with clients in their field and continuing professional development in their working lives. As Alvesson points out:

> Access to occupations like computer expert, (university educated) engineer, management consultant, university teacher and advertising executive are not formally regulated and thus the level of uniformity may become less than for the 'real' professions such as lawyer and chartered accountant. 'The occupational identity of the former may be somewhat less likely than the latter to successfully compete with organizational membership as a source of identification.
>
> (Alvesson, 2000: 1109)

FIGURE 1.3 Managing consultants.

In other words, looking at the requirement for specialist skills and conversance with IT equipment most jobs require workers who can contribute their expertise within the business with a minimal amount of introduction or training. Such workers may well be self-employed and their stay with the organization therefore temporary.

The challenge for employers is that such workers are harder to manage in the traditional supervisory way. It is hard to step in and criticize another for working too slowly or not achieving the job more cost-effectively when we have no idea what needs to be done, nor how to do it. The only answer is the consultancy approach to management (see Figure 1.3).

As a manager, I know that I cannot manage the *process* in the traditional way of overseeing and intervening if things are not going to my satisfaction. So, the focus is on the two other parts of the model:

> *Input*: Drawing up an accurate contract will require accuracy and realistic goals and they should focus around the efficiency factors:

- time
- quantity
- quality
- cost.

> *Output*: This part should focus on effectiveness factors:

- end-user/customer satisfaction.

Tacit knowledge

So, what happens during the course of the working contract is that the knowledge worker gets experience not just of the systems being worked with or developed, but sometimes with the company's customers as well. This is part of any learning organization (Senge, 1990), though in truth it might be accurate to describe it as organizational learning (Easterby-Smith *et al.*, 1999). Efforts have been made to try to get experts to share what is sometimes called tacit knowledge (Nonaka and Takeuchi, 1995), what knowledge workers know and sometimes take for granted about doing their job but will not always willingly divulge however much companies try to encourage it (McKinlay, 2003).

For the company there may be no trace of what was learned so that when transient workers leave, the knowledge they acquired about company processes and customers goes with them. Knowledge is eminently transferable. It enhances the knowledge and skill of the consultant or contractor and can provide them with opportunities to promote themselves and develop business contacts elsewhere later on.

The virtual organization

Does it matter where you work today? Could we spend less time commuting to work and work from home? Do we need to go out to a shop to get what we need? We know what the answer to these questions is: IT makes it possible to work remotely. Organizations do not always admit that they like to supervise workers, which is why they insist that their workers travel in and out to work each day. This is sometimes referred to as 'presenteeism'. We can allow that there are some services that require an immediate presence: medical services would be a case in point. Though even here, NHS Direct has taken more of the advice-giving function away from medical practices, particularly as an out-of-hours service.

We are used as consumers to going online to find what we want. We do not always need to talk to others face to face. If we trust the brand and know the product then who delivers it is immaterial. How many people work for Amazon? Does it matter? Do we care? Certainly the delivery driver will be a subcontractor. But that does not need to concern us provided we get what we wanted on time.

Of course we do not feel that about all services we are offered: most people are terrified of having to change their dentist. If they are good we will not want to lose them or risk swapping to someone who is not so good. So, in a sense, what we see here is the combination of the Shamrock organization – the mixing of different status staffing levels combined with online contact. It makes for a very different world of work and a different consumer experience. It also makes a difference to the work of HRM.

So what of HR in the future?

We can probably agree that a fragmented experience of work will remain the primary focus of the individual's working experience. If this is so, then the case for *organizational commitment* being the lynchpin of HRM theory must be less certain. The alternative is to ensure that everyone who works for the company has the best experience of care and support that HR is capable of giving them.

So, going back to Guest's model, how far has HR delivered on the promises of its outcomes (strategic integration; commitment; flexibility and quality)? We have already discussed how difficult that is to achieve in the fragmented working experience that faces many people today.

How far has HR been able reinforce the organizational outcomes – the measurables that are found in the third column of Table 1.1? Again the answer might be that the outcomes are less likely to be measurable in the way that was possible in the traditional organization with static employment levels aiming to offer a job for life.

So what remains for HR in this virtual world? Well, Handy says that you cannot do business with people you have not laughed with. So, negotiation is hard to do at a distance. Face-to-face contact is the only way to breed trust and loyalty, or, as was taught in selling: people buy from people they like. So, when we look again at the HRD list nothing has changed in essence. As the bridge between the individual and the organization, HR has an important role to play and may increasingly become the key face of the organization at important times in a person's career through contact that is achieved within organizations. The *psychological contract* remains important at the relational level of loyalty and trust (Macneil, 1974; 1980; Rousseau, 1990). It is a major support of organizational commitment.

Six years ago I applied for a job at two universities. As it happens both invitations to come for interview arrived on the mat on the same day. The only difference was that there was a week between the dates for the interviews.

Following the first interview I was offered the job but was concerned that I had accepted the second interview elsewhere. I explained to the chair of the panel that I felt obliged to go along but said that if HR got a contract to me by 1pm the following day, I would sign it and withdraw from the second interview. I said this because I had never known a university to produce a contract within a six week period, so thought that I could safely go to the second interview and see what happened there.

In the event, the contract arrived by 1pm the following day. I signed it and am still at that university. I will always remember that HR manager. Their care of people has been equally demonstrable since. I hope we will never lose such professional dedication from HR departments. They play an important part in engendering *organizational commitment*.

References and further reading

Alvesson, M. (2000) Social identity and the problem of loyalty in knowledge-intensive companies. *Journal of Management Studies*, 37(8): 1101–1123.

Argyris, C. (1976) Single-loop and double-loop models in research on decision making. *Administrative Science Quarterly*, 21(3): 363–375.

Argyris, C. and Schon, D. (1974) *Theory in practice: Increasing professional effectiveness*. San Francisco, CA: Jossey Bass.

Beer, M., Spencer, P., Lawrence, D., Quinn Mills, D. and Watson, R. (1984) *Managing Human Assets*. New York: Free Press.

Blyton, P. and Turnbull, P. (1992) *Reassessing Human Resource Management*. London: Sage.

Bowden, J., Hart, G., King, B., Trigwell, K. and Watts, O. (2000) *Generic Capabilities of ATN University Graduates*. Canberra: Australian Government Department of Education, Training and Youth Affairs.

Chia, R. (1995) From modern to postmodern organizational analysis. *Organization Studies*, 16(4): 579–605.

Drucker, P.F. (1954) *The Practice of Management*. New York: HarperCollins.

Easterby-Smith, M. (1997) Disciplines of organizational learning: Contributions and critiques. *Human Relations*, 50(9): 1085–1113.

Easterby-Smith, M., Burgoyne, J. and Araujo, L. (1999) *Organizational Learning and the Learning Organization: Developments in theory and practice*. London: Sage.

Fombrun, C., Tichy, N.M. and Devanna, M.A. (1984) *Strategic Human Resource Management*. New York: Wiley.

Georgiades, N. (1990) A strategic future for personnel? *Personnel Management*, 22(2): 43.

Gillespie, R. (1991) *Manufacturing Knowledge: A history of the Hawthorne experiments*. Cambridge: Cambridge University Press.

Guest, D.E. (1989) Personnel and HRM: Can you tell the difference? *Personnel Management*, 21(1): 48–51.

Handy, C. (1985) *Understanding Organizations*. Harmondsworth: Penguin

Handy, C. (1989) *The Age of Unreason*. London: Random House Business Books.

Handy, C. (1994) *The Empty Raincoat: New thinking for a new world*. London: Arrow Books.

Iles, P. (1997) Sustainable high-potential career development: A resource-based view. *Career Development International*, 2(7): 347–353.

Knox, A. and Walsh, J. (2005) Organisational flexibility and HRM in the hotel industry: Evidence from Australia. *Human Resource Management Journal*, 15(1): 57–75.

Legge, K. (1995) *Human Resource Management: Rhetorics and reality*. London: McMillan.

Leishman, F. (1995) On screen – police on TV. *Policing*, 11(2): 143–152.

Lewin, K. (1946) Action research and minority problems. *Journal of Social Issues*, 2(4): 34–46.

Lewin, K. (1947) Frontiers in group dynamics. *Human Relations*, 1(2): 150–151.

McKinlay, A. (2003) Surveillance, electronic communications technologies and regulation. *Industrial Relations Journal*, 34(4): 305–318 (with P. Findlay).

Macneil, I.R. (1974) The many futures of contracts. *Southern California Law Review*, 47: 691–816.

Macneil, I.R. (1980) *The New Social Contract: An inquiry into modern contractual relations*. New Haven, CT: Yale University Press.

Mayo, E. (1933) *The Human Problems of an Industrial Civilization*. New York: Macmillan.

Mulholland, K. (2004) Workplace resistance in an Irish call centre: Slammin', scammin', smokin', an' leavin'. *Work, Employment and Society*, 18(4), 709–724.

Nonaka, I. and Takeuchi, H. (1995) *The Knowledge Creating Company*. Oxford: Oxford University Press.

Peters, T. and Waterman, R. (1982) *In Search of Excellence: Lessons from America's best-run companies*. New York: Harper Row.

Revans, R. (2011) *ABC of Action Learning*. Gower: Farnham.

Robertson, M. and Swan, J. (2003) Control – what control? Culture and ambiguity within a knowledge intensive firm. *Journal of Management Studies*, 40(4): 831–858.

Robertson, M. and Swan, J. (2004) Going public: The emergence and effects of soft bureaucracy within a knowledge-intensive firm. *Organization*, 11(1): 123–148.

Roethlisberger, F.J. and Dickson, W.J. (1939) *Management and the Worker*. Cambridge, MA: Harvard University Press.

Romme, A., Georges, L. and van Witteloostuijn, A. (1999) Circular organizing and triple loop learning. *Journal of Organizational Change Management*, 12(5), 439–454.

Rousseau, D.M. (1990). New hire perceptions of their own and their employer's obligations: A study of psychological contracts. *Journal of Organizational Behavior*, 11: 389–400.

Rowlinson, M. and Hassard, J. (2011) How come the critters come to be teaching in business schools? Contradictions in the institutionalization of Critical Management Studies. *Organization*, 18(5/6): 673–689.

Senge, P. (1990) *The Fifth Discipline*. New York: Doubleday.

Storey, J. (1992) *Developments in the Management of Human Resources: An analytical review.* London: Blackwell.

Taylor, F.W. (1911) *Principles of Scientific Management.* New York and London: Harper & brothers.

Trist, E.L. and Bamforth, K.W. (1951) Some social and psychological consequences of the long-wall method of coal-getting. *Human Relations*, 4(1), 3–38.

Weber, M. (1947) *The Theory of Social and Economic Organisation.* Translated by A. Henderson and T. Parsons, ed. T. Parsons. New York: Free Press.

Wheatley, D. (2012) Work–life balance, travel-to-work, and the dual career household. *Personnel Review*, 41(6): 813–831.

Wickens, P. (1987) *The Road to Nissan: Flexibility, quality, teamwork.* Basingstoke: Macmillan.

GRADUATE ATTRIBUTES

Most universities have now begun to develop *graduate attributes* in order to encourage their students to understand and enter into the wider world of work and acquire the skills and knowledge that make that possible. Modern managers have been used to management competencies for several years but their practical application has been sporadic in its development.

In the final part of each of the chapters of this book we have put together some exercises that will enable students and tutors to follow through from the academic overview of HR topics into their relevant application within the graduate attribute framework.

So what are these graduate attributes and how are they analysed? One definition that is frequently used attempts to describe what they are:

> Graduate attributes are the qualities, skills and understandings a university community agrees its students should develop during their time with the institution. These attributes include but go beyond the disciplinary expertise or technical knowledge that has traditionally formed the core of most university courses. There are qualities that also prepare graduates as agents of social good in an unknown future.
>
> (Bowden *et al.*, 2000)

Institutions have their own descriptors for describing the elements and the main areas into which they fit. The authors have used the framework offered by their own university while acknowledging that these may be offered differently elsewhere. The four main areas are:

- academic excellence
- critical thinking and communication
- learning and personal development
- active citizenship and engagement in the wider world of work and society.

These areas are further broken down into their respective elements in Table 1.2.

TABLE 1.2 Graduate attributes, University of Aberdeen

Academic excellence	*Critical thinking and effective communication*
In-depth and extensive knowledge, understanding and skills at internationally recognized levels in their chosen disciplines	A capacity for independent and creative thinking
A breadth of knowledge, understanding and skills beyond their chosen discipline(s)	A capacity for problem identification, the collection of evidence, synthesis and dispassionate analysis
An ability to participate in the creation of new knowledge through research and inquiry	A capacity for attentive exchange, informed argument and reasoning
A contextual understanding of past and present knowledge and ideas	An ability to communicate effectively for different purposes and in different contexts
An intellectual curiosity and a willingness to question accepted wisdom and to be open to new ideas	A diverse set of transferable and generic skills

Learning and personal development	*Active citizenship*
An openness to, and an interest in, lifelong learning through directed and self-directed study	An awareness and appreciation of ethical and moral issues
An awareness of personal strengths and weaknesses	An awareness and appreciation of social and cultural diversity
A capacity for self-reflection, self-discovery and personal development	An understanding of social and civic responsibilities, and of the rights of individuals and groups
	An appreciation of the concepts of enterprise and leadership in all aspects of life
	A readiness for citizenship in an inclusive society

In the activities that follow each chapter we will seek to offer activities that support and develop these attributes. It may be that an activity supports more than one attribute. It is also likely that there are some attributes that require more investment of time in outside activities that cannot be covered in a traditional written format.

General guidelines for critical thinking

This activity will address the following graduate attributes:

- a capacity for independent, conceptual and creative thinking;
- a capacity for attentive exchange, informed argument and reasoning;

- an ability to communicate effectively for different purposes and in different contexts.

Being critical and arguing

You may all think you are critical and some of you may argue a lot but you will find that what you do is not what is expected in a learning situation. It is a very common problem for many engaged in the study of business that there is a lack of experience in critical analysis and the construction of arguments. Both of these are vital skills for those pursuing academic study. What we are going to look at, briefly, here are the basics that you really need to know in order to tackle some of the exercises in this book and help you with what will be expected of you in assignments and examinations.

What is critical analysis?

Let us begin by looking at the two elements that make up critical analysis but let's reverse them.

Analysis

Analysis is the skill of reducing information into elements or component parts.

Critical

Being critical, in the academic sense, is to make careful judgement about information and evaluate the quality of the data.

Critical analysis is thus about your ability to be critical, to evaluate information and to make your own judgement about that information. Critical analysis is about evaluating the validity of any theory, model, idea or practice in the context of the proposition (the problem posed).

At this point you may have some questions such as, "Don't we think critically naturally?" The answer for most of us is, sadly, no. We have our own internal biases which cause us to tend to rely on partial information. In our day-to-day life we frequently find ourselves too busy to take the time to develop fully this necessary skill.

The ability to undertake critical analysis is a skill that is required for everyone, because life is about problem solving. We will be faced with tasks and challenges as we proceed through life at work, at home and while learning. Developing your ability for critical analysis will benefit you in all of the listed environments.

Using critical analysis

Assignments and exam questions will require you to perform the task of critically analysing a specific topic before you begin to write about it. Good critical analysis is about reading as much as it is about writing. Certainly your critical analysis will feed into your argument but before you can begin your argument you require knowledge upon which to base it.

Let us look now at using critical analysis in dealing with a question. There are stages that must be gone through to construct your argument successfully in answer to the question.

Stage 1: Identify the focus of the question

Before you begin to address any question, whether an assignment or an exam question, you need to engage your critical thinking faculty and determine exactly what the question is asking you to do. While this may seem obvious, many writers fail to read and analyse a question fully before attempting to answer it. They get caught up in the drive to answer without fully understanding what they are being asked to answer. All questions are set with certain expectations in mind; to answer them successfully you need to consider what these expectations may be.

Stage 2: What do you think and why do you think it?

What's your perspective on the question? What position do you take on the topic/s the question covers? Why do you hold the positions you hold? Here you are undertaking critical analysis not just of what the question is asking you but also of how you have processed the material that it is necessary for you to be aware of in order to attempt it (in the case of the exercises in this book: how you have critically analysed the content of the associated chapter or, in a taught course at a college or university, the material presented in lectures and the related reading).

Stage 3: Persuading others of your point of view

Okay, by this point you know what you are answering and you know what you think about what you are answering but now you need to convince others of your point of view. While you may find what you think convincing, others may not; this links back to the problem of personal bias. You need to construct your argument.

Argumentation

In everyday life having an argument may be viewed as a bad thing, upsetting to you, your friends and family, but argument is integral to academic life. When we talk of argument in this book we don't mean the sort of argument you have over whose turn it is to take out the rubbish, we mean argument as well-constructed academic persuasion.

Argument is a form of influence or persuasion that involves claims, evidence and assumption rather than just opinion. Let us look at an example of what I mean.

- Dr A is a great writer.
  - Opinion (You may think this but where is the evidence?)
- Dr A is a great writer because he can write on a wide variety of topics.
  - Reasoned judgement (Better but he could write badly on a wide range of subjects?)
- Dr A is a great writer with several prestigious publications and awards to his credit.
  - Factual claim (There is evidence of his ability as a writer judged by relevant others)
  - Verifiable (The awards and publications are on record, they can be examined).

Argumentation is linked to critical analysis and, as previously stated, involves the following.

Claims

Claims are statements that require support (Dr A is a great writer). An argument will contain any number of supporting claims and one supported claim (Dr A's publication on bat guano in Tibet has been hailed by Dr Y and Dr Z as the authoritative work in the field; this demonstrates that he is a great writer). The supporting claims are the *premise* of the argument and the supported claim is the *conclusion*.

Evidence

This is quite simply information that supports the claim. Once again this is about your opinion not being enough. It may be my opinion that football is the dullest sport in the world but what evidence do I have to support that as a claim?

- facts
  - verifiable statements
- statistics
  - numbers demonstrating data
- examples
  - specific cases that support your argument
- expert opinion
  - the judgement of authorities (Dr Y and Dr Z support Dr A's conclusions).

To cite or not to cite, that is the question?

- Why cite?
  - support argument with evidence
  - acknowledge quotations
  - avoiding plagiarism
- in-text referencing

- write the surname of the author and the date of publication, in brackets (Gilmore and Williams, 2013)
- use letters after the date to distinguish between books by the same author published in the same year (Gilmore and Williams, 2009a)
- direct quotes, use speech marks and you should state the page number of the source in the reference (Gilmore and Williams, 2009: 10)
- secondary citation
  - Leitch (2006, cited in Gilmore and Williams, 2009) called for a tripartite approach.

Assumption

The underlying perspective that ties evidence to claims – in essence, your point of view. This will be informed by your critical analysis of the available data.

Things to avoid

- begging the question
  - treating an opinion that is open to question as if it were already proved or disproved
- non sequitur (it does not follow)
  - drawing a conclusion from irrelevant evidence
- argument ad hominem (to the man)
  - a claim or argument is rejected on the basis of some fact about the person making the claim (Dr A is left-handed so his results must be wrong).

Engaging with the attributes

Exercising the above guidelines will address the third element of the critical thinking and effective communication section:

- a capacity for attentive exchange, informed argument and reasoning.

The activities offered at the end of each chapter can be developed into both discussion and presentation formats. This will develop the elements that follow:

- an ability to communicate effectively for different purposes and in different contexts;
- an ability to work independently and as part of a team.

A combination of these elements will contribute to the final part:

- a diverse set of transferable and generic skills.

They also sustain the final element of the academic area:

- an intellectual curiosity and a willingness to question accepted wisdom and to be open to new ideas.

Together these attributes provide the vehicle for the other two areas:

- life-long learning and personal development;
- active citizenship.

These attributes provide the building blocks for a career that can extend itself through change and uncertainty, providing the opportunity to take advantage of new challenges and fresh prospects that may not have been chosen but can be taken proactively and developed.

Tutor guidance

Tutors running discussion groups can refer to the *graduate attributes* both at the beginning and the end of the exercises that feature case studies or debrief activities. Pointing out where speakers have used any of the attributes can enable students to become more reflective and analyse their own and other's contributions to class discussions of student feedback. They can also make notes in their Personal Development Plan. Knowledge and expertise develop together as individuals enter into a group discussion. It fulfils the famous phrase of Karl Weick: 'How do I know what I think till I hear what I say.' Such attributes encourage constructive teamwork and further the development of the organization by involving those who work together in organizing (Chia, 1995).

The general guidance to all participants in feedback sessions to others is:

- say what it is you like about what another has said or written, saying why it is good, identifying its contribution to the argument;
- say what you think could be improved or changed, being critical in a way that makes clear why you think another way might be better;
- give helpful example(s) if relevant. Alternative lines of argument are best illustrated by helpful examples.

Topics for discussion

- Does the rise of the knowledge worker mean the end of organizational commitment?
- How does the increasingly fragmented employment experience of many workers affect the validity of the theory of HRM?

2

STRATEGY AND STRATEGIC INTEGRATION

Topics

- introduction to human resource outcomes
- outside-in and inside-out approaches to strategy
- management by objectives
- market-led and resource-led approaches.

Introduction

Strategy and strategic planning are more often misunderstood instruments within a company. Setting targets for growth is commonly found but relating them to a changing context is not so well applied. Changing markets and new entrants are a constant in a developing world and knowing what change means can be a challenge even for those used to a market and its operation. But *strategic integration* is one of the HR outcomes and in the last chapter we looked at Guest's diagram of HRM theory in which it plays a central role (see Table 2.1).

In this chapter we will look at how *strategic integration* may be developed in an organization. In order to do this we need to give some thought to what is strategy and how it should be developed in a company.

Strategy is derived from a word that originally meant a plan. It was associated with armies engaging in conflict. The General or leader needed to define a plan of action that would then be devolved down to the smaller units in the army and so dictate the tactics – what each unit had to do to fulfil their part in the overall plan or strategy. So, for example, if the leaders were to decide that the strategy in pursuing a war is the unconditional surrender of the other side, then those fighting each battle in that war know that it is to be fought to the bitter end with no negotiations to cease hostilities part way through. This may mean incurring far more casualties on both sides as this strategy is followed through to its logical conclusion.

TABLE 2.1 Overview of links in human resource management theory

HRM policies	Human resource outcomes	Organizational outcomes
Organizational objectives Management of change	Strategic integration	High problem solving/ change
Recruitment/selection/ socialization	Commitment	Innovation and creativity
Appraisal, training and development	Flexibility/adaptability	High cost-effectiveness
Communication of standards/ targets	Quality	Fewer customer complaints Low turnover/absence/ grievance

Source: Adapted from Guest (1989) in Blyton and Turnbull (1992: 21).

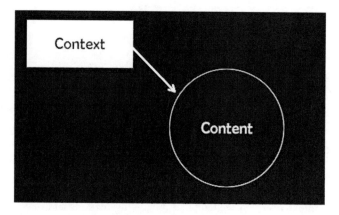

FIGURE 2.1 Outside-in (market-led) approach.

Winning or losing raises the same concerns for companies as it does for armies or countries at war. How will the overall plan or strategy secure the future success of the company? There are many ways of approaching this exercise and, as we shall attempt to show, they do sometimes cross over one another. De Wit and Meyer (2010), for example, use the terms outside-in or inside-out. By that they mean either a *market-led approach* or a *resource-led approach*.

The authors describe working from the *context* in which the firm finds itself as a market-led approach (see Figure 2.1). It focuses on the effectiveness factors of the organization:

- the customers
- the competition.

As we shall see, such strategies may require a root and branch review of what the company is achieving and seek to evaluate whether something very different is required – which could mean recruiting a different profile of staff who are able to produce what is wanted in the future. This might lead strategists to assess whereabouts in that market the company currently sits, and where they want it to be over the period of the plan.

Fit between environment and organization

This could include:

- pursuing markets with high growth potential;
- improving channels of distribution;
- reducing cost structure through the application of modern technology.

There will obviously be implications for organizing how the organization goes about achieving this:

- the scope of activities (broad spread or tight focus in terms of marketing);
- achieving advantage over the competition (unique selling proposition/USP);
- fit: market niche (going for value-added sales and maximizing margins, for example);
- using the core competencies, skills and knowledge within the organization (in a much more focused way).

This suggests that outside-in approaches always have a knock-on effect within the organization's processes and the people who manage and operate them. But, the driving force is surpassing what is currently being achieved in the market and being flexible in the face of market change (Boxall and Purcell, 2003).

In contrast to this there is the inside-out approach:

In Figure 2.2 *content* is the starting point – what is currently being produced internally. The emphasis here is the efficiency factors:

- time
- quality
- quantity
- cost.

Improving targets will depend on developing the systems and the people operating them and training for incremental change will often be the preferred combination to achieve the strategic objectives.

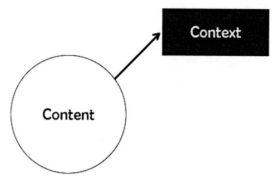

FIGURE 2.2 Inside-out (resource-led) approach.

So we come to an important distinction in management terminology. The distinction between *efficiency* and *effectiveness*. In simple terms we might say that the distinction can be summarized as follows.

Effectiveness

If we take Steve Jobs as an example, his approach at Apple could be seen to be customer focused. He always attempted to stay ahead of the competition by giving customers newly developed products that would do more than the competition could offer. It could be said that over the years his company achieved totemic status in the market and he became an iconic figure.

Similarly, for Richard Branson the emphasis has been the same: take a share in a new market and seek the best chief operating officer to run it. When he set up Virgin Trains, Branson secured the services of Chris Green, an outstanding innovator in the days of British Rail, who had set up both Intercity and Network South-east – both brands that arguably paved the way for the railways to be privatized in the UK in 1993. The concept of the tilting train which had been abandoned by the Government in 1986 was brought back successfully to the West Coast main line between Euston and Glasgow by Virgin Trains and has proven to be highly successful (Green, 2001).

For the company itself, the inner workings of how they go about addressing the new needs of customers to retain their loyalty now becomes important. This brings us to efficiency.

Efficiency

There is always a lag between the expectancy of the market, driven by new options presented by the competition, and the delivery of more efficient products and services. It is this gap that managers need to keep in mind all the time and seek to close if the company is to develop and succeed in its sector. The product lifecycle has a finite limit both in terms of the market and the customer. Reinvention of what we do and how we do it is the gauge of success and speed to market is vital.

BOX 2.1

In the early 1980s GEC took over a well-known family firm that had been manufacturing weighing equipment since the late eighteenth century. The Chairman of GEC, Lord Weinstock, noted that it took on average seven years for the company he had just acquired to get from research and Development to new products available to the customers. The company had just produced the first electronic weighing machine for retail use, which was highly successful with customers. However, Weinstock realized that the competition was not far behind and was liable to catch up and overtake the company's efforts. He therefore decreed that in future the time between planning of products and their launch in the market should be no longer than two years.

Since that time, computer-aided design, computer-aided engineering and computer-aided manufacture have reduced that lead time to a matter of months. For managers, the market does not sleep. How long a product model can be sustained is largely a function of what else becomes available and what its features offer by way of advantages and benefits to those who are in the market to invest, buy and develop the way the results they require are achieved.

Prescriptive approach to strategizing

Approaches to strategic change have included much that could be described as prescriptive: a view of what needs to be addressed by successful companies leading to correct conclusions for implementation into a plan of action. This can lead to different lists of activities that managers are encouraged to check to ensure that they have considered and addressed the critical elements – a bit like a pilot's pre-flight checklist. We outline some of these approaches below.

Traditional steps of strategic planning:

- scan environmental conditions;
- evaluate the organization's strengths and weaknesses (SWOT analysis);
- develop objectives and goals (to fulfil the mission statement);
- develop strategies (to fulfil the objectives and goals).

If there was ever a logical, step approach to strategy formulation, then something like the above list would be typical. If we draw on the example of GEC and Lord Weinstock, then it is clear that on acquiring the weighing machine manufacturer, his awareness of their slowness to develop new products put them in danger of being left behind by their competitors. Redefining the parameters of design and production within a defined schedule was intended to ensure that the company did not fall behind their competitors.

Organizations need to consider:

- the threat of new entrants;
- the bargaining power of suppliers;
- the bargaining power of the customers;
- the intensity of rivalry among competing firms.

For the weighing machine manufacturer the competition were about to launch weighing and counting machines for industrial use; weighing and scanning equipment for use at electronic point of sale in retail outlets; and weighing and labelling for use at fresh produce point-of-sale applications. The market requirements never stay still. In the case of weighing and counting equipment, the company had to buy in equipment manufactured abroad and rebadge them with the company's logo, thereby greatly reducing the margin that their sales might otherwise have yielded. This reinforces the idea that a situational approach is necessary in devising strategy (Dunphy and Stace, 1992).

The descriptive approach

What successful people have done to achieve success for their companies is an alternative approach to exploring strategy formulation. Most of the books on airport book stalls would be part of this genre: hagiographical accounts in which the successful leader or team gives an account of how they put together the winning plan that assured them of success. Victor Kiam's catch phrase was typical of this genre: 'I liked the shaver so much, I bought the company.' The problem for those who seek to emulate this vision is the unlikely possibility that such an opportunity will recur in the same way.

Vision

Whoever generates the vision of the future offers an overview that others are encouraged to envisage and embrace. It offers a general direction in which the company wants to go, allowing a degree of freedom within which employees can decide how to act – the tactics that will enable the vision to be built step-by-step. In some accounts this would be described as autonomy or the discretion allowed to individual staff to make decisions.

BOX 2.2

Following the privatization of the railways in the UK, one operator, Virgin Trains, sought to give their staff more discretion to sort out customer problems without needing to go through to higher authority. One such initiative allowed station supervisors to authorize a taxi where the railway had failed to make a connection between services. One such example allowed by a station supervisor authorized a taxi for a missed connection from London to Scotland. The fare came to over £600. Needless to say this hit the headlines in the national press and provided the train operator with free national advertising.

Richard Branson was relaxed. He reckoned that a single page spread in one paper would have cost him £35,000. For £600 he hit all the newspaper headlines.

For Richard Branson the strategy has always been to appoint the manager with the best track record within the sector to run his business successfully. His own contribution has been in finance and in brand-awareness activities, rather than in day-to-day running of the businesses he sets up. In his airline, Virgin Atlantic, he gave his mobile number to all his pilots. They might need help from the boss in an emergency – there is nothing like cutting through bureaucratic levels to get instant action.

Learning

Let people respond to customer need.

Senge (1990) said that this means transforming people into problem solvers rather than followers of procedure. A learning organization seeks to capture the organizational learning that goes on formally and informally during working time. The secret is to capture the learning so that it can be made available to others in the team. There is another debate as to whether the learning organization is an accurate description of the learning that goes on between individuals and groups. Individuals and groups may learn both formally and informally at work. The organization needs to capture that innovation and learning so that others may benefit from it, too. So, a more accurate description might be *organizational learning*. Organizational learning goes on all the time, wittingly and unwittingly, but the managers are not always aware that it has taken place (Easterby-Smith, 1997). Capturing it requires a deliberate strategy.

Feedback and evaluation are equally to be fostered and valued in any company that seeks to delight the customer. The search to deliver the best performance lies at the heart of every professional's commitment. Sharing that commitment with the peer group becomes important and can support the mentoring and coaching roles that develop others in the organization. How individuals achieve success is essential to share with others, particularly those coming up in their early career with the company. This is sometimes referred to as tacit knowledge – unspoken knowledge that good operators know and take for granted. Sharing it can make others more effective, too.

Power

Negotiate with power groups – and get them involved.

There has been a marked trend to involve members of unionized industries in the decisions made about the way they work. What once was negotiated between representatives of management and unions is now more often communicated directly to all those affected. Collective bargaining has sometimes been eroded by separate deals done directly with particular groups of workers. It marks a significant change from traditional approaches to dealing with power groupings.

BOX 2.3

In the railway industry strikes by drivers were frequent occurrences in the days of public ownership – usually over pay and conditions. Annual rates were on a par with drivers in other parts of the transport sector, which already suffered from high staff turnover, especially among younger workers. On taking over at privatization, one operator (Virgin) offered three times the going rate and since then that has governed pay throughout most of the industry. Strikes have now become the exception rather than the rule.

The McNulty Report (2011) suggested that staffing costs need to be reduced on the railways. But the benefit of enhanced pay has been very few strikes by drivers and a willingness to accept that other rail workers can progress to the driving position, too (something that would never have been countenanced by the unions in the publicly owned industry).

Culture

Work within the dominant culture, before attempting to move it on (we have seen an example of this in the previous case study).

As we will see when we consider culture in more detail, the simple early definition offered by Deal and Kennedy (1982) was 'the way we do things round here'. Anyone joining a workforce for the first time will be made aware of the parameters of acceptable behaviour by fellow workers (the peer group). Imposed change is often resisted precisely because it impacts on custom and practice among groups of workers. However, such changes may be the only way for an organization to survive in the context of radical changes within a sector or industry. Winning round the peer group will be important to achieve in order to avoid resistance or alienation (Nadler, 1993). Repeating yesterday's formulas at work do not usually lead to easy adaptation to required change.

Management by objectives

Translating strategic objectives into new ways of doing things at the functional end of the business is not new. Peter Drucker (1954) laid out a series of steps as follows:

- *Organizational objectives*: profit; market share; technology implementation needs to be translated into:
- *Departmental goals*: in finance; production; marketing; sales departments needs to be translated into:
- *Key tasks*: individual standards and targets in the employment contracts of each individual in those departments.

So, for example, a company looking to increase net profitability by a stated per cent would need to consider the implications for the different *departments* involved:

> *Production*: if the emphasis is on increasing sales, then more will need to be produced – but how much and which products, exactly?

> *Sales*: likewise, where are the sales increases to be targeted and what may be the effect on prices and margins? Are there particular products or services that will lead the sales focus?

> *Marketing*: what sort of promotional strategies will be needed to promote the extra growth in sales? How much will that cost the company? Are we looking for a 'pull' (advertising) or 'push' (direct approach) strategy in the market?

> *Finance*: well, the implications here will follow from the answers to the questions raised above. Increased production will need financing and investment; there will be extra costs in production; more salespeople needed; increased investment in marketing. The finance needs to come from somewhere: share issues/loans/selling off assets?

Once answers to these questions have been drawn up, the final step will lie in changes to *individual key tasks*. If we take the sales department as an illustration, where will the growth in sales come from? Traditionally, there are wide variations between yields from different territories. Sales in large cities tend to be higher because of concentration of customers. And then there are the salespeople to consider: experience and aptitude will govern what new targets may be agreed with those whose job contracts will now be affected.

So, in a sense, the traditional organization with its different levels would suggest that this cascade of changing standards and targets would concern only those whose level of responsibility strategic change applies to. So, the executive level devised the *organizational objectives*. Different departments would need to address the implications for their *departmental goals*, before turning to the implications for change *to individual employment contracts*.

FIGURE 2.3 The traditional bureaucratic layers.

In theory, this could be a top-down approach to management, in which there is little or no consultation of those lower down who will be affected by such a change to their terms and conditions (Figure 2.3). However, this is where the theory of HRM sought to change the cascade, top-down approach. *Strategic integration* requires that everyone is familiar with the three levels: organizational objectives; departmental gaols; and individual key tasks and how these levels interlink with one another and therefore aware of how crucial their contribution is to be to make the organization more effective.

BOX 2.4

Three stone masons were found on site chipping away as they worked on a new building. An observer who was interested in what they were doing approached the first mason and said: 'What are you doing?'

The first mason answered: 'I am chipping away at this stone.'

The observer moved to the second stone mason and ask the same question.

The second mason answered: 'I am building a column that will support one of the main arches.'

Finally, the observer moved to the third mason and asked the question again.

The third mason replied: 'I am building a Cathedral to the glory of God.'

Strategic integration requires workers to be aware of all three answers.

There is the functional level of *content* (what am I doing?); the *context* in which it takes place (why am I doing it?); and the overview or *big picture* of the final outcome (the big picture or overview to which my efforts contribute).

Strategic integration requires that every worker in the organization is able to understand all three aspects of their work and explain it to others.

Competitive advantage approach

First, SHRM (strategic human resource management) means adopting the correct strategies to support the corporate goals.

As we saw in Chapter One, this means that the only management interventions that can be made to alter the strategy of an organization lie in the *Human Resource Development* list:

- recruitment and selection
- induction training
- supervision
- management
- review
- appraisal
- reward
- development
- structure
- communication.

As we shall see, changing performance or behaviour is one challenge. But changing attitudes may be even more difficult to achieve, unless we adopt more radical approaches to staffing such as is offered by *business process re-engineering*. We might also note that the career path suggested by the HRD list is difficult to envisage in the context, say, of Handy's Shamrock organization. For, while the *core employees* will expect the full range of support outlined in the list, those in the *subcontract* segment will be recruited, trained and managed by their contracting company while those in the *consultancy segment* of the organization will necessarily have other work demands in other organizations. So, the full range of HR management interventions might not apply to all sectors of the Shamrock organization.

Linking strategy to innovation and creativity

As we saw in Guest's diagram, Table 2.1, he emphasizes all of these as *organizational outcomes*. Quality enhancement and innovation are difficult outcomes to support consistently, and there is no guarantee that they will coincide with cost reduction – particularly if these reduced costs give rise to interference or opportunity costs because of increased staff turnover, sick absence and grievances. Indeed there are some claims that quality enhancement requires more investment rather than less and that the search for perfect quality may even be outweighed by the costs involved in the search to achieve 100 per cent quality outcomes (Wilson, 1992).

HR practices must be in harmony with the strategic objectives

That seems an obvious assertion to make. However, some of the more radical approaches to change, such as business process re-engineering, adopt a macho approach to people management. In such environments, one of the dangers of the HR manager being on the Board of Directors is that when deciding on strategies that require staff reduction, it is HR who must implement the redundancy programme. This makes it difficult for HR staff on the Board to be seen as impartial in the management process. Indeed, the danger is that they may then be seen as the agents of management.

Certain types of behaviour are required of employees

Of course change programmes require changes in *behaviour* and these can be reinforced by training and validated after the training by measuring changes in behaviour back at work. However, deeper changes involving *attitude change* may be more difficult to manage. Here the issues of potential, ability and aptitude come into play. It may be that what is now required by the strategy is beyond the aptitude of the individuals involved. For some companies the radical change required meant starting afresh with new people away from the previous site so that no part of the previous culture was allowed to carry over to the new site.

Vertical integration is achieved when this connection is made satisfactorily

This statement sounds as if it is suggesting that *strategic integration* is a function of the behavioural requirements reinforced through the management interventions outlined in the HRD list. However, attitudes are much more difficult to change by training. In some cases the company may need to relocate elsewhere and start again. This strategy is sometimes referred to as moving from a 'brownfield site' to a 'greenfield site'.

BOX 2.5

In the 1980s Jaguar motors was spun off from the British Motor Corporation and set up as an independent car maker again. The managing director, John Egan, realized that the lessons derived from Japanese manufacturing, such as quality circles and kaizen were important in establishing a quality marque at the value-added end of the market. Sales of Jaguar cars increased in its major market (at that time the USA), but Egan, in spite of his charismatic management style, was unable to get more than 45 per cent of his workers to take part in quality circles. Eventually the strength of the dollar made the cars unacceptably expensive. But it is possible that the increased efficiency factors that Egan was trying to achieve might have given them more time selling at a reduced price while retaining a reasonable profit margin to survive the price erosion of international currency exchange with the US dollar, which was their main market (Storey, 1992).

Use hard or soft techniques as appropriate

The tradition of personnel practice certainly focused more on the softer side of people-handling techniques. The influence of HR management, where the emphasis is on managerialism or performativity is likely to focus on hard techniques, too. Many consultancy companies monitor the time spent in carrying out different tasks by their staff. These tasks are banded into, say, customer interface (highest yield to the business); back-office work (marginal but necessary cost); and routine tasks (low value-added in terms of client value-added). The ratio achieved by any individual may be the basis of a technique referred to as 'up or out'. That is, within a stated time (three years, say), the individual consultant is assessed as either fitted for promotion or they are dismissed depending on their yield to the company assessed at the three levels over that period.

The best fit approach

Staffing the organization by using the best fit model suggests that each job role will have a profile of knowledge, skills and experience that will need to be satisfied by candidates filling the job. In the case of workers' qualifications, there will be examples where this has already been done in virtue of their training, for example, most of the professions or trades. However, the basic knowledge and skills may not be sufficient. The company may need other skills that require previous experience in, say, negotiational skills, or linguistic skills. These would be complementary skills over and above those required for the basic job role requirements.

We have mentioned in passing the difficulty of changing attitudes – sometimes referred to as commitment. The terms refer not just to competence – can you do it? but 'do you want to do it?' And this is where some of the more radical approaches to change such as *business process re-engineering* come in. One of its proponents put it quite bluntly:

- Don't live too long with people who refuse to change their behaviour.
- This applies to managers as well as workers.
- Don't expect people to change their behaviour unless you change what they do.
- Don't expect cultural change to happen immediately.
- Don't articulate new values and then delay re-engineering management processes to make it happen.

(Champy, 1995: 109)

The first point here suggests that there is little or no place for those who do not adapt quickly to the new requirements. Similarly, in his book *The Road to Nissan*, Wickens (1987) recounts the opening of a greenfield site in Sunderland. He notes that there were many competent car workers who applied for one of the 2000 jobs on offer in their new factory. But they chose workers who had

had no union involvement, thereby setting up a unitary organization rather than the pluralistic organization with its tri-partite relations between management, union(s) and workers.

BOX 2.6

In one inner city school which was renowned as a sinking educational establishment in a difficult area the government of the day decided to set up a City Academy, with funding from a donor in the private sector. A new Head was appointed who inherited 48 staff, many of whom had got used to the undemanding ways of many of their pupils and their parents.

The new Head decided to offer all staff who wanted to stay a new contract: in future all teachers would teach to a new target – all pupils would leave the school in future with at least 5 GCSEs achieving at least grade 3.

Four of the original 48 teachers accepted and came back to teach under the new regime.

'Don't expect cultural change to happen immediately.' But in this case the Head articulated the new values and then promulgated them.

All the doors in this newly target-focused institution open from the inside.

All of this suggests that strategy needs to be devised around employee role behaviour, which will in turn suggest the relevant HR policies for the company to pursue (Schuler and Jackson, 1987).

Pfeffer (1998) suggests seven practices for gaining advantage through people.

Good selection practices (competency based)

So we are back to the first step of the HRD list. Good recruitment and selection. The focus is on the three factors that are the function of competency:

- knowledge
- skill
- experience.

It should be noted that training courses often include all three of these elements and because they are measurable they lend themselves readily to standards and standardization that can be validated at the end of the training. So, this part of the selection process is more likely to be accurate, reliable and testable.

BOX 2.7

In training for pilots the approach to landing is governed by a three-degree flight path to the runway; plus or minus 50 feet above and below the centre line; and not more than 2.5 degrees either side of the centre line to the runway. So pilots can be tested on simulators in varying weather conditions or with engines out of action to test whether they are still capable of executing a landing within those parameters. Training, validation and licensing are all dependent on the implementation of these standards.

Secure employment opportunities (life-long service)

This aspect becomes more difficult to retain as time goes on, for reasons that we have seen demonstrated in Handy's Shamrock organization. Change in global patterns of manufacturing and offshoring have even affected the Japanese aspiration to offer such security to their workers. If Handy is correct that core workers will find full-time employment between 27 and 35 years of age before being required to relocate in subcontract or consultancy work, then lifelong employment in one organization will be difficult for the individual to sustain. Indeed, it has been suggested that the *portfolio career* will see employees evaluating how far a job enhances their knowledge, extends their skills and increases their experience, so that they will be more employable when their time with the company runs out (Iles, 1997). In HR, increasing numbers of staff are on an interim contract with a fixed term. So even here, a lifelong career is not guaranteed.

BOX 2.8

A sales force selling US-produced printing machines in the UK found that they were confronted by competition from a foreign producer. This organization had carefully reproduced their key product, carefully avoiding violation of patents and offered it free as long as the customer signed a five-year deal on servicing, paper and ink supplies. At a sales meeting the salespeople asked to be given a similar deal so that they could compete. The director of marketing said: 'I don't want to hear any of this negative mental attitude. Anyone can sell what we haven't got. I need people who can see what we have got.' Shortly after this announcement, several of the sales force were looking for another job elsewhere.

A climate of sharing information (kaizen)

Kaizen is based on quality circle members meeting regularly to discuss with the members of other quality teams what they have learned for improving the *efficiency factors* of what they do (Imai, 1986). The intention is to encourage the sharing of these improvements found in one team to all the other teams. Less often are the effectiveness factors discussed (is our product satisfying the customer, or not?). Such questions are for management, not workers, to consider.

Active fostering of learning and development (L&D), supported by well-resourced training (basis of quality circles)

Technology seldom stands still in any sector. So, incremental change and supporting training become important stepping stones for keeping a workforce up to date and efficient enough to compete effectively in their marketplace. Senge (1990) introduced the concept of the 'learning organization' which caught the popular imagination among many managers. We have already seen how kaizen was used to further such learning in the manufacturing sector while noting that the remit can sometimes be confined to workers criticizing their own efficiency. However, in the professional sector, such learning is difficult to stimulate and attempts to get such groups to take part in shared knowledge has been found to be unlikely to be embraced whole-heartedly by knowledge workers (McKinlay, 2002).

More in keeping with the need for individual development has been *continuing professional development*, which is required by most lead bodies whose members want to retain their professional membership (Marchington and Wilkinson, 2006). Companies that support their consultancy and professional staff to pursue their CPD plan by allowing time off or helping with costs may find that their commitment to the organization is reinforced, as leaving the organization might lose them the support they need to achieve their CPD goals.

Reward systems that are firmly related to performance (PRP/PRP)

Performance related pay has been part of the pay structure key to incentivizing staff in sectors such as sales. The system has a surface validity that appears to relate ability and effort to reward. It appears to reward those who are at the top of their professional life in terms of their competence and commitment. Much, however, depends on the customer perception of the company's products and services and the demand in the marketplace, as does the potential that can be derived from a particular sales area or territory. Various schemes can be put in place to ensure that the company does not have to pay out too much to salespeople, including what are known as 'house accounts', where the large organizations falling within a territory are reserved to the company rather than the individual in whose territory they actually fall.

BOX 2.9

In one company the sales incentives were banded according to monetary levels. So, whatever sale was made up to £500 enjoyed a commission of 5 per cent. From £500–£1500 enjoyed a commission of 2.5 per cent and anything over £1500 at 0.25 per cent. This led to a sales person selling a £50,000 weighbridge receiving well under £100 for his pains. The company argued that it meant that sales people selling in areas of low priced products were not disadvantaged by colleagues in higher yielding markets. Not many salespeople were convinced by this argument.

A reduction of status differentials among the employees (consensus approach)

Profit related pay, by contrast, could be described as reinforcing team efforts. Such examples as John Lewis Partnership operate on that basis. Everyone is rewarded for their efforts, rather than those who happen to be high performers. Not many companies adopt this approach to incentivizing their team members and in some examples there has been evidence that workers in large organizations receiving shares at, say, privatization noticed no correlation between their hard work and the share price. They might work hard and see the shares fall, while the opposite could also be the case. Lack of correlation between effort and reward may mean that workers become uncertain about the value of holding on to their shares (Dunn *et al.*, 1991).

Extolling the virtues of teamwork and well-managed teams (TQM philosophy)

When we look at matrix organizations and we will see that integrated interdisciplinary teams are a function not just of flatter organizations, but also of *flexibility*. Using people when they are needed and moving them from project to project as need requires is something that appeals to organizations in which, as Drucker noted, the highest outgoing is staff costs. He noted that while in the car industry Honda had achieved a staff cost of 11 per cent, in the service sector it remained as high as 75 per cent. We might note that the financial sector's rush to adopt call centres, internet banking and hole-in-the-wall dispensing of cash were all intended to reduce the biggest unit on-cost they face: branches and staff in the High Street.

Technology will continue to erode even skilled and professional roles and make flexible working even more flexible. It offers opportunity for small companies to compete with larger competitors effectively without investing in the overheads born by their larger rivals.

BOX 2.10

The BBC has offered a benchmark for broadcasters worldwide and continues to market its products wherever they are appreciated; 24-hour broadcasting, like supermarket opening, is not going to go away. Interestingly, then, smaller rivals have adopted technology that allows night-time broadcasting on some radio stations to take place from the presenter's home. It is yet another example of telecommuting, avoiding the cost and inconvenience of staff travelling to distant locations at unsocial hours.

Best practice

Another approach to recruiting the right staff to implement the strategy is to look for best practice and high commitment in the staff attracted and retained. Pfeffer (1998) suggests that choosing the right selection of HR practices appropriate to the strategic need will reinforce the profile required to achieve success. It will be clear that the choice of HR practices now becomes critical. A mix of best fit and best practice approaches would suggest that a contingency approach is relevant. The HR strategy needs to support the external dynamics of the market requirements while being focused inwardly towards individual and group needs. That makes HR a bridge between the outside context and the internal content governing required performance and standards to achieve the organizational objectives (Huselid, 1995).

Best practice model

This practice is based on the belief that generating *organizational commitment* transforms staff into ambassadors of the organization.

But what are these best practices?

1   *Good selection practices (competency based/assessment centres)*

As we have seen, the clarity and accuracy of recruitment and selection will be the gauge of success here. Competencies often can be measured or tested according to the required standard and above-average performers are then more easily identified. Clearly, psychomotor tests, provided they are valid, are always reliable. As we saw with pilot training, the reflexes of the candidate can be quickly measured and they rarely deteriorate until late in life.

Less certain are the requirements for commitment, or what used to be called 'the right sort of attitude'. Unfortunately, effective tests are neither valid nor reliable. They can be manipulated by those who know how they work. Similarly, interviews are among the least reliable ways of choosing people who have 'the right sort of attitude'. This may account for why school or family background can sometimes suggest to interviewers that he or she 'is one of us' (Toplis *et al.*, 1994).

2   *Secure employment opportunities (lifelong service/Japanese car companies/IBM)*
    During the post-war period of the 1950s the majority of Britons left school,
    joined an organization and spent the bulk of their employment there until
    retirement. Most industries were structured to allow gradual progression
    through the levels of the organization leading to a gold watch and retirement.
    One example would be the railway industry, in which the new recruit joining
    after leaving school would become a cleaner in an engine shed, the trainee
    would be expected to progress through the grades from fireman to driver and
    then on through 'the links' of goods and passenger train operations, attaining
    the 'top link' of express driving at 60 for the last five years of his (they were
    all male then) working life. Fewer than 11 per cent of Britons would now fall
    into that long-term employment in one organization category and most of
    those are probably nearing retirement.
        Today's world of work offers a fragmented and diverse series of opportu-
    nities to move around, redeploy and find employment based on a portfolio of
    knowledge and skills acquired through diverse experience and often involving
    frequent changes of employer and retraining.

3   *A climate of sharing information (kaizen/Monday morning meeting devoted to improv-
    ing efficiency)*
    We have already seen this aspect offered as an example of the learning organiza-
    tion. An alternative suggestion has been *organizational learning* (Easterby-Smith,
    1997). The idea of *tacit knowledge* has been examined over the years (Nonaka
    and Takeuchi, 1995) and examples of it can be found in most organizations.
    Internalizing any process requires aptitude, ability and practice, after which
    it becomes second nature and is rarely questioned. The challenge remains to
    communicate it to develop others less experienced.

4   *Active fostering of learning and development, supported by well-resourced training (basis
    of quality circles/job rotation/mutual improvement classes)*
    The significant aspect of L&D at work is not new and certainly predates
    TQM. Apprenticeships are themselves opportunities to learn with someone
    skilled and experienced in a trade or profession. The peer group can support
    L&D at both the formal and informal levels for newly recruited staff. That can
    be both a strength and a weakness, particularly if a strongly reinforced culture
    requiring change responds with resistance.

5   *Reward systems that are firmly related to performance (PRP/PRP – performance
    related/profit related pay)*
    Either of these options can be advantageous in the best practice model. Though
    Fletcher (1993) makes the point that it is better if the pay assessment is done
    at another time than the appraisal, and preferably by an outside agency with
    a special competence in comparative salary assessment. His view is that once
    individuals realize they are not to receive what they thought they deserved
    they have a tendency to switch off from the rest of the appraisal process.

6   *A reduction of status differentials among the employees (consensus approach/single canteen/no pre-set parking spaces)*
Flatter organizations mean 5/6 levels only from functional to executive levels. Deconstructing privilege can be useful in reinforcing a work ethic, reinforcing solidarity, or realigning priorities in an organization.

BOX 2.11

When General Bill Slim took over the XIV army in Burma during the Second World War he discovered among other things that the main complaint of the soldiers was lack of mail and the sporadic supply of cigarettes. So he decreed that these items would be sent to the front-line troops first as a priority and that should there be any lack then the Headquarters supply staff would go without first.

He noted that following his decree there was never a lack of cigarettes as HQ staff made absolutely sure that mail and cigarettes were supplied as a matter of urgency.

(From Slim, 1958, *Defeat into Victory*)

---

7   *Extolling the virtues of teamwork and well-managed teams (TQM philosophy)*
As we noted earlier, teams remain an important vehicle for promoting matrix or interdisciplinary working. However, all working practices need eventually to improve or up rate. Achieving standards of performance does not guarantee quality, which is not an absolute but is always relative to what the customer can get elsewhere from the competition. Furthermore, teams themselves need occasional changes of personnel as they rarely survive a three-year period (Procter and Mueller, 2000).

Resource-based model

The inside-out model, as we have seen, assumes that the current workforce can be developed to accomplish new levels of efficiency in achieving the organization's objectives. An initiative such as TQM is one example of this approach. The underpinning assumptions are simple:

- Focus on the internal competencies and processes that govern the *efficiency factors of the organization*:
  - time
  - quality
  - quantity
  - cost

- *Value*: focus on creating value for the customer; enhancing efficiency; meeting customer needs.
- *Rarity*: the skills profile is unusual enough to be special (perhaps a mix of talents that are difficult for the competition to emulate). Anyone with perceived outstanding skills can take full advantage of their rarity value, as top-class international footballers soon find out.
- *Inimitability*: Follows on from the previous factor (as we saw earlier in this chapter, sometimes referred to as the unique selling proposition – USP). Sadly, however, there are few things that cannot be replicated fairly quickly, and unscrupulous, low-cost producers often find a way to capture new markets with lookalike products or services.
- *Organization*: horizontal integration facilitated by HRM processes that coordinate the disparate nature of different departments, particularly with regard to: employee resourcing; development; performance management; rewards and employee relations.
- This may be seen in action in a TQM context where the focus is on internal processes that set up and reinforce the desirable set of standards in the production and distribution areas (Oakland, 1989).

Processual change

Processual change has traditionally focused on the systems in use within the organization to achieve its objectives. Each industry adopts its own approaches to how things are done which reinforces the custom and practice that governs most people's working lives. In the traditional triangle which represents the hierarchical approach to management functional workers moved into supervisory roles and then on into management functions. This meant that those who managed and those who supervised workers knew from experience what the workers were supposed to be doing and could intervene proactively when things went wrong to remedy the situation. There are still industries in which this remains the case. Flying continues to be run on strictly processual lines and older and more experienced fliers are paired up with those who are just starting out on their flying careers.

But there are situations where this is no longer the case. The Shamrock organization suggests that there will be a variety of staffing inputs that are occasional or sporadic based on the expertise needed by the business at the time. IT interventions require expertise which managers do not share. If they did, they could arguably have done it for themselves. So, another approach is needed to manage such professionals in what they contribute to the organization.

Managing consultants

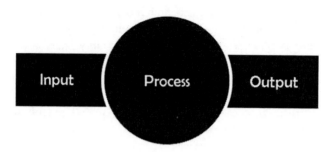

FIGURE 2.4 Managing consultants.

In this case (Figure 2.4) the *inputs* need to be closely defined by the management of the organization. They will be part of the contract agreed before work begins and should specify:

- time
- quantity
- quality
- cost.

The *outputs* similarly need to be defined closely and may relate to the effectiveness factors of end-user use, whether internal or external. Where relationships often go wrong is when change in specification is insisted on and the contract changes. The construction of the Scottish Parliament is a good example of this. So also is the Edinburgh tram system. Unanticipated change can have serious implications that put the original contract at risk. To recover it will usually require more time, effort and cost.

There are other initiatives that can assist in keeping positive relationships alive between parties to consultancy contracts:

- it can emphasize *employee involvement* which suggests that consultation is the mode of managing and people's ideas are encouraged (pioneered by Jack Welsh in GE – who, it should be noted, also sacked the lowest performing 10 per cent of his staff every year, perhaps to encourage the others);
- it can increase the information both the individual and organization have about each other (*strategic integration again*);
- it can emphasize the impact of grass-roots practice in the modification of policy and procedures (*kaizen: focuses on efficiency improvements*);
- *inputs* focus on the efficiency factors. Specify time, quantity, quality and cost closely if you want control of those whose process you do not know, so cannot manage;

- *outputs* focus on effectiveness factors: what it will mean for the end-user; how it will out-play the competition;
- redolent of Deal and Kennedy's (1982) dictum: 'It's the way we do things round here' (*but notice how this focuses on behaviours*);
- the pragmatic approach to research in organizations (*the need to turn data into information*);
- though could encourage diversity around different managers and hence divergence rather than convergence (*unless standards are specific and enforced*).

It will be seen that there are specific similarities between best practice and processual change. Lying behind both approaches are the efficiency factors (time; quality; quantity; cost), the outcome of *quality* being the last of Guest's HR outcomes.

Psychological contract – Macneil, 1985; Rousseau, 1990

There are many references in management literature to the *psychological contract* that, it is suggested, exists between the individual and the organization. It relates to staff retention, for example, and therefore maybe the gauge of how well we are doing in our HR/management interventions.

Denise Rousseau suggested two levels at which the individual may be bonded to the organization:

- *transactional elements*:
  - time and effort in return for money and reward (employment contract conditions)
  - we might consider this to be the content of the normal employment contract
- *relational elements*:
  - loyalty, trust, commitment, development, personal aspirations to get on
  - here, the link suggests more personal contacts in which well-liked and respected managers are able to call on the loyalty of their staff, having built up a relationship of trust.

Guest (1998a, b) spent much time and effort trying to establish evidence to support the links in the psychological contract and came to the conclusion that the contract between individual and organization is difficult to sustain in the way the theory suggests. He argues that a contract is usually between two people and that an organization cannot reciprocate the kind of loyalty suggested by the theory. Rather, the feeling of loyalty is generated between individuals, most importantly with their immediate manager – although their employment contract is drawn up in the name of the organization for which they work.

BOX 2.12

A well-known retailer in the DIY sector had 106 stores UK-wide. They undertook a programme of training for managers, deputies and shop-floor supervisors in management competencies. During the programme the provider discovered that all the deputies who succeeded to management positions had come through one of six stores. Observation suggested that these six managers spent time developing their deputies and reflecting informally with them on what had happened in the store at the end of each day. This kind of mentoring clearly marks out the informal development that supports learning and leads to confident application for the final step up to store manager.

One particular deputy, Tom, had had a number of run-ins with previous managers and was eventually sent to one of the six managers, Dave. Dave did his usual mentoring on Tom who eventually turned himself round and became a good manager himself. Later Tom described Dave's style as follows: 'If you were in trouble and Dave sent for you, he could give you a rollicking, but when you came out you knew he was still your friend.'

Of course, in the context of the *Shamrock organization*, it is possible to provide such support to the core workers, and managers should be trained and encouraged to mentor their staff. But there are question marks over the other two sectors of the organization.

So, for example, how likely is it that the full psychological contract is within the remit of the Shamrock organization for its subcontract workers? For those working in the subcontract sector the relational element might well be less apparent as their employer is, strictly speaking, their subcontractor responsible for recruiting, training and supervising their work. As they have no guarantee that the contract will be renewed at the end of its term, long-term commitment would be unrealistic, even if they built up a good rapport with the customers they serve.

The same might be said of the consultancy sector within the organization. The transactional element of their psychological contract will be partial, largely because if consultants work for more than 75 per cent of their time for one organization they will lose their legal right to declare themselves self-employed for taxation purposes. They will usually be well trained in their discipline, so training is not an issue for them. Consultants are under contract so they must be self-managing to meet the standards and deadlines of their contract. So, what would reinforce their commitment to the organization?

The answer might well be *continuing professional development*. Most professional bodies require their members to offer a rolling programme of self-development in order to retain their membership of the profession and, still more so, to progress to higher levels of the profession. Organizations that offer help in preparing submissions, evidence of projects worked on, or references for work successfully completed could well encourage organizational commitment in a group who would otherwise expect to be peripatetic.

Seeing HR as an investment

HRM professionals are seen as business partners

This is a difficult concept both to envisage and realize. It comes close to the old idea of internalization in which individuals can be trusted to do what is needed to satisfy customers, if necessary, using their own discretion (*EI – employee involvement – approach*) (Wilkinson *et al.*, 1992).

Developing a professional profile for people whose jobs might have been perceived previously as a 'trade' or even lo-tech/no-tech jobs might require training, status, recognition and reward. It requires the development of people in understanding the business dynamics along with continuous communication between managers and staff (features, advantages and benefits).

BOX 2.13

In the latter days of British Rail the Board decided to introduce customer care training for all guards on trains at a cost of £3 million. These (mostly) men had been used to guarding the train in the event of breakdown; protecting the train in foggy or poor conditions; knowing what to do in the event of the train separating etc. Grafting customer handling skills onto functional skills did not appeal to all participants. So, BR set up a new grade: senior conductor, with a special uniform, terms and conditions, and employed them on Intercity trains. Since then, most guards have now adapted to that role and are now allowed to move on to driving duties (something that would have been unheard of in less flexible times).

Employees are continually updating their knowledge, sharing it with others, learning and developing themselves (*organizational learning*). The problem is, managers may never find out what this tacit knowledge involves. Quality circles and kaizen tried to institutionalize such practices (though tended to focus on *efficiency factors*).

BOX 2.14

There are some companies where directors are encouraged to spend two weeks on the shop floor doing a routine, functional job, perhaps on the checkout in a retail store. This even covers contact with customers, too (*effectiveness factors*). There is nothing like first-hand knowledge and experience of what business challenges are today.

Effectiveness focuses on the *end-user evaluation* (companies are not good at this).

BOX 2.15

Universities are good at validation: exams are double marked and sent out to external examiners at other universities. Appeals procedures are taken seriously and investigated fully. However, they are not always as good at evaluation. They use alumni groups to solicit money or arrange occasional meetings when faculty are travelling abroad, for example. But if they were serious about evaluation they would ask their students at least every three years: 'Did anything we teach you make a difference to your business career?'

HR is a team job: it depends on line managers to be effective and it has always proclaimed that this was the important link to establish. To parrot the phrase that *People are our most important resource* wears thin when it is demonstrated to workers that this is obviously not the case. Zero hours contracts and reduced human rights (often referred to by politicians as 'unnecessary red tape') do not improve trust in organizations or their stakeholders.

Competency and knowledge are only seen as the means of *adding value* if the customers and clients perceive that this is the case. It could be as well to check from time to time. Retail stores have mystery shoppers, but how many other businesses do the same thing?

BOX 2.16

A managing director wanted to test out how good his staff were at answering the phone following his investment in customer care training. He wanted to see whether they had got the hang of being helpful or not. The voice answering said gruffly: "ello'. He asked: 'Could I speak to Mr Jones, please?' The voice replied: "e ain't 'ere'. The MD persevered by asking: 'Can you tell me when he might be back?' and the reply came back: 'No, I don't see him, do I?'

Eventually the MD said: 'Do you know who is speaking to you?' The voice said, 'No'. 'This is your MD speaking,' he stated. There was a silence and then the voice asked: 'Do you know who this is?' And the MD said, 'No'. The voice replied: 'Thank God for that' and put the phone down.

Training does not always change attitudes.

Leadership and teamworking are crucial to the endeavour to provide the links between the theory and practice of HR. Behaviours and outcomes should be recognized and rewarded and the link to *quality standards* reinforced throughout the organization.

In this way individual and organizational goals can be aligned. Otherwise they may be slipping apart.

Industrial best practice

The company needs to aim to be seen as the 'employer of choice' in its sector (Marks & Spencer). Detailed best practice focuses attention of potential customers on the organization (Mercedes) so that it is regarded as a benchmark of quality in its sector.

HR as business partner (Ulrich, 1997)

Four key roles of HR

1   *Strategic partner*: HR managers entering into collaborative partnership with line managers should raise standards in connection with strategy formulation and execution. This means collaboration at all levels with HR providing expertise and support to managers in the critical interviews (recruitment; disciplinary; grievance) and managers sharing concerns that may need to be addressed by revising company policy, procedure and practice.
2   *Change agents*: responsible for bringing about organizational transformation and cultural change. Given that most change is coercive for organizations (that is the driver is the law of the land) updating the company's policy, procedure and practices is the primary duty of the HR department. All other relevant documents need to be adjusted accordingly, especially the staff handbook, personnel and training manuals and operations directories. Any disparity of detail between these key documents will give problems should an employment appeal tribunal or court case be impending.
3   *Administrative expert*: constantly improving organization efficiency by re-engineering the work and HR processes. A difficult role that requires tact and trust between HR and operational managers. Experience helps and joint problem solving may be even better at bringing about understanding and insight.
4   *Employee champion*: as employee advocate, the HR developer focuses on day-to-day operational matters. The balance to be struck here is crucial to the impartiality that is necessary for HR to be held in high esteem by everyone. HR should never be perceived by staff as the managers' spies. Nor should HR become an unofficial union for the staff. Discretion is all and confidentiality vital.

Competitive advantage models

This is more proactive in its aspiration to acquire staff who will take the business forward into the future. One of the classic questions that facilitators ask of groups of workers during emergent change sessions is: 'What are the challenges you face as a business in the next three years?'

The answers will often be indicative of people's awareness of risk and challenge facing their business, but also of opportunities for change that may prove worth pursuing (action learning).

Using staff to their best advantage in the roles to which they are best suited was mentioned by McGregor as the hallmark of the Y manager. Some workers like constant challenge and change. They are sometimes referred to as initiators. Their interventions are usually insightful even if not always welcome to their managers. They are harder to keep, however, and can be difficult to retain once the initial impetus of innovation is firmly established in day-to-day business.

BOX 2.17

Retail stores often use initiators as store opening or store revamp teams. They lead and enervate the staff who will have to stay on and keep it going after the initial surge of interest from customers has died down a little.

Initiators may also make good trainers and coaches. Challenge and change are usual and indeed, needed by them.

Finally, we might remind ourselves of the classic cycle of management that governs all concerted efforts that want a chance of achieving success (see Figure 2.5).

Wherever that break comes in the cycle, there the strategy will break down and managers and staff need to intervene to restore the links between what we plan to do and following it through to completion.

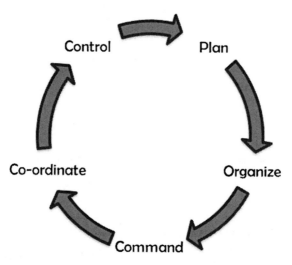

FIGURE 2.5 Management cycle.

Source: Adapted from Fayol (1949).

Back to Guest (1989)

- *Strategic integration*: means staying in touch with everyone about changes in the business objectives. Strategic plans rarely remain intact. Events conspire to divert, distract or derail plans. At that stage they need to be readdressed and represented to the team, so that everyone knows what they are doing.
- *Commitment*: means developing staff through job/work/career and organizational commitment. As we have seen, that may be different for different people in the fragmented organization that includes core workers, subcontractors and consultants. They will have different needs and HR needs to address these directly.
- *Flexibility*: means time/number/cost – but don't forget *functional flexibility*. Reward is important to consider as we develop individuals and groups. Taking on more responsibility should be acknowledged. If that means acquiring knowledge and skill to enhance business opportunities and decision making, then that should be rewarded and acknowledged.
- *Quality*: standards, targets and training. But remember, these often appear as absolutes (ISO standards; Investors in People etc.). In fact they are relative, and they are relative to the value-added that they offer to the end user. *Effectiveness* is all and it lies in the perception of the customer.

'Assumptions about human resource strategy, whether explicit or implicit, will have an influence on what organizations actually do. Assumptions will limit what are seen as legitimate choices' (Torrington *et al.*, 2011: 73).

References and further reading

Blyton, P. and Turnbull, P. (1992) *Reassessing Human Resource Management*. London: Sage.

Boxall, P. and Purcell, J. (2003) *Strategy and Human Resource Management*. Basingstoke: Palgrave.

Champy, J. (1995) *Reengineering Management*. New York: Harper Business.

Clegg, S., Carter, C., Kornberger, M. and Sweitzer, J. (2011) *Strategy: Theory and practice*. London: Sage.

Deal, T. and Kennedy, A. (1982) *Organization Cultures: The rights and rituals of organization life*. Reading, MA: Addison Wesley.

De Wit, B. and Meyer, R. (2004) *Strategy: Process, content, context*. London: Thomson.

De Wit, R. and Meyer, R. (2010) *Strategy: Process, Content, Context*. Andover: Cengage Learning.

Drucker, P.F. (1954) *The Practice of Management*. New York: Harper and Row.

Dunn, S., Richardson, R. and Dewe, P. (1991) The impact of employee share ownership on worker attitudes: a longitudinal case study. *Human Resource Management Journal*, 1(3): 1–17.

Dunphy, D. and Stace, D. (1992) *Under New Management: Australian organizations in transition*. Roseville, NSW: McGraw-Hill.

Easterby-Smith, M. (1997) Disciplines of organizational learning: Contributions and critiques. *Human Relations*, 50(9): 1085–1113.

Fayol, H. (1949) *General and Industrial Management* (trans. C. Storrs). London: Pitman.

Fletcher, C. (1993) *Appraisal*. London: IPM.

Green, C. (2001) *Phoenix from the Ashes* (ILT Sir Robert Reid Lecture 2001).

Guest, D.E. (1989) Personnel and HRM: Can you tell the difference? *Personnel Management*, 21(1): 48–51.

Guest, D.E. (1998a) Is the psychological contract worth taking seriously? *Journal of Organizational Behaviour*, 19: 649–664.

Guest, D.E. (1998b) On meaning, metaphor and the psychological contract: A response to Rousseau. *Journal of Organizational Behaviour*, 19: 673–677.

Huselid, M. (1995) The impact of Human Resource Management practices on turnover, productivity and corporate financial performance. *Academy of Management Journal*, 38: 635–672.

Iles, P. (1997) Sustainable high-potential career development: A resource-based view. *Career Development International*, 2(7): 347–353.

Imai, Masaaki (1986) *Kaizen: The key to Japan's competitive success*. New York: McGraw-Hill/ Irwin.

McKinlay, A. (2002) The limits of knowledge management. *New Technology, Work and Employment*, 17(2): 76–88.

Macneil, I.R. (1985) Relational contracts: What we do and do not know. *Wisconsin Law Review*, 5: 483–525.

McNulty, R. (2011) *Realising the Potential of GB Rail: Report of the Rail Value for Money Study*. Department for Transport: Crown copyright.

Marchington, M. and Wilkinson, A. (2006) *Human Resource Management at Work (People Management & Development)*, 3rd edn. London: CIPD.

Nadler, D.A. (1993) Concepts for the management of strategic change, in C. Mabey and B. Mayon-White (eds) *Managing Change*. London: The Open University/Paul Chapman Publishing, pp.85–98.

Nonaka, I. and Takeuchi, H. (1995) *The Knowledge Creating Company*. New York: Oxford University Press.

Oakland, J. (1989) *Total Quality Management*. Oxford: Butterworth Heinemann.

Pfeffer, J. (1998) *The Human Equation: Building profits by putting people first*. Boston, MA: Harvard Business School Press.

Procter, S. and Mueller, F. (eds) (2000) *Teamworking*. London: Macmillan.

Rousseau, D.M. (1990) New hire perceptions of their own and their employer's obligations: A study of psychological contracts. *Journal of Organizational Behaviour*, 11(5): 389–400.

Schuler, R.S. and Jackson, S.E. (1987) Linking competitive strategies with human resource management practices. *Academy of Management Executive*, 1(3): 207–219.

Senge, P. (1990) *The Fifth Discipline: The art and practice of the learning organization*. London: Random House.

Slim, W. (1958) *From Defeat to Victory*. London: Pan Military Classics Series.

Storey, J. (1992) *Developments in the Management of Human Resources*. Oxford: Blackwell.

Toplis, J., Dulewicz, V. and Fletcher, C. (1994) *Psychological Testing: A manager's guide*. London: Institute of Personnel Management.

Torrington, D., Hall, D., Taylor, S. and Atkinson, C. (2011) *Human Resource Management*. FT Prentice Hall: Harlow.

Ulrich, D. (1997) *Human Resource Champions: The new agenda for adding value and delivering results*. Boston, MA: Harvard Business School Press.

Wickens, P. (1987) *The Road to Nissan: Flexibility, quality, teamwork*. Basingstoke: Macmillan.

Wilkinson, A., Marchington, M., Goodman, J. and Ackers, P. (1992) Total quality management and employee involvement. *Human Resource Management Journal*, 2(4): 1–20.

Wilson, D.C. (1992) *A Strategy of Change*. London: Routledge

GRADUATE ATTRIBUTES

In this exercise you will develop:

- a capacity for problem identification, the collection of evidence, synthesis and dispassionate analysis;
- a capacity for attentive exchange, informed argument and reasoning;
- an ability to communicate effectively for different purposes and in different contexts.

In this exercise you will be asked to use the knowledge you have gained from Chapter 2: Strategy and strategic integration, as well as your critical analysis skills. You are presented with a business scenario and are asked to place yourself in the role of a human resources manager asked to define the way ahead in a difficult situation.

Accomodare DIY superstore

It is 09.00 on a grey September morning and you, the HR manager of the Accomodare DIY superstore chain, are summoned by the managing director for a meeting. The managing director is very concerned about the 80 per cent staff turnover among the shop-floor workers. The managing director stresses to you that each checkout person that leaves costs the company £1,500 in lost training, uniforms and the need to re-advertise and recruit a replacement member of staff. As HR manager it is your job to address this problem; promising that you will make it a priority, you leave the meeting determined to get to the bottom of the matter.

After conducting a staff survey and interviews you discover that morale is low among the staff. The survey confirms that the composition of the superstore chain's staff is 80 per cent part-time, older females (the shop-floor workers). Survey results and interviews clearly indicate that the shop-floor workers feel resentment at being pushed around by the shop-floor supervisors (mostly young, male, full-time employees). The survey results also show that on average shop-floor supervisors must wait two years before they receive a management training course. You decide to write a report recommending a pilot training scheme for your key store with an option to roll it out to all of the stores in the chain if it is successful.

The key store

The Accomodare DIY superstore chain's key store has 100 staff and a staff–supervisor ratio of 1:8. This means that the key store has 12 shop-floor supervisors to 88 shop-floor staff. The composition of the staff in the store matches that confirmed by your survey and the store's turnover rate of shop-floor workers matches the chain average of 80 per cent. So you have a store that is a perfect model for what is happening across the chain.

Your tasks as the HR manager are these:

1   Design a series of courses that will last no more than two days each (management will be anxious not to have the staff absent from the store for too long)
that will reinforce professional behaviour in the core competencies that govern the shop-floor supervisor's job responsibilities. The aim of these will be to
reduce staff turnover to 40 per cent.
2   Demonstrate to senior management that training is a cost benefit by illustrating how good training costs less than the interference costs the store is
currently suffering through the high staff turnover.

Questions you should ask

Before beginning this task you may wish to ask yourself some questions.

- If the key-store has 88 shop-floor staff and a turnover rate of 80 per cent what
  will the interference cost be?
- What kind of training will the supervisors require to assist the reduction of the
  turnover rate?
- What are the main issues that the training must address?
- Would you consider:
    - instructional training techniques?
    - interview skills techniques?
    - leading and building teams?
- Why would these be appropriate or inappropriate to deal with the issues?
- What issues may the composition of the shop-floor staff, 80 per cent older
  female, part-time workers, have for your training programme?
- What methods will you put in place to validate and evaluate the training
  programme?
- Would 360-degree feedback be appropriate?
- What about exit interviews for staff that leave?
- What are the advantages and disadvantages of these or other approaches?

Costs

Given that there are 12 supervisors in the store and that ten days training spread
over six months should suffice, then with a cost per day of £1,000 for the trainer
plus £1,000 in marginal and interference costs (loss of supervisor's time in store;
travel and support) what will the total cost be to the chain?

- Will the training costs, if the training aim is successful, be worthwhile to the
  chain?
- What should you include in your narrative?
- What do you need to include in your report to make it convincing to the
  senior management?

No organization can afford to throw money and time at training and hope it is relevant and that it sticks. The Accomodare management are no different so you must be sure to include some of the following in your narrative:

- absence management
- training needs analysis
- training evaluation levels
- performance appraisal
- development appraisal level
- hard HRM calculations.

At the end of the exercise you may be asked to write a written report or make an individual or group presentation to a suitable audience, being ready to answer questions at the end of your presentation.

Tutor guidance

This exercise can be done in stages or as a report writing/presentation exercise, depending on the objectives set for the tutor groups. If you want to divide it up then there is scope for brainstorming in the group. Students may not be familiar with speaking out as ideas come to them. Putting them to work on the ideas in smaller syndicate groups may encourage them to generate ideas before you run a plenary session and get the ideas down in written form. Writing up requires a facilitational role which can be done by any member of the group and may be best done by one of the group rather than the tutor.

Topics to address can include:

- the training need
- choice of management competencies
- learning objectives for each course
- training methods to develop knowledge and skill
- validation and evaluation issues
- cost–benefit analysis.

Presentation skills are addressed at the end of the last chapter, so the exercise can be combined with these if a presentation is to be set as the final outcome. The benefit of the exercise is that line managers and HR managers should not only be knowledgeable but also skilful in presenting their findings to other managers and to their staff. Management is both an art and a science. The science can be learned from books or lectures. But the art can only be acquired by practising the skills as closely as can be replicated to conditions in the workplace.

3

THE BUSINESS ENVIRONMENT AND HUMAN RESOURCE MANAGEMENT

Topics

- evaluating the business environment and cultural context
- influences on organizations for change
- labour market changes
- some current challenges
- coordinating change of approach in business.

Introduction

Our concept of *strategic integration* should alert us to the fact that much that impacts on a company is *contextual* – sometimes referred to by writers as *exogenous*. The problem with this dimension of outside influences is that it is often outside management's attempts to influence it. Controlling any process requires *access* to the levers that control a process and gaining *control* over the levers. Without this it is impossible to manage an operation. So, with contextual or outside factors affecting the company, it is likely that managers may have less access and less control over the influences that affect their future prospects.

It is sometimes the case that if we take the definition of culture as 'the way we do things round here' (Deal and Kennedy, 1982: 231) then it can be both a benefit and a constraint. Repeating routines that have satisfied past need may not be the ready base for creative thinking required in a crisis. New wine needs fresh skins.

BOX 3.1

A consultant was asked by the training manager of a large manufacturing company whether he could lay on some training for his functional staff to make them more creative and innovative. The factory faced big changes if it was to survive but the HR manager's attempts to engage his staff in blue-sky thinking had not been very successful.

The consultant looked at the recruitment procedures that the company used for selecting their staff and discovered that they used a selection method that distinguished job applicants into 'A' or 'B' types. This categorization was devised by the medical profession to discover those who are more likely to have heart-related problems against those less likely. So, 'A's are generally proactive, questing, people who test the boundaries of any situations that they find themselves in. In contrast, 'B's are more passive and wait to be led or told what to do. The company had selected 'B' types for their functional staff.

The consultant advised the training manager that training would be unlikely to change 'B's into 'A's and that basically he would have to recruit such proactive people – though they would be harder to manage and to retain in routine jobs.

Far-sightedness is a rare but sometimes necessary part of a manager's life. Indicators of what may be about to impact businesses are difficult to read, though there are traditional checklists that are offered to encourage a comprehensive assessment of the factors that could be significant and therefore need to be thought about. Such checklists encourage the manager to be systematic in the way that assessment is made of the factors likely to affect the company's future.

One such model is PESTLE:

- political
- economic
- sociological
- technological
- legal
- environmental.

The CIPD fact sheet introduces the idea that companies operate in what they call 'meso-economic and macro-economic environments' (www.cipd.co.uk/hr-resources/factsheets/pestle-analysis.aspx).

It is indeed true that in order to manage a business those responsible need both access to and control of whatever is influencing that business. Money supply, resources, competitor pricing, can all be influences outside a manager's control.

However, being aware of the likely factors that may influence the organization is part of the prophetic role that all leaders need to play. It was Rosemary Stewart (1992) who, after a long career researching what made managers effective, came to the conclusion that most of what good managers do is intuitive. Perhaps we might also add that intuition is fine tuned by experience. For the cyclical nature of business may suggest that constant trends are not to be relied upon. This means that part of strategic analysis includes assessing the economic context, looking for tendencies suggesting a change in trends.

Another commonly used mnemonic is SWOT analysis:

- strengths
- weaknesses
- opportunities
- threats.

Here, the factors affecting the organization can be evaluated and placed in the appropriate category according to how they are judged in terms of their benefits and constraints to the company. Brainstorming can be a useful opportunity for groups within the company to consider how their working lives will be affected by the factors affecting the organization in the immediate future.

Such lists, sometimes referred to by academics as taxonomies, are useful in prompting discussion or research into a topic, though they are likely to yield data rather than information. This suggests that even with the data, we still need someone to interpret and convert it into relevant information. The question arises, how do experts interpret data? Do they recognize symptoms from past experience? Or, interpret the signals incorrectly and therefore implement incorrect procedures for dealing with the crisis.

If situations are genuinely new, how are they recognized and interpreted correctly?

BOX 3.2

Global warming is hotly disputed in the press and in political circles alike. There are those who believe what they think is the evidence of their senses and interpret what they see and feel accordingly. A hot summer and drought conditions may reinforce beliefs that global warming is a reality that needs to be confronted with radical action.

But sometimes there are other reasons why drought affects parts of the UK. In one water authority area the managers are complaining of an immediate need for 75 million gallons of water. *Private Eye*, a satirical magazine, pointed out that this authority loses 75 million gallons of water every year through leakages in ancient pipework which they do not even want to consider replacing because the costs would be prohibitive and deeply reduce their profits. This suggests that we are getting water, but not conserving it properly (though this is not a reason not to take the global threat seriously).

Leadership is prophetic and the prophet is not just a seer into the future, but someone who can see where the present situation will lead and initiate discussion (if there is time) and stimulate action to implement the necessary change of strategy to counter the perceived threat.

Neo-institutionalism

DiMaggio and Powell (1983) identified what they described as three areas within sectors where industries were likely to share a similar or the same form (isomorphism). They suggested that the drivers for these forms can be included under three main headings.

Coercive factors

The first is *coercive* factors: usually those that organizations are forced to implement or observe. The obvious one would be *law-driven* regulation. If we consider, for example, *health and safety at work* legislation, we are made aware of the comprehensive rules that govern our everyday lives, not just at work, but wherever the public is likely to go. Risk assessments are a regular part of managers' lives and as an organization we are singly and jointly responsible for overseeing a safe working or public environment, wherever we are, and whatever our status and responsibilities may be. Companies have to appoint their own health and safety officers, who are responsible for inspecting the premises regularly and keeping accurate records of what they find and the action they have taken. Organizations that disregard the health and safety laws risk being summarily shut down and can face significant fines, if found to have contravened the law. In a sense we could say that regulation of this kind affects and impinges on all organizations and governs the policy, procedure and practice that they are required to implement.

Political bodies themselves are often responsible for devising different laws and tax regimes. Sometimes legislation can be intended to constrain companies, at other times it can be intended to encourage companies to come in and develop in their local market. *Political bodies* may be less open to managers' influence, although it is not unknown for retiring politicians to take up positions as non-executive directors in order to use their expertise and contacts to benefit the company with inside information and contacts about government intentions to intervene in a market.

BOX 3.3

The Arab Spring is a revolutionary wave of demonstrations and protests that has taken place in the Arab world. It began on Saturday, 18 December 2010. We have seen rulers forced from power in Tunisia, Egypt, Libya and Yemen; civil uprisings have erupted in Bahrain and Syria; major protests have broken out in Algeria, Iraq, Jordan, Kuwait, Morocco and Oman; and minor protests have occurred in Lebanon, Mauritania, Saudi Arabia, Sudan and Western Sahara. Clashes at the borders of Israel in May 2011, as well as protests by the Arab minority in Iranian Khuzestan have also been inspired by this regional Arab Spring.

The protests have shared techniques of civil resistance in sustained campaigns involving strikes, demonstrations, marches and rallies, as well as the use of social media to organize, communicate and raise awareness in the face of state attempts at repression and internet censorship.

Many demonstrations have met violent responses from authorities, as well as from pro-government militias and counter-demonstrators. A major slogan of the demonstrators in the Arab world has been 'the people want to bring down the regime'.

For those doing business there, the results have been devastating. How do you manage in the midst of such chaos and civil war? As we see in Iran, the cost of introducing a trade embargo can mean higher prices at the petrol pumps. Politicians want to be re-elected; businesses need reasonably priced raw materials and free access to markets. Any slide towards war would not be welcomed by those who need to sustain business as usual, and war itself is phenomenally expensive on the public purse and uncertain in its outcome.

Keeping ahead of such challenges means having alternative options, which is why *scenario planning* is a discipline that encourages managers to think the unthinkable and then plan their way out of it or around it.

As we have said, it should not be thought that government is always about legal imposition and regulation. There is also a facilitative role that governments can undertake:

- free trade in liberal democracies (laissez-faire), though with an eye to regulating for fair competition;
- competition and regulation (light touch), though with an awareness that excessive red tape can mean unfair interference costs for business;
- incentives for incoming businesses (from abroad), putting in infrastructure and offering tax incentives;
- fiscal policy and its knock-on effects in business (tax breaks for companies entering the market);

- legislative changes to foster flexibility (reducing red tape or restrictive practices that might constrain business from achieving success);
- managing performance to achieve economic growth, low inflation and low unemployment (government cannot stand back and let the market take over – that kind of laissez-faire after the banking crisis now looks like gross irresponsibility on the part of government, who have a primary responsibility on behalf of its electors to exercise a regulatory function on behalf of their citizens).

Mimetic factors

Industries in all sectors are famous for copying what is regarded as best practice in the business operations of other operators in the sector. Ideas of how to organize are freely available as staff move from one company to another. Knowledge workers take their experience with them. The way we do it round here is frequently challenged by incoming managers whose experience elsewhere now becomes available to the company that receives them. Organizing is therefore a constantly changing kaleidoscope of incremental changes, of what may have been experienced elsewhere and then adopted by the home organization. One of the benefits of employing managers from outside the organization can be because they bring with them new ideas and different practices that it is hoped will improve the efficiency or effectiveness of the organization. Bringing in outsiders is one way of challenging a culture that has become set in its ways. The public sector has sometimes sought to do this in order to bring in fresh blood. New ideas, and innovative ways of doing things, always challenge the traditional working methods that insiders have become accustomed to (Randall and Procter, 2008). There is certainly an opportunity for challenge and change derived from mimetic influences.

In this respect the allure of improvements to efficiency or productivity can be an irresistible influence on industry practice in general terms. The move to one-person operation in public transport is one example. Conductors on buses disappeared as soon as the unions agreed to one-person operation in the late 1950s. No competitors could then hold out for long, paying wages for two-person crews against competing operators with only half the wage costs to pay. It made business sense for all operators to adopt the same practice as their competition.

Technology is very quickly, and sometimes uncritically, acquired once it is known that the competition have adopted it. Managers may be heard to say: 'If they (the opposition) have got it, we have to have it, too.'

Normative pressures

The third set of influences that can affect institutions are derived from pressure groups, which have a strangle-hold or monopoly over a sector of knowledge or skills-led activities. These are sometimes referred to as 'communities of practice' or 'embedded communities'. They are often responsible for training their own members, licensing them when qualified, and censuring or striking them off if they are found to have contravened the profession or trade's rules or regulations. The boundaries between the professions and perceived outsiders are often stoutly defended against intrusion or change (Nicolini *et al.*, 2008). And once the threat of imposed change has been warded off, the dominant profession returns to its previously ascendant position within the sector (Reay and Hinings, 2009).

BOX 3.4

The British Medical Association has decided to ballot doctors for industrial action over the government's reform of the NHS pension scheme.

The ballot is the first time that doctors will have voted on such action since 1975.

The decision followed an overwhelming rejection by doctors and medical students of the 'final' offer on pensions.

The BMA said the changes would see younger doctors paying more than £200,000 extra over their lifetime in pension contributions and working eight years longer, to 68. The highest earning doctors' contributions would rise to 14.5 per cent.

Officials urged the government to reopen talks with the health unions, but said neither the Treasury nor the Department of Health had signalled any change to their position.

The health secretary, Andrew Lansley, said the NHS pension scheme is 'amongst the best available anywhere' (Guardian.co.uk, Saturday 25 February 2012 11.51 GMT).

However, government needs to keep these professionals on-side. There are many countries elsewhere happy to offer employment to medical practitioners.

Impact of changing contexts on organizing

As we have seen, classic organizing focused on the triangle (Figure 3.1) illustrates the levels of the traditional hierarchy with a span of control of 1:8 or thereabouts between the different levels within the organization. Any large body of people working together to achieve a common objective, it could be argued, needs as many levels as it takes to provide adequate command and control between leader and led.

FIGURE 3.1 Traditional bureaucratic layers and functions.

For Weber (1947) a bureaucracy is characterized by similar factors that establish both the hierarchy and command and control of the many by a few:

- clear definition of duties and responsibilities
- maximum specialization
- vertical pattern of authority
- obedience to authority
- post-holders rely on technical knowledge
- maximum use of rules
- impersonality in administration
- remuneration determined by rank and responsibility
- promotion determined by seniority or achievement as judged from above
- clear separation between ownership and control.

Fewer examples of this structure now exist in sectors that have organized more flexibly, though it should be said that in the public sector the traditional institutional format is still more likely to be apparent. The drive for private sector sell-offs or subcontracting may merely erode the numbers involved at the core level, though within that core there is still evidence of traditional levels of management with closely defined areas of responsibility and a cascade approach to the direction of communication to those below them in the hierarchy.

Historical principles of organizing

- *division of labour*: classical in its derivation from Adam Smith (2009 [1776]) and fundamental in its subsequent influence on factory management in the

Industrial Revolution, also adopted by bureaucracies in the service sector – and we would find similar hierarchical control in the big financial institutions;

- *unity of command*: much more like the army in its top-down cascade of management directions to others lower down, privileging a top-down style of promulgating rules, commands and strategic plans;

- *authority and responsibility*: authority based on knowledge of the business frequently derived from going up through the ranks and acquiring the requisite experience, knowledge and skills. This is one example of a culture that is likely to reinforce and support a consensual view of what works and what does not and a core commitment to replicating that order, which is difficult to reinforce in more fragmented organizations;

- *span of control*: how many people is a manager asked to manage? It is usually considered that 1:8 is a reasonable span though the average in some factories could be as high as 1:13 since economies have taken place. In Marks & Spencer it is 1:4 so that a supervisor is never far away from a member of staff in need and this in turn is intended to improve the quality of the customer experience;

- departmentalization:
  1. functional – finance, production, sales, marketing etc.
  2. product or service – separate lines for different models of car
  3. customer – retail/wholesale divisions
  4. process – paint shop/welding/assembly/final checks
  5. geographic – often sales and other such territorial divisions
- centralization/decentralization (control from the centre or devolved budgets)
- strong board control (little delegation versus delegational release of control through unbundling or delayering).

Large organizations frequently use a model that found favour in most contracting industries and has now been adopted in many technology-led businesses that require smaller teams working across disciplinary boundaries. As can be seen in Figure 3.2, the level of the team leader is not always defined by discipline, although the discipline leader/director at head office will still be responsible for the management of his/her own staff within the discipline in such matters as appraisal and review of performance. This can sometimes lead to conflicting loyalties between line managers and the professional loyalties experienced by their staff servicing their clients (Robertson and Swan, 2004).

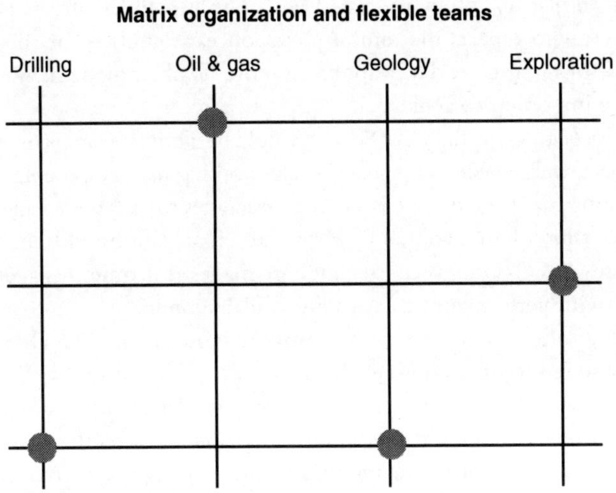

Matrix organization and flexible teams

FIGURE 3.2 Matrix organization and flexible teams.

In some technology-led companies the team projects last a matter of weeks and months at the outside. This can make appraisals difficult to carry out when several projects have been supported and different team leaders have been responsible for the smooth running of each one. Promotion and development still depends on the discipline head though the experience of the individual will have been experienced by the different project managers he or she has had.

So, here, once again we can observe the HR outcome of *flexibility* in the workplace. These are supported by technology where it allows monitoring of performance at a distance.

- *technology and structure*: stability in the environment favoured mechanistic, formalized, centralized organizations with limited upward communication;
- *in less stable periods* an organic structure was considered more appropriate in which there is:
  - greater degree of horizontal differentiation;
  - lesser degree of formalization;
  - responsibilities less clear cut;
  - communication more likely to be through networking;
  - community of interest more significant than contractual obligations;
  - interdisciplinary teams responsible for innovative projects.

There are now a variety of structures that have allowed adaptation to different business needs and facilitated the management of different functions within a business sector:

- *simple structure*: usually owner–manager small business – better able to communicate with networks and computer-based business;

- *machine bureaucracy*: often associated with Fordism (lines of cars passing each operative who repeats the same process on each unit) – for these giants of manufacturing, the need to respond to more flexible, niche markets can now be more important to achieve;
- *professional bureaucracy*: the Civil Service would be a prime example in which flexi-time was a well-established practice – tele-working may be possible so that time commuting can be saved and family responsibilities for carers are easier to fulfil;
- *divisional form*: often favoured by corporate organizations with many different businesses (GEC/Unilever) – technology makes real-time management more feasible with performance data readily available online;
- *ad hocracy*: often associated with creative environments, R&D, partnerships –ideally suited to off-campus exchanges;
- *missionary*: apostles – people sent out to convert sales or convince clients – only *similar objectives* would find anything in common between their ways of working. However, instant messaging makes the exchange of current information much more feasible. The first news feed of important incidents, for example, may not be formal news organizations, but informal social media.

All of this suggests that *technology* offers the consistent underpinning network that supports joined-up communication to business and the community. It offers immediacy of data and therefore the possibility of current information for all those involved in business. If this is successfully managed, *strategic integration* ought to be possible to achieve for everybody in the organization.

- *Long-linked technology*: tasks that flow in a particular sequence and are inter-dependent, but allow organizations to be widespread geographically. The linkage of stock exchanges would be a prime example of a global industry that could not operate as it does without IT connections.
- *Mediating technology*: links between clients and services (as in cashpoints and internet banking). We might also include here the online sales of products and services which in some sectors is 25 per cent and rising – thus depressing high street trade at such traditional times as seasonal and holiday trades.
- *Intensive technology*: tasks are geared to tackling problems in unpredictable conditions. Examples of this might be flight-deck technology in which weather and flying conditions are monitored and keep an aircraft stable at optimum speeds using auto-pilot systems.
- *New technology*: ICT systems tend towards centralization. It gives senior managers access to information about performance that would have been impossible before the advent of such supervisory technology. It has made possible such initiatives as just-in-time ordering, stock order control, and monitoring of business outputs through their people.

The possibility of informing everybody in the organization about the impact their job has on the organization ought now to be feasible. Information about performance now gives functional workers the discretion to adapt and adopt practices to adjust the business outcomes to suit the business need as it becomes apparent. It also makes possible different ways of organizing structures that support the work too:

- *virtual organizations*: through ICT systems; increased the numbers teleworking (4 million in 2000). By 2007 6 per cent of the EU workforce and 20 per cent of the US workforce were teleworking. Savings in onsite facilities can be between 40 and 60 per cent, according to IBM;
- *size and structure*: findings suggest (Pugh, 1968) that size affected likely structure in most organizations. Increase in numbers leads to greater horizontal diversification and greater vertical differentiation to facilitate communication between specialized functions;
- *strategy and structure and HRM*: notice the interlinking of these factors since the days of Chandler (1962). The only difference now is that IT makes it possible to connect easily across the world, so that people do not have to be housed together in order to work efficiently and effectively.

BOX 3.5

How many people work for Amazon? Is it hundreds or thousands? And where are they based? A recently opened new establishment in central Scotland offers jobs for 3,000 people. It is a very large storage facility, the size of a large aircraft hangar.

But who delivers your book to your door? A subcontractor's driver in a hired van, probably.

The fact is, the Shamrock organization is flexible enough to give instant service without the on-cost of core staff running every part of the business.

Job done.

The implication for power, control and structure

- Finally, dominance depends on influencing abilities. On the basis that knowledge is power that may mean that the dominance of *expert power* has come into its own (French and Raven, 1959).
- Tall organizations may well mean greater horizontal and vertical differentiation as necessary.
- Flat organization means the vertical layers are diminished (5/6). Fewer levels are needed to supervise a larger body of people or systems.
- Expertise power predominates where there is dependency on particular high-tech or professional skill areas (lawyers, doctors etc.) and, indeed, IT-led activities of all kinds.

- Power is distributed between all stakeholders who have access and control over the system and here the importance of contracts and agreements on the levels of service is underlined – clearly defined inputs (efficiency factors) and outputs (effectiveness factors).
- The manager does not need to understand the process anymore, still less to intervene to control it.

Three outcomes now become possible more immediately: *flexibility*, *cost control* and *evaluating the HR contribution* (Torrington et al., 2011).

Technology facilitates the gathering of data concerning the performance and therefore allows the closer validation of budgeted against actual costs. Error and wastage rates are indicators of loss of control and varying quality in any process at work. But often no costing of these classic interferences was ever made available to those responsible for the operations until long after the event. What is needed is immediate feedback on the impact of interference as it occurs so that steps can be taken to alleviate the problem by the operators.

Finally, the evaluation of HR's contribution is monitored through calculating how far the interference costs of staff turnover, sick absence and intermittent absence are affected by the effects of change and the implementation of staff investments such as training and development. The *evaluation* of the value-added that staff bring to what they do lies with the end-user or customer. It is not as frequently assessed as the more measurable outcomes are and may account for higher levels of turnover as staff cease to be aware of the difference they make to the lives of the people they serve.

The shifting labour market

The move in numbers of workers involved in different occupations changed within the last half of the twentieth century. The traditional roles that would have been found in the bureaucratic hierarchy of the business organizations saw significant shifts. Table 3.1 expresses this change.

With the exception of employers and proprietors, which have fallen over the years, the top half of the table has increased significantly as a proportion of the workforce. In contrast, the bottom three occupations have reduced in number as a proportion of the workforce. There are those who would see this as part of the de-skilling of the traditional workforce which has been the outcome of applied technology in the workplace (Braverman, 1974). Technology obviates occupations that would once have been done by human operators and this has become particularly apparent in the manufacturing sector.

In contrast, there are those who see this as an evolutionary change in which traditional workforces are transformed into higher value-added occupations which are themselves dependent on individuals receiving a higher education on which to build a professional or managerial career. More recent data from the National Census in the UK has adopted slightly different occupational titles for workers in the twenty-first century (see Table 3.2).

TABLE 3.1 Shift in occupational levels in the UK, 1951–1999

Occupation	% in 1951	% in 1999
Higher professionals	1.9	6.4
Lower professionals	4.7	14.9
Employers and proprietors	5.0	3.4
Managers and administrators	5.5	15.7
Clerks	10.7	14.9
Foremen, supervisors and inspectors	2.6	3.1
Skilled manual	24.9	12.7
Semi-skilled manual	31.5	23.0
Unskilled manual	13.1	5.9

Source: Labour Force Survey statistics accessed at www.statistics.gov.uk.

TABLE 3.2 Shift in occupational levels in the UK, 2001–2011

Occupation	% in 2001	% in 2011
Managers and senior officials	12.9	15.3
Professional occupations	11.7	13.2
Associate professional and technical occupations	13.2	14.6
Administrative and secretarial	14.9	10.8
Skilled trades	9.5	10.4
Personal services	7.5	8.7
Sales and customer services	8.6	6.6
Process, plant and machine operatives	8.7	6.2
Elementary occupations	13.2	11.1

Source: Office of National Statistics: Labour Force Survey statistics accessed at www.statistics.gov.uk.

Once again the top three occupations continue to expand as a proportion of the labour force, while the bottom three continue to contract. Skilled trades are holding their own and increasing marginally. But administrative/secretarial and sales/customer services have reduced, perhaps because the range of technology now available has replaced secretarial services and made fast-moving consumer goods salespeople less likely on the ground servicing customers as sales transfer online.

Continuing demographic trends

- *population change*: demographic towards older/retired generation (but society needs them to keep working);

- *social behaviour*: obesity, drug dependency, lifestyle choices (increasing the likelihood of health care, so self-imposed conditions will be charged to the patient);
- *social trends* (towards later retirement, declining marriage rates and house ownership);
- *immigration/emigration rates* (as demand for skill sets varies throughout the world and can be attracted or deterred by government action);
- *lack of key skills* in the workforce (outside-in approach needed, e.g. attracting nurses from third-world countries);
- trend towards *further and higher education* prior to employment (delaying entry into the workforce);
- *interim management* (an increasing part of the expertise workforce, e.g. HR; IT);
- *telecommuting* (6 per cent of the workforce currently but set to rise).

Implications for wider society

Population change

Ten per cent of the population in the UK is over the age of 65. A long-lived generation has been in receipt of good health care and is able to sustain a longer life than many previous generations (males 77; females 84). This gives governments a challenge: how to pay pensions over the extended period of life of individual citizens and/or getting them to work longer before retiring.

When the NHS was set up in the UK in 1948 people lived between 18 months and two years after their retirement from work. The post-war generation worked hard, many in physically hard environments, or even hostile environments such as mining, where reaching retirement age at all could be considered an achievement. The National Insurance levy was spent on government expenditures rather than invested to provide for future pensions needs, as it was assumed that the current working generation would always be able to pay for those who had retired. At that time six people supported each pensioner. It has now reduced to three people supporting each pensioner.

But if you work on you can lose pension benefits which, in any case, are taxed in the normal way. So, you earn money and get taxed on it, invest in a pension and then get taxed on that as well. Politicians have failed to see the constraints put on their older citizens to continue working and earning by failing to address a balance of fairness between opportunity and reward.

Health care

A related area is health care. As more people get older, they become more likely to draw on the resources of the NHS. Governments realize that the cost of treatment may not be so easy to sustain as 'free at the point of use'. As demand for health care increases and resources to fund it become restricted, there might be a case for charging for some types of medical treatment. And what of people whose lifestyle inherently involves abuse of their own health (smoking; excessive drinking; drug abuse)? Should they be charged for the treatment for damage that they have done to themselves? For those of us in the West the cost of health care may be unsustainable in the face of our competitors who do not provide such cover for their own citizens.

Skills and movement of populations

Globalization involves people and money passing freely across borders. Economists would see this as a simple function of supply and demand. But how many immigrants can a country let in before its own population objects to more incomers? It is alright if we need them for essential services, but otherwise the indigenous population does not always want to let any more people come in and draw on its services. Such immigrants are sometimes referred to as 'economic migrants' – meaning that the incomers want to come here to make money. It could be argued that the New World of the USA was largely founded by such people – though now resisting incomers from bordering countries.

Turning perceived threat into opportunity will continue to be the challenge of the future. For example, the needs that govern required competencies throughout the world require us to accept that we need a skilled workforce to achieve economic success. And that acceptance of difference will necessarily mean a more cosmopolitan society.

Underlying this is a need to readdress how we support education in our society to increase the understanding of the problems globalization presents us and take the steps we need to overcome them. So, management is concerned not just with getting goods out of the door and delivered to customers; neither is it just turning up each day to make sure that the company continues to function. It now requires an interest that is worldwide in its breadth of understanding. What happens in one place is liable to impact on areas on the other side of the world. And all this takes place in a world of diminishing resources. How do we support nine billion people on this planet of depleting resources? Those who have made a serious investment of their time and effort into understanding and conducting management will need to address the question seriously. It will impact on all of us.

Case study: Karren Brady – business environment and HRM

It is not often that the lives of business managers are open to close scrutiny. But when they are there is an opportunity to analyse how the issues that arise in a business are influenced by context and an awareness by a manager of the possibilities for doing things differently.

Those who have seen the television series *The Apprentice* will know that one of Lord Sugar's assistants is Karren Brady. Karren's day job is as CEO of West Ham

Football Club. She related her story to the *Financial Times* on 15 March 2012. As you read it, make notes of how strategy and the tactics of running a business link with HRM and organizational outcomes:

'After leaving school I got a job at Saatchi & Saatchi in London and went on their graduate programme even though I was only 18 – which, unfortunately, probably can't happen today because everyone seems obsessed with university degrees.

'I had the most brilliant time. At 18, I couldn't believe people hated going to work. I just thought it was the best place in the world, full of genius.'

But struggling to make ends meet, she moved to London Broadcasting Company – now LBC Radio: 'I meant to go there, earn more money, then re-apply to Saatchi at a higher level and better pay bracket,' she explains.

She was tasked with selling adverts for a notoriously unpopular slot and had the idea of asking David Sullivan to advertise his Sport newspapers: 'He said radio doesn't work and put the phone down. But to me, I'd made a connection so I went to his office and waited for hours until eventually he said I could have five minutes.

'I offered him a deal – if your sales don't go up, you don't pay. Within six months he was spending £2m on radio advertising.'

Impressed, Mr Sullivan offered her a job. Within a few years the pair were looking for a new business venture and settled on Birmingham City. Ms Brady, at 23, became the first woman to run a top-flight football club. The sport was unsure how to respond.

Sales has traditionally been the seed-ground for entrepreneurs and negotiators who go on to run their own business. Spotting a business opportunity means putting together a prospect with a proven benefit offered by a different approach to business, as Karren demonstrated to her future backer. But, the next move might not have been so easy. Running a business needs both functional skills and aptitude, and ability to appreciate and act on new markets for a mature business.

'No one had thought of football as an industry before. The business of football hadn't been fully explored – and its ability to build relationships and a brand was something that really interested me,' she says.

'It was a difficult job because Birmingham City was in administration; it was literally falling down. The club had run out of money, so everything was done on contra deals – it would offer season tickets in return for fixing the typewriter. I think the worst was to swap an executive box for black bin bags. I think only a man could do that.' She smiles again.

Surveying its run–down state she saw only opportunities: 'I decided we had to be close to the community. I developed schemes like "kids are a quid", the family stand, and a school dinners deal, so that kids in my area that qualified for free school dinners got free tickets. Families that get free school dinners are on the poverty line and they could never afford luxuries for their children like tickets.

'We also set up a lone parent deal so a single mother or father could come with two kids to football for a fiver. In the end we had nine full-time teachers working with the community and 35 full-time community officers going across Birmingham teaching kids anti-drugs, healthy living. Those became the things we stood for.'

She says when she, Mr Sullivan and his long-time business partner David Gold sold the club in 2009 it made money, had no debt, and 75 per cent of its senior managers were female.

Vision is combined with insight as once again a different approach is taken to an old-established business, whom some would have said was just a sport. The community around the club is perceived as central to the future development of local involvement, the context that must be tapped into otherwise the future could be bleak.

In January 2010, she took over at West Ham after its purchase by Mr Sullivan and Mr Gold, the club's joint chairmen. She makes crystal clear that she runs the business, despite her title of vice-chair:

'I am the CEO. But when I came here there was a CEO, so I was the vice-chair. It's a nonsense title, but having had the business cards printed ...' She laughs.

With the business cards came business principles: 'It was a male, blokey environment, not a professional working place where there is expectation and ownership of projects.

'I think that's part of the change in the culture, which is why West Ham for two years on the trot has made the first trading profit for as long as anyone can remember – because suddenly there's no hiding place. It's not, as I called it when I came here, the West Ham country club.'

She has torn down office walls and created a light, open-plan office buzzing with people; she stresses the importance of environment: 'The whole office was painted burgundy, it had green carpet, there were no windows and there were offices for one person each – a whole row of cells.

'You would come in full of energy and in two hours you wanted to throw yourself off the ledge. I like to work in an open space and I love the feeling of being with people. My door is never closed – nothing is more important than being able to communicate.'

Has Ms Brady had to behave more like a man to be successful in the male-dominated world of football?

'I once worked for a female boss who wanted to be a man – a ruthless, relentless type of personality and I was desperate that I would never be that kind of person,' she says.

'I'm a promoter of diversity. I believe in promoting from within, nurturing people. I think women and men are very different types of managers and I think those differences should be celebrated.'

Context is balanced by content. An appropriate working environment means a different way of doing business. The country club becomes open-plan and diversity is the watch-word that governs decisions made about people in the business. Gender is less important than competence and fitting into the new business approach.

> She copes with the 'conundrum' of having 18-year-old ticket office staff paid up to £15,000 a year and teenage footballers earning £15,000 a week, by creating a culture in which both feel valued, with a chance to progress.
>
> Her test of staff motivation is the rate of annual sick leave ('here we have the lowest sick leave of any company I've worked for'); and she still hopes to lead West Ham to a new home at London's Olympic Stadium – 'As long as it can be a world class stadium for our discipline,' she says. 'We won the Olympics on the legacy plans – and the East End of London could do with that legacy, particularly for its young people and opportunities for jobs and education.'

So, for Karren, building relationships and building a brand coincide in her overview of what she is trying to achieve for the company. She appreciated that the Birmingham Football Club existed in isolation and set about involving the local community, especially disadvantaged families and children.

She adopted a similar approach at West Ham Football Club where she notes ominously that it was not 'the West Ham Country Club'. Her eye for disparities of reward among her staff team is quick to note that a ticket clerk may be earning £15,000 a year while a footballer may be earning the same amount in a week. For Karren it was a question of 'creating a culture in which both feel valued with a chance to progress'.

We might also have noticed that Karren monitors the organizational outcomes that Guest outlined: staff turnover, sick absence etc. She notes with some satisfaction that 'here we have the lowest sick leave in any company I've worked for'.

Her future plans include the Olympic Stadium and along with that a continued commitment to the local community which she had shown at Birmingham City FC.

But all is not as easy as it sounds and her family also engages her attention and requires her to consider work–life balance seriously:

> So far, Ms Brady has come across as fearless and determined. But pressed on how she combines business and motherhood, emotional stress flickers towards the surface. She has been married to Paul Peschisolido, former footballer and now manager of Burton Albion, since 1995 and the couple have two children. The family home remains near Birmingham, and Ms Brady has a small flat in London.
>
> 'Well, it's definitely not easy and this belief that there are superwomen with perfect jobs, perfect children, perfect husband, perfect lives is absolute bull, frankly,' she says.

There is real feeling now. 'It's hard. My son's not well today. He's in the Midlands and I'm here. All the time I'm thinking should I be at home, should I be here, should I go home after this, should I not do that meeting, should I wait to see how he is?

'It's a horrible stretch. If I'm at sports day, am I missing a board meeting? If I'm at a board meeting, I miss sports day. I can never get it right.

'The key for me was accepting I can only do what I can do. I have two personalities – one for home and one for work and the trick is not to allow one to drain the life out of the other.

'I never say yes to anything – I don't go to parties. You'll never see me falling out of nightclubs. I work and I go home. Those are the two most important things in my life and I don't want to give either of them up – so I stretch myself, not my children and not my business.'

With today's strong focus on the need for more women to take on senior business roles, I ask how much less 'blokey' West Ham now is: 'I brought in three senior women,' Ms Brady replies. 'I like people who aren't afraid to question our business and I think you get that by employing people from different education systems, different backgrounds and different genders.'

We might note here that Karren is not interested in reverse discrimination: appointing women to a level or quota in order to achieve an artificial balance between the genders. The criteria for someone to be on the Board is 'people who aren't afraid to question our business'. Only diversity of talent can establish that broader base of understanding and commitment that the business needs to develop its potential effectively.

Implications for organizations

- *Porous boundaries* suggest that organizations are influenced at all times by outside influences. The football clubs or any other businesses do not exist in isolation; they exist as part of a local and wider community and the links with those communities need to be proactively set up.
- *Organizations* are therefore more malleable than might appear from the way they are structured. Karren's interest in relationships and branding, which had been reinforced early on in her first job in public relations, gave her a different way of thinking about the business she subsequently ran.
- *Changing customer tastes* is an excellent example of what can then happen to previously popular products and services. Traditional football supporters were older males and the facilities provided were rudimentary with few seats and little by way of facilities. Bringing in a family audience means several people come instead of one. But this can only be done by offering more facilities catering for children and families. Karren understood that and responded to it.
- *Serious new competitors* cannot be ignored. Predictions might have suggested that football would cease to be a major spectator sport as watching matches

on television became more prevalent among the population. Certainly the gate numbers for some clubs have gone down during recessions or economic downturns. However, the market has moved into a new constituency group, the family, attracted by better facilities and investment and the emphasis on entertainment and comfort.

- *Threats to sources of people*, energy or key staff can be equally significant to the organization's ability to retain its service and quality consistency. So, keeping staff on-side is a necessary part of enhancing the product and service and preserving the consistency of the public's experience. Businesses that have neglected this have done so at their peril. One example would be banks that have encouraged internet banking, ATMs and call centres and reduced their customers' contact with their local manager.
- *Successful companies* are structured to satisfy the demands of their home markets. Birmingham may not be West Ham. But for Karren Brady the same principle of engagement with the local community was in the forefront of her strategy of embedding the company in the local community.
- *Challenge* may mean adopting a more organic/dynamic/flexible structure for staff and customers. This may mean a change of culture from the West Ham Country Club to something more flexible where people contact is vital to fostering a team approach to customer care.
- We might say that *environmental influence* modifies the balance between technical and social subsystems. In other words that will mean that effectiveness factors (the customer and the competition) will dictate the balance needed between people and technical systems (efficiency factors).
- The *technical system* is concerned with transforming inputs into outputs. But the efficiency with which that process is managed will be lost if the output is ineffective as far as the potential end-users are concerned.
- The social relates to the *interpersonal aspects of life* in the organization (Trist and Bamforth, 1951). For Karren that has meant staying away from home and being involved in the work family. Value-added starts at the top of the organization and management interest in the staff sustains their interest in customers.
- The answer is suggested as *autonomous working groups* (the original concept underwriting TQM). But their effectiveness is closely related to the *strategic integration*, the first of the HR outcomes offered in Guest's diagram of HRM theory.

Organizational trends

- *CEOs need to ask challenging questions* and listen to the replies – not comfortable but in the end challenges the individual to think 'outside the box'. As we have seen from Brady's account, this is something that she encouraged her Board members to do when they served with her. She considered that diversity of background was important for giving different perspectives and opinions to the strategic discussions that necessarily take up the Board's time.

- Need for *faster more creative action* in most organizations. When Lord Weinstock took over W & T Avery in 1980 he acquired a world-branded company known for its expertise and experience in the weighing industry. He discovered that their time from R&D to launching products on the market took up to seven years. He determined that this should be reduced to no longer than two years.
- Closer relationships with *the stakeholders*. This term is frequently used in the HRM literature and can be used to mean shareholders, or anyone with an investment of stake in the company. But it also means a wider group who are affected by what the company does. The people of Florida were stakeholders in the Gulf of Mexico oil spill in 2010. The people of Bophal were likewise stakeholders in the operations of Union Carbide in 1984. The effects of mismanagement continued for those local people for years afterwards. Companies are more likely to be risk-averse, with health and safety policies in place now. The cost of not having them and then being faced with a serious accident could spell disaster for the company through compensation actions in the courts and loss of reputation in the wider market.
- *Free of cumbersome bureaucracy and more alert to changing customer need*. It could be argued that most organizations are not so encumbered with structured bureaucracy in the way that they once were. The flat organization of 5/6 levels has impressed itself in most organizations following the example of Japanese manufacturing companies. Similarly, being more alert to customer need has been reinforced throughout companies in the private sector, especially those affected by online sales. The public sector, however, is another question altogether. Here the willingness to unbundle or delayer organizations has been somewhat slower and governments have had to resort to such initiatives as compulsory *competitive tendering* and *market testing* to try and achieve economy and flexibility. There is a natural resistance to what is seen as attempts to deprive members of their rights. For example in the police forces, the Sheehy Report in 1993 suggested rationalizing ranks in the police to reduce the number of tiers in the different forces. Such is their political muscle in the political arena that the recommendations were shelved by the government of the day. However, the Scottish Parliament has now accepted a single police force in Scotland and discussions are taking place in England and Wales to amalgamate forces. Budget cutbacks may finally have required a reassessment of efficiencies and effectiveness that govern publicly funded policing.

Team structure

- *Working across boundaries* now becomes vital to interdisciplinary working and problem solving. As we have seen, both matrix management and the use of interdisciplinary teams make teamworking an essential vehicle for achieving organizational outcomes using people flexibly.

- *Training* is needed to sustain team roles in the organization and groups. But *development* is also a necessary function of being able to chair meetings and to act as a facilitator in discussions and brainstorming for creative teams. Shadowing those who are good at these roles can be an excellent way of gradually undertaking more demanding team roles.
- Encouraging people to cross boundaries, particularly *interdisciplinary boundaries*, is vital in progressing learning between groups and encouraging previously separate professional groups to engage with colleagues from other disciplines and departments. Understanding difference can mean less contention and argument between different functions.

Lean production

- *Customer-focused* operating units enable professionals to become exposed to the market that supports them. In the pharmaceutical sector, some companies have moved from the development of compounds to conducting lab-based research for customers and clients. The role of the team leader becomes one of negotiation with the clients on the productivity factors governing the work contract agreed. It must then be closely monitored by the team for timely delivery.
- *Devolved decision making* started with quality circles, when teams were made responsible for their own development and job rotation along with their production targets within the requisite period.
- *Stream-lined management control/tighter financial control* – allowing teams discretion does not mean that the company gives up on analysing what is sometimes called *profitability metrics*. Individuals are assessed for time spent in different cost-allocated activities and the results then govern whether they are allowed to travel to meetings or take part in training events.
- *Business process re-engineering* is a more radical approach to managing people. We have already discussed the outside-in approach to strategy, or market-led approach. Here the decision to seek people with the right employment profile dominates the decisions about developing existing staff and presages a fundamental shift in HR thinking. There is much evidence to suggest that even staff retained can feel aggrieved that their colleagues dispensed with were treated in that way (Hallier and Lyon, 1995).
- Establishing a connection between organizational actions and decisions and shareholder value requires achieving a careful balance between dividend and retained profits needed to reward the shareholders but at the same time enhance future investment in the company.
- *Change* is now an enduring fact of life for everyone in their working lives. The traditional company as defined in the nineteenth century is probably in need of a radical overhaul. For individuals the company is unlikely to provide the vehicle for their employment throughout their working lives. Aware of that, individuals may make their own decisions about the value-added that their

employment experience yields. They will be aware of the three classic questions posed by one international business school which suggests that continued employment depends on the answers to the following questions:

1   *How much do I cost?* For those of us working within the context of a welfare state, our costs will be higher than populous, emerging countries who do not afford their citizens the same employment, health and safety, and health-care rights. Their productivity factors will therefore be lower in cost than ours will.

2   *How much do I yield?* This comes back to profitability metrics which we discussed earlier. What is it the company rates highly and which of my tasks contributes directly to generating that profit?

3   *How does that compare?* There are people around the world doing a similar job in a similar sector. How much do they get rewarded and what are their overheads in terms of housing and living standards? In manufacturing offshoring is a well established phenomenon. It is likely that other sectors will follow.

Reviewing the HRD list

- recruitment/selection
- induction training
- supervision
- management
- review
- appraisal
- reward
- development
- communication.

If we return to the Shamrock organization we can ask whereabouts the focus of HR should fall.

As far as the *core employees* are concerned it would clearly require the application of every step in the process. But how far does that apply to the other segments of the Shamrock organization?

If we look at the *subcontract workers* first, then we might ask where in the list the core company should apply its efforts. It is clear that once the contract for a service is signed with the subcontractor then they are responsible for recruiting their own staff, training them, and managing and supervising them day to day. It may be that even appraisals are done by the subcontractor which leaves only the day-to-day monitoring of the performance of the contractor's staff to be reviewed at the end of the term. The only day-to-day major concern of the core company would be the training of subcontract staff in health and safety and customer care matters.

For the *consultancy workers* the issues of HR involvement become a little more difficult to assess. Clearly, consultants are usually engaged for the prior knowledge and skill that they have in the area for which they are retained. Induction training would be less of a need for them, apart from health and safety requirements. They will obviously report to a manager from the core group; however, their progress will need to be reviewed and, depending on how long they are with the company, may include an appraisal.

The question of their development may then become an opportunity to offer support for what is an increasingly demanding need in most professionals' lives. *Continuing professional development* is a requirement for retaining membership of most lead bodies today and is certainly required for advancing through the grades above membership. For most professionals, then, the opportunity of putting together a portfolio of work undertaken or projects managed can be an important step to increasing their visibility with their professional sponsors. Career commitment will be uppermost in their mind and any organization that supports that is likely to win their continued commitment to the company that provides such opportunities.

The external environment will continue to be challenging to organizations. Strategic plans will need to be reviewed more frequently, rather than less. But the implications that change has for organizations comes down to the HR interface with individual workers. Flexibility began its life as a way of extending the utility of the individual to the organization's changing and sporadic requirements. Increasingly, that assessment of mutual benefit will apply to key knowledge workers whose expertise is required by the organization.

References and further reading

American industrial enterprise. Cambridge, MA: MIT Press.
Braverman, H. (1974) *Labor and Monopoly Capital: The degradation of work in the twentieth century.* New York: Monthly Review Press.
Chandler, A.D. Jr. (1962) *Strategy and Structure: Chapters in the history of*
Dawson, P. (2003) *Understanding Organizational Change: The contemporary experience of people at work.* London: Sage.
Deal, T. and Kennedy, A. (1982) *Organization Cultures: The rights and rituals of organization life.* Reading, MA: Addison Wesley.
DiMaggio P.J. and Powell, W.W. (1983) The iron cage revisited: Institutional isomorphism and collective rationality in organizational fields. *American Sociological Review*, 48:147–160.
French, J.R.P. and Raven, B. (1959) The bases of social power. In D. Cartwright and A. Zander (eds) *Group Dynamics.* New York: Harper & Row, 607–623.
Hallier, J. and Lyon, P. (1996) Job insecurity and employees' commitment. *British Journal of Management*, 7: 107–123.
Handy, C. (1989) *The Age of Unreason.* London: Hutchinson.
Nicolini, D., Powell, J., Conville, P. and Martinez-Solano, L. (2008) Managing Knowledge in the Healthcare Sector. A Review. *International Journal of Management Reviews*, 10(3/4): 245–263.
Porter, M.E. (1979) How competitive forces shape strategy. *Harvard Business Review*, 57(2): 137–145.

Pugh, D.S., Hickson, D.J., Hinings, C.R., and Turner, C. (1968) Dimensions of Organization Structure. *Administrative Science Quarterly*, 13: 65–105.

Randall, J.A. and Procter, S.J. (2008) Ambiguity and ambivalence: Senior managers' accounts of organizational change in a restructured government department. *Journal of Organizational Change Management*, 21(6): 686–700.

Reay, T. and Hinings, C.R. (2009) Managing the rivalry of competing institutional logics. *Organization Studies*, 30(6): 629–652.

Robertson, M. and Swan, J. (2004) Going public: The emergence and effects of soft bureaucracy within a knowledge-intensive firm. *Organization*, 11(1): 123–148.

Smedley, T. (2012) On my agenda: L & D is back on the agenda. *People Management*, July: 37–39.

Smith, Adam (2009 [1776]) *The Wealth of Nations*. Blacksburg, VA: Thrifty Books.

Stewart, R. (1992) *Managing Today and Tomorrow*. Basingstoke: Macmillan.

Torrington, D., Hall, D., Taylor, S. and Atkinson, C. (2011) *Human Resource Management* (8th edition). London: Pearson

Trist, E.L. and Bamforth, K.W. (1951) Some social and psychological consequences of the Longwall method of coal getting. *Human Relations*, 4: 3–38.

Weber, Max (1947) *The Theory of Social and Economic Organization*. Translated by A.M. Henderson and Talcott Parsons. New York: The Free Press.

Whitehead, P. (2012). Superwomen? It's absolute bull, frankly. *Financial Times* 15 March. Reprinted with permission.

GRADUATE ATTRIBUTES

In this exercise you will develop:

- an intellectual curiosity and a willingness to question accepted wisdom and to be open to new ideas;
- a capacity for attentive exchange, informed argument and reasoning;
- an ability to communicate effectively for different purposes and in different contexts.

Please read the following imagined case study on L&D in a bureaucratic setting. At different points in the narrative you will be asked to stop and answer questions. Please make notes so that you can contribute to a group discussion.

Two years ago Helen Carter led a L&D team in the Department of Agriculture that was 2,500 strong and which was only a part of a larger HR team consisting of 12,300 people. Now only 200 L&D staff remain and Carter presides over 45 of them. Carter has a new role at the head of the newly formed internal organization, the Department of Agriculture: Learning and Development (DALD).

Helen's journey began in the reorganization of 2009 under the banner of net generation HR. With the dawn of the credit crunch a new approach to L&D was heralded. It became quickly clear to Helen that there would be efficiency demands coming and that it would be necessary to explore how better to deliver services across the department in all areas of HR. While there were aspects of the removal of redundancy (duplication of services and wastage) there was also a hard look at how the quality of services could be enhanced.

The exploration revealed a situation that was far from satisfactory. It appeared that no one had ever before attempted to assess the yearly L&D spend of the Department of Agriculture (DoA). More worrying still were the difficulties of being able to track this spend. Records just simply seemed to be unavailable. At the end of the exploration period a best guess figure was arrived at of around £305 million.

The process revealed massive duplication of effort was taking place within the department. There appeared to be thousands of L&D programmes ongoing with almost no communication between them. Carter discovered 178 teamworking programmes, 316 leadership programmes and 523 negotiation skills programmes all running within the department. She also discovered that nearly 75 per cent of programme delivery was entirely classroom based.

Very clearly something needed to be done to address the situation. If a functional L&D approach was to emerge post cutbacks, sweeping changes were required. Carter made a decision to centralize generic learning and this resulted in the introduction of a common curriculum: a new commitment to e-learning and blended learning and, crucially, procurement of market provided, rather than internal solutions.

Questions:

- **What was the external driver for L&D in the DoA?**
- **Why might there be concerns that classroom learning could be 'out of touch with the world'?**
- **In what ways might market-provided procurement of training be more effective for the DoA?**
- **How could external training provision be more cost-effective for the DoA?**

In Carter's view the spending review in government during 2009 saw L&D spend plummet and the DoA's former system close. It was clear that the cuts following the spending review would result in the various departments contained in the DoA closing down their own L&D resources. This spurred the decision to ensure that there was some central team coordinating L&D provision, which led to the creation of DALD.

Questions:

- **Why would it be necessary to set up a central team?**
- **What would be their main function?**
- **How would they evaluate their effectiveness?**

DALD was launched on 16 May 2011 and became fully operational in June 2012. The purpose of DALD was to serve the generic training needs of the whole of the department with only its staff of 45. Carter had this to say about DALD:

> We wanted to ensure that from DALD's inception we were not creating yet another monolithic structure; rather, we were committed to keeping it small and efficient. The aim was to produce an enabling organization. Rather than being the provider, DALD's responsibility would be to act as the middle man.

The common curriculum for L&D was divided into three core areas:

1 working in the DoA
2 leadership and management development
3 core skills.

A menu of broad courses across these three areas was created and then divided vertically by a seven-tier grade structure. All DoA staff can register for the DALD Learning Portal, and see the courses applicable to their level, that of their direct reports or the level of their aspiration. The courses consist of 73 one- or two-day workshops, 126 e-learning programmes and over 5,000 learning resources available from physical and electronic sources.

Questions:

- **What is the function of DALD in the DoA?**
- **How do the courses provided reflect the level of responsibility held by the trainees?**
- **Is DALD providing training or a resource centre?**

Some departments within the DoA make more of a demand on L&D than others. This is based around what is required of the department. Some have direct contact with the public, visiting farms etc., while others are more policy development based. What is genuinely unknown at the moment is what the demand will be like. What we do know is there will be a demand and it will start to increase.

Questions:

- **Will departments continue to provide their own training needs?**
- **How will DALD be able to assess that demand for their services is reasonable?**
- **How will they be able to evaluate their services?**

DALD is funded through contributions from the various departments within the DoA. These contributions equate to roughly £25 per member of staff. This means that DALD has a budget of around £8.5 million a year in total. This budget pays for everything online, the services of DALD and a procurement contract with Capita. Built into the Capita contract is a requirement that over 50 per cent of our business must be with SMEs – niche consultants, coaches, whatever is necessary. Capita therefore can only claim 49 per cent of the actual delivery. So far 58 per cent of DALD's delivery has been from the SME sector.

Prices within the contract are fixed for the next three years with an option of extension for a further two. So far they are already seeing savings in cost of 60–70 per cent in some areas with no loss of quality.

By the autumn of 2011, DALD was already realizing £60 million annual savings through a combination of headcount reductions and procurement controls. Carter's comment on this was that her target of £90 million seemed achievable:

> There are two ways of looking at savings – the variable factor is that activity has gone down from where it was two years ago, so the real measure of value over the next two to three years will be unit cost, and we've started to track this now in the form of a 'learning hour'.

In Carter's opinion only the number of hours devoted to learning in the workplace, on e-learning and in the classroom will be a true measure of success.

Despite the classroom-based learning falling from 67 per cent to around 6 per cent of the total, Carter claims it is wrong to think the new approach is all about self-managed learning.

Questions:

- **How will DALD evaluate the learning events put on by Capita's contractors?**
- **How might 'unit cost' and 'learning hour' be calculated?**
- **How could the learning impact of these courses be evaluated and compared between departments?**
- **Whose voices are currently missing from the accounts given so far?**

'During the initial spending review a lot of discretionary budgets were just brought to a halt. L&D was just one of those areas where we saw a fall in terms of spend from the previous year.' The result, Carter adds, is that 'people have lost the habit of learning'. It's now her job to help them find it again.

One attempt to do this is through an internal communications campaign. Its tagline is: 'The time to train is past, it's time to LEARN.' Carter's role is to spread the word that L&D has not gone away and is in fact better than ever, while undeniably changed. There are certainly cynics in the DoA that need to be won over to the changes in L&D.

> My biggest challenge is to really embed this new approach, to build commitment and belief in our line managers, in particular. Many of them will never

have experienced L&D outside the classroom and will cling to the idea that real learning happens only in the classroom.

Another perception that some hold could prove damaging is that the cuts being made to the HR and L&D headcount mean that these functions are no longer important to the DoA. The HR ratio was 1:48 two years ago and is now 1:80, and the aim is to get it to 1:100. But despite having a much reduced team at her disposal, Carter claims that it has not been difficult to do more with less.

Questions:

- **Why might managers be cynical about training in the DoA?**
- **How can DALD support a learning organization in the DoA?**
- **What are the main objections that might be made about online learning?**
- **How far will the present initiative be seen as yet more cutting of training budgets?**

By mid July, 46,000 staff were registered on the DALD website, which leaves 53 per cent outstanding. Admitting that winning over the cynics and getting the L&D engine up and running will take time, Carter adds, 'We don't know what the impact has been of under-investment in L&D over the last two years on an organization that is going through profound change and will continue to do so over the years ahead.'

Carter is convinced that the DALD model is precisely the one needed to deliver better learning for the Department of Agriculture: 'We are heading into a different world and L&D is going to be one of the levers and enablers to get us there. It then only makes sense to dispense with what has gone before and to begin again.'

Summary

Identifying where the challenges of supporting value-added in a business remains the crucial focus of management, particularly during radical change. It is easy to see that reducing budgets and staffing is a priority during government drives for austerity. Drucker's view that service sectors would struggle to equal the gains manufacturing achieved through automation have been realized. But the search to reduce headcount in the service, particularly in the public sector, has not abated. The danger with reducing headcount in the service sector means that there are less people around to be of service to the clients (as all users of call centres can attest).

Online learning may well be a way forward for those who enjoy self-learning and IT-led programmes (on average probably less than 10 per cent of the population). But for those who need the interaction with another human being to validate learning, lack of contact may make it more difficult to achieve the learning objectives and feel enthused by the path of development.

Local managers may resent the levy made on them by the DALD, the broker. They may feel that there are benefits to dealing with the contractor directly. DALD will need to work hard to reinforce the message that they fulfil a vital role in the training plans of the civil service in the future.

Tutor guidance

Two things arise from reading or indeed listening to such accounts. First, spotting and exploring the *basic assumptions* that lie behind the thinking of the authors. As Schein says, these can be beliefs, norms or ideas about job, work, career, management and organizational issues. Given that such assumptions are used to evaluate experience, derive meaning and ascribe value to those events, surfacing basic assumptions can be vital when working with an organization as an agent of change.

Second, accounts can be used to raise the political issues that HR faces. Making effective decisions depends on a number of factors, including autonomy and available resources and these are not always as adequate or as comprehensive as HR might like in order to achieve the set objectives.

Some guidance from the tutor will be useful as each section and their questions should be addressed in feedback from the syndicate groups to the plenary group at the end of the discussion.

4

HUMAN RESOURCE MANAGEMENT IN AN ORGANIZATIONAL CONTEXT

Topics

- organizational development and change
- resistance to change
- the beginnings of emergent change
- working towards continuous change.

Introduction

The word 'organization' is difficult to define or identify clearly as, strictly speaking, there is no such thing as an organization (as often we associate an organization with the building/structure that houses it). The phrase: 'the organization sacked 50 workers' therefore makes no sense, though such statements are often used in everyday conversation. But, closer scrutiny would suggest that it is not strictly accurate. Organizations have no eyes, no ears and no brain, so they cannot make the kind of decision described in that way. It would be more correct to say that the senior managers or the Board of Directors decided to sack 50 workers. Academics sometimes refer to such usage as 'personification' – we are creating the image of something animate from something essentially inanimate (Nadler, 1993).

So, when we speak of 'the organization' we are conceptualizing something that exists only in our minds. One illustration would be: what happens to the organization when everyone leaves the building in which it is housed? Does it still exist in the same way as it does during the working day when there are lots of staff about and the place buzzes with activity? Again the answer would be no. But, as we have seen in the *Shamrock organization* (Chapter 1, p. 17, Figure 1.2), in these times it may be that a significant number of those working for the organization are not core staff. This means that they are not there all of the time and sometimes not at all.

The virtual organization is supported by people who are working elsewhere and perhaps have no day-to-day contact with other staff. And yet their efforts may be as vital to the organization's success as those who are there on site under a core staff, full-time contract.

This has given rise to a debate among researchers about the use of the word 'organization' in management parlance. Some writers suggest that a more accurate description would be 'organizing' (Chia, 1996). In other words, there are activities that we can designate as part of the means whereby the organization is supported (or even the reverse: where the organization is put at risk, say, by activities that detract from its ability to enhance value for its customers).

The sporadic nature of human interventions supporting organizing would suggest that there is constant change inherent in the organization. The consistent appearance of stability, which is often a combination of what Schein (1985) refers to as visible artefacts, is not much more than appearances. The fact that everything is in the same place and not much appears to change may convince us that there is consistency and familiarity from day to day. And yet we might also acknowledge that there are incremental changes that affect the organizing ability of those involved in seeking to achieve the organizational objectives. Staff leave or retire and new recruits are inducted. But this is a minimal change which does not usually demonstrate itself too evidently. New faces quickly become familiar and are then part of everyday living. Even more radical changes can be assimilated over a long enough period of time, after which it is difficult to remember what the previous practice was like.

Continuous change happens so gradually that its emergence is sometimes taken for granted. Organizing change is just part of updating what we do: there is a software update; a new division of sales territories; new customers come on board or we lose older ones. While we are reorganizing to adapt to incremental changes these soon become familiar and staff support each other in coming to terms with what is different.

Organizing is the process of arranging collective effort so that it achieves an outcome potentially superior to that of individuals working alone. This is sometimes referred to as $2 + 2 = 5$ – we achieve more together than we do individually. Organizing common tasks reinforces not just cooperation between individuals, but also commonly held beliefs about 'the way we do things round here'. It is here that HRM can play a vital role. The HRD list provides the opportunity for the organization to intervene positively in the lives of the individuals on which the organization depends. In this sense it is a systematic approach to reinforcing the values that the organization's success depends on.

So, organizing requires a degree of control to monitor progress against original objectives and to make appropriate adjustments as business changes. Another familiar word for this would be *managing*. This means that we do the things that contribute to the common goals of the organization. It also means that we think for the organization: why are we doing this; is this the best use of our time at the moment; how have our efforts made a difference to the organization today, this week, this year? Change is normal and we accept that *flexibility* is required if organizations are to continue to develop successfully in changing market conditions. But how these changes affect individual staff members now becomes even more critical to monitor and review, and it is here that the HR department will be vital in the part that it plays.

Principles of organizational design

When we looked at Weber's ideal type of bureaucratic organization we noted that it included the following.

A clear hierarchy of offices

We illustrated this by the traditional triangle which contains the levels within the organization enabling one person at the top to control the efforts of all those levels of staff for which he/she held responsibility. The number of levels depended on a span of control that traditionally has been held to 1:8. Responsibility is devolved down through the levels and the type of communication that characterizes this is sometimes referred to as a cascade, each level of managers passing on required information to those in the level below. This is sometimes referred to as a command and control style of managing.

Specialization of job roles

Job descriptions were often functional: driver; clerk; mechanic; supervisor. The title itself illustrated clearly what function that individual was hired to attend to during their working life. The first two steps of the HRD list would be intended to cover this aspect of competence and commitment in individual workers: recruitment/selection and induction training.

The world of work has moved into a more fluid phase since then, as we have noted. The often heard statement in the past of 'I am just a driver, don't ask me about management – ask a manager, that's what they're paid for' is a lot less sustainable in current circumstances of flexible markets and a global economy. Whoever is front-facing with our customers needs to know more than just their job function. Customers judge the organization by the information and support that they receive from the contact they make with the organization's staff, however that contact is made, be it by phone, email or any of the many ways now available in ICT technologies. That is why *strategic integration* is the most important of the four HR outcomes as illustrated in Guest's diagram. Knowing where individual efforts fit into the organization's strategic plan becomes the gauge of how good staff are at relating what they do for the customer and answering the questions about their service that is offered. So, the aim for HR's induction training is to cover not just the job and how I do it, but why I am doing it that way, too. This is sometimes referred to as double loop learning (Argyris and Schon, 1978).

The importance of impersonal considerations in reaching decisions

Strictly speaking, one of the important changes that bureaucratization brought to the period of industrial revolution was impersonal, objective considerations in coming to fair and equitable decisions in public life. It is still the case that the civil service in the UK will seek to adhere to an objective assessment of need for their clients and an objective and fair service in a way that was once described as 'without fear or favour'. This may sometimes give rise to a certain rigidity of response to clients. If the rules say that the form must be filled in triplicate and the yellow copy lodged at the office within three working days, then lodging it on the fourth day and trying to get it accepted is unlikely to meet with success. So, everyone is treated the same under bureaucratization, no special favour is offered to friends, relations or those prepared to offer bribes to get round the rules.

If we go back to Peters and Waterman (1982) and their emblematic book *In Search of Excellence* then we can see how the popular saying 'delighting the customer' began to win adherents. HRM was not long in following with some of its proponents stating that 'people are our most important resource'. Both sayings place a premium on the individual 'delighting the customer', or 'going the extra mile'. The employee should now be 'empowered', if necessary, to offer more than would normally be offered. This suggests that bureaucratic objectivity which characterised service in the past has been superseded by a more responsive, positive and discretionary style of managing customer relations. So, not just what we offer, but the way we offer it to customers, becomes equally, if not more, important.

This suggests that the widespread use of formal rules and procedures to govern the conduct of office holders is less likely to delight the customer. The emphasis is not just on competence but on commitment. Staff are now considered to be the company speaking, acting and thinking. So, they must be fully appraised of management decisions moment by moment. One way of judging how well this has been achieved is observing staff when things go wrong. We have seen examples such as when Terminal 5 opened at London Heathrow Airport and baggage handling came to grief. Those in the front line often knew no more than the customers and therefore could not give accurate advice and help. Staff became as demotivated as everyone else involved, largely because their lack of information made them the target of ill-tempered customer outbursts which they could not counter with the requisite information. The attempt to coordinate and control organizational activities through managerial hierarchies and formal rules (Hales, 2002) is found wanting when it is unable to respond in an emergency and come up with alternative options for its clients. Comprehensive training and adequate management skills lie in the hands of HR through the provision of sufficient training for staff that have been selected for their aptitude when they were recruited. This means budget allocation, the calculation cost of interference costs and return on investment.

The implications for organizational change

Demands for change can include:

Restructuring initiatives such as mergers, and acquisitions are often associated with rationalizing premises, particularly where the merged company inherits more than one venue in a single location that had previously belonged to competitors. The implications for rationalizing staff numbers will often be a prime objective and part of the reason for the merger – thereby introducing economies of scale and establishing one outlet instead of two.

Efforts to alter the culture of the organization: changing the dominant values that govern the behaviour of the staff. The dominant culture often seeks to impose itself on its smaller partner – not just uniform changes or rebranding, but 'the way we do things round here' (Deal and Kennedy, 1982). The implications for promotion will be watched by all staff to see which of the two sides in the merger come out with more promotions to management positions after the merger takes place.

BOX 4.1

A consultant was engaged to conduct training and development with managers in a timber business with branches UK-wide. Arriving at one venue in the country he was introduced to the supervisors. It became apparent that they had all been with the company for over 30 years during which time they had experienced several takeovers.

Listening to their reminiscences, the visitor kept hearing the name 'Stanton's' referred to and eventually noticed an old truck body parked in the yard being used as a garage with the same name just visible on the side. That was the name of the company they had all joined and its name was still alive and well regardless of the three ownership changes that had taken place since then.

A greater emphasis on quality with responsibility devolved to all staff. This sort of initiative was established in manufacturing through TQM in the 1980s and since (Oakland, 1989). It had been established early on in the car industry in Sweden and Japan and was brought over to the UK as foreign car companies were encouraged by the government of the day to open manufacturing plants in the UK. It was based on quality circles in which dedicated manufacturing teams could between them cover the many functions that previously would have been in the hands of the trade or one specialist group. It can be seen, then, that this practice was based on *functional flexibility* and in the opinion of some had about it an anti-union purpose of breaking down inflexible working practices. Neither industrial action nor absenteeism which bedevilled car manufacturing in the 1970s would ever again come to dominate and obstruct car manufacturing thereafter (Storey, 1992) in the way that it had before.

Reorganization of work around empowerment and teamworking initiatives. From the previous paragraph it will be seen that empowerment and teamworking were central to the TQM approach. Wickens (1987) relates in his book *The Road to Nissan* the quest to recruit car workers who had had no active part in union activity in their past working life. The pluralistic world of management, union and workers was replaced by the unitarist model of management and staff. In some manufacturing plants everyone, including the managers and directors, was expected to wear the same uniform and go to the same canteen – something that would have been unthinkable in a British factory prior to such initiatives. Interestingly, John Egan, on becoming managing director of Jaguar attempted to bring in quality circles on the brownfield site that he inherited. However, the research suggests that no more than 45 per cent of his staff were prepared to make this transition to the new mode of teamworking and job rotation (Storey, 1992). In comparison, Nissan had opened a greenfield site and could therefore choose those they believed would adapt to the new practices wholeheartedly. This led to world-beating manufacturing targets being achieved by them in Sunderland.

Redesigning processes to add value to the firm's offering and being more responsive to individual customer need. Adding value to a service most often means investment in training – yet again an important intervention that is most often to be managed by the HR department. The Handy report of 1987 drew comparisons between the UK's investment in training in comparison with the major international competitor countries. The result was dispiritingly lower in the UK, suggesting a figure of 0.35 per cent of GDP compared with between 5 and 7 per cent for our major competitors. Proper, competitive investment in training is the only guarantee of value-added services and it has to be said that in the public sector commitment to training staff was always held in high esteem in spite of government cuts to budgets in which training was often the first victim.

Resistance to change

There are sometimes *personal reasons* why people may resist changes proposed or imposed at work. Nadler (1993) suggests a number of reasons why individuals may feel threatened by proposed change. He suggests that individuals may perceive that the proposed changes are likely to threaten workers' expertise, undermine their influence, dilute their power base and reduce the resources currently allocated to their department.

Nadler explains resistance to change as being based on:

- loss of control over the job
- loss of organizational control
- loss of status for individuals.

So he suggests three needs arise:

1 the need to motivate for the change;
2 the need to manage the transition;
3 the need to shape the political dynamics of change.

Nadler suggested 12 steps that address these concerns directly and that include involving those affected in the training, offering support during the training and thinking carefully about rewards for those embarking on new skills:

Action steps

1   assure the support of key power groups;
2   use leader behaviour to generate energy in support of change;
3   use symbols and language;
4   build in stability;
5   surface dissatisfaction with the present state;
6   participation in change;
7   rewards for behaviour in support of change;
8   time and opportunity to disengage from the present state;
9   develop and communicate a clear image of the future;
10 use multiple and consistent leverage points;
11 develop organizational arrangements for the transition;
12 build in feedback mechanisms.

His is one of the first n-step approaches that addressed the perceived fears that individuals may have when faced with change to their working lives and suggests interventions that can obviate resistance and reinforce confidence through involving people at work in their own development.

Lack of trust between management and employees may also be significant in obstructing organizational development. In traditional workforces there were often long-service members of staff whose memory stretched back to previous attempts to alter the security of job tenure or erode trade union, pension or earnings rights. Privatizations of public services have a long track record of attempting to achieve exactly that. Increased profits have been drawn from reducing staff and closing services while proclaiming increased efficiencies. For managers this will be perceived as smart management. For workers it will be perceived as getting fewer people to do more for less.

There may be divergent views on the advantages/disadvantages of the proposed changes. Most people can agree on the effectiveness factors that govern a business or service. Everyone lays claim to wanting to delight the customer. The problem comes over agreeing how this should be achieved. For those involved in fronting up the business it will seem obvious that job security and reasonable rewards are the guarantee of reliable and good service. For managers, the search for efficiencies will predominate and so neither side will agree what is the best way forward.

BOX 4.2

While visiting a factory minting coins a consultant was advised by the manager that the target for workers in each working period was 76,000 coins per working shift. Going down to the shop floor the visitor observed a largely ethnic workforce inserting a sheet of metal into the stamping machine, pulling a lever to activate the stamping head and then throwing the residue metal into a bucket. The best performer was achieving 55,000 coins during the shift.

On returning to the manager the consultant remarked on this disparity between target set and best performance to be told by the manager: 'They could do it, if they wanted to.'

People have a *low tolerance for change*, unsurprisingly, especially if the drivers of change intensify and the rewards become sparser or non-existent.

BOX 4.3

Working for a government department for several years, a consultant observed that each year HQ would launch a new training programme. They were always labelled with a title: The Manager as Trainer; The Manager as Coach; Empowering your People; etc.

Training was laid on for all staff (referred to by the staff as 'sheep-dip training'). At the end of the year no evaluation of the training took place to measure the improvements to their business as HR were busy launching the next training initiative. Unsurprisingly, staff quickly became cynical about the constant annual training initiatives.

Change upsets established routines

There have been enough change initiatives to establish that change to routines, though necessary from time to time, does need careful planning and implementation. Sometimes what looks easier and more efficient to designers and managers does not always feel that way to practitioners who have to adapt to new ways of doing things. The benefits are not always immediately apparent to the users.

BOX 4.4

Fly-by-wire technology was introduced to aeroplanes to make piloting easier and more efficient. Gone was the traditional yoke to be replaced by a short, power-assisted control stick. The profusion of dials and indicators was replaced by a single screen containing all the required flight data.

Early planes containing this new technology suffered a number of incidents in which pilots trained on the old equipment found themselves confused and uncertain with the flight information the single screen was presenting to them. They missed the feel of the weight of the plane through the controls and had been trained to scan the bank of analogue instruments, systematically picking up the information they needed. Looking at a single screen was not as easy for many older pilots as the designers had hoped.

The new technology is now well embedded. It just took longer for pilots to familiarize themselves to it than the designers had thought.

Proposed change challenges cherished values and beliefs

Deeply held values and beliefs can be the hardest to shift and are rarely moved by training. The developmental route may be more effective, but usually takes longer. It may be that mentoring, coaching, shadowing and discussion groups with peers will be the beginning of a journey that will take time and patience. Piderit (2000) researched what she described as three levels that can give rise to ambivalence in the face of change:

- cognitive
- emotional
- intentional.

She suggested that though individuals may be convinced intellectually at the need for change they may be either emotionally unconvinced or may experience a reservation at the moral or intentional level ('this should not be happening'). Instructional training courses find it difficult to address such reservations convincingly, largely because they focus on doing rather than emotional or intentional responses to management and change. Only developmental courses based on discussion and led by those who are experienced and committed to the new way of doing things are likely to work.

People are concerned about their ability to grasp new competencies/training

We have remarked on this aspect already as this was one of the fears addressed by Nadler (1993). The solution he suggests is giving support to people during their training. There can be a genuine concern about aptitude where individuals have not been required to exercise the newly required skills in the past. For those embarking on leading such initiatives it may be worth considering what are the options for those who genuinely find themselves unable to adapt, despite their best efforts. Dispensing with people's services without thought about their future could diminish good will among those workers left behind when their colleagues and friends have had to leave (Hallier and Lyon, 1996).

Fears about job security, income, ambiguity and uncertainty

This has certainly proved to be a significant problem where individuals expected or were assured when they started work that they would have a job for life. Certainly that was the case with individuals in the *public sector* and in some of the professions too. So, learning that this job security may no longer apply to their work can come as an unpleasant surprise and engender strong feelings of antipathy towards the managers and change agents instituting such programmes of change. This reinforces a point that comes through strongly in the literature on change management: bottom-up/emergent change may be a more fruitful route to take to allay fears and reassure those about to undergo change at work (Pettigrew, 1985). This takes us back to the T groups that Lewin used to run at the outset of change programmes in organizations (Lewin, 1947).

People feel a sense of apathy and powerlessness and the problem with this is that fear is a poor foundation for entering into proactive and demanding training. It may also erode the *psychological contract* at its deepest level: referred to by Rousseau (1990) as the *relational* part of the contract. Here she is referring to the trust and loyalty that underwrite the *transactional* level of the terms and conditions in the employment contract. Plagued by fears about their job security, individuals may give up or feel alienated from managers whom they trusted in the past.

Individuals are influenced by peer group/group norms

Just as individuals learn from the peer group about the culture on joining the organization, so they are likely to share a common response in the face of radical change in the organization. Schein (1985) remarks that external threats tend to surface basic assumptions, as often those assumptions have been threatened and defended in the past and the peer group retains a determination to hold out against change, alerting others who have joined since of the need for resistance. It is likely that unionized work environments will set about mobilizing their members more effectively to counter such threats of change.

Organizational systems are elaborate with an inbuilt resistance to review and change

This brings us back to Deal and Kennedy's (1982) saying that culture is based on 'the way we do things round here'. Not all change is resisted. But the response to it will depend on the way in which change is perceived by those on whom it is imposed. Modern technology should be a welcome relief from the labour-intensive methods that used to dominate some working lives. Sometimes, however, it is interpreted as the 'spy in the cab'. Only if trust and honesty govern the working relations between staff and managers will there be a loyalty that positively influences both effective training and willingness to embark on change.

Psychological responses to change

Psychological impact

Psychologists suggest that there are identifiable stages in the way individuals deal with change. They suggest that those stages can include the following steps which are often referred to as the coping cycle (Carnall, 1990):

- *'denial'*: this cannot be happening; I don't believe it; wake me up when it's all over;
- *'defence'*: being defensive is a way of obstructing change with all the reasons why it shouldn't happen;
- *'discarding'*: once change is seen as inevitable people come to terms with need for change;
- *'adaptation'*: gradual movement towards considering the options on offer;
- *'internalization'*: following training and new ways begin to be taken on board.

The underlying assumptions here would seem to be that individuals will adapt to change in the end. Managers and change agents just need to give people a chance to grieve about the lost past before coming to terms with the inevitable future.

The question then arises: how can the process of going through these stages be given a context in which individuals and groups can be allowed to give vent to their feelings and at the same time learn about the need for change and its possible benefits for them?

Time to take thought

One of the earliest models of change is the *force-field model*. Lewin's ice model contains three steps: *Unfreeze–Change–Refreeze*. As we will see, his was the first of many, what are sometimes referred to as n-step approaches to change. We have included a model of the force-field analysis based on the need to diet. It is illustrated in Figure 4.1.

Lewin's initiative was based on using what he referred to as *sensitivity or 'T' groups*. He gathered workers into smaller groups and used interactive groups to get individuals and groups to probe and examine the assumptions that they held about their job, work, career, managers and the organization. We could describe this technique as a means of surfacing the norms and beliefs that people hold about themselves and their working lives. This is sometimes referred to as identity (Corley and Gioia, 2004) and is said to include the questions 'who am I?' and 'who ought I to be?'

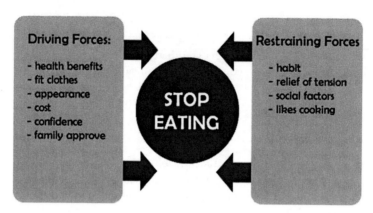

Driving Forces:

- health benefits
- fit clothes
- appearance
- cost
- confidence
- family approve

STOP EATING

Restraining Forces

- habit
- relief of tension
- social factors
- likes cooking

FIGURE 4.1 Force-field analysis.

What follows is the move to the second stage of bringing about a change of view about job, work and the future needs of the company. So, in a sense the selling or influencing part is based on outlining the future clearly and reassuring people that their working lives would change but that there are benefits for them in collaborating with the change. The overall aim, as the diagram illustrates, was to reduce the restraining forces and reinforce the driving forces, thereby bringing about a movement towards change in the required positive direction.

The third stage, refreezing, was based on the reinforcement that all training seeks to engender. It might be reward, control, measurement, review or any combination of the management strategies that are traditionally put in place to ensure that changes of behaviour are permanent and enduring.

In a sense, Lewin was the father of change management initiatives. There were many famous academics and consultants who succeeded him, who had worked with him in facilitating the T groups. They included Chris Argyris, Edgar Schein and Douglas McGregor, all of whom in different ways continued to develop Lewin's work, building on his interactive techniques with groups of workers facing change at work.

What this suggests is that overcoming resistance requires a deliberate programme that addresses the concerns that people may have about their future after the change takes place, and their ability to be successful in any new skills and knowledge that they are required to achieve. It answers the two questions that arise for individuals during change: what am I facing and what can I do about it? (Lazarus and Folkman, 1984).

Two approaches are offered here.

Communication: openness is the best policy. Next to that are consultation and review. Most people like to have a chance to air their views about the need for change and even to offer solutions of options that managers may not have thought of (Revans, 1980).

Bullock and Batten (1985) offer what they call four phases that apply to all n-step approaches to change:

- exploration:
  - – need awareness
  - – search
  - – contracting
- planning:
  - – diagnosis
  - – design
  - – decision
- action:
  - – implementation
  - – evaluation
- integration:
  - – stabilization
  - – diffusion
  - – renewal.

Bullock and Batten examined more than 30 n-step approaches and pointed out the fact that for many of them the one stage most often missed out was the *exploration phase*. For them, the difference between steps and their phases was that with steps, as the word suggests, there is a logical sequence and that each is discrete, finishing before the next step begins. For Bullock and Batten, the phases can overlap, which means that each can feed into the next in a seamless way, offering an opportunity for groups to feed into the planning phase as part of the exploration exercise – a subtle form of *employee involvement (EI)*. Similarly, following the training, comments for change or adjustment can be implemented so that subsequent groups can benefit from the previous group's experience.

Negotiation: 'What's in it for me?' is a natural feeling and response to management demands for change, however much the need for change is acknowledged. Managers need to think through what the benefits are for the workforce and how they will reward people for adopting and adapting their lives to fit in with new organizational needs. Again using the four phases, the question of rewards can be part of the exploration phase at the outset, meaning that change agents are made aware early on of how the groups feel about the best prospects for reward, validation and evaluation. As far as those subject to change are concerned, what staff think will work is a good start for gaining their commitment and good will. If it fails they will be the first to say so.

Organization Development (OD)

Interventions in organizations to achieve change have been crucial to change agents since the initial work of Lewin and his collaborators. There have been many variations which we have already referred to as n-step approaches that have about them a predictive nature. Typical would be the following:

Kotter's model

- establish a sense of urgency;
- establish a coalition;
- create a vision and strategy for change;
- communicate the vision and strategy;
- remove obstacles;
- produce visible signs of progress;
- stick to the change process;
- nurture and shape a new culture.

(Kotter, 1996)

The short bullet point layout can easily disguise just how difficult it can be to imagine how a change agent would implement the steps outlined. How, for example, might one establish a sense of urgency? This is not clear from that simple statement, and it would be reasonable to ask who the coalition in the second bullet point includes, exactly. Creating a vision and communicating it does seem to suggest that the brains behind the vision have come up with the idea themselves and are then intent on passing it on to others, and though removing obstacles may resonate with Lewin's restraining forces in his force-field analysis, it would be difficult to maintain that a new culture was in place merely because new behaviours had been imposed.

OD – a developing field

Over the years since Lewin, OD has not been static in its understanding of the issues that it needs to address. The search for changing a culture was more important as employee involvement became central to the change endeavour. Doing things to change organizations structurally necessarily came to impact on the people working in them. Where once 'the hands' referred to in *scientific managerialism* were passive absorbers of change, increasingly, people working with specialized knowledge and skill came to realize that they had power over their own destiny.

So, an interventionist strategy which at first focused on the structural changes required by a changing organization became modified to take into account the feelings and responses of the people working in them. At first this awareness was focused on those with specialist or rare skills and knowledge. Their training made them valuable and without them value-added and quality products and services were difficult to achieve.

BOX 4.5

A visit to a small factory on a rural industrial estate in the early 1980s revealed a workforce of highly skilled engineers working on specialist industrial weighing and counting machines. At that time union membership was beginning to be questioned by those keen on the unitarist approach to management.

The CEO asked his staff whether they wanted to remain union members or not. They replied: 'Oh no,' because they knew that they earned more by opting out of collective bargaining.

Workers in high-tech industries realized that they had choices that previous generations had not benefited from. Knowledge and skill gave them discretion and autonomy over where they worked and under what conditions. This reality was acknowledged in the soft side of HRM practice. At that stage career development, coaching and personal development plans became more important to them. In *Process Consultation*, Schein (1967) offered a model of managing change that included, as its title suggested, exploring and developing the personal preferences of individuals and groups at work. Hofstede (1991) offered a similar approach to managing change.

The search for the HR outcome of *quality* and the example of Swedish and Japanese car companies encouraged initiatives such as TQM (Oakland, 1989) and more radical approaches to change were to be found in *business process re-engineering* (Champy, 1995) which drove the change agenda in many companies in the 1980s and 1990s and required a commitment of their workers that had not been considered by employers before.

Then came the learning organization (Senge, 1990), and knowledge management (Nonaka and Takeuchi, 1995). These new ideas brought about a focus on people learning at work but presented managers with a challenge: how does the company get to know what its workers are learning at work? Various ideas were tried and they varied from kaizen type meetings, anonymous help lines, and team sharing of new ideas and ways of doing things. No one doubted the validity of what went on in interdisciplinary teams: it was self-evident that people would share with one another – that was the basis of brainstorming and open group learning. But what is learned can become carefully secured from those not in the team and is thereafter a tacit knowledge that is not willingly divulged (Nonaka and Takeuchi, 1995). What is found to be useful may later also be valuable and not all of those involved in the consultancy segment of the Shamrock organization may feel obliged to divulge what they have learned at work (McKinlay, 2002).

Latterly, there has been a danger of change fatigue, particularly in the public sector where initiatives have come annually. But the principles underlying these initiatives have remained much the same as traditional OD practice. They are often based on the assumption that changing attitudes can be achieved by training everyone in the organization.

Task: where tasks are no longer needed, job redesign is necessary. Such changes may lead to *training needs analysis* and appropriate support to those staff affected.

One popular method of checking what needed to be done has been *GAP analysis* in which a list of the original tasks undertaken within the job description was compared with the new competencies required in the revised job analysis. New elements or units of competence were then designated for training and support.

Individual/group

Sensitivity training: Lewin believed that involvement of staff was vital to the success of change agency. He used sensitivity or T-groups which encouraged staff to be perfectly frank about their feelings and beliefs about their jobs, work, career, managers and the organization. Not all national cultures appreciate the invitation to be openly critical – considering it to be a career-limiting risk. However, it must be said that what Lewin describes as the first of his three steps – unfreeze – could be seen as an early attempt at what Bullock and Batten (1985) refer to as the *exploration phase*. They conducted a comparison between several n-step approaches and concluded that this exploratory phase was most often missing from the steps advised by the change agents.

Process consultation: This approach was developed by Schein (1967). It will be noted that Lewin employed several researchers as facilitators and some of them were to become famous in the subsequent work that they did. Chris Argyris, Douglas McGregor and Edgar Schein all took part as facilitators in Lewin's T-groups. So, it is unsurprising that they continued to develop the work that he had begun. Schein (1967) takes the technique further than the original idea of frank and open discussions to what might now be viewed as coaching, counselling or mentoring managers at work to achieve the required change. This he described as process consultation. The emphasis is on facilitation and confidence based on asking questions and listening. It is intended to draw out problem areas through discussion and make the groups and individuals aware of commonly held views during change programmes.

Survey feedback: many organizations have regular staff review questionnaires that are closely monitored by managers and HR to see whether from year to year trends or tendencies are emerging among the workforce. It is customary to insist on anonymity and confidentiality. But that in itself can mean that staff responding to the questionnaires take the opportunity of downloading negative comments and views. It is always worth checking staff turnover figures, intermittent absence and sick absence to see whether the concerns raised by staff are reflected in a higher incidence of negative organizational outcomes mentioned by Guest (1989).

Team building: There are few jobs that do not require teamworking and many jobs include in their assessment centres a team-based test, such as Belbin (1980). The demise of the traditional hierarchy, the reduction of levels in the organization and the unbundling of business within large organizations has combined with the need for functional flexibility, so there is no more ideal vehicle for cross-disciplinary cooperation than teamworking. When used as part of the review method, emergent change is much more likely to occur in such interdisciplinary teams. Questions to ask at initial briefings to achieve feedback include:

- What group practices are worth preserving?
- What behaviours are undermining the effectiveness of the team?
- What are the team's proposals for improving the team's overall effectiveness?

It should be noted, though, that teams that change frequently are both more difficult to keep track of and more difficult to review. Procter and Mueller (2000) note that few teams (about 3 per cent) are allowed to choose their own leader by the company. Another good investment is to vary the chairing role within the group. But not everyone is always comfortable with this as a practice. It is difficult to see how the complex skills required can be achieved unless some exposure to the role is allowed prior to confirmation in a post requiring it as a competence.

BOX 4.6

A training consultant with a group of managers decided to vacate the chair and ask one of the managers on the course to take over while he sat in the body of the group. The manager chosen was very uncertain about assuming the role, but he discharged the chairing role well.

At the end of the discussion the consultant pointed out that he had lost no power or influence as he was quite capable of making his views known if that was necessary.

The manager who conducted the discussion perfectly commented: 'Yes, but you should still have been in the chair.'

So, change and employee involvement is not always easy to manage. But it is worth striving for as an external change agent.

Intergroup development: it is a good investment during change to breech the boundaries between departments and include a mix of people from around the company. This will ensure different insights into the organization and different opinions and perspectives. Groups that contain only one discipline may lack the insight to offer more than their own perspective on the way the company works ('if only marketing would get their act together, we would actually make some sales'). Review sessions particularly benefit from the broader representation that mixed groups bring to discussions about future strategy, particularly on how to implement the change programme.

Appreciative enquiry: instead of being critical, the facilitator comments on the many positive things and strengths of the organization and its people. Then comes the final question: how do we reinforce and support those values in the future? Evaluation lies in the hands of those left behind to continue the work.

Discovery: qualities and strengths of the organization. Is there a company identity which is obvious to outsiders but taken-for-granted by the insiders? Outside feedback can be a useful opportunity for insiders to consider the image that they enjoy from those they need to influence to be successful.

Dreaming: what sort of organization would we like to be? Blue sky thinking is allowed and encouraged even if it inhabits the realms of the idealistic. Brainstorming may be a technique that reinforces ideas' generation, so encouraging ideas' generation will be an important role for the facilitator to play here.

Design: how would we go about building this dream? The *exploratory phase* that Bullock and Batten (1985) refer to should lead seamlessly into their second phase: *planning*. The advantage of this as part of emergent change is the involvement of the staff in what happens next in the change programme. It allows managers and change agents to remind people when progress is lapsing: 'Remember, this is what we promised ourselves we would try and achieve.'

Destiny: the future can be now reinforced, provided that we embark on changing something that we do each day. The proponents of radical change always say: 'Don't expect people to change their views, if you don't change what they do' (Champy, 1995). Reflection of what this has meant will also be included as part of evaluation.

Role of change and development in HRM: a number of drivers

Cross-boundary working requires people to work with different cultures. It was a misfortune to the UK economy to see the British car and motor bike industries go under to foreign competition. It could be argued that this could have been remedied by allowing British workers to see the conditions under which their competitors worked. As Oakland (1989) points out, in the opinion of the quality management gurus, 85 per cent of responsibility for quality management lies with senior managers. Such visits to competitors might also have alerted them to the need to improve their own techniques.

Mergers and acquisitions require a blend of ways of working. It has to be said that this is rarely worked out sensitively or thoughtfully. It is more likely that the dominant or larger body takes over and suppresses the smaller constituent part of the merged body, eroding the way that things have been done in the past rather than celebrating them (Randall and Procter, 2013).

Partnership is the key idea to gain commitment from everyone and prevent cliques of privileged groups emerging and imposing their views. But partnership means sharing knowledge, communication (this includes listening) and cultivating a culture that embraces everyone. As Bullock and Batten (1985: 386) suggest, this is a long-term view of change rather than a quick fix.

There is a need to improve and enhance performance through HR interventions. We have already recalled the HRD list and will return to it many times in the future. All of our joint policy, procedures and practices need to be looked at and revised to capture the best practices, whichever area of the company they come from.

How OD is applied

Identifying a need for change

This is not always as self-evident as might be assumed. That results are poor for a company may be obvious, but why that should be the case may be more difficult to identify. Falling sales may just be due to a contracting market. So, no amount of promotional activity or staff training may make any difference to driving up sales. And yet there are still decisions to be made about restructuring or redeploying resources to cope with contraction. It may be that staffing becomes a challenge. There is not only staff turnover but also the retention of staff and the attraction of the right calibre of staff to be considered. Demographics can work against companies seeking to attract the right people in a situation of depleting resources or more attractive employment prospects elsewhere.

Select an intervention technique (usually appoint a change agent external to company)

This would be a traditional approach to what we call the problem-solving approach. It is assumed that the problems can be fixed and that there will be a right way of doing this. As we have seen, training is often offered as a solution to problems within the organization. But, again, as we shall see in subsequent chapters of this book, its success is based on a number of prerequisites: do the trainees have the aptitude and commitment to embark successfully on the training? Is the competence required actually trainable? There are some trainers who would argue that training does not change attitudes. This is especially the case with such topics as customer care; teamwork; and leadership. There are some behaviours that can be trained into individuals: knowledge can be enhanced; skill can be improved; experience can be consolidated. But, there is no guarantee that individuals will change what they think or feel about imposed work processes and in interacting with other people in the business.

Gain top management support

This ought to go without saying. However, it is not always the case. New managing directors or chief operating officers often have plans to institute change that may not be shared by those they have inherited around the boardroom table. That makes for quite a lack of consensus which, when attempts are made to engage the doubters in change initiatives, can find them less than supportive. Unfortunately, such lack of enthusiasm will often be sensed by their staff who are then less likely to join in the change programme proactively, either.

We will be talking more about the need to engage in bottom-up or emergent change. Getting doubts, concerns and objections out into the open is an important part of resolving conflict and suspicion. So, too, can involvement in the planning and exploration of a change programme be crucial to its acceptance.

Plan the change process

The crucial question is who, exactly, is involved in making the plan? We cannot assume that change agents will have a ready answer. But even if they think they have, wise change agents will seek to bring in others from within the company as internal change agents. In many sectors those with experience will also add credibility to the composition of the change team.

BOX 4.7

External change agents are often faced with mixed groups meeting for the first time to discuss change prospects.

In any such forum it is likely that the external change agent will be asked: 'Are you a Doctor (Nurse/Customs Officer) yourself?'

The implication for the external agent is obvious, but can be overcome by involving those within the organization who are on-side with the prospect of change. Such internal change agents are flag fliers and champions of change.

Overcome resistance to change

There are always objectors to change. Sometimes their previous experience of change warns them that change has not always been well managed in the past. Sometimes there have been forcible redundancies affecting friends and colleagues during past change programmes (Hallier and Lyon, 1996). Sometimes, there was no conviction that the previous change was worthwhile or even achieved its goals at all. Often there will be those who will want to download their frustration at perceived mismanagement of past change. These interventions are worthwhile and should be encouraged.

BOX 4.8

Outlining the need for change, an external change agent facilitating the meeting found himself confronted by a challenger from the back of the room.

'I've been here 35 years,' said the objector, 'and I have never seen any change programme work successfully here.'

The facilitator invited the objector to come out and join him in the front and then asked him to explain to the group how he thought successful change should be managed.

He thereafter became a very positive internal change agent on the programme both as a supporter and (after training) a very good trainer.

Evaluating the change process

We need to return to our HRM and organizational outcomes diagram from Guest (1989) (Table 4.1).

The measurement of success in HRM is to be gauged by the outcomes in both columns two and three. Sometimes companies have not been particularly good at keeping accurate measurements in the past. This may mean that evaluation has to be part of the change programme. Indeed, involving individuals and groups in their own self-assessment can be a good way of gaining commitment and ongoing monitoring for the company.

We might also point out that evaluation does include the end-user. Customer surveys, questionnaires and feedback/focus groups can be an excellent means of finding out how a change programme has impacted on those receiving the service.

Finally, *exit interviews* should be mentioned, too. The views of those who have left the organization and gone to work elsewhere can give an important insight into why people left and whether the events that may have triggered their leaving have now been addressed successfully.

Post-bureaucracy and HRM approaches

Emphasis on greater flexibility

We have already seen that one of the HR outcomes that Guest's diagram includes is *flexibility*. As we have noted, this can include:

- time
- number
- cost
- functional.

TABLE 4.1 Overview of links in human resource management theory

HRM policies	Human resource outcomes	Organizational outcomes
Organizational objectives Management of change	Strategic integration	High problem solving/change
Recruitment/selection/ socialization	Commitment	Innovation and creativity
Appraisal, training and development	Flexibility/adaptability	High cost-effectiveness
Communication of standards and targets	Quality	Fewer customer complaints Low turnover/absence/ grievance

Source: Adapted from Guest (1989) in Blyton and Turnbull (1992: 21).

The first three would feature in any organization's attempt to get more production for less overhead (efficiency/productivity factors). But it is the fourth flexibility that has been the focus of many of the more recent change initiatives, such as TQM, in which job rotation is sustained by team members being trained to do one another's jobs and thus to cover for each other when occasion demands.

Decentralization of activities

The *Shamrock organization* offered an illustration of how companies could change the employment status of their staff while retaining their services under more flexible terms and conditions. A similar movement would be unbundling where large organizations either divest or float parts of the organization to be run as independent businesses. Both could be described as strategies that are *panopticon*: they enable the senior managers a much clearer view of who makes what contribution to the bottom line day to day.

Contraction of hierarchies (5–6 levels/flatter organization)

Delayering, as it is sometimes referred to, is facilitated by flexible working. Not only are establishment/staffing costs reduced by this strategy, but technology allows supervision of more people by fewer managers, even if their staff work off-site. The traditional span of control is no longer necessary as all aspects of the organization's operations are monitored remotely and accurately 24/7.

BOX 4.9

Modern aircraft are monitored as they fly to detect any unusual or abnormal usage. This means that both pilot and meteorological conditions can be tracked during flights so that servicing staff can attend to any defects detected as soon as the aircraft lands.

Inappropriate flying can also be tracked so that pilots putting equipment under strain or passengers at risk can also be monitored and dealt with appropriately immediately upon landing.

Cross-functional project arrangements

There are many examples of such organizing of people's efforts in groups. They feature in all companies that have embarked on matrix management and gone on to extend their influence beyond manufacturing into the service and IT industries. Project management becomes an important expertise to be able to employ to manage such flexibility effectively. Not only are group outputs important to monitor, but so too are the individual contributions that have made that achievement possible.

Reduced command and control structures

It may be necessary to define individual targets clearly in an organization that seeks to reduce supervisory and management levels. Traditional management born of having been through the job oneself is less and less likely to apply to core managers tasked with monitoring consultants and subcontractors. This brings us back to our original diagram of process management (see Figure 4.2).

Where managers do not know the process involved in what people do for them, their only access and control is defining the *inputs* of the working contract accurately:

- time
- quality
- quantity
- cost.

And *output*:

- outcome for the end-user.

As can be seen from daily occurrences in the contracting business, particularly with government organizations, it is not as easy to define these as tightly as might be hoped. This means that cost overruns may be incurred or penalties invoked, or the worst scenario: the consultant walks away from the contract and no other consultant wants to take it on.

Erosion of boundaries between organizations/professional groups

In-house professionals are always more biddable than those who have a choice of employer or can work for the highest bidder. Independent operation is always more feasible for those whose skills are in short supply, or jobs for which specialist skills are in demand. This will apply increasingly to all forms of knowledge work. Professionals who do not depend on an organization for CPD are unlikely to exhibit *organizational commitment* which HRM theory strives to engender. This is one of the conflicts between the HR outcomes that have gone largely unremarked: *flexibility* can militate against *organizational commitment* (Blyton and Turnbull, 1992).

FIGURE 4.2 Managing consultants.

Decline of traditional organizational careers (portfolio)

Related to the last point is the question of *career commitment*. Portfolio careers are the ability of those with relevant skill sets to move frequently so that they are dependent on one organization and can advertise their diversity of experience to those with whom they wish to work. Their only concern is to ensure that their current work enhances their knowledge, increases their skill and consolidates their experience. In this way they will feel more employable working on interim contracts (Handy, 1989).

Participative working arrangements that give workers greater influence over decision making

Autonomy is most feasible for those who are able to determine how they go about their work. The exercise of autonomy is dependent on the discretion to approach a job in a particular way without reference to the original contractor. It is a good example of the team empowerment and reinforces the idea that knowledge is power for those who possess it.

Teamworking and empowerment initiatives

Job rotation (TQM initiatives)

As we have noted, this is fundamental to the introduction of flexible working in the manufacturing industry, particularly the car industry. But then its principles began to commend themselves to other sectors as well. It should be said that its effectiveness depends on *comprehensive training, job rotation* leading to *functional flexibility*.

Work rotation (functional flexibility)

One ready example of work rotation is the accelerated promotion path that exists for graduate management trainees in some large organizations. In such cases it is not uncommon for trainees to spend a period of time in each of the major departments. At the end of the experience they will be assessed for their aptitude and ability and a decision will be made about where they finally settle in the organization.

Work rotation can also be used to develop likely candidates into jobs that offer more prospects or development and promotion by acquiring the necessary knowledge and skills in supporting roles. One example of this would be working as an administrator/secretary in a sales office. Over the course of time contact with customers, other salespeople and product range awareness would develop a familiarity with much of the threshold knowledge necessary for going out to negotiate with customers face to face. This can be done both by further training in negotiational and sales skills and accompanying current salespeople in the field. Eventually, such a developed candidate would be able to 'go on terms' as a salesperson in their own right. It could also avoid the interference costs of waiting to fill a position by people from outside the organization.

Responsive to customer requirements (delighting the customer)

This term found its way into popular usage in the early 1980s with Peters and Waterman's *In Search of Excellence*. It has become somewhat hackneyed since, but does occasionally raise its head unexpectedly and not always where there is a ready reward on offer.

BOX 4.10

Following a day of delays at Heathrow Airport, weary passengers embarked on their shuttle flight home.

Once moving, the pilot announced that the plane was thirty-eighth in line for take-off. The effect on the passengers can be imagined. However, nothing daunted, the pilot asked the passengers to look at the elliptical wing shape they could see outside the windows as the planes in front turned onto the runway and took off. He proceeded to explain how the Bernoulli brothers began experiments on air flow and lift, finding that with increasing speed the pressure on the top of the wing reduced, thus allowing the plane to lift off and fly ...

Needless to say, by the time the pilot had finished his talk he was able to announce that they were now at the head of the queue and next in line to take off. He received a spontaneous round of applause from the passengers – he had certainly delighted his customers.

Allowing those with the expertise to manage the outcomes of a project

We already referred to this when we mentioned moving the leadership of the team around to allow those with the relevant expertise to take the lead when their skill is most in need. But to be able to do that with confidence requires more than just the expertise to solve a part of a problem. Coordinating others becomes a complementary set of skills that have to be developed in most people to find them competent in people-handling skills. This is particularly true of an interdisciplinary group where all are at the same level of responsibility.

This brings us to the basis of power in working groups and how it operates. There are different definitions and it is a difficult concept to understand fully as its context will be relevant to success.

Getting someone to do something they would not otherwise have done

Another popular definition is 'getting things done through other people' (Follett, 1942 [1927]). The problem with this definition is that it could apply to persuasion, or it could apply to force. In other words, the power could be mandatory or it could be discretionary. The definition as stated does not distinguish between the two. So power over others can rest on different contexts.

Authority vested in law (coercive power)

We have already noted that neo-institutionalization identifies three drivers that have an effect on organizations adopting similar forms (the word used here is iso-morphic) (DiMaggio and Powell, 1983). The first driver referred to is coercive. Here the organization has no choice but to adopt or adapt to the law, for example. Health and safety would be a prime example but it would be equally unwise to ignore most employment law.

The power of influence (peer group) mimetic power

There can be many drivers that are copied by others in a sector or field. Fashion would be one ready example that can drive copying what is put up as the right thing to do or the fashionable thing to do. The drive for open offices took on an influence of its own – though significantly very senior people always seemed to garner an office of their own.

The power of professional bodies (normative power)

We have already mentioned the credibility that professional power brings with it. There is also evidence that professional boundaries can be stoutly defended against change. The present government is currently finding this out as they attempt to privatize the National Health Service in the UK. Doctors and nurses have their own professional bodies and these can be intransigent in their opposition to change (Nicolini *et al.*, 2008). Disregarding this aspect of professional power is always a risk for those who depend on the services involved.

French and Raven (1959) outlined five different types of power which included the following.

Coercive power

As we saw earlier the tenor of this power lies in the force that can be brought to bear on the subject of the power. It could be a legal contract that binds both parties to adhere to the conditions contained in the contract, for example.

Reward power

It doesn't have to be money but it could involve setting up a need inherent in the relationship. Good or acceptable behaviour is rewarded in a way that is both expected and therefore appreciated.

Legitimate power

As its name suggests, this includes all relationships that involve rightful demand based on mutual duty and responsibility. The employer–employee relationship could well be used to illustrate how this relationship works. Both sides have duties and responsibilities that they owe to the other. Failure to fulfil one's contract could lead to disciplinary action.

Referent power

People give power to others freely not only because they are bound to by external or legal constraints. Role models are accorded a power of influence that can be freely given but is just as influential as are other more coercive or legitimate relationships. Being related to someone in power may be just as influential to others as formal positions of power within the hierarchy.

Expert power

The power of the consultant or professional worker to dictate the terms and conditions under which a relationship develops is based on their expertise. As with other forms of power they are dependent on the continued effective exercise of such expertise. Governments are perceived as powerful when they deliver to the expectations of their electorates. They are deemed weak and rejected when they fail to deliver satisfactorily.

Ongoing HR role

There are many interventions that can be made by HR to ensure that individuals and groups are encouraged to become involved in their own development. *Strategic integration* is not a one-off annual event or a rolling programme that is solely in the hands of senior managers. It is an ongoing evaluation of where the company is and where it needs to be, followed by an attempt to plan out the way in which this progress will be implemented.

HR needs to address issues around *flexibility* of labour and resources, ensuring that people are available according to need and are involved in the *quality* outcomes that the company needs to achieve in order to succeed. All of this requires *organizational commitment*. Though, as we have seen, the very success of flexibility in organizations has meant that the relationship between interim and contracted workers makes commitment less likely, due to job insecurity and the need to plan for a future that will probably be elsewhere. Knowledge workers have learned that their advantage lies in acquiring further knowledge, skill and experience. Without that their continued employment must become less certain.

References and further reading

Argyris, C. and Schon, D.A. (1978) *Organizational Learning*. Reading, MA: Addison-Wesley.

Belbin, M. (1980) *Management Teams: Why they succeed or fail*. Oxford: Butterworth Heinemann.

Blyton, P. and Turnbull, P. (1992) *Reassessing Human Resource Management*. London: Sage.

Bullock, R.J. and Batten, D. (1985) It's just a phase we're going through: A review and synthesis of OD phase analysis. *Group and Organization Studies*, 10(4): 383–412.

Carnall, C.A. (1990) *Managing Change in Organizations*. Englewood Cliffs, NJ: Prentice Hall.

Champy, J. (1995) *Reengineering Management*. New York: Harper Business.

Chia, R. (1996) Metaphors and metaphorization in organizational analysis: Thinking beyond the thinkable. In D. Grant and C. Oswick (eds) *Metaphors and Organization*. London: Sage, 127–145.

Corley, K.G. and Gioia, D.A. (2004) Identity ambiguity and change in the wake of a corporate spin-off. *Administrative Science Quarterly*, 49:173–208.

Deal, T. and Kennedy, A. (1982) *Organization Cultures: The rights and rituals of organization life*. Reading, MA: Addison Wesley.

DiMaggio P.J. and Powell, W.W. (1983) The iron cage revisited: Institutional isomorphism and collective rationality in organizational fields. *American Sociological Review*, 48:147–160.

Follett, M.P. (1942 [1927]) *Dynamic Administration*. New York: Harper & Brothers Publishers.

French, J.R.P. and Raven, B. (1959) The bases of social power. In D. Cartwright and A. Zander (eds) *Group Dynamics*. New York: Harper & Row, 607–623.

Guest, D.E. (1989) Personnel and HRM: Can you tell the difference? *Personnel Management*, 21(1): 48–51.

Hales, C. (2002) 'Bureaucracy-lite' and continuities in managerial work. *British Journal of Management*, 13(1): 51–66.

Hallier, J. and Lyon, P. (1996) Job insecurity and employee commitment: Managers' reactions to the threat and outcomes of redundancy selection. *British Journal of Management*, 7(1): 107–123.

Handy, C. (1989) *The Age of Unreason*. London: Hutchinson.

Hofstede, G. (1991) *Culture and Organizations: Software of the mind*. Maidenhead: McGraw Hill.

Kotter, J.P. (1996). *Leading Change*. Cambridge, MA : Harvard Business School Press.

Lazarus, R. and Folkman, S. (1984) *Stress, Appraisal and Coping.* New York: Springer Publishing Company.

Lewin, K. (1947) Frontiers in group dynamics. *Human Relations,* 1(2): 150–151.

McKinlay, A. (2002) The limits of knowledge management. *New Technology, Work and Employment,* 17(2), 76–88.

Nadler, D.A. (1993) Concepts for the management of strategic change, in C. Mabey and B. Mayon-White (eds) *Managing Change.* London: The Open University/Paul Chapman Publishing, pp. 85–98.

Nicolini, D., Powell, J., Conville, P. and Martinez-Solano, L. (2008) Managing knowledge in the healthcare sector: A review. *International Journal of Management Reviews,* 105(3/4): 245–263.

Nonaka, I. and Takeuchi, H. (1995) *The Knowledge Creating Company: How Japanese companies create the dynamics of innovation.* New York: Oxford University Press.

Oakland, J. (1989) *Total Quality Management.* London: Heinemann.

Piderit, S.K. (2000) Rethinking resistance and recognizing ambivalence: A multidimensional view of attitudes toward an organizational change. *Academy of Management Review,* 25(4): 783–794.

Peters, T. and Waterman, R. (1982) *In Search of Excellence.* New York: Harper & Row.

Pettigrew, A.M. (1985) *The Awakening Giant: Continuity and change at ICI.* Oxford: Basil Blackwell.

Procter, S.J. and Mueller, F. (2000) *Teamworking.* London: Macmillan.

Randall, J.A. and Procter S.J. (2008) Ambiguity and ambivalence: Senior managers' accounts of organizational change in a restructured government department. *Journal of Organizational Change Management,* 21(6): 686–700.

Randall, J. and Procter, S. (2013) When institutional logics collide: reinforcing dominance in a merged government department. *Journal of Change Management,* 2(13): 143–158.

Revans, R. (1980) *Action Learning: New techniques for management.* London: Blond and Briggs.

Rousseau, D.M. (1990) New hire perceptions of their own and their employer's obligations: A study of psychological contracts. *Journal of Organizational Behavior,* 11(5): 389–400.

Schein, E.H. (1967) *Process Consultation: Its role in Organization Development.* Reading, MA: Addison Wesley.

Schein, E.H. (1985) *Organizational Culture and Leadership.* San Francisco, CA: Jossey Bass.

Schein, E.H. (1990) Organizational culture. *American Psychologist,* 45(2): 109–119.

Senge, P. (1990) *The Fifth Discipline: The art and practice of the learning organization.* London: Random House.

Storey, J. (1992) *Developments in the Management of Human Resources.* Oxford: Blackwell.

Wickens, P. (1987) *The Road to Nissan: Flexibility, quality, teamwork.* Basingstoke: Macmillan.

GRADUATE ATTRIBUTES

In these exercises you will address the following graduate attributes:

- a breadth of knowledge, understanding and skills beyond your chosen discipline(s);
- an ability to communicate effectively for different purposes and in different contexts;
- a diverse set of transferable and generic skills.

Assertiveness

In work we may often find ourselves thinking that 'if I just keep my head down and get on with it my work will speak for itself'. In my experience, as good as your work may be, it is never that eloquent on your behalf. In practice, some level of assertiveness is necessary not only for good communication but also for coping with the stresses that may build (particularly if no one gives you due credit for your good work).

What does it mean to be assertive?

Being assertive is about expressing yourself. It is about making your personal rights and feelings clear to others. Assertiveness is an attitude and a way of acting in any situation where you are required to express your feelings, ask for what you want or say no to something you do not want. Assertiveness is about self-confidence. It is about having a positive attitude towards yourself and towards others. It is about standing up for your needs and interests in an open and direct way.

Being assertive is about:

- focusing on your goal
- being self-aware
- building self-esteem
- being yourself
- being honest.

An assertive person stands up for things that matter to them while at the same time respecting the things that matter to others.

Why should you be assertive?

The way in which you interact with others can be a source of considerable stress in your life. This is nowhere more true than in your working environment. Developing the ability to be assertive can alleviate stress, make you feel more relaxed and help you develop self-respect and self-worth.

You should be assertive because doing things you do not want to do tends to create resentment which can become the source of conflict in your relationships with others. Assertive people look after their own needs and interests but also recognize the needs and interests of others. Being assertive helps them to achieve the proper balance between their interests and those of others.

Assertive people use open, direct and honest communication with others. When they feel angry or upset, they confront the source of their anger in an objective way. They take responsibility for their decisions and behaviour. They admit to their mistakes and accept their part in them.

To become assertive is to undertake a mode of behaviour and communication that will provide the most effective means of operating to reach their goals. It creates a confidence not only about yourself as an individual but also about your place in the world. It will manifest itself in how we speak, how we stand and in our use of language. It is about being aware of and accepting how we are now and about taking the steps necessary to getting to how we wish to be.

When are we assertive?

- when we can say no;
- when we are not afraid to ask for clarification;
- when we can disagree openly;
- when we can express our likes and dislikes freely;
- when we experience greater relaxation in interpersonal situations;
- when we can talk about ourselves unselfconsciously;
- when we can accept compliments;
- when we stand up for our rights but do so in such a way that the rights of others are not violated.

The road to assertiveness

So, now we know the benefits, what we need to know is how to get there. How do we find the road we need to become assertive? Well, we must begin by looking at the three basic styles of interpersonal behaviour:

- aggressive
- passive
- assertive.

Aggressive

Examples of aggressive behaviour would include elements such as fighting, threatening, accusations, blame and generally acting towards people without regard for their feelings. The advantage of this form of behaviour is that people tend not to try to push the aggressive individual around. The disadvantage is that people also tend not to want to be around them.

Aggressive people have little or no reluctance in imposing their views on others, or even harming the interests of others while in the pursuit of their own. Rather than collaborate with others, the aggressive person prefers to dominate the situation. This may be by the use of organizational authority, threats or even bullying when they feel that it will achieve their aims. They are frequently the sort of manager who wants to micro-manage everything that their staff does because they want everything done their way. Further they have a tendency not to care about the opinions of those within the organization that have less power than them.

Passive

A passive person is quite likely to allow other people to manipulate them. They tend not to stand up for themselves, do what they are told to do regardless of how they actually feel about it. They are inclined to be quiet, even timid, and they are quick to apologize, often for things they didn't do. If there is any advantage to being passive it is that you rarely experience direct rejection or conflict with others. However, the disadvantage is that the passive person will be taken advantage of by others. This can result in a burden of heavy resentment that can lead to internal conflict that may manifest in resentment and anger.

To be passive is to be in a condition characterized by submissiveness and by an unwillingness to stand up for your needs and interests. The passive person will hold themselves back from the attempt to influence others. They will rather allow others to influence them and to disrespect their individual rights and boundaries. Due to the fact that the passive person does not assert their views or put forth arguments to support them, their views are generally either unclear or completely unknown to others. The end result of this is to make dialogue and ideas sharing a virtual impossibility.

Assertive

The assertive person stands up for themselves and expresses their feelings. They refuse to let others take advantage of them but are, at the same time, considerate of the feelings of others. Indeed, the advantage of being assertive is that you can get what you want, usually, without making others angry at you.

When you are assertive you can act in your own best interest and not feel guilty or wrong about it because although you are pursuing your interests you are also attempting to avoid disadvantaging others. The aggressive behaviour of attack and blame, the passive behaviour of submissiveness and withdrawal are seen for the inadequate strategies of escape that they are. It becomes clear that such strategies create more pain and stress than they prevent.

A quick quiz

To be assertive you have to:

(a) put the needs of others before yours
(b) aim to win no matter what the cost may be
(c) stand up for your needs and interests in open and direct ways
(d) be both passive and aggressive in equal measure

Answer: (c)

You are being aggressive if:

(a) your aim is to dominate others
(b) you are listening to others and making an effort to keep the peace

(c) you always to admit your mistakes
(d) your aim is to give balanced compliments and constructive feedback

Answer: (a)

You may be passive if:

(a) you often find yourself saying no to people
(b) you are known for bringing your influence to bear
(c) you frequently find yourself doing things you really don't want to
(d) you act in your interests and feel no guilt

Answer: (c)

What's that signpost up ahead ... next stop The Assertive Zone

The road to learning to be assertive can be a hard one because it involves working on yourself in six distinctly signposted areas:

- developing non-verbal assertive behaviours;
- recognizing and being willing to exercise your basic human rights;
- becoming aware of your own unique feelings, needs and wants;
- practising assertive responses;
- being able to be assertive whenever needed.

Learning to say NO

All six of these areas can be uncomfortable for you to develop. It is amazing how many people have difficulty with a one syllable word such as NO. Learning to say this simple word can lead to a reduction in stress as you assert your rights and needs. It is easy to say yes to yet another piece of work for a quiet life but you need to think whether it is more appropriate to say no. Saying yes may not only be the worst thing for you, it may not be the best thing for the organization. If you are stressed and overburdened by your workload, then you are probably not producing to your potential.

Saying no

When you are saying no you are not rejecting the person, only the request. It is okay to ask for more information in order to decide whether you want to say no. You have to accept the responsibility for saying no and not blame the other person for making the request.

If you are taken unawares by the request or you feel that you don't have sufficient time to think when asked, then say, 'I will have to think about that and let you know.' Give yourself time to think about what you want to say.

Body language *or 'What on earth do you mean by non-verbal?'*

You don't need to be aware of all the minutiae of body language to use it. In fact much of the literature on body language fails to convince me but that doesn't mean that it is all nonsense. Let's look at some things you can do to be assertive with body language.

Make sure that you look directly at another person when addressing them. Looking away conveys the message that you're not quite sure about asking for what you want. It suggests insecurity and often untrustworthiness. So look at the person when you are making your point.

Don't back off or move away from the other person while in dialogue. Standing your ground really applies when being assertive.

Try and be open – open body language consists of having the arms and legs uncrossed, hands open with the palms and the insides of the wrists exposed; the body, feet and face point at the other; the face is exposed and unobstructed. Stand erect rather than slouching.

Humans have a requirement for a certain amount of space around their bodies in order to feel comfortable and not threatened. Distances vary with individuals and the cultures in which they were brought up. Violating this personal space can be seen as an aggressive action so try to avoid it.

Stay calm – try to use calm measured body movements, don't wave your arms frantically. Avoid angry outbursts.

This is by no means the end of body language and its influence on being assertive but it gives you some food for thought. Communication is not just about what you say. It is quite possible that you may be saying one thing while your body language is undercutting the effect you want.

What do you mean by rights?

What is your Personal Bill of Rights (PBR)? Look at the list below, consider which you think should be part of your PBR and tick the box.

- ❑ I have a right to be treated with respect as a human being.
- ❑ I have a right to be treated as an equal.
- ❑ I have a right to decide how I wish to spend my time.
- ❑ I have a right to ask for what I want.
- ❑ I have a right to ask for feedback on things such as my performance.
- ❑ I have a right to be listened to.
- ❑ I have a right to be taken seriously.
- ❑ I have a right to have an opinion.
- ❑ I have a right to say No without feeling guilty.
- ❑ I have a right to make clear my needs.
- ❑ I have a right to set my own priorities.

- ❏ I have a right to express my feelings.
- ❏ I have a right to make mistakes.
- ❏ I have a right to hold religious beliefs.
- ❏ I have a right to my emotions.
- ❏ I have a right to change my mind.
- ❏ I have a right to fail occasionally.
- ❏ I have a right to ask for information.
- ❏ I have a right to be successful.
- ❏ I have a right to adhere to my own set of values.
- ❏ I have a right to take time to make decisions.
- ❏ I have a right to hold political opinions.
- ❏ I have a right to privacy.
- ❏ I have a right to not know.
- ❏ I have a right to be an individual.
- ❏ I have a right to take responsibility for my own decisions.
- ❏ I have a right not to assert myself.
- ❏ I have a right not to be dependent on the approval of other people.
- ❏ I have a right to place value on my own worth.
- ❏ I have a right to choose how I respond in a given situation.
- ❏ I have a right to be independent.
- ❏ I have a right to be angry.
- ❏ I have a right to develop as a human being.
- ❏ I have a right to choose whether or not I get involved in other people's problems.
- ❏ I have a right to decline to be responsible for the problems of others.
- ❏ I have a right to look after my own needs.
- ❏ I have a right to have time for myself.
- ❏ I have a right to be me.

Now have a look back at what you have ticked. Why did you choose those? Why did you leave out some? Would what you have picked be appropriate in all contexts? Would you expect to have the same PBR at work as outside? If not, why not?

You need to be clear what you consider your rights to be before you assert them.

Work and assertiveness

Are you happy at your work? Not, do you get paid enough or do you have good prospects for promotion, but are you happy? The fact is that for many of us our workplace is an important place in which to meet new people, to make friends and to create a social support network. To be happy at work you have to have a good environment and you are part of creating that environment.

Let's think about rewards. What sort of rewards do you get from your work? Is it just the pay cheque at the end of the day/week/month or is it more? Do you get satisfaction from helping people, solving problems or just using your skills to their maximum? What would you like to be getting from your job that you are not getting?

Let's think about how you can move from where you are to where you want to be in terms of your work. What assertive skills could you exercise?

Career

In the current environment it is very unlikely that you will have one job for the whole of your life. We talk now of portfolio careers. A portfolio career is composed of different kinds of jobs pursued successively or simultaneously. Nowadays you may need to retrain once or more in your working life and to pay attention to the development of your career path in ways that were previously unnecessary.

To be aware of, and to plan, your career path is a vital assertiveness skill. You need to view your career as an ongoing process and plan it to meet your needs.

Workplace

Charity may begin at home but your career path is guided in the workplace. Learning to be assertive in the workplace is a vital part of being successful. In the workplace you will need not only to be aware of your achievements but also to have the ability to make others aware of them. If you can't do this you are likely to miss out on opportunities. When you face your promotions review, the facts as to what you have, or have not, achieved will emerge, or rather they will have the opportunity to emerge. These reviews tend to be formal and in many organizations there is a review of each individual's progress every year. It is then important that on attending your review you go equipped with the facts about your progress and achievements over the previous year and are prepared to assert them. Don't make the mistake of leaving this task to your line manager. They may be genuinely unaware of what you have accomplished in the past year. You must speak up and share your views, make the case for your achievements and take constructive criticism with good grace. The review is a situation where you need to be your own champion; you can't wait for others to speak up on your behalf for if you do you may be deafened by the silence.

Remember that being assertive in the workplace, just as elsewhere, doesn't mean trampling on others and it certainly doesn't mean letting others trample on you. You need to make your case without belittling the work of others but also without giving them undue credit for your successes.

Make a record of your achievements throughout the year leading up to your review. The best time to make a record of your achievements is as soon as possible after you have achieved them. Keep a running record of what you achieve because you will find this a lot easier than trying to remember later, when you are already involved in your next project. Record the difficulties you had to overcome related to the work but not personal difficulties. Your record of achievements should be task focused as that is what the reviewer will be looking for.

Remember that while it may feel virtuous to respond to the question 'how have you got on this year' with 'I think I've done all right' and demonstrate your humility, it is unlikely that this is a quality that your manager is looking for in those they may wish to promote. You must sell yourself and your achievements while being honest about them. You must also be honest about your mistakes – we all make them – as to admit to them rather than conceal or pass blame demonstrates that you are capable of learning from them.

A friend of mine called me to say that they hadn't been promoted and they were furious about it. When I asked why they hadn't got the promotion they said it was because other people had been given credit but their work had been ignored. Now, while I felt great sympathy, as it was one of my friends, and said comforting things about how awful the management must be not to recognize their work, I couldn't help but think that if they had been more assertive their contribution may not have been overlooked.

A thought exercise

Imagine yourself living your life assertively, making your own decisions and creating the life you desire to have.

Think about what actually happens in your life currently. Where does it fail to match your desires? Why haven't you got to where you want to be – are you too passive or too aggressive?

In what situations would you really like to be more assertive? Think about them and make a list so you remember (this is the first step to action).

Consciously make and affirm a decision to be more assertive. How are you going to implement this decision? What should you do next? It's up to you.

Summary

For managers the ability to reflect and help others be reflective is a necessary prerequisite to being successful with people. The skills set required has as its foundation assertiveness which is the basis of good negotiation skills. It is complemented by listening skills which enable us to take in what others are trying to say to us. Such skills cannot be trained into us, but we can learn to develop them.

Mentoring can be an excellent way of developing in interactive listening and discussion skills. We hear and we forget. But when we listen there is a chance that we will learn to understand.

Tutor guidance

There are several ways of setting up exercises for teams to work with assertiveness. Writing up prompt cards that contain roles for staff and managers can be a useful way of engaging a tutorial group. Divide the tutorial into groups of three or four.

Each group receives a card explaining the situation that has arisen from the point of view of either the member of staff or the manager. There can be as many situations as there are teams.

Each team discusses the situation on its prompt card and works out how it would approach a conversation/interview to follow through on the subject matter raised on the card.

The tutor calls on two teams to send forward one of their members so that there is someone presenting the manager's brief and someone presenting the staff brief. The interview should be recorded/videoed ready for playback afterwards.

Should any interviewer suffer a blank moment or feel unable to go on they can tag another member of their team to take over the interview. That person can decide to continue from where the previous team member left off or opt to start the interview again.

Getting the other person talking is a key skill that interviewers need to develop. As we know, asking open questions can be a good way of doing this. Such questions might be:

- Tell me about ...
- What do you think about ...?
- What do you feel about ...?

Members of the team not involved in actual interviewing can be asked to note how many open/closed questions were asked during the course of the interview and what the ratio of the talk was between the two people involved.

Debriefing at the end, after or during play-back, can focus on:

- the direction the interview took;
- questions asked during the interview;
- defining moments in the interview (when the interview took a turn for the worse or better);
- whether the interview achieved a rapport between the parties;
- alternative approaches to such an interview.

As always, a few points to guide feedback should be adhered to by all those giving it:

- say what was successful and why, giving details if possible;
- say what could have been done differently;
- offer positive and helpful examples of how this could be done differently relating them back to the key principles of assertiveness.

Practising assertiveness depends on setting up practical exercises that can be used in groups. Setting up realistic scenarios that occur regularly or are offered by the group make the topics dealt with current and relevant and therefore encourage engagement from those taking part.

Two briefs should be drawn up for teams taking part and the position of each role player should be made clear on the card. These conditions should be adhered to as they keep the role players on track and require self-discipline and assure consistency within the exercise.

Teams of three can be given a card and plan how they intend to present the material they have been given. Once they have had time to do this each team sends forward one of their members to conduct the interview. This can be usefully recorded so that play-back can take place and feedback given. The tutor may choose to take the role of a difficult member of staff or the role of a good manager. These roles can then be reversed so that trainees learn from the tutor how to proceed assertively.

Feedback should focus on:

- what went successfully in the interview(s);
- what did not succeed;
- learning points arising for future encounters;
- reinforcement of the principles of assertiveness.

If there are more than two teams, increase the number of scenarios you write up to engage each pair of teams with their own scenario.

5

MANAGING CHANGE/ CHANGING MANAGERS

Topics

- culture and cultural change initiatives
- cultural change – behavioural change
- commitment levels and motivation
- quality initiatives
- Shamrock organization, flexibility or fragmentation?
- Hofstede and national cultural stereotypes.

Culture and culture change initiatives

Culture is a difficult concept to explain clearly and succinctly and yet most staff members and managers will assume that they know what it means. If we take the simple definition of 'it's the way we do things round here' (Deal and Kennedy, 1982), then we can see just how simple and obvious that sounds. And yet, why we do things the way we do them, even when working in groups, invites a closer look at the assumptions that might be being made.

First, it may be that we are referring to everyone doing things in the same place, in the same way, at the same time. Such uniformity might be obvious if we were observing military manoeuvres or parade ground precision of movement among a body of soldiers. Such an approach would also be observable in highly disciplined environments such as flying, where, for example, the BUMFICHH checks (brakes; undercarriage; mixture rich; fuel on, and sufficient; carb heat on; hatches secured; harness tight) are drilled into pilots during their training to be rigorously followed as part of the procedure for the approach before a landing. Such behaviours are often initiated by instructional techniques, regularly practised and validated by examination and regular checks.

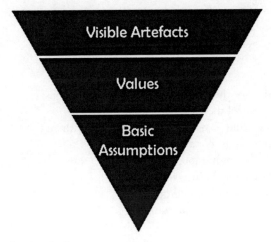

FIGURE 5.1 Three levels of culture.

Source: Schein, 1985.

If we refer back to Schein's cultural layers model (Figure 5.1) then we can see that most of what is observable lies in the top layer of visible artefacts. It usually includes what we would see on entering a business premise when we first visit, or when we enter for the first time as a consultant or change agent. We may observe uniform patterns of behaviour – trained into people so that they perform in particular ways. These may be procedures and practices that support the business objectives in a way that is intended to reinforce productivity or efficiency factors (time; quality; quantity; cost).

As observers, our challenge lies in penetrating the two layers that lie below the visible artefacts: values and basic assumptions. No matter how uniform behaviours may appear, it is unwise to assume that everybody in the organization thinks the same or believes the same things about their job, their work, their career or the organization. At these deeper levels individuals may have certain beliefs about the meaning of the way we do things around here. These may be work priorities: given a series of demands on my attention now, which would I choose to attend to first, as a matter of priority? It may be that there is an answer to this that members of the peer group know and perhaps communicate to those who join them as new recruits. It is part of fitting in with the group values, and individuals that do not comply might find it difficult to fit in long term.

Discussion group

What makes a good manager/group leader?

Here are a few statements that you may want to consider. When you have had a chance to make up your own mind, discuss with others in the group whether you agree with them or not. How far does your answer depend on how you interpret the statements? You can refer back to the previous chapters to elements covered in the exercises on critical thinking, argumentation, assertiveness to refresh your memory on the factors that are important.

A good manager/group leader:

- always leads by example;
- derives influence through respect for others' opinions;
- steps in to control the group when necessary;
- lets the group find its own level and leaves it to them to make decisions;
- is never directive or confrontational;
- has a good sense of humour;
- is a good listener and learns from the group;
- works for consensus in the group;
- is always loyal to the organization;
- speaks up for those in the group under attack;
- disciplines people that step out of line;
- brooks no nonsense from time-wasters.

Even more difficult for the outside observer to penetrate would be *basic assumptions*. If there are beliefs and norms that govern how people think about their lives and what is right and wrong/good or bad then there may be a range of beliefs among individuals within a working group that account for variations in individual approaches to working with others. Religious groups offer many examples of this divergence of belief in practice. There can be many observances that are interpreted in different ways: by some adherents very strictly, but by others more leniently. These judgements are a function of interpretation and lead to ascribing meaning to events at work.

Most of the statements above are deliberately vague. As in the case of the first statement: what is it that the leader is seeking to achieve? Are we referring to setting standards for the group by personal example or something else?

For some of the statements a definition would need to be agreed before discussion could take place in any meaningful way. Many of the words are highly subjective and depend on the definition adopted by the reader. In the case of question 4: what sorts of decisions are being left to the group (whether they do assignments and exams, for example)? And in the case of question 6: sense of humour is very individual and what makes one person laugh may offend others.

All of this suggests that working groups (or any other groups) may have a variety of beliefs that they feel strongly about but which may or may not influence their work. Only when work directions contradict basic assumptions will resistance be evident and probably clearly expressed. As we shall see, this aspect of perceptions lying at the heart of basic assumptions may not be accessible to managers or agents of change until after a challenge to them (wittingly or unwittingly) has been made.

It is possible for individuals to survive in an environment hostile to their personal beliefs, in which they appear to espouse a corporate belief in order to survive or continue in membership there while retaining a personal belief at variance with the socially acceptable construct. However, as Legge remarks:

> Corporate culture – that shared by senior management and presented as the 'official' culture of the organization – may be only one of several subcultures within an organization, and may be actively resisted by groups who do not share or empathise with its values. If the corporate culture makes no sense of the organizational realities experienced by the employees other than senior management, it will not become internalised outside that small group.
>
> (Legge, 1995: 187)

This suggests that managers and change agents need to consider how changes in values and basic assumptions can be achieved through change programmes and whether it is possible to change strongly held basic assumptions. There are many examples of managers who have attempted radical changes in production procedures in the car industry, for example (Storey, 1992), but found that worker resistance made it difficult to achieve and it was impossible for the whole group. The attempt by John Egan, then managing director of Jaguar Motors, to introduce quality circles found that no more than 45 per cent of workers were willing to adapt to the new production regime. This brownfield (old established) site can be compared with the approach of Nissan in Sunderland where careful choice of competent and committed workers on a greenfield (newly opened) site made adaptation easy to achieve and brought about worldwide record-breaking production targets (Wickens, 1987).

BOX 5.1 CHANGING CULTURES – BEHAVIOURS AND ATTITUDES

- Accepted and appropriate patterns of behaviours are defined by values and basic underlying assumptions.
- Successful organizations tend to be those where the values and basic assumptions encourage practices and behaviours that match the organization's strategies.
- Where values and basic assumptions are incompatible with an organization's strategy, successful cultural change may be difficult to achieve.
- If an organization is contemplating change it first needs to establish whether the strategy necessitates a shift in values and basic underlying assumptions.
- Prior to any cultural change, senior management must understand the implications of the new culture for their own practices, artefacts and espoused values and be involved in all main change phases.

- Adequate resources need to be allocated to support cultural change and maintain it once it has been achieved.
- Culture change programmes must pay careful attention to the organization's power bases and opinion leaders such as trade unions and employees' associations.
- Cultural change programmes must pay careful attention to the organization's existing practices or artefacts such as recruitment, selection and retention, performance management and employee relations.
- In order to create a change in culture, organizations need to decide how practices or artefacts will be amended to support the newly espoused values and contradictory practices removed.
- Every opportunity should be taken to reinforce the practices and artefacts and restate the espoused values of the new culture's values and basic underlying assumptions.

(Developed from Beckhard and Prichard (1992)
and Hassard and Sharifi (1989))

Box 5.1 contains a list of general guidance for successful cultural change. It can usefully be explored more fully.

The first statement would seem to reinforce Schein's levels: if the values and basic assumptions are in accord with the behaviours required, then there should be no problem with success in achieving organizational objectives through people. The second statement reinforces the need for consistency between the three layers. The third statement raises the question of radical change in the organization's objectives and where that leaves the workforce whose values and basic assumptions may need radical change to achieve the company's new objectives. An example of this might be the requirement for aptitudes that were never required of staff before. An example may illustrate this.

BOX 5.2 COSMOS PHARMACEUTICALS

A well-known pharmaceutical company found itself subject to a takeover by a larger competitor who evaluated the worth of the business on each site and started to make some strategic closures. One such site designated to close worked extremely hard to put together a management buy-out – without success. Eventually, they were taken over by another pharmaceutical company. The new company introduced management metrics to monitor what researchers did throughout their working days. The PhD chemists previously dedicated to developing compounds were redirected to undertake contracted research work, which required negotiating work rates and dead-lines with prospective clients as well as managing the work and their teams.

Questions for discussion

- What would you think the responses were from dedicated PhD chemists to this change to their working role?
- How would managers best support such a change to working practices?
- How would you respond to management metrics as described in the case study?

(Developed from Beckhard and Pritchard (1992)
and Hassard and Sharifi (1989))

Discussion

Highly trained professional workers spend a considerable time becoming qualified and their dedication to developing a compound for the specialized pharmaceutical market requires a lifetime's dedicated work. The change to more reactive, client-responsive roles might find them struggling to acquire the required competencies.

You might also have listed the elements of the competencies. The chemists would be required to deal with clients in the sector in a more reactive and respon-sive mode: negotiational skills; listening and probing skills; closing skills; handling concerns and objections, are just some that you might have mentioned. It should be said that these competencies do require a measure of aptitude on which training can be built. Without such ability, the prospects for successful adaptation to the new business-driven role would be difficult to achieve. Managers can only offer training and support, but that of itself may not enable an individual to feel com-mitted and competent in such a radically different role.

The final question will depend on your own feelings about being followed closely by a monitoring regime. It would be taken for granted in some sectors such as sales, telesales and consultancy, but might be resented by those who regard themselves as professional knowledge workers.

Points 6 to 11 on the list become very relevant in the situation just described. Radical changes in work roles may find few current practitioners with the aptitude to undertake very different but critical knowledge and skill-led roles. The simi-larity here lies with the example given earlier of the brownfield site. As we shall see, there are other approaches that would suggest a completely new approach to recruiting the people needed from outside and finding alternative roles for those who may feel unable to adapt successfully.

Commitment levels and motivation

Corporate endeavours have always required managers to encourage their people to work together consistently and accurately. Those with a minimal view of why people work will often advance the belief that it is money – overlooking the fact that people seem to work very hard at hobbies, sports, interests and charities, for none of which are they normally paid. Apart from that there are well-paying jobs that individuals may decide that they would prefer not to do and that raises the question of commitment as well as competence. Competence answers the question 'can you do it?' Commitment raises the question: 'do you want to?'

In the days when workers chose a job and tended to stay in it until they retired, it made sense to ask questions about motivation and consider the popular theories that were used to underwrite it. Students of business studies are usually well schooled in the work of the theorists whose names are common currency, such as Mazlow, Herzberg, McClelland and Alderfer. However, the world of work has changed somewhat since the period when these writers developed their theories. We have only to consider the different work contracts that are available in organizations together with the shorter life of organizations to question how useful some of the theories of motivation still are.

One writer whose books have been remarkably prescient if not prophetic is Charles Handy. In his book *The Age of Unreason* (1989) he describes the Shamrock organization which can be illustrated as shown in Figure 5.2.

Here, Handy suggested that core jobs would be available to qualified workers between the ages of 27 and 45, after which they would have a choice between the professional/hi-tech sector of consultancy or the subcontract sector of routine, no-tech/lo-tech services. In a later work, *The Empty Raincoat* (1994), he suggested that the age of moving out of core work might in many sectors have reduced to 35. This kind of radical change suggests that for many workers the prospect of working for one organization could well look much less likely than would have appeared to their predecessors at work. That being the case, a more likely concept to consider would be commitment. This also coincides with the theory of HRM summarized in Guest's illustration in Table 5.1.

TABLE 5.1 Overview of links in human resource management theory

HRM policies	Human resource outcomes	Organizational outcomes
Organization objectives Management of change	Strategic integration	High problem solving/change
Recruitment/selection/ socialization	Commitment	Innovation and creativity
Appraisal/training/development	Flexibility/adaptability	High cost-effectiveness
Communication	Quality	Fewer staff complaints Low turnover/absence/grievance

Source: Adapted from Guest (1989) in Blyton and Turnbull (1992: 21).

FIGURE 5.2 Segments of the Shamrock organization.

Source: Adapted from Handy (1989).

If we look at the central column the four *human resource outcomes* can be seen and they include commitment; in the original generation of the philosophy of HRM commitment was often assumed to be *commitment to the organization* – hence in the right-hand column it can be seen that one of the organizational outcomes of a well-run organization is low staff turnover. The theory suggests that if the HRM policies are applied correctly, outcomes such as *organizational commitment* are reinforced.

However, commitment is a term that can be used in different contexts and as far as work experience is concerned it may be worthwhile considering the different types of commitment that are often referred to.

Job commitment

Porter *et al.* (1974) suggested that job commitment is often formed in the early months of settling into a new job role. We might believe, then, that should job fit/ suitability not be apparent within that period, the individual will either leave or not receive a permanent contract (Shore and Martin, 1989).

Work commitment

We might consider here the wider interest in a working environment than just the first job within the business. A new joiner in the hospitality sector may have job commitment in bar work, but be interested in a working environment that can lead to a management or tenancy position. 'While customer service is an important value, it is willing engagement with a highly scripted, efficiency-oriented work process that makes it happen, not a more empowering form of work design' (Boxall *et al.*, 2011).

Career commitment

At this level particularly those involved in vocational training or qualifications may experience career commitment. So, in the medical profession, a doctor or nurse may move around practices or hospitals but describe themselves by their specialism rather than the organization that they work for ('I am a doctor/nurse and I specialize in paediatrics'). They will move to whichever organization will advance their career (Meyer and Allen, 1997).

Organizational commitment

The final accolade for the successful organization: workers who would never contemplate leaving to work elsewhere because they consider that the prospects they have could never be equalled, still less bettered, by rivals in the sector. There are famous retailers whose workers would not willingly consider moving off to competitors. Their commitment is secured through the benefits that they perceive in remaining and developing their career within the organization, sometimes reinforced by profit-related pay (Meyer and Allen, 1991).

However, these commitment levels need to be placed in the context of organizations as they appear today, both the fragmentation within organizations that the Shamrock organization suggests, and the uncertain duration of ownership and management that is apparent in many sectors worldwide.

For those working in the *subcontract* sector both job and work commitment depends on the contractor. Fear of non-renewal of the contract at the end of the year may make career and organizational commitment in the organization worked for much less likely. So, such workers may well experience job commitment, but the focus of their organizational commitment may be their immediate employer, the subcontractor, rather than the company whose customers they are dealing with.

BOX 5.3 DISCUSSION

Many airlines have been busy outsourcing jobs which once would have been core to the organization. Baggage handling; checkout desk staff; food preparation specialists – all now are likely to belong in Handy's subcontract world. Each year their employer, the service provider, will be expected to resubmit a tender for another year's contract with the airline.

Questions:

- Who is responsible for recruiting and training these workers?
- Who is responsible for supervising and appraising them?
- Who do they feel committed to – the subcontractor; the airline; or the airline's customers?

If we look at the *consultancy* sector a similar situation is likely:

> The best that we might expect is that while the consultant is working for a client their commitment must be total. The second question raises concerns when the consultant works for more than one company in the same sector. Experience of several clients in a sector confirms competence and extensive expertise. But it can also give rise to concern that confidential information may be unwittingly passed on to competitors.

BOX 5.4 DISCUSSION

Working as a self-employed management consultant will mean balancing a portfolio of work divided between different clients. Indeed, to work more than 75 per cent of your time for one client would put your status as self-employed at risk.

One such consultant worked for a government organization, a retailer in the DIY sector, and a public utility in the process of privatization. You might like to consider the following questions:

Questions:

- To which of the clients will the consultant feel most committed?
- Could there be a conflict of interest in working for several clients?
- In speaking to client's customers should the consultant explain his status or allow the customer to believe that he/she is part of the core staff?

The third question may be the most difficult dilemma and requires careful handling at all times. We have only to consider how we feel when speaking to call centres to know that trust in the organization is not improved by constant changes in people answering questions or trying to solve problems on the phone. *Trust* is generated through a designated contact. Whether the consultant can offer that point of contact is debatable if he/she is on an interim contract.

Managing the Shamrock organization may require acceptance that individual workers have different levels of commitment and that *organizational commitment* may be fleeting due to the temporary nature of a working contract. Consistent approaches to customers will need careful consideration and constant monitoring.

Shamrock – fragmentation and flexibility

Before we move on to consider the implications of Shamrock's fragmentation of the core workforce, we can consider one of the four other HR outcomes described by Guest (1989): *flexibility*. As with commitment, flexibility can be considered under four headings and we can consider them now.

Time flexibility: there are industries that have always used time flexibility as a core part of their business strategy. We can consider transport, for example, where commuter flows concentrate in the early hours of the morning into work and then again in the early evening as commuters return home. Keeping staff on duty all day means that for much of the day their work will be reduced or they will be idle. One technique for dealing with this is the system of split shifts, where drivers book off after the morning rush hour and have time off before booking back on ready for the evening rush hour.

Number flexibility: allied with time periods served is the number of staff available at any one time. In retail the number of part-time can outnumber the full-time staff. The secret of managing part timers is to ensure that they are there when customer flows are likely to increase. Both duty managers and checkout supervisors are acutely aware of the numbers in queues at checkouts. In the case of one well-known multiple chemists the rule has been that where there are more than five customers in a queue, another checkout should be opened immediately by the duty manager.

Cost flexibility: both time and number, obviously, have implications for managing costs. In earlier times dock workers were hired on a casual basis according to need so that no more were paid for than the work available warranted. Companies that are good at estimating time and number accurately according to customer flows and are good at securing the best margins from their suppliers usually exhibit the best performance in terms of the company's net profitability.

Functional flexibility: lastly, the ability to use staff in several roles and functions has been the hallmark of breaking through the inflexibility exhibited when single union agreements precluded others from undertaking union members' work functions. As we shall see, the automobile industry revitalized itself on the basis of functional flexibility as at the heart of its organization lay quality circles and job rotation. We will examine the philosophy that lay behind this movement in the present chapter.

To illustrate the points that we have made so far about commitment and flexibility we will look at two popular movements that were enthusiastically adopted in different sectors and examine how effective they were.

Quality initiatives

Before the advent of TQM in car factories, certain car makes had a habit of breaking down even when new. They were popularly referred to as 'Monday' or

'Friday' cars because these were the days when in some places workers were liable not to turn up for work. Managers then had the problem of finding a stand-in for someone with a particular skill or expertise and sometimes had to make do with someone who lacked the full skill or knowledge to do the job effectively – hence the premature breakdowns. Supervisors were expected to identify faulty units, but could only do this on an occasional basis. Oakland describes that situation:

> The cause of the decline is that management has walked off the job of man-agement, striving instead for dividends and good performance of the price of the company's stock. A better way to serve stockholders would be to stay in business with constant improvement of quality of product and of service, thus to decrease costs, capture markets, provide jobs and increase dividends.
>
> (Oakland, 1989: x)

The answer lay in setting up quality circles whose members shared the knowledge and skills needed to manufacture a car. The function of the team leader was not to direct and supervise, but to ensure that all members were trained to enable *job rotation* within the team. They would be jointly responsible for the quality of what went out (so no need for a white-coated quality inspector) and each vehicle was numbered so that any faults would be traced back immediately to the team that had produced it.

At the heart of TQM lay a philosophy that included a market-led approach. Wilson (1992: 94) expresses the links between the stages of the TQM process as shown in Figure 5.3.

Defining customer need

At first glance it might seem that this is the most obvious element of Wilson's model. But the quest needs to start by asking which market is being targeted. When Toyota first launched the Lexus car they had asked customers what the perfect car would contain and then built to that specification. Unfortunately, the resulting car appealed to older buyers who were used to Oldsmobiles but not the Mercedes and BMW owners whose business they were aiming to attract. Later on, they remod-elled around 4WD models and achieved the success they were looking for.

Improve organizational quality towards meeting those needs

The obviousness of the second step might well be taken for granted in manufac-turing and service industries today. But the question of how much this will cost also needs to be taken into account. There is always a cost to be incurred for new equipment and investment in training to achieve the required quality standards. The secret will be to ensure that the expected gain in sales will outweigh the inter-ference costs that arise from seeking higher standards of production.

FIGURE 5.3 Steps in the Total Quality Management cycle.

Source: Adapted from Wilson (1992: 94).

Reduce costs

There may be an assumption here that the more rigorous organization of the manufacturing process and training of team members to adhere to the standards of production will eliminate the wastage and error rates previously pertaining to production processes. If so, it should be noted that there will be a limit to how far economies can be made on such historical losses. In other words once the company is operating at 100 per cent efficiency, there are no more savings to be made.

Productivity improves as quality increases

We can follow the logic of this assertion with the points we have made earlier: the improvement here will achieve a level of improvement to the point where the quality standard is achieved. If, say, ISO 9000 has now been achieved in both process and output, then that is where our cost base now consolidates. The initial take-up of the process of improvement may indeed offer improved savings while it is still in the process of being implemented. Once achieved, however, unless further improvements over and above the standard aimed for can be made, further productivity improvement will be limited.

Gain increased market share

At this point the assumption made should be correct provided that the improvements made to product and service now coincide with what the customer wanted. However, this takes no account of the fact that while the improvement process was being put in place the customer's requirements could have changed. It may also be that another supplier could have achieved or surpassed the standards and got to the market sooner. In this case the expected yields in terms of sales may be less than anticipated.

Growth of the business

How business grows may be a function of internal factors such as extra production capacity or external factors such as increased market share. Both could indeed be the outcome for a successful supplier of product or service. However, neither of those outcomes is guaranteed. A market may become saturated – in which case there is no more growth, however good the product may now be. On the other hand, there may well be demand but the capacity is not within the company's capacity to deliver it.

BOX 5.5 QUESTION

Spend some time looking at the links between the stages in the TQM cycle. See whether you can discover the flaws that might underlie the assumptions being made here.

Discussion

Define customer need

This brings us back to our first point. But it again begs the question: how exactly is this need assessed. Achievement of an industry standard can become an end in itself and the effort to rethink and start the cycle all over again may be more than the managers want to embark on.

There are those who claim that the system's benefits outweigh its disadvantages:

> Quality and productivity improvement through standardization and statistical process control is a modern success story. Economically feasible methods for controlling the uniformity of output enabled the use of interchangeable parts, which, in turn, made possible industrial mass production, economies of scale and improvements in wealth and welfare (Womack *et al.*, 1990).
>
> (Lillrank, 2003: 215)

It would be fair to say that the initiative that Deming and his colleagues put in place commanded considerable attention during the 1980s both in the USA and throughout the industrialized world. However, there are some other concerns that have arisen during the experience of the many companies who have embarked on TQM and we can consider them briefly as follows.

Intangible benefits

The focus of some efforts to achieve a stated standard such as BS 5750 or ISO 9000 can become an end in itself rather than a means to the end of quality achievement. The focus of steps and stages of inspection and outside intervention can distract attention from the transformational process, which proponents suggest is the main benefit of undertaking TQM.

Sectional interests

TQM can find a disparity between managers who are very committed and those who are not. Some writers suggest that this increases the chance of fragmentation and localizes commitment to the overall strategy (Cyert and Marsh, 1963/1992).

The customer comes first and is also judge

Sometimes the effort to achieve internal standards can conflict so that the need to satisfy current customers is perceived as a distraction. Response times become slower and problem solving can be resented by those who are tasked with implementing change.

The sponge phenomenon

Managers may find that resources and time are required to effect the required changes. The training needed takes longer to bed down; courses need to be extended; extra tuition is needed in areas that had not been foreseen and so on. The programme is a consumer of financial resources and the time taken to deal with problems. Both can easily become a significant interference cost.

Re-creating the rigid organization

Achieving the industry standard and acquiring the plaque or award becomes an end in itself and once achieved leaves individuals feeling that nothing more need be done. Changing customer needs now takes a back seat as we have satisfied the need to validate the standard and no further change is needed.

The distinction between means and ends becomes blurred

During the programme the end result can be lost sight of by participants, as the elements needed to achieve the end (achievement of the standard) are focused on as an end in themselves. Achievement of the standard becomes an end in itself rather than a means to the end of offering better quality than the competition.

TQM can make things worse

Diverting attention from an inherent problem not necessarily directly connected with the quest for an industry standard award could be just enough to distract the company away from developing to answer a further market need.

Lack of evidence

It is always difficult to support causal connections between validation and evaluation. The fact that training has been conducted to a standard does not ensure that success in satisfying the customer is guaranteed (Wilson, 1992: 101 ff.).

All of these possibilities need to be considered before organizations embark on root and branch changes, however well intentioned. Managers and consultants owe it to themselves and their clients to raise these issues before a commitment is made to radical and far-reaching change. In the words of researchers who published an article entitled 'Mixed results, lousy process: The management experience of organizational change':

> The argument advanced here suggests that an adequate theory of organizational change should take into account not only organizational process and context, but also the lived experience of those involved in processing change initiatives and the pressures, tensions, contradictions and constraints under which they function.
>
> (Doyle *et al.*, 2000: S72)

Business process re-engineering

What we have looked at so far is based on what is sometimes described as a resource-based strategy (inside-out). Managers work with the people they have and seek to develop their knowledge and improve their skills through training, in such a way they will be able to achieve consistent quality results to a predefined industry standard. But, as we have seen, on some brownfield sites, managers have found it difficult to gain commitment from all those in a long-standing, pre-existing workforce. This presents managers with a problem: what do we do with those who are unwilling or unable to adopt or adapt to new practices?

A more radical approach was signalled during a commercial air traffic controllers' strike that threatened to paralyse the USA in 1980. The new president sacked the strikers and put military air traffic controllers in their place. This signalled a different approach to resistance among an existing brownfield workforce.

> So dealing with failing companies is straightforward in the minds of BPR's proponents:
> Here's our definition of a laggard: A laggard is a company where senior management has failed to write off its depreciating intellectual capital fast enough and has underinvested in creating new intellectual capital. A laggard

is a company where senior managers believe they know more about how an industry works than they actually do and where what they know is out of date.

(Hamel and Prahaled, 1994: 55)

So, managers can try to inspire their workforce with a new and different vision of what needs to be done in the brave new world of successfully satisfying burgeoning customer need. They can do all the things that managers do who are attempting to implement TQM. However, they may find that there are some who do not respond to the new regime as laid out – as we saw in the case of Jaguar Motors. So what to do, then? A proponent of business process re-engineering (BPR) explains:

Don't live too long with people who refuse to change their behaviour, especially if their work is important to achieving your re-engineering goals. Your tolerance of old behaviours signals that you are not serious about the change.

The above applies to all people, managers as well as workers. This is a new democracy.

Don't expect people to change how they behave unless you change what they do; that is, their work must be designed to allow them to act differently.

Don't expect cultural change to happen immediately. Although you may achieve some early results, a complete cultural change is measured in years (hopefully just a few) rather than in months.

Don't articulate a new or updated set of values and then delay re-engineering your management processes to support them.

(Champy, 1995: 109)

So, now we can see the clear strategy of disposing of those who do not achieve the required new standards. The problem now becomes what happens to those who are left behind? There is evidence to suggest that those left behind may well be aggrieved that friends and colleagues have been dispensed with in such an arbitrary way (Hallier and Lyon, 1996). There are also those who warn that 70 per cent of BPR initiatives have failed to achieve their declared objectives: 'Business process re-engineering is revealed as essentially political in rhetorical and practical manifestations. Its claims for newness are exaggerated and its application generally less startling in its outcomes than its promotional literature predicts' (Willcocks and Grint, 1997: 105).

We have so far mentioned radical changes affecting a company's workforce and the likelihood of resistance and unease among those affected, including those who stay. But there are also situations where smaller changes of behaviour can be required by managers and even monitored by surveillance systems. Recording company phone calls with customers is a routine practice in call centres and we, as customers, are made aware of it before we start speaking to the operator responding to us. In the retail sector there are also examples of checkout operators being required to smile at customers and being checked on camera (Ogbonna and Harris,

1998). One research subject said that she had not thought that she was required to be an actor when she joined the retail sector. In the USA such edicts from management were, in one case, met with refusal from the mostly female staff who 'claimed that it increased their exposure to sexual harassment from customers' (Zeidler, 1998 in Fineman, 2000: 3).

Hofstede and national cultural stereotypes

Increasingly, global businesses and freedom for money and people to cross borders will bring a mix of national cultures into the workforce. There has been much comment on national cultural differences and how they manifest themselves. None is better known by students than Hofstede. His primary research was conducted among research subjects working for IBM, an American multinational company (MNC) with offices throughout the world. Hofstede thought he had identified what he described as five key dimensions:

- power distance
- individualism/collectivism
- masculinity/femininity
- uncertainty avoidance
- Confucian dynamism.

Without going too deeply into each dimension in turn, we can say that the dimensions were intended to allow the researcher to assess whereabouts national groups score similar to the way in which constructs were measured and compared in individuals (Kelly, 1955). The way in which national subjects behave may well be both identifiable and distinct, thereby allowing the observer to place subjects within such categories and then draw conclusions about national profiles. However, it should be said that such behaviours can also be learned. Gender typing alone should alert the researcher to the difficulty of identifying particular basic assumptions held by men compared with women. Perceptions can change over time so that expectancies that might have applied some years ago (gentlemen always give up their seat to a lady on public transport) now no longer apply in the same way today. Such subtle changes make it hard to apply the masculine/feminine dimension with any hope that it will consistently identify a national type that can distinguish between, say, Scandinavians and Asians.

Behaviours, however similar, may be indicative of basic assumptions, but they are not necessarily predictive. The danger with linking action to belief and ascribing it to national culture makes it difficult to distinguish between what is open to management to influence and what may always elude the influence of both researcher and manager. There have been significant attempts to highlight exactly why such research is flawed and its findings questionable. Foremost among them is McSweeney who summarizes his article as follows:

The failure of Hofstede's stories – once unpacked – to show a causal link between his dimensions of a particular national culture and a specific national action is not surprising, given the earlier critique of his construction of his national cultural cameos. But, in the event, how credible is the notion of systematically causal national cultures? The critique above of Hofstede's identification methodology did not rely on a counter supposition that such causal national cultures did not exist. The analysis was agnostic on that issue. Here, however, I want to raise some doubts about the notion of national cultural social causality and so to suggest that the failure of Hofstede's model goes beyond the technical. Hence, the implication is not to devise improved identification of national cultures, but to abandon the notion of a mono-causal link between national cultures and actions within nations.

(McSweeney, 2002: 109)

This is not to deny the relevance of difference between cultures, nor to suggest that such differences are irrelevant. It does mean that managers need to be aware not just of differences in behaviours (which, as we said, can be learned), but also of the underlying values and basic assumptions that underwrite the behaviours and are more difficult both to surface and to change. Fineman mentions examples of what he calls the pervasive requirements of transnational organizations, such as:

McDonald's insistence that staff in its Moscow branch should serve Big Macs with a smile, despite the wider cultural predilection to greet customers with a scowl. Or the smiling training for Inuit employees ... the Inuit have no tradition of smiling or greeting others with a 'hi' or 'hello'.

(Jones, 1999 in Fineman, 2000: 3)

Taking all these points into account of the difficulties faced by change agents, consultants and managers seeking to bring about change, there follows an account of change which begs some questions that you can now consider and discuss.

References

Beckhard, R. and Pritchard, W. (1992) *Changing the Essence: The art of creating and leading fundamental change in organizations.* New York: Jossey Bass.

Blyton, P. and Turnbull, P. (1992) *Reassessing Human Resource Management.* London: Sage.

Boxall, P., Ang, S.H. and Bartram, T. (2011) Analysing the 'black box' of HRM: Uncovering HR goals, mediators and outcomes in a standardized service environment. *Journal of Management Studies*, 48(7): 1504–1532.

Champy, J. (1995) *Reengineering Management: The mandate for new leadership.* London: Harper Collins.

Cyert, R.M. and March, J.G. (1963/1992) *A Behavioral Theory of the Firm.* Blackwell: Oxford.

Deal, T.E. and Kennedy, A. (1982) *Corporate Cultures.* Reading, MA: Addison Wesley.

Doyle, M., Claydon, T. and Buchanan, D. (2000) Mixed results, lousy process: The management experience of organizational change. *British Journal of Management*, 11, Special Issue: S59–S80.

Fineman, S. (2000) *Emotions in Organizations*. London: Sage.

Guest, D.E. (1989) Personnel and HRM: Can you tell the difference. *Personnel Management*, 21(1): 48–51.

Hallier, J. and Lyon, P. (1996) Job insecurity and employee commitment: Managers' reactions to the threat and outcomes of redundancy selection. *British Journal of Management*, 7(1): 107–124.

Hamel, G. and Prahaled, C.K. (1994) *Competing for the Future*. Boston, MA: Harvard Business School Press.

Handy, C. (1989) *The Age of Unreason*. London: Business Books Limited.

Hassard, J. and Sharifi, S. (1989) Corporate culture and strategic change. *Journal of General Management*, 15(2): 4–19.

Jones, L. (1999) Smiling lessons end service with a scowl in Greenland. *Guardian*, 23 October: 21.

Kelly, G.A. (1955) *The Psychology of Personal Constructs*. New York: Norton. Reprinted by Routledge (London), 1991.

Legge, K. (1995) *Human Resource Management: Rhetoric and realities*. Basingstoke: Palgrave MacMillan.

Lillrank, P. (2003) The quality of standard, routine and nonroutine processes. *Organization Studies*, 24(2): 215–233.

McSweeney, B. (2002) Hofstede's model of national cultural differences and their consequences: A triumph of faith – a failure of analysis. *Human Relations*, 55(1): 89–118.

Meyer, J. and Allen, N. (1991) A three-component conceptualization of organizational commitment. *Human Resource Management Review*, 1(1): 61–89.

Meyer, J. and Allen, N. (1997) *Commitment in the Workplace: Theory, research and application*. Thousand Oaks, CA: Sage publications.

Oakland, J. (1989) *Total Quality Management*. Oxford: Butterworth Heinemann.

Ogbonna, E. and Harris, L.C. (1998) Managing Organizational Culture: Compliance or Genuine Change? *British Journal of Management*, 9: 273–88: 221–226.

Porter, R., Steers, R.M., Mowday, R.T. and Boulian, P.V. (1974) Organizational commitment, job satisfaction, and turnover among psychiatric technicians. *Journal of Applied Psychology*, 59: 603–609.

Schein, E.H. (1985) *Organizational Culture & Leadership*. San Francisco, CA: Jossey Bass.

Shore, L.M. and Martin, H.J. (1989) Job satisfaction and organizational commitment in relation to work performance and turnover intentions. *Human Relations*, 42(4): 625–638.

Storey, J. (1992) *Developments in the Management of Human Resources*. Oxford: Blackwell.

Wickens, P. (1987) *The Road to Nissan: Flexibility, quality, teamwork*. London: Macmillan.

Willcocks, L. and Grint, K. (1997) Re-inventing the organization? Towards a critique of business process engineering, in I. McLoughlin and M. Harris (eds) *Innovation, Organizational Change and Technology*. London: International Thomson Press, pp. 87–110.

Wilson, D.C. (1992) *A Strategy of Change*. London: International Thomson Business Press.

Womack, J.P., Jones, D.T. and Roos, D. (1990) *The Machine that Changed the World*. New York: Free Press.

Zeidler, S. (1998) Don't have a nice day – workers protest smile rule. Los Angeles: Reuters, 16 November.

Further reading

Alvesson, M. (2002) *Understanding Organizational Culture*. London: Sage.

Anthony, P. (1994) *Managing Organizational Culture*. Buckingham: Open University Press.

Bate, P. (2000) Changing the culture of a hospital from hierarchy to networked community, *Public Administration*, 78(3): 485–512.

Beer, M., Spector, B., Lawrence, P.R. and Mills, D.Q. (1984) *Managing Human Assets*. New York: Free Press.

Beer, M., Einstat, R.A. and Spector, B. (1990) Why change programmes don't produce change. *Harvard Business Review*, November/December: 158–166.

Collins, D. (1998) *Organizational Change, Sociological Perspectives*. London: Routledge.

Cottee, P. (2006) Change of heart. *People Management*. London: CIPD.

Dawson, P. and Andriopoulos, C. (forthcoming) *Managing Change: Creativity and innovation* (2nd edn). London: Sage.

Formbrun, C.J., Tichy, N.M. and Devanna, M.A. (1984) *Strategic Human Resource Management*. New York: Wiley.

Frost, P.J., Moore, L.F., Louis, M.R. and Lundberg, C.C. (1983) *Organizational Culture*. Beverley Hills, CA: Sage.

Genus, A. (1995) Re-engineering business processes in practice, in I. McLoughlin and M. Harris (eds) *Innovation, Organizational Change & Technology*. London: International Thomson Business.

Giorgiades, N. (1990) A strategic future for personnel? *Personnel Management*, 22(2): 43.

Goffman, E. (1959) *The Presentation of Self in Everyday Life*. New York: Doubleday.

Greenhaulgh, L. and Rosenblatt, Z. (1984) Job insecurity: Towards conceptual clarity. *Academy of Management Review*, 9: 439–447.

Gregory, K. (1983) Native view paradigms: Multiple cultures and culture conflicts in organizations, *Administrative Science Quarterly*, 28(3): 359–376.

Grint, K. and Case, P. (1998) The violent rhetoric of re-engineering: Management consultancy on the offensive. *Journal of Management Studies*, 35(5): 557–577.

Hallier, J. and Lyon, P. (1995) Middle managers and the employee psychological contract: Agency, protection and advancement. *British Journal of Management*, 7: 107–123.

Hammer, M. and Champy, J. (1995) *Re-engineering the Corporation*. London: Nicholas Brealey Publishing.

Hampden-Turner, C. (1990) *Corporate Culture for Competitive Edge*. London: Hutchinson.

Handy, C. (1993) *Understanding Organizations*, 4th edn. London: Penguin.

Handy, C. (1994) *The Empty Raincoat: New thinking for a new world*. London: Hutchinson.

Hofstede, G. (1980) *Cultures Consequences*. Beverley Hills, CA: Sage.

Hofstede, G (1991) *Cultures and Organization*. Maidenhead: McGraw Hill.

Isabella, L.A. (1990) Evolving interpretations as a change unfolds: How managers construe organizational events. *Academy of Management Journal*, 33(1): 7–41.

Knights, D. and McCabe, D. (1998) Dreams & designs on strategy: A critical analysis of TQM and management control. *Work, Employment & Society*, 12(3): 433–456.

Knights, D. and Willmott, H.C. (1987) Organizational culture as management strategy: A critique and illustration from the financial service industries. *International Studies of Management and Organization*, 17(3): 40–63.

Legge, K. (1989) HRM a critical analysis, in J. Storey (ed.) *New Perspectives in HRM*. London: Routledge.

Lewin, K. (1947) Frontiers in group dynamics. *Human Relations*, 1: 5–41.

Louis, M.R. (1980a) Surprise and sense making: What new comers experience in entering unfamiliar organizational settings. *Administrative Science Quarterly*, 25: 226–251.

Louis, M.R. (1980b) Career transitions: Varieties and commonalities. *Academy of Management Review*, 5: 329–340.

McCabe, D. (1998) Making sense of quality: Towards a review and critique of quality initiatives in financial services. *Human Relations*, 51(3): 53–73.

McKinlay, A. (2002) The limits of knowledge management. *New Technology, Work and Employment*, 17(2): 76–88.

Martin, J. (1992) *The Culture of Organizations: Three perspectives*. New York: Oxford University Press.

Martin, J. and Frost, P. (1996) The organizational culture wars: A struggle for intellectual dominance, in S. Clegg, C. Hardy and W. Nord (eds) *Handbook of Organizational Studies*. London: Sage.

Martin, J. and Meyerson, D. (1988) Organisational cultures and the denial, channelling and acknowledgement of ambiguity, in L.R. Pondy, R.J. Boland Jr. and H. Thomas (eds) *Managing Ambiguity and Change*. New York: Wiley.

Meek, V.L. (1988) Organizational culture: Origins and weaknesses. *Organizational Studies*, 9(4): 453–473.

Meyerson, D. and Martin, J. (1987) Cultural change: An integration of three different views, *Journal of Management Studies*, 24: 623–648.

Noon, M. (1992) HRM: A map, model or theory, in P. Blyton and P. Turnbull (eds) *Reassessing HRM*. London: Sage.

Ogbonna, E. and Wilkinson, B. (1990) Corporate strategy and corporate culture: The view from the checkout. *Personnel Review*, 19(4): 9–15.

Pascale, R. (1990) *Managing on the Edge*. London: Viking.

Pettigrew, A.M. (1979) On studying organizational cultures. *Administrative Science Quarterly*, 24(4): 570–581.

Pettigrew, A.M. (1992) *Shaping Strategic Change*. London: Sage.

Pondy, L.R., Frost, P.J., Morgan, G. and Dandridge, T.C. (1983) *Organizational Symbolism*. Greenwich, CT: JAI.

Revans, R. (1980) *Action Learning: New techniques for management*. London: Blond and Briggs.

Rousseau, D.M. (1998) The problem of psychological contract. *Journal of Organizational Behaviour*, 19: 665–671.

Schein, E.H. (1990) Organisational culture. *American Psychologist*, 45(2): 109–119.

Smircich, L. (1983) Concepts of culture and organizational analysis. *Administrative Science Quarterly*, 28(3): 339–358.

Storey, J. (1995) *Human Resource Management: A critical text*. London: Routledge.

Turner, B.A. (1990) *Organizational Symbolism*. Berlin and New York: de Gruyter.

Van Maanen, J. (1978) People processing: Strategies. *Organizational Dynamics*, 7: 18–36.

Weick, K.E. (1998) Improvisation as a mindset for organizational analysis. *Organization Science*, 9(5): 543–555.

Whipp, R., Rosenfeld, R. and Pettigrew, A. (1989) Culture and competitiveness: Evidence from two mature UK industries. *Journal of Management Studies*, 26(6): 561–585.

Wiener, Y. (1988) Forms of value systems: A focus on organisational effectiveness and cultural change and maintenance. *Academy of Management Review*, 13: 534–585.

Wilkins, A.L. and Ouchi, W.G. (1983) Efficient cultures: Exploring the relationship between culture and organizational performance. *Administrative Science Quarterly*, 28: 468–481.

Wilkins, A.L. and Patterson, K.J. (1985) You can't get there from here: What will make culture change projects fail, in R.H. Kilmann, M.J. Saxton and R. Serpa. (eds) *Gaining Control of Corporate Culture*. San Francisco, CA: Jossey Bass, pp. 262–291.

Willmott, H.C. (1995) The odd couple? Reengineering business processes and managing human relation. *New Technology, Work & Employment*, 10(2): 89–98.

GRADUATE ATTRIBUTES

At the end of this exercise you will have addressed the following graduate attributes:

- a capacity for problem identification, the collection of evidence, synthesis and dispassionate analysis;
- a capacity for attentive exchange, informed argument and reasoning;
- an ability to communicate effectively for different purposes and in different contexts.

Case study: change can be the hardest word

Please read the following piece. At different points in the narrative you will be asked to stop and answer questions. Please make notes so that you can contribute to a discussion.

> *Part A*
>
> 'Our aim in this change was not to produce incremental change. Rather it was our intention to alter the way the business functioned from the ground to the penthouse. That's why we refer to it as Project Scratch. We are starting from nothing,' said Tom Burbank, corporate services director at the Aberdeen-based Teller Oil Company. The organization's plan involved bringing four regional offices to one central building, restructuring the way oil pipeline services were provided to customers and procuring new information and communication technology (ICT).
>
> 'In essence we have completely dismantled the business into its component parts and we are rebuilding them in a different way. Think of LEGO bricks, that's what is going on. We are taking it apart to build something new, a new organization. We saw that we need to streamline the business, reduce over-heads and transfer cost-savings into service delivery.'

Questions:

- **What sort of change is being contemplated here?**
- **When you hear this sort of comment from a manager, what might be your fears as a member of staff?**
- **When you hear this sort of comment from a company, what might be your fears as a customer?**
- **Why are people inside and outside organizations suspicious of radical change?**

> *Part B*
>
> The restructuring of Teller Oil will make it one of the country's largest oil support businesses, managing more than 24,000 oil drilling locations. It

provides support for companies all around the world operating in many specialized environments. The need to make the business more efficient was not the only reason behind the change programme. Another factor lurking in the background was the desire finally to escape from the scandal of 2007 that had seen two employees jailed for property fraud, resulting in massive damage to Teller's reputation.

Questions:

• **What are the important needs that oil companies operating in specialized and hazardous environments might have?**
• **How might these customers become aware of improved efficiency?**
• **How might the change envisaged obviate fraud?**

Part C
The first stage of Project Scratch was to bring the local offices together and create a new customer services team. Four offices meant four receptionists, four switchboards and unnecessary overheads. As well as this we did a customer survey which revealed that 80 per cent of them preferred online or telephone contact with us to visiting our offices.

Questions:

• **What is the biggest overhead in the oil support industry?**
• **If you were one of the four receptionists or office staff what concerns might you have?**
• **Where have many companies located their telephone customer service teams?**
• **How would you satisfy workers that radical change will not mean loss of jobs?**

Part D
During the second stage of Project Scratch, Burbank and his team carried out a complete business audit. We discarded all of the preconceptions we held about the business. We classified every individual business function to produce a current state and then moved elements around to get to our desired future state. The next task was to transfer 445 people from the old structure to the new one. The acronym for this crucial stage was AMAN:

• as you are
• move to a different team or location
• absorb a new role
• new post.

Questions:

- As HR managers, what would be your main concerns about this change plan?
- Can an organization require a member of staff to take a new post/move office?
- What is the technical legal term for change that makes it difficult or impossible for an individual to continue working?
- How can HR overcome concerns and objections about such job changes?

Part E

Around 130 professional services staff in head office, such as accountants, stayed in their existing roles, leaving 315 staff to be reassigned. The exercise also identified 58 roles that were no longer needed, although an immediate recruitment freeze and termination of temporary contracts helped minimize permanent staff losses. The organization did not offer voluntary redundancy as it wanted to retain key skills.

The HR manager, Keera Hall said, 'It was very difficult to construct a process that would move staff into new roles. We needed to move the right staff across. We knew there would be a synergy between the old and new roles, but we needed a new mix of them.'

Questions:

- If you were the HR manager, how would you go about doing this?
- How much consultation and negotiation would be involved?
- Where would you start?
- What safeguards would you put in place?

Part F

Hall and her staff examined the current job descriptions. 'We required that there was at least a 60% match between the old role and the new one, as we could have faced constructive dismissal cases if we had moved people to roles they were not capable of doing. We identified 15–25 competencies and each absorb a new role candidate had a one-to-one meeting with the OD staff. We explained the assessment process and outlined the particular roles we recommended they go through A & D for. Staff were invited to apply for up to three roles. A Safety Officer could move into the customer care centre – dealing with client enquiries; business support, working on income collection or become a relationship officer supporting clients.'

Questions:

- **If you were a safety officer how would you feel about the three choices?**
- **How closely would they need to coincide with your previous experience?**
- **What might be your concerns about undertaking one of the new roles?**
- **What would be your ultimate fear about such a transfer of roles?**

Part G

Assessments included two or three exercises and lasted half a day. Exercises varied from mathematical aptitude testing to leadership and communication skills. One such exercise was a simulation of a small medical clinic, where the candidate had to deal with various crises thrown at them. The exercises gave the staff the opportunity to demonstrate skills they might not have been displaying in their current roles.

Questions:

- **What are the dangers of doing such assessment tests?**
- **Which are the valid and reliable aptitude tests for human subjects?**
- **Who are the assessors of the test results to be?**
- **What sort of feedback should candidates be given?**

Part H

William Konner, a former safety officer, who is now a customer care coordinator, recalls his initial shock at 'having to apply for my own job'. He decided to embrace it positively and now on the other side of the new role can see the sense of the AMAN process. 'My role has changed significantly for the better,' he says.

Helen Jefferies did not find the road so smooth. Believing she had failed at the assessment centre she applied for another job elsewhere. In fact she had passed with flying colours but the feedback came too late for her. 'Fortunately, six months on I've returned to allocations, doing a job I love,' she says.

Questions:

- **How could this mix up have been avoided for Helen?**
- **What were the risks for William?**
- **How could HR have handled this differently?**
- **What is the main learning point about how people settle successfully into a new job role?**

Part I
Organizational results are as follows:

- overheads have been reduced by £1.6 million;
- a survey of clients indicates satisfaction levels are the same as before the changes;
- staff turnover has reduced by 2 per cent;
- internal processes identified the weak spots where fraud had occurred;
- 65 jobs were lost;
- 315 jobs were reassigned.

Will this be the end of change for a while? 'It's not in the nature of our organization. We are about evolution.'

Questions:

- **Did they achieve their original objectives?**
- **Where for them is the link between efficiency and effectiveness established?**
- **What will they have had to do for the 65 who left?**
- **What lessons could there be for companies embarking on similar radical change?**

Summary

Change programmes often encounter misunderstanding and misconception by those whom it is meant to benefit. Bringing people into the change event from its inception is more time-consuming and therefore more costly. However, top-down change may miss out on the important step of *exploration*. Understanding the background of change and the expectations of those involved in it may avoid some of the undesirable outcomes that too often accompany change programmes.

Key people leaving the organization because they are uncomfortable with change is not only an interference cost to the organization but also leaves those who are left behind feeling less secure and uncommitted to the organization. HRM theory made great play of organizational commitment. Sadly it can too often be put at risk by unacceptable or poorly prepared change programmes.

Tutor Guidance

Case – change can be the hardest word

Part A questions:

What sort of change is being contemplated here?
The initial sentence gives a clue to the company's approach to this change: Project Scratch, starting from scratch. The change could be described as radical. However,

the corporate services manager does indicate that the intention was to change the way the business functioned from top to bottom.

It is possible to argue that the focus here is on efficiency (time; quality; quantity; cost). The supporting evidence for this point lies in the second paragraph (ICT driven). Also in the third paragraph reference is made to streamlining the business, reducing overheads and transferring cost savings into service delivery.

When you hear this sort of comment from a manager, what might your fears be as a member of staff?

An obvious answer here, as with most change proposals, is the question 'will I still have a job?' Again, as Drucker points out, 75 per cent of a service industry's overheads lie in the staff costs. So, when streamlining and cost reductions are mentioned in the same sentence, it might suggest that there will be less people around after the streamlining has taken place.

When you hear this sort of comment from a company, what might be your fears as a customer?

Most of us have been held in a queue on the phone waiting to be answered, while listening to music and the occasional announcement saying that we are now in a queue and will be answered by the next available operator. ICT is excellent in theory but often less easy for customers to use in practice. There are some customers with personal problems who prefer to come in and talk to someone they know – and a local office is ideal for that purpose.

Why are people inside and outside organizations suspicious of radical change?

Perhaps experience teaches us that claims of efficiency improvements often end up reducing the service/and therefore staffing levels. And claims made that ICT will be so much more immediate and easy for customers may not be as simple to use as their designers have claimed. The stories of claimed improvements can often lead to other problems for customers and staff. New rolling stock on the railways was claimed to have more room for passengers in the rush hour. This was true: the railway company had removed several seats from each of the carriages to allow more standees. Customers are usually not fooled that easily especially when their second largest single outgoing is an annual season ticket.

Part B questions:

What are the important needs that oil companies operating in specialized and hazardous environments might have?

We could say support, and access to assistance in emergency. Probably both mean for the clients promptness and closeness of people they know and trust. Closing four offices down to one will mean that the three closed offices will no longer be able to offer that kind of local presence appreciated by some clients.

How might these customers be aware of improved efficiency?

The online and telephone links will become vital. The company claims that the majority of their clients prefer that point of contact anyway. However, the company will need to monitor call flows and answer rates closely to ensure that their clients are not kept in a queue or when they are answered, passed from hand to hand among the staff.

How might the changes envisaged obviate fraud?

Fraud is usually based on review of people and systems within the company and therefore customers will be unaware of what such procedures are. The only exception to this might be new rules that affect customers – as is the case with opening a bank account when an appearance at the branch with many forms of identification is now required and even the staff seem confused about how the system works.

Part C questions:

What is the biggest overhead in the oil support industry?

We have already seen that staff costs in service industries can be as high as 75 per cent. This compares with manufacturing where similarly high costs have been significantly reduced by automation and the elimination of semi-skilled jobs (such as welding). In Honda, one of the leading examples in the automobile industry, the staff cost has been reduced to 11 per cent. Service industries have striven to emulate this (banking online and cash withdrawals from the hole in the wall are just two examples of this in the financial sector).

If you were one of the four receptionists or office staff what would worry you?

Will I still have a job after these changes? At very least I might have to move to another post and then the question of will I be able to do the job arises. Will the company provide training and support, and what happens if I don't like the new job? For those moving to the new central office there is the question of how much time and money will the extra commuting cost.

Where have many companies located their telephone customer service teams?

Most people will know that the answer is offshore. But even keeping them locally could mean a subcontracted secretarial service organization – the subcontract segment of Handy's Shamrock organization. But extra links in the chain between the company and the client leave us open to misunderstanding, and sometimes delayed responses. Service air staff who deal with booking on and boarding passengers are often unaware of why delays are occurring as the airline has not told them so they cannot pass on information to the passengers.

How would you satisfy workers that radical change will not mean loss of jobs?

In some companies the staff turnover is significantly high and therefore what is sometimes referred to as 'natural wastage' may help in alleviating the fears expressed here. However, the right staff do not always go, and sometimes those who could be dispensed with want to stay. The assurances that the next available job will be offered are part of the normal requirement in a redundancy programme. However, not everyone wants to do a different job to the one they joined to do.

Part D questions:

As HR managers, what would be your main concerns about this change plan?

Perhaps you will have said that it all sounds as if the change is laid down by the managers. Where is the staff involvement? There might be some who would welcome a new position, a different post or a move away from their present place of work. Bottom-up or emergent change is difficult and time-consuming to arrange, but it does mean that we can respond to some of the individual aspirations that lie within most working teams.

Can an organization require a member of staff to take a new post/move office?

Redundancy is based on the fact that the duties being exercised are no longer required in the company. It is then a question of being offered the next available, suitable job. This is the difficult part: individuals need to feel that they have the ability or potential to try the new position/post. If the answer is that they do not then the redundancy pay-off would be the next option. So, there is an element of negotiation here and it is something that change agents do well to invest time on.

What is the technical legal term for change making it difficult to continue working?

In situations where change is imposed and this finds the individual in difficulties with adapting to the required changes, then this could be construed as 'constructive dismissal'. What that means is that the individual finds it virtually impossible to undertake the different terms and conditions required of him/her. The employment contract is key here: what was it that the individual was taken on to do? Changing that in any significant way without taking into account the wishes and aspirations of the individual could have serious legal implications.

How can HR overcome concerns and objections about such job changes?

We have already mentioned negotiation/consultation. The rest is training and support during an induction period and possibly offering the services of a coach or mentor to see individuals through to undertaking their new position successfully.

Part E questions:

If you were the HR manager, how would you go about doing this?

A full-scale *manpower inventory* might be a good start, assuming that the company does not already have one. This can be followed up by a GAP analysis that identifies the competencies that will no longer be needed and the new competencies that will support the new roles. Sometimes this can indicate who is most likely to be able to make the required moves most readily.

How much consultation and negotiation would be involved?
Probably extensive, since even if the complementing competencies that straddle
the gap may seem obvious to a professional HR adviser, staff directly affected
by it may need time to think about it and consult family and friends. Sometimes
the obvious candidates are not willing to make the move, or alternatively see the
opportunity of accepting redundancy payment as too good to turn down.

Where would you start?
I think we have answered this in the previous two answers.

What safeguards would you put in place?
Training, support and counselling would be the three key words here. The services
of a redeployment company might also be a good investment. At least it makes staff
feel that they can discuss matters about their career with those who are competent
and objective.

Part F questions:

If you were a safety officer how would you feel about these three choices?
It sounds as if remaining a safety officer elsewhere is not an option. Professional and
objective advice on complementary skills and aptitude would be strongly advisable
here, as most staff will want to feel that they have a good chance of fulfilling the
new role with the reasonable prospect of success.

How closely would they need to coincide with your previous experience?
The answer would probably be more than 50 per cent of the role should be familiar to the new incumbent.

What might be your concerns about the new roles?
Most concerning would be skills that the candidate is not used to using or finds
uncongenial, in spite of the training. Sales and negotiation or cold-canvass phon-
ing are skills that require intensive training but also aptitude. Competence does not
guarantee commitment. You may be able to do it, but still hate doing it.

What would be your ultimate fear about such a process of transfer?
Definitely it is similar to the previous question and its answer. The thought that
if the new post doesn't work out, is there any way back and what are the options
then? HR needs answers to these questions, as they will most likely be asked.

Part G questions:

**What are the dangers of doing such assessment tests?/Which are the valid
and reliable tests for human subjects?**
There are people who are good at tests and the evidence is that those who practice
doing tests increase their chances of getting better results. So, tests of themselves
may not tell us very much about what employees will be like in the job we want
them to do. There are different types of test available to employers and their validity and reliability need to be carefully assessed to ensure that they satisfy both.

TABLE 5.2 Different test: validity and reliability

Type of test	Validity	Reliability
Cognitive tests	?	✓
Psychomotor tests	✓	✓
Affective tests	?	?

As we can see from Table 5.2 only psychomotor tests (such as are used in simulators for pilot assessment and training) are likely to be both valid and reliable.

Cognitive tests are often reliable but are difficult to relate to the complex functions most jobs now entail. There is, therefore, no necessary correlation between IQ tests and performance in most jobs.

Affective or personality tests are suspect because they usually depend on self-perception and can be easily skewed by the subjects taking them.

The exercise medical centre, like most problem-solving exercises needed to be closely related to the job being offered. That may or may not have been the case here. An in-tray exercise is often used in assessing candidates for managing and prioritizing activities within the context of a specific job.

There is an ethical discussion to be had about whether it is fair for employers to use testing to assess employees for different job roles. Individuals learn in their own way and in their own time so it may be that in a one-off test they fail to do themselves justice, as Helen obviously believed.

Who are the assessors and does that matter/What sort of feedback should candidates be given?

Assessors should ideally be appointed from outside the organizations. They should be qualified and experienced in the sector in which they are working. Candidates have a right to feedback and should also be given any test papers that they have filled in.

Part H questions:

For Helen the exercise reinforces the point that we discussed above in the previous section. Clear feedback would have avoided her leaving the test believing that she had failed. It was fortunate that there was a job for her to return to which reinforces the point that a probationary period with an option to return is always a good investment to encourage open-mindedness and secure people in their continued prospects with the organization.

William was lucky and in some ways aptitude can only be tested by trying the job out. Perceived benefits and an extended role made for a successful outcome for him in the end in spite of his reservations at the outset.

Part I questions:

Did they achieve their original objectives?

Well, they certainly reduced the overhead. However, they also attempted to focus on their customers. The client satisfaction levels were the same as before the change took place. That could be interpreted as a positive sign as no difference was noted so no disturbance to customers ensued. Alternatively, it could be interpreted that not much had been achieved by the changes apart from reduction in overheads for the organization.

Where for them is the link between efficiency and effectiveness?

The end-user is the final arbiter of whether a business has made this link. As we saw with the Lexus example, a highly efficient car is not necessarily perceived as a highly effective one nor one that is desirable to buy. For housing services, for example, the idea of competition is not particularly relevant as the clients are usually not able to exercise choices for going elsewhere.

What will they have had to do for the 65 who left?

Redundancy payments should have been paid at very least. Hopefully, they also assisted by paying for job placement services for those who had the challenge of looking for another job elsewhere. As we have noted, the way leavers are treated often affects the attitudes to the company of those who remain in the workforce.

What lessons could there be for companies embarking on similar radical changes?

The answer to this question should be the basis for the presentation exercise that the students undertake. The main point here will be that change, particularly radical change, needs to take people with it rather than be imposed by managers of external consultants. Managers are often enthusiastic about the efficiency factors that can be improved through change programmes. They are less often sensitive to the need to reinforce change in a way that makes its benefits apparent early on to those who must carry it through.

Bottom-up or emergent change may take longer and therefore be more costly in terms of time and cost. But the cost of imposed change getting it wrong may be higher in terms of staff turnover and the demotivation of those who are left behind in the organization.

A good presentation will take the time to address this issue of perceived benefits for those undertaking to adapt to the changes imposed. Advice on presentation skills can be found at the end of Chapter 12.

6

EMPLOYEE RESOURCING

Topics

- job development and assessing job competency needs
- HR planning for job needs
- monitoring performance
- business planning and HR.

Introduction

Finding the right people for business has always been a challenge and sometimes a problem. At present more than 80 per cent of companies in the EU complain that they cannot find the people they need to staff their business effectively. This is in spite of the highest unemployment figures that have been seen in the EU countries since the great depression of the 1930s. So what is going on in the employment market?

We have already noted that the tendency of large companies to delayer and unbundle their businesses has been complemented by the trend to outsource areas of functional parts of their business to subcontractors or to use consultancy workers as and when required (Shamrock organization, Handy, 1989). That ought to have bought with it the benefits of flexibility in all its forms:

- time
- cost
- number
- functional.

Employee resourcing, then, is the process for ensuring that the HR requirements of an organization are identified and plans are made for satisfying the requirements for staffing a company effectively (Bulla and Scott, 1994). It might be thought that the flexible arrangements, which are now possible, would have made this easier to achieve rather than more difficult. So, what lies at the heart of this problem?

The first challenge for recruiters is to explore who is out there and how do we know? Again, it might be thought that there is a plethora of data on the internet which ought to make recruiters more aware of their options not less. And yet precisely because there is more data, does not mean that there is more information. It has sometimes been said that the world is data rich and information poor. And to turn data into information requires effective interpretation of the data presented to us.

Often that means some knowledge of what is available needs to be complemented by what is realistic.

BOX 6.1

Consider the roles which are required by the average academic working in a university:

- Lecturing and tutoring students; researching and writing academic papers; administration and management; pastoral counselling.
- Consider the competencies required of each element of the job.
- How likely is it that one person will be excellent at all of them?

Making demands on people is part of hiring them. We like to be challenged in our jobs normally; otherwise we may get bored and look for fresh opportunities elsewhere. In her book *Managing Today and Tomorrow*, Stewart (1991) remarks that within three months the job that we have accepted has usually grown to assume larger duties and responsibilities than we thought we would have to undertake. She illustrates it diagrammatically as in Figure 6.1.

Now these extra job duties can come from the manager, colleagues or subordinates, and when we accept them, our core duties still have to be completed. This may account for why managers in the UK routinely take work home or work 60–70 hours a week. So, we might say that traditionally people have done whatever has been asked of them, perhaps because they did not want to refuse, or because they thought it was a means of gaining more experience and being seen as fitted for promotion.

We might also consider the types of change that have traditionally been identified in organizations:

- incremental change
- punctuated equilibrium
- continuous change.

Technology requires incremental change of us all the time now. Software updates, for example, are regular interventions that everyone using computers has to come

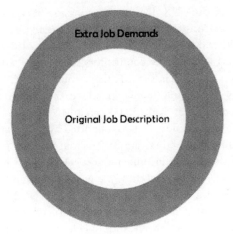

FIGURE 6.1 Growth in job demands in the first few months.

Source: Adapted from Stewart (1991: 15).

to terms with. Changes in staffing and new faces in the working team can also give rise to the need for change and adaptation to different human dynamics at work.

And then there are the changes at work that may require significant reorganization, which may demand a sudden change, such as the relocation of a plant or office, or radical changes in working patterns to reconnect with market demographics.

Finally there is continuous change, which can be easily demonstrated by the requirements of CPD, which all professional lead bodies now require for continued membership or progression through the grades within the body itself. There is no end to learning and development during a working life and career and the traditional early training and qualification in any area of knowledge will therefore require individual planning and implementation to sustain future employability.

What follows from that is that employers have a high expectation of what their people can do and it may be that the cry that they make that there are not the skilled people that they need 'out there' is partly due to their own high expectancies that applicants for jobs will be able to demonstrate knowledge, skill and experience in all the fields that they require. Drawing on our example of the requirements expected of an academic we can see that it is very unlikely that any individual will excel in all the areas designated. Most students will accept that lecturing standards vary enormously within and between members of the faculty who teach them. It is not unknown for academics in receipt of research monies to begin their research by buying out their teaching and funding a teaching fellow to undertake it. If writing and research is your primary interest, it may be that teaching is not an area of interest, or indeed an aptitude that is readily available to you (Kristof, 1996).

So recruiting people from outside can be difficult, largely because we have no idea whether they will be able to adapt to the culture of the organization, nor whether they will be able to respond to the demands of the business in the future. All of this raises another question: can we develop our talent in-house?

It has to be said that the UK does not have a good track record at investing in training. The Handy/Constable reports in 1987 suggested that only 4 per cent of managers in the UK had a business qualification against 24 per cent of our major competitors and that whereas our competitors spent anywhere between 5 and 7 per cent of GDP on training, in the UK the amount was 0.35 per cent. In 1980 the British Foundry Association (highly skilled workers engaged in making engine blocks for cars and aeroplanes) had 120,000 members supported by 6,000 apprenticeships. Their numbers are now 60,000 supported by 390 apprenticeships. In our own sector of business studies there are 2,000 about to retire (or at least of retirement age). Behind the present incumbents are 594 PhDs qualified to take up the posts we vacate (and 90 per cent of those are non-EU citizens).

All of this suggests that the UK has traditionally succeeded by recruiting trained people from the opposition, which seems to have reinforced the idea in some employers' minds that if you train your people, they only leave and go off to the opposition (so do the same rather than train and then lose them). In other countries in Europe the tax system reinforces training, particularly for those in their first six months of employment, by monitoring investment and adjusting corporate tax advantages accordingly. So, firms that train gain a tax advantage, while those that neglect training may end up being penalized by having to pay more in corporation tax.

Investment in training is the principal path to improving productivity. It requires people who are willing and able to respond to the training needs required of them. It therefore depends on ability, potential and aptitude, for which there are few valid and reliable tests.

Manpower inventory

Manpower inventories are a graphic way of illustrating who exercises which competencies currently in their job and can also include the competencies needed in the future so that those already trained and experienced can be complemented by those designated for training or trained or awaiting further experience to consolidate their newly trained skill(s).

Appropriate training can then be designed around the elements of the personnel profile:

- knowledge
- skill
- experience
- attitude.

Standards can then be drawn up that satisfy the following guidelines:

- they are stated in *behavioural* terms;
- contains the *conditions* under which that behaviour must be exercised;
- contains the *standard* that applies to the context of the behaviour.

The question of flexibility may then be considered, as contractors or consultants may be better value for money than core workers in the organization. If we consider Guest's HR outcomes, then we have already addressed *flexibility* and *quality*. The answers to how specific we can be about staffing levels depends on *strategic integration*: we need to know how accurate we can be about where we want the company to be over a defined period.

Hard and soft HRM

Early writers sometimes made the distinction between hard and soft HRM. The distinction between them is straightforward.

Hard HR planning

Based on quantitative analysis to ensure the right number and sort of people are available when needed, it analyses cost–benefit analysis and works on the bottom line of the organization's desired outcomes. In other words, the question of how much production or service will cost depends on the three classical cost headings:

- *establishment* costs (predominantly wages, especially in service industries);
- *marginal or variable* costs (light, heat, travel, accommodation which may vary over the year);
- *interference* costs (paying for the unexpected such as breakdowns; staff turnover; absence etc.).

Most companies are unaware of the extent of their interference costs. The negative organizational outcomes, which Guest lists, are therefore worth examining to discover just how much staff turnover and intermittent absence are costing the company. Such items are rarely expressed in the company accounts and when raised usually focus the minds of senior managers if expressed accurately. Commitment to resolving those problems causing the cost overruns will often then be given.

Soft HR planning

In contrast, this aspect is more explicitly focused on creating and shaping the culture of the organization so that there is a clear integration between goals and employee values, beliefs and behaviours (resource-led approach). How people are handled becomes more important in terms of the calculations made about their terms and conditions. So, companies that care about their staff may offer services that are subsidized or free, whether travel or catering or personnel services. All of this is intended to convey the message of being a caring employer.

There is no necessary contradiction between hard and soft HRM and they are not mutually exclusive. What things cost and whether they yield what we expected will remain important to calculate, though it must be said that good will is often difficult to estimate and evaluate and easy to lose, sometimes over things that might have been considered trivial by managers.

Throughout this book we have given equal consideration to both hard and soft HRM. It was a popular debate in the 1990s, but professional HR managers have probably moved on since then.

BOX 6.2

A new CEO took over a large organization and decided to set an example of economy and cost cutting from the outset.

One of his first acts was to have all personal paper baskets removed from all rooms thus saving costs in cleaning.

In their place were recycling points at the end of each corridor where individuals could dispose of their own waste appropriately.

You may want to consider how much time was spent by professional staff making that journey and how much that interference cost was in comparison to the amount saved on the cleaning bill with subcontractors.

Three steps of HR planning

1 Forecasting future people needs

The faster a business gathers pace, the harder it is for individuals to predict with any certainty what their staffing needs will be. Organizations that have a stated staffing complement may well find themselves running below full staffing levels as those leaving or retiring are not readily replaced or are replaced by part-time/temporary staff. There will always be a question over quality and consistency in such cases.

BOX 6.3

A retiring academic was given a part-time contract to conduct student tutorials. His rates were £30/lecture or £18/tutorial.

He left home using his senior citizen's pass at 9.30am to avail himself of a cheap fare, arriving at the institution at 1pm to work through till 6pm.

He then had a similar length of journey to return home.

His teaching hours were from 1pm–6pm (5 hours in all at tutorial rate) and his fare reimbursed. However, his full time away from home was more than 12 hours.

Needless to say after one term he did not return.

2 Forecasting the future availability of people

In the early 1990s the National Health Service in the UK worked out that if all the UK females aged 18 were trained as nurses, there would still not be enough to staff the burgeoning needs of an ageing population in which 10 per cent is over 65. This meant for them a search for nurses from other countries, especially the third world. Needless to say this denuded third world countries of qualified nurses whose training had been paid for by their home country.

More recently, the government in the UK, aware that there was popular discontent with immigrants from abroad, put in place visa restrictions to make it difficult for non-EU citizens to get into the country. It is estimated that there has been a 6 per cent drop in immigration in the groups targeted and this has had the effect of reducing student applicants to universities by 21 per cent, thereby seriously curtailing an £85 billion business on which the UK depends.

These two illustrations indicate that our calculations of who is available depend not just on who is available in theory but also on political factors that can obstruct recruitment and over which HR has little or no control.

3 Drawing up plans to match supply and demand

It sounds easy but it does mean working in a dynamic market. For some universities it has meant setting up campuses in other countries. There are ways round immigration limits, but they require ingenuity and patient alternative planning.

This requires constant investigatory activity by which HR requirements can be explored and the effects of alternative policies and actions can be investigated. Only 6 per cent of Boards of Directors include a representative from HR. So, it is difficult for HR planners to contribute at first hand to the discussion and consensus of the Board of Directors. Often managers request staff recruitment at very short notice. This means that the chances of discussing long-term staffing needs are therefore less likely (Boxall and Purcell, 2003).

Gap between theory and practice

Impact of outside-in change and difficulty of predicting the future business requirements

If we go back to *outside-in* or *market-led* approaches to change, then it is clear to see that predicting the movement of available staff in any sector may be hard to calculate accurately for any period of time. Who would want to attempt to predict what the world will look like in five years' time? The foundations of business are themselves unstable: the burden of debt borne by governments has got to the stage where it is no longer sustainable by further borrowing; this is compounded by the financial sector which has lost sight of its original purpose of being a means to the end of financing business and become instead an end in itself as it seeks to maximize its own assets and profits. There are no clear voices indicating how to resolve this impasse.

Perhaps we should also consider that the proponents of HRM theory devised the theory during a relatively stable period of growth and continued development of industry which would sustain individuals who wanted to devote their energies to a career in the organization. We can remind ourselves of just how important an outcome *organizational commitment* was at that time.

And yet, as we have seen, the movement away from permanent employment in one organization or sector has increased as the fragmentation of long-term organizations has continued apace. The search for *flexibility* in all its guises reinforces productivity, efficiency and profitability at the expense of *commitment* as an HR outcome. Coupled with this is the growing awareness that the knowledge worker has the advantage that skilled workers in the past did not have: the ability to move on, taking their knowledge with them. Businesses dependent on knowledge and expertise need people who answer the profile required by the business to sustain their competitive edge in the market. This emancipation that knowledge brings individual workers gives them an advantage that the agents of organizational flexibility and change could never have foreseen or imagined when HRM theory was first developed (Alvesson and Willmott, 1992).

Shifting kaleidoscope of policy and strategy in organizations

We return to the challenges of formulating *strategic integration* in the organization. Who is responsible for deciding in which direction the organization should go? If we go back to the types of change we can ask whether *incremental change* is a safer approach – building on the successes of the past and allowing individuals to take stepped changes that are within their capabilities and tolerance of change itself? Or is the *punctuated equilibrium* approach called for, in which only a few of the people we have will find radical change either congenial or acceptable? If we consider that mergers and amalgamations can often be perceived as radical change, then the figures for retention of key people can be as low as 25 per cent over the subsequent three-year period (Willcocks and Grint, 1997).

Finally, there is the condition of *continuous change* which probably represents what most organizations face in a world whose changes become ever more fast-paced and unpredictable. It begs the question of how long change can be sustained by the individuals who need to bring to bear their competence and expertise on markets that are subject to worldwide forces.

Distrust of managers in the theory of planning

The demands on managers change from day to day. So, it is not surprising that pragmatism rules in decision making. Replacing people who leave, retire or go off on leave of different kinds must take precedence over the longer term considerations of HR planning. What is desirable is countered by the demands of the immediate need of staff to get business done to deadlines. Anything else has to wait. Time spent on meetings is usually resisted as it detracts from time spent in managing crisis and covering for absences or lack of required resources (Lavelle, 2007).

Lack of evidence that HR planning works (Rothwell, 1995)

Taking the above into account, the task of the HR planner is a difficult one. But there are benefits to be found in keeping records of organizational outcomes as outlined in Guest's diagram: which departments suffer from high staff turnover; sick absence and intermittent absence? What are the comparative results between departments? Where are the areas that give rise to continual problems? As we have already noted, interference costs can be calculated for all of the problem areas relating to staffing. Perhaps the occasional update to Board members might encourage them to apply themselves to the challenge of staff planning with their HR colleagues.

Reasons for HR planning

Planning to optimize the use of resources

If Deal and Kennedy (1982) are correct in describing culture as 'the way we do things round here' then we need to ask whether that is a benefit or a constraint. On the positive side, consistency in any area of business at least reassures customers that there is a benchmark and that they will not be needlessly surprised by unpredictable change. On the other hand, we could also argue that sameness can lead to lack of innovation, resistance to change and performance that does not pleasantly surprise customers.

If staff are challenged to think about the business there may be just a chance that they will feel their contribution is important; their ideas are respected; and that the idea of empowerment might just be welcomed rather than ignored. Good managers are developers and facilitators – they make it easy for staff to think the unthinkable – such as, how can we do things in a way that delights the customer and maximizes our chance of getting return business. Discussion is the basis of education. It develops the power of thinking, challenges the traditional and encourages envisaging the future.

Planning challenges assumptions and liberates thinking

As we have said, a good manager can stimulate and encourage positive thinking in others. It has to be one of the primary vehicles for mobilizing *strategic integration*. Doing the job and doing it well is the foundation of any professional performer. However, getting the best out of people also means engaging their brain. Most people have ideas while doing jobs that come to them easily. It may be how to do the job more quickly or thinking laterally about why we do things the way we do. Brainstorming in teams or groups can be an effective way of releasing such thoughts and encouraging others to think about future prospects for the business, too.

Managers who take the time and trouble to do this both one-to-one and in groups encourage others to stretch their mental horizons and think about pro-actively managing themselves and the people around them. Ideas are the basis of planning and idea sharing is the basis of consensus about the future, which makes change programmes easier to initiate and run.

Planning gives an opportunity to link HR and business plans

This is critical for the achievement of *strategic integration*. It allows staff to explore proactively the issues that face the company and to discuss those issues in the light of future prospects for the business. The idea is to think the end and then come back with suggestions for meeting that end (which, of course, may mean some options are not open to us because employment law or health and safety constrain it). Using flip chart sheets can be a useful way of both working with ideas and keeping a record of what has been raised for future sessions (Taylor, 2008).

BOX 6.4

The governors of a further education college met to consider a staff disci-plinary case. Unusually, given that all political parties were represented, the decision at the end of the session was unanimous that the member of staff should be dismissed.

The Clerk to the Governors, the Local Authority's lawyer, said, 'This is not a sacking offence.'

An HR manager and board member replied: 'We will decide what needs to happen. You will tell us how we can do it.'

The member of staff was later removed but given a job in another part of the college. Political accommodation won in the end.

What sort of things might be discussed

Internal labour market

Where will the business be in two years time? What will the needs of that business be then? How will customer expectancy have changed by then? What implications will that have for the staff required to satisfy that need?

It also needs to consider the stocks and flows of people available to be promoted, trained and redeployed to meet future need. Who has the potential and ability to be developed for more responsibility within the company? A few years ago there was much discussion about the need for succession planning. The idea was that if a key member of staff should leave, the organization would have someone whom they considered a suitable successor. It has to be said that often events moved so slowly that by the time the moment for change came, the appointed successor had themselves moved on, or proved beyond doubt that they were not suitable for the new job's demands now required by the changing context of the business.

BOX 6.5

Changing the perceptions of people above you is arguably the most difficult challenge in an organization. Often, early perceptions die hard, or remain stuck in people's minds over the long term.

Demonstrating competence does not always overcome early beliefs that individuals 'do not have what it takes'. Though if pushed, they would be hard put to it to substantiate their views.

Choosing candidates for jobs once we know and have worked with them can be difficult to do. Stereotypes die hard for all of us and breaking the barriers requires subtlety and care.

BOX 6.6

The post of deputy head teacher came up in a secondary school. There were two candidates:

One was Head of English, a 56-year-old, considered the heir apparent by his older colleagues. The other was a 32-year-old, a younger more dynamic teacher.

The discussion among the governors moved in favour of the older teacher, largely as a reward for long service and a belief that he deserved to succeed to the job. And then one governor intervened: 'Describe to me the qualities of the person the school needs to do this job,' he asked the group.

The discussion then moved to the idea of someone innovative, committed to the children, and, above all, young and dynamic. They went ahead and appointed the younger candidate.

He had a difficult time with some of the older members of staff. But he got on well with the students and was a very effective deputy head.

External labour market

Who is out there and what do we know about them? It could be said that there is more data available about people in all sectors that can be accessed through the diverse media now available that shows profiles, expertise and experience. Once professional sites such as LinkedIn become well established, then it becomes easier to access relevant information about potential candidates in local, regional, national and international markets. This must be a boon to head-hunters who can pick out likely candidates much more easily.

Probably, word-of-mouth still remains a significant factor in most sectors, particularly within professional networks. People who have moved around in their careers tend to have acquired a reputation that is known well by their colleagues. These colleagues move around themselves. So in most sectors, the local group can between them come up with insightful comments about people they have worked with and what they experienced.

BOX 6.7

A well-published, internationally renowned academic spent his career moving from university to university every two years or so. At conferences he appeared affable, charming and encouraging to up-and-coming young colleagues.

His arrival at any institution was always greeted with enthusiasm and for him there was a honeymoon period which was appreciated by everyone who met him. However, problems arose when he was asked to play an active role in teaching or administration.

This always led him to a move to another university. Not surprisingly his track record became well known through all who had served with him.

Competence and experience are rightly highly rated by interview panels and appointment bodies. However, the question of fit does not just depend on knowledge, skill and experience. Fitting in with colleagues will also be an important part in integrating well and being readily accepted by fellow members of staff. Socializing and informal management styles can therefore be significant factors in integrating well in new organizations (Becker *et al.*, 2001).

BOX 6.8

A senior officer retired from the armed service and took up a position of chief executive of a local authority. His style was command and control and he tended to send memos and post notices that summoned managers to meetings and indicated that decisions had already been made. This approach was extremely uncongenial to senior members of his staff.

After three months he lost the cooperation and good will of his colleagues and left the job.

He then became managing director of a debt collecting company where his style was a perfect fit and went down well with his staff, many of whom were ex-service personnel themselves.

Summary checklist

How many people are we likely to need in our key operational and functional areas?

As we have seen, core workers are expensive, and it may be that our needs could be satisfied by consultants. In BPR terminology we could describe these operators as *expertise managers*. Lawyers, IT staff, HR managers are increasingly either on an interim contract or they are hired in for particular functions which may be occasional or ad hoc. Similarly, functional areas are often effectively covered by subcontractors. They are responsible for recruiting, training and managing their staff on behalf of the company they serve, so there are no management overheads for the core company once the contract has been signed. If it is an annual contract, there will be ample opportunity to seek expertise elsewhere should performance be less than satisfactory over the period of the contract.

What skills are we likely to need in the future?

For managers, increasingly, the BPR title *enterprise manager* best expresses the role that most core staff have in the organization. As most consultants will know, it is significant that many managers still do not know the key data that governs the success of their company until the end of year report brings it to their attention, or the company experiences a crisis.

CPD ought to underwrite this need for continuous change and development in the organization's key people. Smaller groups or teams are more likely to have the chance to discuss such matters informally together. Hiding from the unpleasant or uncongenial does not solve the underlying problem. And, usually, problems ignored do not diminish, they become more critical over time if unaddressed.

Will we be able to meet the needs from our existing resources?

We have already considered this aspect and noted that lateral thinking is required to overcome what can otherwise be a predictive approach to staff development. So secretaries become senior secretaries and salespeople become sales managers. The practice of *work rotation* may offer transfers from traditional employment silos across job or group boundaries. Secretaries in sales offices are often known to customers, aware of the company's products and services, and aware of company procedures and practices. For those who would like to represent the company face to face, the acquisition of the requisite skills and support is not difficult to develop and support – especially if the resumption of the previous job is still available should the transfer not be as successful as had been hoped.

This can on occasion be more successful than engaging a salesperson from another company, who will take some weeks, if not months, to become familiar with the company's procedures, products and services before becoming effective in the field.

If not, where will we be able to find them?

We have already talked about the need to access outside resources and the easy access to information about prospective staff available on the internet. We have also mentioned the need to network in the relevant fields which may yield useful contacts and word-of-mouth references. The rest is always being open to offers and prospects. We may not need a particular post at the moment. But, in the event that we might in the future it would be useful to have some contacts to call on.

What do we need to do to develop or extend our skills base?

Two things summarize our considerations so far: developing our *internal resources* and seeking to enhance the staffing complement by *judicious recruitment*. We accept that for many professions and job functions, the employment market has become more fragmented. There is, therefore, less expectancy that jobs and the organizations that offer them will be permanent. That means that efforts to retain good staff will be a constant challenge (Sisson and Storey, 2000).

BOX 6.9

Recruiting high-flying staff can be a constant challenge. For universities, for example, academic staff with good research publication profiles are eagerly recruited before the regular research assessment exercise takes place. Shortly afterwards, however, they may find better offers elsewhere.

The temptation to move again will often be difficult for such individuals to resist, leaving the institution back where it started in the need of attracting and retaining high-flying staff.

Scenario planning

Tries to open the minds of executives to a range of possibilities that organizations may have to confront

Playing 'what if' has been developed into a management technique that engages the minds of senior and specialist team members in thinking about future possibilities in the world or sector in which they operate. It can be organized as a brainstorming session and works best when the facilitator accepts all answers and puts them up where all can see them clearly.

Following on from that, the team can choose which options they think are feasible and whether they want to take a step-by-step approach to planning. This can be played by seeking the logical consequences and asking 'what then?' after each step is discussed.

This process builds up a picture of the consequences in the production or supply chain as it affects the company in a logical and consistent way. The next step is to look at the organization of the change steps and the resources required to respond effectively to the new challenge. That may well affect:

- people
- investment
- strategic alliances.

On the question of the last item in the list, a recent article in the *Financial Times* pointed out that there are 40 airlines in Europe. Experts in the sector believe that there is room for four or five viable aircraft companies there. Michael O'Leary of Ryanair may not be the most loved chief executive in the aircraft industry, but he has been in the forefront of discussion about the future shape of the airline industry and how his company would respond to different challenges in the future. His own decisions about pricing, destinations and aeroplane requirements have rarely been found wanting, annoying though his style may be to others.

BOX 6.10

The oil industry has been a prime user of scenario planning in seeking to respond to what is a volatile market in the commodity. Prices must necessarily rise as the resources run down. But this natural depletion worldwide is disturbed frequently by political forces in countries that produce the oil.

So what if oil rises to $200 a barrel?

Well we might see a downturn in usage, of course. But in general petrol products are price elastic until viable alternative energy resources become available. So, what we can see is that such a price rise would trigger:

- search for alternatives;
- increased revenue for drilling in currently costly venues (Falkland Islands; Western coast of Scotland etc.).

We could say that innovation and creativity is not just dependent on entrepreneurs or genius inventors. Thinking ahead can also help staff to enter into dialogue with one another and encourage inventiveness and responding to challenges that may lie ahead (Bowman *et al.*, 2013).

Demand forecasting

Basis: annual budgeting

BOX 6.11

Let us assume that a company wants to increase its profitability by 2 per cent. What are the implications for the rest of the organization?

Sales: What sort of increase in volume and/or prices would be required to achieve this company objective?

Marketing: Whatever the answer has been to the previous question, stimulating extra sales will require some increase in marketing activities. So where are these new sales going to come from, and where will we need to focus our efforts? Most importantly, what will this cost us?

Production: Sales people rarely sell everything that the company produces. So, it is likely that more will be required, or perhaps an increased range of products to attract different clients or customers. Are we ready to launch this increase in production?

Finance: All of this new activity means finance and investment. But will it be justified by the return on the investment?

Trends analysis techniques

Ratio-trends analysis

Most organizations are aware of the employment trends that pertain to their sector. If we take the example of the retail sector, the ratio between full- and part-time workers can be as high as 20:80. We have already commented on flexibility as one of the HR outcomes looked for by HRM theory. We can appreciate that part-time workers satisfy the need to be accurate in estimating number of staff; time; and costs in allotting staff as flows of business change throughout the seasons of the year, or even during the working day itself. But it also means functional flexibility: and that is a function of training. If we want people to cover more responsibilities, then we owe it to them and the customer to see that they are properly prepared and supported to offer different services.

Work study measurements

There is nothing new under the sun and time and motion studies have been a staple technique of OD. The emphasis on time; quality; quantity; and cost has been central to the search for increased efficiency or productivity factors. For some writers this is the heart of what is referred to as managerialism or performativity. Managers seek to get their staff to do more for less, if they can do it without alerting staff to the fact that they are being closely monitored. For some writers the movement that reinforces close supervision is sometimes referred to as panopticon (all-seeing). And there are those who would say that the computer is a very effective way of monitoring performance, without the need to employ a supervisor to do it. So, home-working or telecommuting can be safely entrusted to the individual to do in their own time. As long as deadlines and quality are met, there should be no problem with direct supervision.

GAP analysis

We have already referred to *manpower inventories* and these can be the first step towards identifying where in the organization potential workers are who could be developed to cover newly required roles and competencies. The technique involves listing the job responsibilities currently undertaken by members of staff designated for change. Side-by-side with this list should be posted the list of competencies required in the new role. It should be clear that some knowledge and skills will be transferable and where the gaps are between current competency and the need for further training.

Filling that gap will mean drawing up a *training needs analysis* for those affected by changes to their job description.

Supply forecasting

As we have seen previously with the health service, calculating the need for nurses and doctors can never be an exact science. However, 10 per cent of the UK population is over the age of 65 and that ratio will rise in the coming years. As we get older we are more likely to need to call on the services of the health service, so there should be a direct correlation between demographic changes and the need to train and employ more professional health workers. At present the trend in public funding appears to be moving in the other direction. Keeping people healthy so that they can continue working would seem to be an important priority for any country that wants to enhance the quality of life that all its citizens enjoy.

Labour turnover index

Calculating how many staff leave in the course of a year and what percentage that is of the overall number employed is an important function for HR to discharge. However, as Guest's diagram illustrates, the organizational outcomes of effective HR practices should ensure that we are addressing the expectancies of our staff in all the areas that affect their well-being at work. If there is an increase in this level then the search for the reasons should be urgent as the interference cost of staff turnover can be extensive (Torrington *et al.*, 2009).

BOX 6.12

Recent figures from a UK retailer suggest that the interference cost of losing front line retail staff is £1,500.

Similar figures for graduate management trainees was calculated as £10,000.

Thirty per cent of graduate management trainees leave within six months of starting their job.

Loss of sales revenue when sales territories are left uncovered can run into several thousand £s. To that figure must be added the cost of recruitment and the time taken for new appointees to become effective, which can take several months

---

Survival rate

Calculating at what point in their career service the majority of staff leave can also be significant. Are there particular roles that are affected or particular departments that tend to shed staff? Is there a point in an apprenticeship or training scheme where staff tend to leave the organization?

BOX 6.13

A retail store had a high refusal of job offers made to prospective staff.

The HR director decided to send in two applicants from an agency to discover what was going on.

The manager sat with his feet on the desk leaning back in his chair in both interviews. In one case he threw the applicant's CV on the floor saying, 'This is a joke'.

The manager was sacked.

Exit interviews

It is a useful and worthwhile custom to seek an interview once people have left and settled elsewhere. Once the need for a reference has been discharged and they are stable in their new career, they may be prepared to speak more frankly about their experiences and the reasons that led them to leave.

Frequently the real reason for leaving may include one or more of the following:

- more pay
- better prospects

- more security
- more opportunity to develop skills
- better working conditions
- poor relations with manager
- poor relations with colleagues
- bullying/harassment
- personal (family, illness, moving).

In some sectors, friendships have built up over the years. So, if one of a circle of friends leaves, it may not be long before others follow. This can be the case particularly among sales forces whose propensity to leave is often higher than other occupations. Company cars, bonuses, commission and rewards are keenly monitored by salespeople and if friends speak well of a new company, the temptation to leave can be irresistible.

We have already mentioned interference costs of staff turnover. The following is a list of items that need to be added into the calculations of interference costs:

- leaving costs
- recruitment costs
- interference costs of recruitment
- induction costs
- interference costs of induction
- training costs
- interference costs of training
- loss of input to sales, support, manufacturing
- loss of new starter input.

The result as we have remarked often runs into thousands of £s. Consultants do well to calculate these before they embark on working with their clients. It is always worthwhile to discover whether the managers are aware of such costs and why they think staff turnover is occurring. The answers will always be enlightening, whatever they are. The next question will be: why have they done nothing about it? (Purcell, 2004).

BOX 6.14

A company manufacturing coins had a production floor full of die-stamping machinery. The operator inserted a sheet of metal, depressed a handle which caused the head of the machine to descend and emboss the coins, dropping them into a receptacle below. The operator removed the remains of the metal sheet and discarded it. The premises were old and poorly maintained. Staff had to work in draughty and cold conditions. The all-female operators were observed working non-stop.

> Asked why they stayed, the staff replied that they and their families all went on holiday together when the factory shut down for two weeks in the summer.
>
> Asked why they didn't look for a job in a more congenial environment they said, 'We would not want to leave our friends.'

Business planning and HR

Involvement in strategy planning is rare

The figure for HR managers serving on the Board of Directors has changed little in 20 years. The figure always hovered somewhere around 6 per cent. Does this mean that, in general, senior managers have little regard for HR as a specialism? Certainly in the case of one well-known retailer, renowned for its staff welfare provision, not only did they refuse to change the name of the department from personnel to HR but after a three-year trial of having the HR manager on the Board, removed her and did not replace her on the Board.

It may be that senior managers consider HR as a specialism with no expertise in strategic decision making. And yet, virtually every decision they make on the Board has a knock-on effect on the staff. Not only that, the effect of decisions made in a downturn may well involve redundancies. These will need to be implemented by the HR department.

Perhaps, one consolation for HR staff is that they can genuinely say, when implementing the less congenial decisions of the Board, that they had nothing to do with the discussions leading to the final outcome. But *strategic integration* would suggest that knowledge is a better strategy

The process is fragmented and sporadic

HR is responsible for monitoring staff turnover and sick absence and the interference costs involved in these trends; this is an important part of evaluation of the company's effectiveness in managing the people on whom the business depends. If we look at the HRD list again, there are few interventions that managers make in the life of the staff that does not have important consequences. As such, constant review of how well the company and its managers are doing should be important to the Board of Directors.

Strategic alliances with good managers may be the only way of ensuring that the messages that the Board needs to hear are made at appropriate points in their discussions.

Portfolio management approach

The search for economies and the movement of work from core staff to sub-contractors has not passed by HR. Many of the day-to-day tasks from pay-roll to recruitment to pensions can and often are contracted out to other agencies. A growing number of managers are on interim contracts, which may not make them feel secure in their employment, or feel committed to the organization.

Of most concern to staff is the opportunity to seek advice and help in difficult situations and know that discretion and confidentiality will be observed. It is difficult to feel a rapport with those who are not part of the full-time management team.

Line managers are suspicious of personnel involvement in manpower/strategic issues

It is ironical that HR, set up to support managers in the difficult tasks they can face in day-to-day management, can find themselves isolated or viewed with suspicion. Policing the organization's HR performance raises issues of diplomacy and tact as such interventions are not always appreciated even when dealt with assertively.

In one large retailer, the general store manager was assisted by three deputies, one of whom was responsible for HR matters. All recruitment and HR matters were dealt with by this deputy and reports made to head office on the progress of the store. The general managers felt that they were excluded from decisions that should have been within their remit. Interestingly, while the management staff turnover in most retail stores was no more than about 20 per cent, in this company it reached 46 per cent.

Developing an involving approach

It is all down to selection: develop a profile of the technical and interpersonal skills that the new work requires

This ought to be obvious, but may need a moment's thought. The key phrase here is 'new work'. The mixture as before may not be the way ahead. What is it that the business needs in the future? In a static period, procedures and processes may be the gauge of good quality and happy customers. 'We do what we know, and we know what we do.' A good example of this is the way in which aircraft companies are regulated: pilots fly the same plane across the same routes so that they are familiar with the patterns of approach and take-off in all weather conditions. That reinforces safety for the passengers, though it is less than flexible for the operator. But as most businesses become more challenged by change they require people who can respond to change fast and effectively. This, of course, means a willingness to learn and undertake continuing training. But it may also mean having an aptitude which was not expected before.

BOX 6.15

A pharmaceutical company developing compounds was dependent on its PhD researchers. These men and women were expert in their field and were responsible for the team under them developing the drug through its various stages.

The company was taken over and their role became changed to negotiating with clients, costing the development work, and securing the business. They were subject to profitability metrics (the close assessment and costing of all aspects of their working day).

Needless to say, for many of them this change was extremely uncongenial, as many of them found they had no aptitude to make this change to their new role.

Remember that an ability to learn may be one of the important capabilities you are looking for

But accept that most learning that we undertake is personal and what is sometimes referred to as 'tacit'. In other words, we ourselves would find it difficult to describe what it is we do when we are successful at a particular skill. This makes it difficult for us to analyse our success, still less teach others how to be successful.

However, it may be that an applicant's CV shows signs that they have welcomed change; have responded to challenges; and have demonstrated the required aptitudes in the past. Look at *free-association*, as well as formal jobs undertaken. Sometimes individuals can have arranged and managed all sorts of relevant tasks in their free time, as a hobby or interest. So, people who have been successful at selling in a jumble sale or sale of work may have just the aptitude that can be developed in a job requiring negotiation (Becker *et al.*, 2001).

Determine what formal testing procedures can tell you about the candidate

There are few tests that are both valid and reliable. Such tests are usually termed *psychomotor tests*. Our hand–eye coordination and our reflexes are stable during our lifetime and can be tested effectively through such tests. So, for those seeking to join an air force as a fighter pilot, the simulator and our responses in it to the different conditions we will experience in flight can be tested effectively.

Cognitive tests, as the name suggests, focus on our mental abilities and can include intelligence tests, verbal reasoning tests, numeracy tests and so on. They are always reliable, but not always valid. In other words, there is no necessary correlation between good results in an intelligent test and performing the job in hand. So, someone with a high Mensa score may not be an outstanding manager or sales person, for example – for the simple reason that the competencies required of a manager or sales person cannot be picked up in an intelligence test.

Affective tests would probably be better known as personality tests. Many of these tests are neither valid not reliable. In some cases once the way the test works is discovered, the results can be skewed by the candidate to coincide with the profile that the tester is looking for (Toplis *et al.*, 2004).

Observe the candidate working under real or simulated work conditions

Difficult to do, but some organizations have adapted to it. For artists, the portfolio of their past work is always telling. For athletes, their performance on the field is easy to track, too. But for managers, the context and culture in which they work is important to their effectiveness and moving companies, even within the same field of work, is not always successful.

BOX 6.16

In some churches, when there is a vacancy for a minister or priest, the selection committee is given the names of three incumbents interested in moving and permitted to go and listen to them preaching in their different parishes.

In some cases the three candidates are then invited to preach at the church that is looking for a parish minister so that the congregation can hear them preach as well.

After this the congregation can make its own decision about who they would prefer to listen to on a Sunday. They could be stuck with the new incumbent for a long time – so they need to be sure that the style and content of preaching suits them.

Broaden the interview process to include team members with whom the candidate would be working

This is certainly custom and practice in most universities, where panel interviews are the norm. Five members include not just the Head of College, and other managers, but also a staff representative. Prior to that, the candidates are invited to address the staff about their research and their likely contribution to the university. At the end of this session they are then questioned about their presentation and their likely contribution to the team.

It should be said, however, that there is no democratic vote as to who should be appointed. And it often happens that the principal and his advisers will have their own ideas on who finally should be appointed.

Don't limit your pool of candidates by requiring past experience

It is easy to say this, but in practice much more difficult to do, especially in the face of more experienced candidates. However, the question, 'Have you done this job before?' is the bane of life to all those seeking their first employment in any post, especially in management. Appointing a candidate who is gifted but needs experience requires supporting them with training and mentoring to ensure they have the best chance of success.

Design the recruiting process to expose your culture to the candidate and treat them as a company member during the process

The candidate should clearly understand what it means to work for your company. That may be difficult to do. But to those moving on to other institutions and not sure which to choose, at very least they should be able to speak to others who are already there and go and see the place for themselves (try ringing up when you are not expected and see whether the response is as helpful and informative as their promotional material suggests).

It was always said that 'People buy from people they like'. So being friendly and approachable has an added bonus: it makes the candidates feel at ease and therefore, hopefully, give the best account of themselves that they can. It also makes them feel that they are joining colleagues who are friendly and supportive to work with (Storey and Sisson, 1993).

Finally:

Jobs today increasingly involve negotiating, interaction, and mutual influence

Team players are a necessary ingredient to the modern organization. Certain jobs may well attract isolates. But increasingly even these jobs now depend on using other's skills and working in teams whose members can complement one another's competencies.

They take place in flexible, self-directed working teams

So team training and team events need to develop the members of a team. The manager is a facilitator but does not need to control every meeting. Indeed, there is a case for moving the chairing role around the team so that others can get experience in developing the key roles that teams need in order to be successful. Such tests as the Belbin test may make it easier for people to discover which their strong roles are. The obverse side of that is that it shows also an individual which roles they are less successful at and need cover for in team events, or in which they need to develop more (Belbin, 1980).

These interactive processes acknowledge the usefulness and appropriateness of a personal and personable approach to people both during the selection process and during induction training. The best teachers are those who have experienced failure or struggled to get on themselves and know what it is to wrestle with learning difficulties.

BOX 6.17

An academic applied for a post and was invited to make a presentation at a stated time.

When he arrived there were no directions, no parking and no indication as to where exactly the room was. He asked the way at different reception areas and was eventually directed up three flights of stairs. He had driven for over two hours, could have done with a drink and a comfort break. A door in front of him opened and a member of staff appeared and said, 'Ah, there you are. Just in time. Come in and get started.'

So, he did. At the end of his presentation he was subjected to intensive questioning critical of his work and told by one staff member that 'writing books was a waste of time' (he had just had one published himself).

He decided not to go back for the interview but then changed his mind and went. He was greeted at the door by a colleague from a previous university who had obviously been speaking to the interview panel about him. The experience of the interview was thoroughly enjoyable and he decided to stay.

First impressions count for a lot with people who have only their own intuition to go on when applying for a job. Good presentation applies not just to job applicants but to organizations, too.

References and further reading

Alvesson, M. and Willmott, H. (1992) On the idea of emancipation in management and organization studies. *Academy of Management Review*, 17: 432–464.

Becker, B., Huselid, M. and Ulrich, D. (2001) *The HR Scorecard: Linking people, strategy and performance*. Boston, MA: Harvard Business School Press.

Belbin, M. (1980) *Management Teams: Why they succeed or fail*. Oxford: Butterworth Heinemann.

Bowman, G., Mackay, R.B., Masrani, S. and McKiernan, P. (2013) Story telling and the scenario process: Understanding success and failure. *Technology Forecasting and Social Change*, 80(4): 735–748.

Boxall, P. and Purcell, J. (2003) *Strategy and Human Resource Management*. Basingstoke: Palgrave Macmillan.

Bulla, D.N. and Scott, P.M. (1994) Manpower requirements forecasting: A case example, in D. Ward, T.P. Bechet and R. Tripp (eds) *Human Resource Forecasting and Modelling*, The Human Resource Planning Society: New York.

Capelli, P. and Neumark, D. (2001) Do high performance work practices improve establishment level outcomes? *Industrial and Labour Relations Review*, 54(4): 737–775.

Deal, T.E and Kennedy, A.A. (1982) *Corporate Cultures: The Rites and Rituals of Corporate Life*. Reading, MA: Addison-Wesley.

Guest, D.E. (1997) Human resource management and performance: A review and research agenda. *International Journal of Human Research Management*, 8(3): 263–276.

Handy, C. (1989) *The Age of Unreason*. London: Century Hutchinson.

Kristof, A.L. (1996) Person–organization fit: An integrative review of its conceptualizations, measurement, and implications. *Personnel Psychology*, 49(1): 1–49.

Lavelle, J. (2007) On workforce architecture, employment relationships and lifecycles: Expanding the purview of workforce planning and management. *Public Personnel Management*, 36(4): 371–384.

Purcell, J. (2004) Business strategies and Human Resource Management: Uneasy bedfellows or strategic partners? Working paper presented at the International Seminar on HRM: What's Next? June, Erasmus University, Rotterdam.

Rothwell, S. (1995) Human resource planning, in Storey, J. (ed.), *Human Resource Management: A critical text*. London: Routledge, pp.167–202.

Sisson, K. and Storey, J. (2000) *The Realities of Human Resource Management*. Buckingham: Open University.

Stewart, R. (1991) *Managing Today and Tomorrow*. Basingstoke: Macmillan.

Storey, J. and Sisson, K. (1993) *Managing Human Resources and Industrial Relations*. Buckingham: Open University Press.

Taylor, S. (2008) *Employee Resourcing*. London: IPD.

Toplis, J., Dulewicz, V. and Fletcher, C. (2004) *Psychological Testing: A manager's guide*. London: CIPD.

Torrington, D., Hall, L., Taylor, S. and Atkinson, C. (2009) *Fundamentals of Human Resource Management*. Harlow: Pearson Education.

Willcocks, L. and Grint, K. (1997) Reinventing the organization? Towards a critique of business process organization, in I. McLoughlin and M. Harris (eds), *Organizational Change and Technology*. London: ICP, pp. 87–110.

GRADUATE ATTRIBUTES

At the end of this exercise you will have addressed the following graduate attributes:

- a capacity for problem identification, the collection of evidence, synthesis and dispassionate analysis;
- an awareness and appreciation of ethical and moral issues.

Ethical problems

Please read the following piece. At different points in the narrative you will be asked to stop and answer questions. Please make notes so that you can contribute to a discussion.

One thing that is self-evident in the modern business world is that all organizations require skilled employees. In this world HR professionals devote much of their time and energy to the task of providing skilled resources to organizations. This means time focused on recruiting, developing, paying for and retaining these skilled employees. With so much time and energy being spent on this area it would be only logical to assume that everyone perceives skill as a positive thing, something to be developed and exploited as much as possible. However, reality isn't like that. Skill has a value and thus some people will seek to restrict it, or restrict access to it.

The majority of organizations will attempt to act to prevent injustice. In most organizations this will take the form of the creation of systems that are designed to ensure fairness. These tend to be systems such as competency and performance management models. However, there is an element of danger related to such systems: they may create false objectivity and mask political behaviours in the organization. It is possible that such behaviours will lead to unspoken practices that subvert organizational value and contentment in the workplace.

Political behaviours that can be envisioned would include: skills monopolies; managers who ensure their favourites get promoted; employees who do nothing to help others up the career ladder; and inadequate job handovers. Examples such as these may assist HR professionals in identifying the signs of skill restriction so that they may take action to reduce the negative consequences.

Questions:

- **Why do personal considerations sometimes overtake the institutional benefits of identifying the best candidates?**
- **How can HR procedures identify value-added more clearly?**
- **Can 'office politics' be challenged successfully?**

Case study 1: skills monopolies

It is a very common occurrence in professional organizations to require candidates for membership to pass exams. While one can see the logic behind this, it is worth looking more closely at the fact that some of these professional organizations require their candidates to pass all their exams in one sitting. If we consider one of the most fundamental economic theories, that of supply and demand, it is clear that restricting the flow of qualified people will result in higher fees for those who are qualified. It can be argued that some of the old forms of apprenticeships amounted to very little more than programmes designed to restrict the number of skilled workers on the market.

One thing is certain and that is there are skill restrictions on a local scale in many organizations. One example reported in the literature was somewhat ironically in a training department. In this department a group of individuals labelled themselves as *The Facilitators* while the rest of the team were considered simply trainers. The Facilitators utilized their elevated status to give themselves the exclusive right to present the prestigious residential courses that the department offered.

The Facilitators believed that their level of self-awareness, a claim that is suspect when you consider the fact that we are unaware of our own blind spots while finding it easy to spot lack of awareness in others, granted them this elevated status.

The manager of the training department took at face value the views of the senior team members that they had this particular trait and the ability to assess it in others.

Questions:

- **Why would professionals seek to restrict access to their special position?**
- **Under what circumstances might restriction of candidates be justified?**
- **Why would the responsible manager not challenge this restriction?**

What we can see clearly in the case of the Facilitators are two characteristics of skills monopolies. The first of these is that of the group holding the monopoly will protect that monopoly through either a tangible but hard-to-achieve qualification or by reference to an abstract quality that they claim to possess. The second is that managers do not want to believe such behaviour can happen in their teams. It is common that when managers are challenged about skills monopoly behaviour, they begin by dismissing the suggestion, but it can happen anywhere and HR professionals must be alert to it.

While not stated in the Facilitators example there is a third characteristic of skills monopolies which is that the supply of the skill is not really limited. Indeed, there would be no need for those deemed skilled to restrict those not deemed skilled if they really were unable to do the projected work. What rather is occurring is that it is the recognition of the skill in others that is being restricted.

It is this third characteristic that causes the most harm to organizations. It means that people who are perfectly capable of doing the higher value work are prevented from doing it and either become trapped in lower status jobs or leave the organization.

Questions:

- **What strategies might HR deploy to overcome restriction of skills?**
- **How might HR appeal to the manager to recognize the problem?**
- **What joint strategy might HR and the manager embark on to change access to those who are restricted in this way?**

Case study 2: protégé path

It is a simple truth that in general managers like to see their own people do well. However, we must also keep in mind that some managers will have favourites that they like to see do particularly well. It is this which brings us to the concept of protégé path clearing, in which a manager eases the way for his or her favourite.

While there is certainly nothing wrong with managers coaching or supporting an employee, in fact it is quite laudable, it becomes dysfunctional if the manager, intentionally or unintentionally, blocks the careers of rivals in order to clear a path for the protégé.

We can imagine a situation in which at a meeting three senior managers are gathered to discuss future roles in the organization. Each of the three feels that their deputy is capable of taking on a more responsible role but when a candidate from outside any of the three managers' teams is suggested as having the potential for promotion they are dismissed as not a strong enough candidate. The candidate's career is curtailed simply due to a conversation between the three. No feedback is given as to the reason for the perceived lack of potential. The candidate remains unaware that the opportunity for further progression is gone.

Of the managers' deputies, whose path had been cleared of a rival, one went on to succeed in a senior post. Perhaps they would have done so anyway but we can never be sure. The others received promotion to a senior role but could not deliver. They did not benefit from having their way cleared. The organization that had to pay them off did not benefit. The person passed over for promotion did not benefit. The organization failed to see that anything wrong had been done.

Questions:

- **How might HR reinforce the message of interference costs?**
- **Where would be the best forum to advertise comparative interference costs?**
- **Who should then take up the responsibility for seeing that this situation is rectified?**

Case study 3: pulling up the ladder

Internal politics can produce some odd effects. Take as an example what can happen when someone manages to break through the glass ceiling but ignores the help they have received on the way and does nothing to reach out and offer help to those still struggling to breach the barrier. What is happening here? It is difficult to know what motivates individuals. In some instances, it may be down to lack of awareness or a disinclination to help others.

What we shouldn't ignore as a possible motivation for this behaviour is that it may in fact be a deliberate attempt to keep potential rivals at bay. Whatever the motive, HR professionals need to be watchful for anyone being constrained. As with skills monopolies, if good people sense their progress is being stunted, they either leave or give up, and could be forgiven for turning in no better performance than is required to keep their job.

Questions:

- **How can the ceiling smasher be used as a role model for those following on?**
- **How can HR reinforce this role?**
- **How can managers become involved in such a developmental role?**

Case study 4: the hurried handover

Another form of skill restriction can happen when someone hands over their job to a successor. While it is true that some people will go to great lengths to ensure a successful job handover there are others who tend to be more sparing. Commonly, this takes the form of giving only the sparsest information to the new role recipient and then becoming busy with other things.

Even when such individuals actually remain within the same organization they become uncommunicative. Phone calls and emails typically remain unanswered. It may be the case that the former occupier of the post simply has no interest in seeing their successor do well. If your successor does a better job than you, what does that say about you?

How you answer the question above will unconsciously influence the depth of knowledge at the handover you provide. While some people are genuinely pleased to see others build on the successes that they have achieved, others resent it. Such people wish their achievements to be the pinnacle of achievement rather than a staging post for others to move further on from.

Questions:

- **How can HR encourage a fair handover between office holders?**
- **Can a development programme be put in place that involves significant parties to the transition?**
- **Should non-cooperators be held accountable?**

Ethics and values have become an increasingly important part of most organizations today. Understandably no organization likes to admit that their organization harbours people who engage in unfair practices and the majority will create systems that are designed to promote fairness. Therein may lie the problem – the very systems designed to address the problem can have unfairness embedded within them.

What we see most frequently in these cases is false objectivity. If we look at the concept of the competency-based grade definition, this is an excellent tool if everyone is doing the job described by the competency model. We must also ask the question, how precise are the definitions anyway? Competency descriptions are open to interpretation. No one can apply a competency description unaffected by their prior view of the person being assessed. We need to recognize this. Decisions based on 'office politics' are easily dressed up as being objective and fair.

Questions:

- **How might a fair system based on competencies be set up?**
- **How can it be consistently applied?**
- **When are there justified exceptions to the competency system?**
- **How can HR ensure that there is flexibility in the selection process?**

- **How can organizations encourage ethics and values in the face of competition in the global marketplace?**

Resources are in a strong position to identify and disrupt these subversive practices. It can act to support stated values and bring an improved level of fairness. Imagine a situation at a *calibration meeting* in which a pool of consultants is discussed to ensure they had the right relative performance assessments. While one consultant is discussed, a manager voices an opinion that they had not done well in some aspect of their work. Unless feedback has been given to the individual concerned the HR manager should ensure that it is not raised in the meeting. There should be no critical comments that have not first been discussed with the person concerned. A rule such as this should be the foundation to any ethical policy for people management. Those seeking to clear a path are forced to justify their denigrations of those they fear will rival their favourites. Those seeking to control recognition of a skill are forced to be open about what they are doing. The rule shines a light on potentially dark practices.

Questions:

- **Are there any situations where the rule of not mentioning key information should be waived?**
- **When should HR probe restrictive practices in selection?**
- **How can policy, procedure and practice be changed to take account of restrictive practices to selection of candidates in the organization?**

Three more ways in which HR professionals can challenge skills restrictions are:

1   It is vital for any HR professional to challenge systems and processes and especially those they own, such as the appraisal and promotions systems. They need to ensure that they are not applied outside their intended application, or are treated as somehow objective when they are not. HR professionals should not pretend that objectivity is possible when applying the assessment processes.

Questions:

- **How can laid down procedures be challenged by those that use them?**
- **How far can discretion to alter procedures or systems of selection be allowed?**
- **How can a manager compensate advantages or disadvantages in the selection procedure?**

2   HR professionals must challenge people:

If a manager suggests his deputy is the best candidate for promotion, challenge for evidence of the specific results the deputy has delivered. Probe beyond the general and the vague. If a manager suggests someone is not ready for a more senior role, first, challenge them for specific first-hand evidence for that assessment; second, challenge them to discuss it with the person concerned. They may prefer not to, in which case they should withdraw their assessment.

Questions:

- **Who has the right to challenge a manager/chair in a selection meeting?**
- **Should a manager declare an interest when his/her deputy is being discussed for promotion?**
- **Should HR chair such discussions to ensure objective assessment is made of all candidates?**

3   HR professionals must challenge themselves:

While it is very tempting to stick your head in the sand and think 'this kind of thing goes on but not where I work', HR professionals cannot simply turn a blind eye just because they may not like what they see. It is a major challenge for all HR professionals to recognize that they may have been party, wittingly or unwittingly, to skill restriction. While this may be a hard thing to have to acknowledge, the other choice is dismissing the possibility of ever putting things right.

Despite the best intentions of HR professionals and the systems and processes they create, unfairness is widespread. Usually the motivation is at an unconscious level. We are all very good at convincing ourselves that what we do to serve our own needs is actually done in the organization's best interests. These unconscious needs vary from a wish to protect high status work to meeting a personal need to be seen as someone who is exceptional in some way. But these actions damage both the people and the organizations. All our competency models and appraisal schemes are not enough: we need to look beyond them to what is really going on, and challenge anything that does not look right.

Questions:

- **Bias is likely in all human judgements. How can it be moderated?**
- **Is HR the watchdog of human rights and fairness in the organization?**
- **How far can individual judgements based on likes be accommodated in the selection process?**

Tutor guidance

HR can be seen as a series of functions within the organization that seeks to influence the interventions managers make in their staff's working lives. Getting it right means carefully drawing up policies and procedures which managers are then supported in achieving correctly.

Less often are the issues of custom and practice brought to the fore and perhaps only when there is an issue that requires addressing formally, such as a grievance interview or a complaint, is possible discrimination during the selection process addressed.

Changing a culture is a long process that takes place incrementally. It requires HR professionals to be alert to the problems to which the way we do things around here can give rise. It also needs moral courage to challenge managers who may be less than pleased to hear that their management style is under question and could lead to strained relationships in the workplace.

The syndicate discussions should focus on this aspect of the politics of recruitment which is not always addressed in the text books. Each of the examples merits a question on how the HR department should intervene to change the culture of management which, wittingly or unwittingly, supports these poor practices.

The final questions invite the discussion of the role of HR as the conscience of the organization and the balance they need to strike between the different parties working together in the organization.

7

DEVELOPING YOUR PEOPLE

Topics

- identifying competencies and training needs
- systematic training cycle and learning objectives
- training methods validation and evaluation
- the learning organization and HR strategies.

Introduction

Training is an important investment

Training is an important investment for all companies. We have already seen that UK companies have not always made that investment as well as their competitors have (Handy, 1987; Constable and McCormick, 1987). Peter Drucker once famously said: 'If you think training's expensive, try ignorance' and yet most people will be aware of the parsimonious approach that governs most training – even the most expensive.

BOX 7.1

In the UK, flying training is expensive and is charged by the hour. Prior to the hour's flying there should be a briefing session in the classroom explaining to the trainee what the instructor intends to cover during the flying session. After landing, the practical flying should be followed by a debriefing session, again in the classroom, explaining what was achieved or what still needs to be practised.

Needless to say, often the previous flying session runs late, the plane lands and the instructor sends the next trainee out to check the plane while having a quick word with the previous student. So the briefing and debriefing sessions are more honoured in the breech than the observance.

In the USA flying training is cheaper and many methods of briefing and debriefing are available – books, videos, DVDs, syndicate groups with other students. Most trainees find this both more flexible and adaptable to their own personal learning preferences

People will remember the way they were treated during their training

There are many trainers who are good at what they do, but have no sympathy with those who find they are struggling to understand something or need extra practice before they become familiar with new knowledge and skills development. *Training for trainers* is an important investment because people learn in different ways, and at different speeds.

BOX 7.2

Most people will have experienced IT training in which there is a classroom full of computers and a trainer at the front of the room. Different functions of a piece of software are demonstrated at the front by the trainer and then the trainees are expected to follow through on their own machine.

Questions are best dealt with one to one. But how does one trainer deal with 12 people, all of whom have different problems or difficulties? Fleeting contact with several people may be more frustrating than enlightening for the trainees.

One-to-one training is expensive. But it may be the only way that people get the time to ask questions, learn by their mistakes and practise until they feel confident to carry on confidently unsupervised. Training budgets will be tight in any organization. But the teacher–pupil ratio remains critical to all learning sectors. In the best universities, for example, that ratio can be as low as 1:4. In more modest HE institutions it may be nearer 1:16 – which means that some tutorial groups contain perhaps 20 students. The chances are that such numbers constrain open discussion and make it difficult for the tutor to gauge whether everyone has engaged with the learning points.

Blue chip companies are usually renowned for their good training of new recruits to the company. Sitting next to Nellie or learning 'on the road' may be useful introductions to those with experience and a realistic appraisal of what the company does in the field. However, it can be light on threshold knowledge – what the good practitioner needs to know to support a consistent and careful performance that offers an insight into not only what we do, but why we do it that way.

Well-trained staff stand out from their less well-trained competitors, who try their best, but are found to be lacking foundation knowledge or enhanced skills. Coping with emergencies; coping with difficult customers; solving problems for clients; all these are areas that may occur infrequently, and therefore require more frequent practice to get right (Hunt and Baruch, 2003).

BOX 7.3

Every pilot is expected to be able to land the plane in the event of a power failure. Setting the plane into the glide, designating a landing spot, and then gently gliding down using the flaps should bring the plane to the landing spot without risk.

Needless to say, this technique is practised frequently, simulated on the test (rather like the emergency stop on a car test). The examiner just turns off the power without warning and watches the trainee pilot undertake the correct manoeuvre, switching the power back on once the final approach has been made.

Pilots who have been away from the flight deck for more than a month are tested in this exercise before being allowed back onto the flight deck.

Our safety as passengers depends on them getting it right first time – and practice makes perfect.

Determining the training need

What is the trainee's threshold knowledge?

We start as trainers with an obvious question, but one that is often taken for granted: what do trainees know already? All of us have been to training sessions where the trainer begins by making a statement such as, 'I am sure you all know the Highway Code, don't you?' Rather than look silly in front of a group of strangers, we might be tempted just to say, 'Yes'. But what does the trainer know about how much we really know (sometimes referred to as threshold knowledge)? Good training begins with asking questions and listening. 'Tell me what you know about the Highway Code' would have been a better question to begin with. That way the trainer will trigger either some information or perhaps none and be able to draw his or her own conclusions about what the trainees know already (their threshold knowledge).

What do they know about the job already?

The statement, 'I used to work for GEC', may or may not be significant and requires further probing. What were they doing in GEC, and what were their results? Is this previous knowledge relevant or not to the present job they are to undertake? Perhaps it would be worthwhile asking the trainee to demonstrate this knowledge or skill in an appropriate way. In this way we have covered the four factors of a qualifying interview (finding out about the other person):

- *P* – probe
- *L* – listen
- *O* – observe
- *D* – decide.

We can then begin to answer the following questions.

How relevant are their qualifications?

This is always a difficult factor to discover and has taxed managers and recruiters over the years. Qualifications directly related to the job may, indeed, be a statutory requirement. In this case there is no option but to make it a requirement for applicants. But how relevant are they to the training being undertaken? Graduates may be no better at undertaking training outside their area of expertise than are non-graduate applicants. The kind of education they received may not be vocationally related to the job they are being trained in. So, they may have no inherent advantages over those who have not enjoyed the same start in life that graduates receive.

What level of experience do they have?

This may be a fairer indication of aptitude and ability than qualification alone. At one time recruiters used to stipulate the number of years of experience that they were looking for. That was legally challenged some years ago and is now no longer used to assess applicants for jobs, on the grounds that the specified requirement of five years' experience could be challenged by someone with only four year's experience claiming that he or she could well have the requisite experience. Numbers used in this way can be arbitrary and subjective. And yet experience can demonstrate some measure of ability and, if tested accurately, may be a significant indicator of job aptitude.

Are there areas that will need to be addressed: company products/company procedures and practices?

Even practised professionals will need time to get used to individual differences between companies they have joined. Perhaps this is where being teamed with more experienced colleagues can be an advantage. Knowledge of procedures is one thing that may be possible to learn online or from a text book. But, application to client need often requires a more experienced colleague who can give advice.

Are we making assumptions?

Experienced managers can easily be assumed to have requisite experience and knowledge already. The question is worth asking: where is the evidence that could support claims made about previous knowledge and experience and how could it be acquired? Certainly, experience can be attested by previous employers. But is the previous experience relevant to the candidate's suitability for the new challenge?

How will the candidate be expected to mobilize job knowledge?

Functional flexibility has already been emphasized as a frequent requirement in modern employment. Knowledge on its own needs to be mobilized by skills, which are sometimes assumed in those who have been professionally trained. However, being good at learning complex or difficult systems of knowledge does not guarantee that the requisite communication skills are there to support them. So, it is worth asking what we require the job applicant to be able to do with the knowledge they have acquired. If customer handling is part of the job, selling and negotiation skills, or coaching or counselling skills may well be needed to mobilize their professional knowledge. Such areas need to be specifically addressed in training (Boyatzis, 1982).

BOX 7.4

In past times, doctors were assumed to have acquired enough professional training to be able to cope with the communicational aspects of their job. So, telling people the implications of the illnesses they had was assumed to be something they could take in their stride.

More recently such assumptions were replaced by proper training in the skills of counselling people with serious or life-threatening illnesses.

These are not easy skills to acquire but training does help professionals cope with such difficult situations.

Skills and shortages gap

Technical and practical skills

There are few jobs that do not depend on key business skills. In fact we might say that the traditional divisions between high-tech and lesser skilled jobs are becoming narrower. This would suggest that Handy's predictions about the rising number of knowledge workers was not exaggerated. Knowledge workers, such as consultants, need to be well grounded in the skills that make them effective in the businesses they seek to serve (Handy, 1989).

Communication skills, customer handling skills, teamworking and problem solving skills

There are few jobs in business that do not require communication skills. Public speaking; interaction with clients; interaction with colleagues; and addressing problem-solving are all necessary prerequisites in most customer-facing jobs today. Functional flexibility requires people who have been trained in these areas. Work experience is complemented by effective training.

Opportunities to gain requisite skills training

Statistics vary on the lack of skills and disinclination of organizations to embark on requisite skills training. As we have noted, in the UK less has traditionally been spent by employers on staff training than by our competitors. We might also note that training provision such as apprenticeships have become less well supported both by employers and by government.

Organizations that are profit-focused are often looking to achieve more with less (fewer resources; fewer people; and less investment). This may lead to the search for trained people from other organizations and diminishes the likelihood that training provision will be realistically addressed. However, when good training is made accessible and affordable there never seems to be any lack of people keen to take advantage of it. We have only to look at such new institutions as the Open University to see evidence of this search for development in distance learning to cope with increasing demand for learning and development.

TABLE 7.1 NVQ SVQ frameworks

Level	Description
Level 1	Competencies that involve the application of knowledge in a range of routine tasks
Level 2	Competence that involves the application of knowledge in non-routine tasks
Level 3	Levels 1 and 2 together with responsibility and control and guidance of others
Level 4	As above but with autonomy and responsibility for people and resources
Level 5	All of the above plus management review and evaluation

Source: QCA (2008).

Finally, the claim that managers have little interest or skill in coaching their staff may be a function not of unwillingness on their part, but of the excessive hours that managers are required to work in the UK. Training and development require time: time to take thought; time to consider options; time to devise workable strategies together. As we have seen above, managers are not trainers, necessarily, but with training they can be very effective in bringing on other team members.

Management competencies

As we can see from Table 7.1, the National Vocational Qualification levels have been laid out and applied to all the competencies defined as applying to management. They were originally developed and adopted by government during the 1990s. It should be said that, in spite of allowing and encouraging staff and managers to keep a portfolio of what they do at work to demonstrate management competencies achieved, the take-up of such work-based learning has not taken root as was hoped.

In part this may be because there is little time for managers to develop themselves or their staff at work. It may also be that the validation of the scheme is dependent on written evidence duly attested by internal and external validation, and that time for such recording exercises is just not available. What should be clear, however, is that developing professionalism in management competencies is vital to the development of people at work. Involving managers in training and its evaluation is obviously important and this can be complemented by external trainers where necessary (Carroll and Gillen, 2001).

Investors in people

One of the initiatives that government introduced in the early 1990s was the accreditation of employers who made significant systematic investment in their people's training and development.

Its purpose was to develop strategies to improve the performance of organizations by demonstrating the link between enhanced knowledge and skill and the value-added that trained people could offer to the business as a result of the training.

The idea of IiP (Investors in People) was based on identifying the training need in the organization and linking it to the overall needs of the business; then defining the training required by individuals and allocating funding to ensure that the requisite training was carried out. All that remained was evaluation of the contribution made by the newly acquired competences to the required business effectiveness and checking that the requisite improvement had occurred.

This process reinforces *strategic integration* using investment in training as a vehicle. It is a variation on management by objectives. It includes *evaluation* – something that traditional training had not always focused on in the past. Training is usually validated, often by testing, examination or demonstration. But it has less often been evaluated by seeking to measure organizational outcomes.

BOX 7.5

Universities are good at validating students' work progress. There is usually a system of double marking within the university after which selected texts (usually critical borderline marks, together with all fails and distinctions) are sent to the external examiner in another university.

Were universities to embark seriously on evaluation, they would need to contact all students after, say, three years asking them whether anything they had been taught had been useful to them at work or in their lives more generally.

Systematic Training Cycle

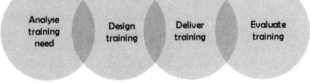

FIGURE 7.1 Systematic training cycle.

Source: Adapted from Gilmore and Williams (2009: 126).

Analysing a training need begins the series of successive steps intended to address efficiency and effectiveness through enhancing what people know and what they do in their jobs (Figure 7.1). So, traditionally training can address three of the four headings of the personnel profile:

- knowledge
- skill
- experience
- attitude.

Training events can enhance *knowledge* and develop *skill* so that both of these are consolidated by *experience* – based on the assumption that the more you practise, the better it goes.

What training cannot address directly is *attitude*, which is largely a function of commitment and aptitude. We will be looking at how attitude can be influenced when we consider the role of *development* later in the chapter.

Learning objectives

We can most easily illustrate the development of learning objectives by looking at an example. Let us assume that we want to devise a standard induction training course in selling. Our objective is to:

- *list out what the trainee sales person will be able to do at the end of the training session (these are sometimes referred to as learning objectives).*

In order to do this we identify the steps involved in what is sometimes referred to as a sales cycle, and they could be listed as:

1 conduct a qualifying sales interview;
2 present the product or service to the sales prospect;
3 put together and explain a proposal/estimate for the prospect;
4 conduct a negotiation;
5 close the sale successfully;
6 handle concerns and objections.

Each of the units of this competency can be broken down into their separate elements. So in the case of the first unit:

Conduct a qualifying sales interview, the elements are as follows:

1 introduce yourself to the client;
2 identify the client's role and budgetary responsibilities;
3 identify current usage of product/service;
4 explore their likes and dislikes of their current usage;
5 identify expected standards;
6 summarise and close, gaining commitment for step two.

Training methods

Most training requires both an element of underpinning knowledge and a level of skill to communicate that knowledge.

Theoretical knowledge may require formal, classroom style instructional technique, laid out in a way that interests the trainees and gives examples and exercises of theory in practice. Stories based on experience can be useful to trainees and are enhanced by trainers who are experienced and knowledgeable in the subjects they instruct in.

Skills development is usually hands-on and experiential. Role-play and filming of activities provide a useful opportunity to exercise the skills in the likely scenarios to be faced in business. Video recording can be used to capture the performance of those involved and allow group and tutor comment and feedback on what has been achieved.

Validation of theory and practice may involve exams, tests and real-life performance. The only stipulation is that it must reproduce realistically the situation that the trainees are likely to face in the work role they will need to undertake (Honey and Mumford, 1989).

Validating the training

At the end of each module a test regime should be set up (always test in the way that the knowledge/skill will need to be demonstrated in the field)

In the case of the training above these might include:

- answering questions about the features of the product/service;
- demonstrating how to handle concerns and objections;
- asking probing questions to extend knowledge of customer need;
- responding to customer signals during negotiation;
- working out what the range of a negotiation should be;
- using appropriate closing techniques at critical stages of the negotiation.

Checking that a performance can be achieved is essential for validating training. However, it is not the whole story. Putting theory into practice in real life is another step for trainees to take and another technique that is referred to as *evaluation* (Hamblin, 1974).

Evaluation

The important thing to remember about evaluation is that it concerns *effectiveness*. This can include asking the end-user whether they have noticed any difference in performance before and after the training initiative. What impression is the organization now giving and how is that enhancing our business outcomes? Are we actually making more sales as a result of the sales training conducted? It does not have to be in monetary terms. It can also be customer satisfaction – do customers notice any difference? If there was a problem with wastage or error rates, are these now reducing over a significant period since the training was completed? If accidents at work were a problem, has the accident rate now gone down since the training? If staff turnover or intermittent absence was on the increase, has it now reduced following the training? In fact, all the organizational outcomes that Guest illustrates in his diagram of HRM theory should show a measurable change following successful training. The search for value-added should begin with the customer or end-user. If they noticed no difference then at least we know that although efficiency may have improved, effectiveness still needs to be addressed (Watad and Ospina, 1999).

The evidence that training has been effective can also establish the reduction in interference costs. This reinforces in the minds of senior managers and board members that HR plays a valuable role for the bottom line of the company.

TABLE 7.2 Training evaluation levels

Level of evaluation	Evaluation question	Evaluation method	Staff involved
Reaction level	What has the individual learned?	Log book/diary Questionnaire Discussion	Trainer Trainees Senior managers
Learning level	What has the group learned?	Testing (exam) Role play/simulations Validation at work	Trainer Senior managers External assessors
Job behaviour	How has job performance been affected?	Challenges Special projects 360-degree appraisal	Trainee Supervisor/manager Colleagues Customers
Organization department	What has been the impact on organizational performance?	Fewer customer complaints Increased productivity Fewer cost–benefit analyses	Departmental team Senior managers Training manager and HR team Board/stakeholders

Source: Adapted from training evaluation levels (Gilmore and Williams, 2009: 130).

Extending the scope of evaluation can involve several levels of research (Table 7.2).

The *reaction level* is most often visited by trainers at the end of their courses. Participants are invited to complete a sheet of comments on the course and return it to the organization.

The *learning level* can involve outside assessors such as mystery shoppers or even applicants sent by an agency to apply for jobs. Both can assess competence and commitment of newly trained staff who remain unaware that they are being observed.

With *job behaviour* the appraisal and its implications for development are addressed. For supervisors and new managers it may be worthwhile getting subordinates as well as managers involved, using, say, 360-degree appraisal. Some input from the trainer(s) can also be useful in outlining what was achieved on the course and indicating where development could most usefully be applied, though again this is less often done where external trainers are employed (Fletcher, 2007).

Team and department involvement can lead to an overall assessment of benefits to the organization. In the retail sector, staff training is sometimes more honoured in the breech than the observance. Some feedback from staff on whether this training has improved since the training would be a useful indicator that newly acquired skills are being used to the benefit of the staff in the store. Once again this can be a useful comparator for HR to use at senior management meetings.

The *organizational level* includes hard HRM: assessment of cost–benefit of the training to the company. It may also identify particular areas in the business that are in further need of training support and development. Keeping interest alive in training initiatives needs support from the senior levels of management. So, feedback and discussion should be a permanent item on their agenda (Pichet *et al.*, 1993).

The learning organization

This term became popular in the 1990s, pioneered by Peter Senge (1990). His idea was that learning should be a corporate endeavour involving everybody in the organization. A similar earlier attempt at learning in the workplace was kaizen in Japanese factories, which was introduced prior to Senge's work. In one sense such team feedback was intended to encourage members of quality circles to share their knowledge of ways of increasing efficiency in production areas with colleagues in other quality circles. That might include new tips for saving time in processes; making available to those who are less skilled or experienced the tacit knowledge that workers acquire as they become more skilled and experienced (Cunningham, 2007).

Centred on the process of learning at work

Learning is an individual endeavour. But, it can be facilitated by coaching from fellow workers more experienced or qualified in the working processes. As the number of knowledge workers has increased in the workplace, the effort to capture the essence of what they do and pass it on to others less experienced has been a constant search in most organizations.

Some initiatives to capture the knowledge and expertise of workers have been set up within organizations. Some of them have been informal groups in which individuals are encouraged to share their tacit knowledge (McKinlay, 2002). However, such initiatives are not always as successful as it was thought they would be. Professional knowledge can sometimes be closely guarded by individuals whose work depends on it. Professional boundaries can be closely defended from attempts to acquire the knowledge by outsiders (Nicolini *et al.*, 2008).

Focus on what people learn at work and how they pass this on to other people

Those more likely to share tacit knowledge are teams whose joint efforts are required for success. As we shall see, profit related pay applied to teams is more likely to encourage such sharing than performance related pay – which can too often be awarded to a few successful individuals at work (Fletcher, 1993).

All of these efforts to share knowledge can be encouraged through coaching, mentoring and shadowing. These initiatives are intended to offer development opportunities using more skilled and experienced individuals or team members.

BOX 7.6

In the early 1990s the Scottish Police College set up a mentoring programme for their Accelerated Promotion Path candidates. These were graduate entrants to the police service who were destined to move from substantive sergeant to inspector within seven years.

They were given a mentor, a superintendent, to whom they had access and were encouraged to meet with regularly to discuss their career progression in the police service.

Rather like the Open University, a student will have many course tutors as they study different modules for their degree. However, they will have one tutor counsellor who oversees the whole of their time with the university and is therefore knowledgeable and aware of difficulties encountered during their time with the university.

The mentor provides that kind of continuity for those on an accelerated promotion path.

Experience of knowledge sharing is crucial to R&D and innovative, creative working teams. Brainstorming can encourage individuals starting with the team to hear ideas from more experienced members and gain confidence to contribute ideas themselves. Such group sessions can be highly useful not just in generating ideas at the outset of organizational projects, but also in gaining feedback throughout the systematic training cycle. Evaluation does not need to be confined just to the end of the cycle. As Bullock and Batten (1985) indicated in their phases of change, the phase of evaluation can be extended throughout the change process so that what is learned in one group can be readily shared with others going through the same steps of the change at a different time or location (Clutterbuck, 1992).

Loop learning

Two authors have done much to encourage managers and trainers to think about the implications of what they are achieving through the individual for the organization. They are Argyris and Schon (1974). Since 1974 they have developed the idea of single, double and triple loop learning that engages people in different levels of learning and increases their involvement with the organization's strategic objectives.

Single loop learning is the method by which individuals are frequently inducted into a job. This is often associated with instructional techniques that involve being told or shown what to do. A good example of this in school days would be learning the times tables, often by rote. Pilots are still taught all basic manoeuvres using mnemonics. For example, prior to landing every pilot is taught to do the BUMFICHH checks:

- *B* – brakes off
- *U* – undercarriage down
- *M* – mixture (fuel) too rich
- *F* – on and sufficient
- *I* – indicators: reset altimeter to field height; check radio frequency is correct
- *C* – carburettor heat on
- *H* – hatches closed and secured
- *H* – harnesses on and fully secured

Such mnemonics learned by heart reinforce the correct procedure to follow preceding a landing (communications from air traffic control; navigation – are we in the right place; count visually number of planes ahead of you; adjust engine for speed levels; lower flaps progressively at the right time). It is easy to miss out a step and rote learning of easily remembered checklists repeated between the pilots on the flight deck can reinforce safety.

It is sometimes said of shop-floor and checkout supervisors in the retail sector that they need to acquire two main skills:

1   diagnose and put right problems;
2   explain the system to other people (staff and customers).

Both of these skills are addressed by *double loop learning*. Basically, this level reinforces learning *why* we do things in the way we do – whether that involves operating machinery; changing till rolls; defusing customer–staff problems; dealing with refunds. This knowledge often requires a raft of skills to support it in action. So, here *interactive training* comes into its own: role-plays; examples; filming and replay; feedback to develop the skill and knowledge required. This satisfies the three steps that trainers learn about imparting their knowledge and skills to others:

- I hear – and I forget
- I see – and I remember
- I do – and I understand.

Interactive training can achieve all three levels, because while knowledge or principles can be taught deductively, the supporting skills are taught and tested inductively. This gives the added advantage of developing knowledge and skill together in individuals and reinforcing group learning at the same time. Shared group preparation for interactive skill learning should give added confidence and more insightful feedback to the individual from the group and trainer (Anis *et al.*, 2004).

Triple loop learning

Reviewing management objectives is the final level of learning for the worker fully involved in fulfilling the organization's objectives. Where in the past staff were not encouraged to concern themselves with organizational outcomes now *strategic inte-gration* requires that everyone understands the contribution their work makes to the profitability of the company. *Triple loop learning* can develop this aspect of assess-ment of enhanced understanding in the individual's day-to-day work. This level of learning should engage all workers in the *strategic integration* that Guest features as one of the HR outcomes emerging from good HR practices.

This learning route encourages individuals to embark on continuing learn-ing that can both enhance their career prospects and increase their commitment through *Continuing Professional Development* and their *Personal Development Plan* (Kram and Isabella, 1985).

Organizational learning

There are some authors who suggest that organizational learning is more accurate in describing the learning that goes on within organizations (Easterby-Smith *et al.*, 1999). The learning organization is less specific about how individuals learn in an organization. In this sense learning happens both formally and informally and is often facilitated both wittingly and unwittingly within the *peer group*. The challenge for managers is how to capture the learning that takes place informally at work in order to understand how learning and understanding of work develop and how this can be passed on to others.

So, managers and HR practitioners will continue to strive to create and foster knowledge transfer in the company. But, how they achieve it is by no means as clear as just stating the need. Where once managers had the power of lock-out (preventing workers from accessing their machinery on which they depended to follow their craft), knowledge workers now have the power to leave the organiza-tion, taking with them all that they have learned.

Transmitting innovative knowledge to others will be a continuing challenge that organizations and their managers need to address, thereby retaining the knowledge of their own business and safeguarding themselves from what has on occasion been described as the 'brain drain'. Successful capture, storage and transmission of this knowledge, once achieved, is an essential resource as the focus of the company's intellectual capital – to be stored and passed on in the company to individuals and groups who succeed those currently in post.

Official attempts to get professionals to download tacit knowledge, as we have seen, is constrained by either lack of ability to expound it clearly or by concerns that professional secrets will mean others taking over their jobs. So, professional boundaries are likely to be stoutly defended both by individuals and the group to which they belong (Nicolini *et al.*, 2008). *Communities of practice* require their members to trust each other to keep professional knowledge within the commu-nity, and that community may still guard entry to others in the organization.

The need to develop the requisite knowledge and its contribution to the aims and objectives of the organization will remain important in supporting *strategic integration*. So much so that the proponents of BPR suggest that managers should be renamed so that:

- senior managers become enterprise managers
- middle managers become expertise managers
- first line managers become people and systems managers
- workers become self managers.

(Champy, 1995)

The knowledge required at work is to be applied in a way that acknowledges the need for proactive involvement in the achievement of the organization's objectives.

Managing performance

All of the above might suggest that managers have less control over their workers than might once have been the case. The days when internal promotion meant that every manager had once been an operator and then a supervisor have generally disappeared. Being an enterprise manager means being dependent on expertise managers.

BOX 7.7

A bank in the UK in 2012 was attempting to exchange a software programme on its customers' accounts. Unfortunately, the changeover was unsuccessful and its customers were deprived of access to their money for days, running into a week or more.

The highly paid CEO was interviewed before the TV cameras apologizing profusely to his customers. But when asked why there had been no back-up systems in place seemed unable to respond to the question.

Perhaps the expertise managers in the IT department did not know the answer either.

Technology continues to drive innovation in all industries which is one aspect of the phenomenon sometimes referred to as *globalization*. Multinational providers continue to attempt to dominate the provision of software and hardware to the world, thereby dictating the standards that must be reached before starting a business or becoming a new entrant to a business sector.

Managerialism and *performativity* combine to reinforce efficiency and effectiveness to delight the customer and outmanoeuvre the opposition. In the process, traditional crafts and jobs disappear to become automated or replaced, thereby deskilling their job holders (Braverman, 1974). Initially, this meant the erosion of semi-skilled jobs in car factories (welders being replaced by spot-welding equipment). But soon precision engineering became displaced, too, and the gap between high-tech and low-tech jobs became ever wider.

Alternatively, managing performance is about individuals, groups and organizations achieving organizational objectives as a consequence of their actions. So, their presence may or may not be needed on site. Telecommuting is a feasible option for many workers. And even those who have to travel usually have access to their laptop and therefore to the business to which they can contribute even on the move. So, management is at once more difficult (immediate supervision is more difficult) but also easier. The connected worker can be on call 24/7 (Strother, 2002).

The role that HR can play

So, how does HR play its part in managing performance in the modern organization? It is necessarily part of expertise management and depends on line managers to manage the enterprise. Its role is therefore facilitative rather than directive, and yet it does have responsibility for people, as its title suggests. There are some areas in which HR can contribute to the achievement of Guest's HR outcomes:

First and foremost, *strategic integration*. As we have seen, only about 6 per cent of Boards have a director of HR as one of their members. The unfortunate part of this as far as strategic integration is concerned is that HR, if excluded, is thereby deprived of the opportunity of being party to the formulation of strategy. It is clear that some of the things on which the Board's decisions will impact are precisely the areas for which HR is responsible. New talent to take the company into a new age needs to be recruited and selected, so being a party to the discussion would be a useful investment for HR. Then there is the role of human capital developers. Newly recruited people need relevant induction training, however well they are qualified in their own specialism. Such training means that they become familiar with the company's policy, procedures and practices that much more quickly.

As expertise managers, HR professionals are there to support their managers. One of the key features of HRM theory was the move of what personnel had traditionally done and its transfer to the line manager. Employment law is constantly developing. It is tested in Employment Appeal Tribunals and sometimes courts throughout the country and the implication of those decisions can affect HR policy and procedure in important and significant ways. The HR manager and team are the functional experts in their subject and their knowledge is vital to managers who become involved in HR situations so that they are properly briefed and, if appropriate, accompanied.

Thus far we have talked about managers' involvement in such matters as disciplinary and grievance interviews. But there will be staff involved on the other side of the table and they have rights, too. So, in a sense, we could argue that HR also has a role as employee advocate. This is particularly the case if staff have knowledge of illegal or illicit practices and want to 'blow the whistle' on poor or illegal management practices. Being the conscience of the organization is not an easy role to play, but it is essential if managers are going to be properly appraised of the implication of events as they unfold.

This brings us back to our first point: the HR leader should be at the centre of the organization's life spanning all areas relating to the HRD interventions. There is a moral and practical balance to be struck between all the stakeholders involved in the organization.

High performance work practices

Continuing professional development

For most professional workers there is a *lead body* responsible for training, certifying, commissioning and developing its members. Gone are the days when doctors could expect to practise medicine from the time they qualified until they retired with little in-service training. The difference today is that the lead bodies require evidence on continuing professional development. On that demonstration of progress in their chosen career development depends their continued membership and advancement through the grades to fellowship and beyond.

The CPD programme is therefore a rolling programme of activities chosen by the member to demonstrate how their work has been specifically developed and what targets they have set themselves over a stated period of time. Their portfolio of work is then examined by the lead body and their progress is evaluated for continued membership or development through the membership grades.

' For professional workers, therefore, being involved with projects that enhance their CPD prospects can be a welcome part of their desire to continue working with the company that provides such opportunities. In contrast, professional workers who feel that they are confined to repetitive work with which they are well acquainted may feel that they are lacking the opportunity to get involved in work projects that will enhance their CPD prospects and that therefore their career development is likely to stall.

'Back to the floor' managers

This approach is sometimes adopted by companies whose managers have come up through from the shop floor, but are some years away from the day-to-day practice of what they first did when they joined the company. So, in some retail organizations directors are expected to spend a week on the checkout; shelf stacking; issuing stores; answering customer queries etc.

It is easy for managers to grow nostalgic about how things were when they started in the business. Twenty or so years later, the context of their business can be very different. They need a reality check on what their staff face day to day and this is one way of getting it. Pilots who wish to remain current in their licences also have to undergo a regular number of flying hours each year. Regular check-rides or simulator practice is part of this familiarization process. Managing other professionals requires the credibility governed by regularly keeping up to speed with the latest initiatives. Those who are led appreciate that commitment in their leaders.

Profit sharing

Directors' pay is much in the headlines at the moment. Golden hellos, golden parachutes, golden goodbyes and share options are all expected by those in high places, even when the share prices go down. It is clear that this has given rise to much resentment, not just within companies, but for the public at large who wonder what it is that the great and the good do that justifies these inflationary amounts of money.

For companies such as John Lewis, all staff are shareholders, and therefore share in the proceeds of the company's success. Over and above that, those who have served for 25 years are given a year off on full pay as a thank you for their loyal service. There are few other organizations that have this openness to sharing their success with all those who made it possible. The customer experience is enhanced compared with their competitors.

Performance related pay

All salespeople will expect performance related pay. Indeed, their terms of condition can range from basic plus commission to commission-only salespeople. The difficulty comes when organizations or governments seek to impose similar terms and conditions on workers who have no background or expectation of this at all.

From time to time teachers or nurses are identified as candidates for these kinds of terms and conditions. Discussions will be had about whether teachers who get more children through their exams should get more money and those who do not should be sacked. Nurses who get a higher throughput of patients should be rewarded and those who do not should suffer accordingly with lower rewards.

There are many who will argue that fair comparison is impossible to make between individuals and groups in either hospitals or schools. Not all pupils have the capability of passing academic examinations, just as some patients are destined not to recover but still need caring nursing. Counting artificially imposed successes across time limits is not good for children learning or patients healing, many of whom need more time and effort which is not always rewarded by the pay system based on targets.

BOX 7.8

A CEO who took over a publicly owned housing department was tasked with bringing it into the private sector as a housing association. She called in a management consultant and said, 'I want you to tell these people (her staff) that performance related pay is good for them.'

The consultant explained that this might not necessarily be true. The CEO said, 'I will pay you the going rate.'

The consultant refused to undertake the role prescribed by the CEO.

The consultancy went no further.

Linking HRD practices

Careful/sophisticated recruitment and selection

We have already discussed best fit and best performance approaches to recruitment. Both approaches require careful consideration of where the company's needs lie and who would best answer those needs. As we have noted, finding those people could be the most difficult test for any recruiter to achieve. Not all competent and experienced candidates will necessarily fit in with the ethos or culture of the organization. The famous 'milk round' in which companies look to recruit the best students from the best universities yields on average a turnover rate of 30 per cent before the induction programme is completed, indicating that perceived competence and testing does not always guarantee a good fit with the culture of the organization.

What we could say is that the attempt to expose the candidate to the company's people and culture is something well worth attempting from the outset of their contact with the company. A realistic appraisal of the culture of the organization presented to prospective employees may make a decision before a job offer has been made and accepted better grounded and so avoid the interference cost of losing them further on in their career.

Job security

This is has been an increasingly difficult area for all employers to address. We might say that the private sector has been exposed to more job insecurity than their colleagues in the public sector. Indeed, the expectation always was that the civil service would provide a secure career until retirement with a good pension, although their wages might be slightly less than those doing the equivalent job in the private sector. We have already mentioned career portfolio and it is here that the seat of security lies for most knowledge workers. Developing knowledge and skill through experience is an important gauge of whether people feel they are likely to be more employable when they do need to leave the organization. This reinforces the points that were made about CPD. Salespeople and IT workers need to feel that they are at the forefront of technology in their work. Falling behind makes them feel less employable and they are more likely to leave of their own accord, if this is not addressed by the company.

Emphasis on providing career opportunities

The phrase 'dead-end jobs' applies to all appointments not just a few favoured professionals. Job rotation and work rotation are not difficult to arrange in most organizations. Sometimes it takes imagination to explore what other people might enjoy as a challenge. If there is any value in the reference to globalization, then it ought to be that opportunities can take people anywhere in the world that their talents and expertise are required. Work rotation provides opportunity to see how other parts of the organization work and contributes to building and developing a career that is exciting in its prospects.

Complementing CPD issues is the *Personal Development Plan*. Learning languages is all part of extending potential employment opportunities. In the UK we have been poor at encouraging this type of development, assuming that we will be working with 'foreigners' usually able to speak English. It may be that in the future other languages may come to dominate world trade. Recently in Hong Kong financial sector recruits were advertised for and one of the conditions was being fluent in Mandarin.

BOX 7.9

While working with a national supplier with a global market a visiting management trainer was introduced to a member of staff who seemed rather depressed on the course. An informal chat revealed that his domestic situation caring for dependents accounted for his rather depressed state. The trainer asked what he did in his spare time. He answered, 'I learn languages.' The organization soon afterwards gave him premature retirement, believing that his active full-time career was ended. He went off and set up in business as a self-employed translator.

A year later the Wall dividing East and West Germany came down. The organization needed translators desperately. He applied and was successful. He found himself earning far in excess of what he had earned there as a full-time employee. Thereafter, he always appeared at work with a smile on his face.

The trainer wondered why no one in the organization had asked about his PDP before.

Appraising each individual's performance and development

Experience suggests that managers sometimes regard the annual appraisal as a bureaucratic chore. The more staff they have to appraise, the more onerous is the paperwork that needs to be filled in. Discussions are often constrained through lack of time and therefore probing for the unexpected aspirations is less likely to take place and be recorded.

Staff, too, are aware of this routine approach to their appraisal and sometimes, provided that they are satisfied with their rewards, will accept what is said, sign the form and leave. The question, 'where do you see yourself in five years time?' is less often explored. Perhaps because managers do not want to raise expectancies which they think are unlikely to be fulfilled.

Clive Fletcher (1993) mentions that there is an argument for allowing individuals to choose their appraiser in the company – perhaps someone they trust and have worked with apart from their manager. This is particularly the case where managers rarely see their staff at work or where they are geographically widely dispersed. Matrix management did not make appraisal easier, as the people in the project working teams are unlikely to be appraising each other. The responsibility for the appraisal may well remain at head office whose managers see staff at work much less frequently.

For professional workers Fletcher mentions the value of the blank sheet of paper in which those who are involved in an expertise whose work is not shared by others should be tasked with drawing up their own appraisal of what they do, how they contribute to the organizational objectives and what support they need in their future CPD.

Training and learning/development

It could be argued that learning is involved in both training and development activities, although perhaps it is easier to observe and measure training outcomes than the longer-term developmental experiences that staff may have. In a sense this brings us back to tacit knowledge: what has been learned and how has development been supported over a period? For knowledge workers, training is less likely to be a need compared with development. Their CPD will be a priority for their membership of their lead body. Having someone to offer support is an important facility that mentoring and shadowing can answer. Having a sounding board that can support and develop knowledge workers answers an increasing need in most organizations. It requires coaching skills (developing skills and knowledge) and sometimes counselling skills (encouraging self-reflection and exploring feelings) and these cannot be assumed in many managers, however experienced they may be in their own job.

Pay satisfaction

This is always a difficult area to assess accurately. There is often a going rate in a job or sector that is well known to those who work in it. Sometimes, there is also a cut-off point beyond which staff will not undertake more work for more pay. There is a balance to be struck with employees about reward which includes money but may also involve other aspects of their life and development. Managers who take the trouble to find out what they are may find that retaining staff is easier to do.

Work–life balance

How much time will people spend at work? What is an expected good day's work? Evidence suggests that working people beyond their limits will only lead to stress or breakdown. But some people are either unaware or have adapted to a long-hours culture at work. Evidence suggests that presenteeism will not guarantee greater efficiency. It could presage the reverse, which means that errors, accidents or poor work are more likely to occur as time at work extends beyond what was agreed originally in the employment contract.

BOX 7.10

One of the first cases of stress to go through the courts was brought against a local authority. A member of staff working with two other colleagues in the housing department found that one colleague was made redundant and he was expected to cover the job. When he went off sick, his wife, who was an HR manager elsewhere, suggested that he keep a time log when he returned to work.

He did return and kept the time log. This time his other colleague was made redundant and he was expected to do his job, too. He eventually had a nervous breakdown and sued the authority, bringing with him the time logs proving how much he had been expected to do.

The authority were found liable for the stress caused.

The staff member was awarded a six-figure compensation, compensating him in full for the wages that he would have earned had he been able to work through to retirement.

Job challenge/job autonomy

Challenging work will necessarily change over time. What is challenging initially may become routine over an extended working life. Rosemary Stewart (1991) remarked that her research into satisfaction at work coincided with individuals being able to take on different, but contingent work that extended their talents for the people around them. Individuals most likely to be dissatisfied were those who were confined to the job description and found themselves unable to extend into other areas that interested them. Similarly, vocational elements of a job are unlikely to sit easily with administration or management responsibilities that preclude work in the originally chosen occupation. As with job autonomy, there are those who want to be able to plan their own work and do it in their own way. That is an aspiration that is fulfilled in many types of job. There are sales people, pilots, surgeons, many of whom are what would be described as solo performers. They are absorbed in their job but are unlikely to enjoy meetings, teamworking or company exercises of any kind.

BOX 7.11

A salesman who had exceeded his quota was told by the company that he would be going on a company holiday with other salespeople who had exceeded their targets.

He went to see the managing director and said, 'If I have made so much extra profit that you can afford this holiday, give me that money to spend on my children who I see little of during the working week.'

> The managing director refused, saying, 'You will not get on in this company with that sort of attitude.'
> The MD was right: the salesman found another job shortly after that.

Teamworking

As organizations unbundled and delayered, teamworking became the desirable style for managing working together on jointly run projects. We have already looked at matrix management and interdisciplinary working teams. These require skills that some workers perhaps unaccustomed to such working may find difficult to adapt to.

Training is a useful investment and awareness of team roles in such exercises as the *Belbin* test can assist in clarifying the team roles that individuals may have (Belbin, 1993). He describes the following roles:

- *plants*: ideas people, good at brainstorming, which often precedes team exercises;
- *resource investigators*: as the term suggests, people who will do preparation and support work for the team;
- *monitor evaluators*: good at monitoring time and resources and reminding the team when it is running up against deadlines;
- *coordinators*: as their name suggests, good at bringing people together, possibly in the chairing role;
- *implementers*: making things happen in the group;
- *completer finishers*: self-evident – but often absent from management teams;
- *teamworkers*: self-evident and good at building bridges;
- *shapers*: a common role to find in salespeople – definitely drivers and several in a team will often lead to clashes;
- *specialists*: again self-evident and may be present in many interdisciplinary teams.

Meredith Belbin who designed and developed the test was realistic about its likely uses. Most people will find four or five of the roles in their profile, which means that we rely on others in the team to complement the roles that are less available to us.

Those who do the test are unlikely to be surprised by the findings. Experience usually teaches us what we can do well and what we are not so good at. Team leaders themselves can benefit from knowing more about the team roles that their team members are comfortable with. As with much else, matching roles to people should find everyone comfortable with the roles they need to play.

Good teams share in taking responsibility for the team's activities, and that means noticing where others in the team are struggling and in need of help and support. The listening role is important for everyone to develop, which is why introverts may be better at developmental roles than their extrovert colleagues (Kolb *et al.*, 1984).

Teams can also encourage more confident decision making – and there is some evidence that teams make more courageous decisions than individual team members might make left to their own devices. In this way information sharing and two-way communication can be crucial in supporting *strategic integration* through teamworking.

The only caveat that Belbin drew from his initial research into the team roles was that too many of the same role in a team could be detrimental to team success. He developed an alpha group containing high-powered executives, many of whom were shapers. They spent much time arguing about how to go about the tasks they were given and therefore always finished behind ostensibly less gifted teams. Evidently, self-discipline is also required where several powerful roles are contained within the group and firm chairing role.

Performance management systems

Below are listed some of the features that characterize organizations that implement performance management systems.

The organization communicates a vision of its objectives to all employees

This brings us back to *strategic integration*. The main thing to note about strategy is that it is always changing because the context in which the organization exists is always changing, too. Nothing is forever, except the very vaguest of aspirations, such as, 'we want to be happy' and too often blue-sky company mission statements are couched in such general terms. The problem is that happiness is a very personal and therefore subjective experience. Arguably, companies could never satisfy all the needs that staff may have. It is better to have temporary objectives that can be changed according to the circumstances surrounding the company. It alerts individuals to the implications of change and the steps they need to take to change direction to achieve the organizational objectives in different job outcomes.

It sets departmental and individual performance targets related to wider organizational objectives

Once again, Drucker's management by objectives is relevant:

- organizational objectives are broken down into
- departmental goal areas (sales, production, marketing, finance etc.) and
- individual key tasks (sales people; service agents; secretaries; administrators etc.).

If we all achieve our individual objectives, then the departments will together achieve the organizational objectives – whatever these happen to be. But changes in direction need to be broken down into revised departmental goals and individual key tasks.

It conducts formal review of progress towards these targets

Monitoring progress is the principal role of the first-line manager. However, as we commented, with *triple loop learning*, staff should be able to do this for themselves. Changing targets have implications for managers responsible for line management and ensuring that staff understand what their new targets are may also mean extra training, support and development.

It uses the review to identify training, development and reward outcomes

Again, appraisal should embrace all these aspects of people's lives. The manager is an initiator and also a facilitator. Making it easy for other people to succeed requires coaching and counselling skills. Those who do best at this aspect of their job spend more time talking informally to their staff, during which they pick up more easily on concerns and objections to enforced change. The classic strategy of monitoring – managing by walking about – is a necessary prerequisite of success at problem solving before matters become too far advanced.

It evaluates the whole process in order to improve effectiveness

Again we can say that a holistic approach to business includes all of the stakeholders. Effectiveness is assessed by those outside the organization. Sadly, for many organizations the awareness of problems comes only when customers complain or shareholders express their displeasure at the Annual General Meeting. Being close to the business means checking that there are no problems in the way the service is delivered.

It uses formal appraisal to communicate performance requirements that are set on a regular basis

And not only appraisal, but any opportunity to discuss at length or briefly what is going on and what it means to all of us in the organization. Lying at the heart of this are the standards and targets that should support all that is achieved at work. But those who do more to support value-added for the customer are not always acknowledged as they should be. The distinction between standards and targets should enable managers to identify those who are capable of more than the job demands made on them (Boxall and Purcell, 2003).

Standards and targets

A standard *is a behaviour or performance that applies to everyone*

If it does not apply to everyone then it cannot be a standard. The amount that people need to produce or sell to cover their costs is a standard: it applies to everyone, and those who fall below the standards are usually on their way out of the organization fairly soon after.

A *target* (in some organizations referred to as a stretch target) is a behaviour or performance that applies to an individual. Here we acknowledge that people differ in their abilities and opportunities and taking that into account encourages them to stretch their performance and be rewarded for it, too.

It should be noticed that some organizations refer to *goals*. This is confusing because it could apply either to standards or to targets. If you work for such an organization it is advisable to find out which these goals are – *standards or targets*. Falling below either should have very different outcomes.

Correctly worded standards

There are three parts to a correctly worded standard:

1 It must be stated in behavioural terms.
2 It must contain the conditions under which the standards should be exercised.
3 It must contain the standard that is being measured against.

We will go through them a step at a time, starting with behavioural terms (Table 7.3).

If a trainer were to ask a group, 'Do you know the national anthem?' They might well receive the answer 'Yes'. The question to ask is do I know whether they know, and the answer to that question would have to be 'No' – because there is as yet no evidence that the knowledge exists.

However, if a concrete word from the list on the left is used, the questioner would discover whether the knowledge was there or not. So, the question should have been: 'State/recite/write down the national anthem.'

TABLE 7.3 Behavioural terms

Concrete terms	Abstract terms
• list	• know
• state	• acknowledge
• describe	• grasp
• assemble	• appreciate
• draw	• consider
• write down	

The second part of a correctly worded standard is the *conditions* which must be clearly stated as part of the standard.

1 *time* – what time is allowed for the behaviour?
2 *quality* – what quality standard must be achieved?
3 *quantity* – what quantity is to be produced in that time?
4 *cost* – what cost constraints are in place?

The more tightly these conditions are defined, the more accurately the standard can be measured.

Standards

1 health and safety law
2 employment law
3 error rate
4 wastage rate
5 accident rate.

The list is endless. It depends on the context in which the original standard is being framed. For example, if production targets are increased it sometimes happens that workers remove the safety guards from the machinery to make it easier to take short cuts and increase the speed of operation. So, the final part of the newly worded standard would include: '*without contravening health and safety regulations*'.

In Table 7.4, the statement on the left is an aspiration at best. The statement on the right does include the necessary details to define clearly what outcome is required in terms of sales performance to the required standard.

Handbooks, policy and procedures; operations directories; personnel ad training manuals should all adhere to the same correctly worded standards. If there are any variations or disparities between the standards expressed, then it will be difficult to convince a tribunal that a case against someone who has not met the standard was justified. Finding differently worded standards in different parts of the company's literature will be seized upon as evidence of confusion and used as a mitigating circumstance for below-standard behaviour.

TABLE 7.4 Correctly/incorrectly worded

Incorrect	*Correct*
Improve your sales performance as soon as possible	Increase your sales by 10 per cent over last year's figures, in the next 12 months, completing all company order forms correctly

- All performances should be subject to correctly worded standards.
- All standards should be related to the company's strategic objectives.
- All performances should be monitored so that we all know what we have achieved and how much more we need to do.

This is how *strategic integration* needs to connect with *quality*, *flexibility* and *commitment*.

Summary

The drive for competitive advantage can only become more critical for all organizations. The opposition from emergent economies depends on lower wage rates, and lower overheads for the workforce will continue to affect countries that carry the costs of a welfare system and universal health care. This means that our costs in the West, particularly Europe, are significantly higher than those of our competitors. Our only advantage lies in focusing on value-added for our customers and ensuring that this is reflected both in the product design and the service and support that we offer. The outcome will depend on managers continuing to support their teams to excel individually and corporately in what they do. CPD is not an option, it is a necessity.

References and further reading

Anderson, V. (2009) Research: Line manager as coach. *People Management*, 21 May, p. 42.

Anis, M., Armstrong, S.J. and Zhu, Z. (2004) The influence of learning styles on knowledge acquisition in public sector management. *Education Psychology*, 24(4): 549–579.

Argyris, C. and Schon, D. (1974) *Theory in Practice: Increasing professional effectiveness*. San Francisco: Jossey Bass

Belbin, M. (1993) *Team Roles at Work*. Oxford: Butterworth Heinemann.

Boxall, P. and Purcell, J. (2003) *Strategy and Human Resource Management*. Basingstoke: Palgrave.

Boyatzis, R. (1982) *The Competent Manager*. New York: John Wiley.

Braverman, H. (1974) *Labor and Monopoly Capital: The degradation of work in the twentieth century*. New York: Monthly Review Press.

Bullock, R.J. and Batten, D. (1985) It's just a phase we're going through: A review and synthesis of OD phase analysis. *Group and Organization Studies*, 10(4): 383–412.

Carroll, S. and Gillen, D. (2001) Exploring the teaching function of the managerial role. *Journal of Management Development*, 21(5): 330–342.

Champy, J. (1995) *Reengineering Management*. New York: Harper Business.

Clutterbuck, D. (1992) *Everyone Needs a Mentor: How to foster talent within the organization*, 2nd edn. London: Institute of Personnel Management.

Constable, J. and McCormick, R. (1987) *The Making of British Managers: A report for the BIM and CBI into management training, education and development*. London: British Institute of Management.

Cunningham, I. (2007) Viewpoint: Sorting out evaluation of learning and development: making it easier for ourselves. *Development and Learning in Organizations*, 21(5): 4–6.

Drucker, P. (1955) *The Practice of Management*. London: Heinemann.

Easterby-Smith, M., Burgoyne, J. and Araujo, L. (1999) *Organizational learning and the learning organization. Developments in theory and practice*. London: Sage.

Fletcher, C. (1993) *Appraisal*. London: IPM.

Fletcher, C. (2007) *Appraisal, Feedback, and Development: Making performance review work*. London: Routledge.

Gilmore, S. and Williams, S. (2009) *Human Resource Management*. Oxford: Oxford University Press.

Hamblin, A.C. (1974) *Evaluation and Control of Training*. Maidenhead: McGraw-Hill.

Handy, C. (1987) *The Making of Managers: A report on management education, training and development in the USA, West Germany, France, Japan and the UK*. National Economic Development Office. London: NED/MSC.

Handy, C. (1989) *The Age of Unreason*. London: Arrow Business Books.

Honey, P. and Mumford, A. (1989) *A Manual of Learning Opportunities*. Maidenhead: Peter Honey.

Hunt, J.W. and Baruch, Y. (2003) Developing top managers: The impact of interpersonal skills training. *Journal of Management Development*, 22(7/8): 729–752.

Kirkpatrick, D.L. and Kirkpatrick, J.D. (2006) *Evaluating Training Programmes*. San Francisco, CA: Berrett Koehler Publishers Inc.

Kolb, D.A., Rubin, I.M. and McIntyr, J.M. (1984) *Organization Psychology*. Englewood Cliffs, NJ: Prentice-Hall.

Kram, K.E. and Isabella, L.A. (1985) Mentoring alternatives: The role of peer relationships in career development. *Academy of Management Journal*, 26(4): 608–625.

McKinlay, A. (2002) The limits of knowledge management. *New Technology, Work and Employment*, 17(2): 76–88.

Nicolini, D., Powell, J., Conville, P. and Martinez-Solano, L. (2008) Managing knowledge in the healthcare sector: A review. *International Journal of Management Reviews*, 105(3/4): 245–263.

Pichet, J.W., Stetson, B.A., Lorenz, R.A., Boswell, E.J., Schlundt, D.G. and Oldham, J.A. (1993) Continuing education on teaching skills for health professionals: Evaluation of training the trainers. *Evaluation and the Health Professions*, 16(4): 400–416.

Qualifications and Curriculum Authority (2008). Official document.gov.uk.

Senge, P. (1990) *The Fifth Discipline: The art and practice of the learning organization*. New York: Currency Doubleday.

Stewart, R. (1991) *Managing Today and Tomorrow*. Basingstoke: Macmillan.

Strother, J.B. (2002) An assessment of the effectiveness of e-learning in corporate training programmes. *International Review of Research in Open and Distance Learning*, 3(1): 3–18.

Watad, M. and Ospina, S. (1999) Integrated managerial training: A programme for strategic management development. *Public Personnel Management*, 28(2): 185–195.

GRADUATE ATTRIBUTES

This exercise allows you to examine the following graduate attributes:

- an ability to work independently and as part of a team;
- an awareness of personal strengths and weaknesses;
- a capacity for self-reflection, self-discovery and personal development.

Teamworking

Let's begin by thinking about what a team actually is. Let's suppose you book into a hotel and in front of you at the check-in queue are a bunch of people all dressed in Star Trek uniforms. When you strike up a conversation with them you discover that they are all part of a Star Trek fan club and they have all travelled together to the hotel to attend a convention for fans like themselves. One of them introduces herself as the club's captain and tells you that she arranged the transport and hotel bookings. As they get their rooms allocated and drift away you are left wondering, were they a team?

The answer is no, they were a group but not a team. Sometimes the words are used interchangeably but they are in fact very different things.

A group is two or more individuals who are joined together by a shared bond or affinity. In this case they all like Star Trek.

A group can be defined as a small group of people with complementary skills and abilities who are committed to a leader's goal and approach and are willing to be held accountable by the leader. The group supports the leader's goals and the leader-dominated approach to goal attainment. Groups have individual accountability rather than shared accountability.

So what's a team? A team can be defined as being a small group of people with complementary skills and abilities who are committed to a common goal and approach for which they hold each other accountable. But wait a minute, how does that make them different from a group? Were the Star Trek fans a team after all? No, the key here is 'for which they hold each other accountable'.

A team is more than the sum of its component parts. To play the game a sports team cannot be just a group of talented individuals. The goal of the group can only be accomplished through the interaction of all members, thus it is not a group but rather a team (see Table 7.5).

Group and team

TABLE 7.5 Group and team characteristics

Group characteristics	*Team characteristics*
A focus on individual goals	A focus on group/team goals
Individual accountability	Group accountability
Goals and work style shaped by manager	Goals and work style shaped by team leader and team members
Groups meet to share information and views	Teams meet regularly for discussion, planning and decision making
Individual work	Collective work

The benefits of a team

Let's consider what benefits working in a team can provide:

- teams increase utilization of the strengths of team members;
- teams have the ability to compensate for individual weaknesses;
- teams value diversity in gifts/talents and skills;
- teams can increase job satisfaction;
- more input leads to better ideas and decisions;
- involvement of everyone in the process;
- increased ownership and buy-in by members;
- higher likelihood of implementation of new ideas;
- expands the circle of communication;
- increased understanding of other people's perspectives;
- increased opportunity to draw on individual strengths;
- provides a sense of security.

Teams are vital in an environment that is growing increasingly ever more complex.

These are of course only some of the potential benefits and the last one is of particular interest. In our increasingly complex and interconnected world, teams and teamwork have become progressively more important because they can offer a swifter response to that changing environment.

But teams are not all the same – they don't all work in the same way. Let's look at some types of teams.

Types of teams

Functional teams

- manager and her/his employees from one functional area;
- attempt to solve problems in specific functional area.

Cross-functional teams

- members come from different functional areas;
- a hybrid grouping of individuals who are experts in various areas.

Virtual teams

- physically dispersed and connected by technology;
- these teams tend to be extremely task oriented.

Virtual teams are becoming very common. The rise of communication technology has made them increasingly feasible and this form of team can easily bring together expertise from across the globe. Their disadvantage can be the difficulty in organizing and motivating people in diverse locations.

Team motivation

Some individuals in fact become less productive when they are members of a team. This is an effect that is sometimes referred to as social loafing. Essentially, the individual takes team membership as permission to be unproductive. These team members will rely upon the other members to achieve the team's goals

However, some individuals work harder when they are in a team, the social facilitation effect. This is simply saying that the very fact of team membership encourages the best work from these individuals.

So how do you encourage social facilitation and avoid social loafing? The social facilitation effect can be maintained and social loafing avoided by encouraging team members to get to know each other and to have the opportunity to observe and communicate with each other in an open manner. It is also vital that clear performance goals exist and that the tasks that individuals are assigned are meaningful to them. Members of the team must be assured by word and deed that their efforts matter to the team. It is also essential that this takes place within a business culture that is committed to supporting teamwork.

Teamwork is best motivated by rewards based on team performance. To achieve the performance that will bring rewards the team must work together effectively.

The effective team

As hinted at above, effective communication among team members is at the very core of good teamwork. Without good communication the pooling of team members' resources will not be available to maximize their efforts. Very simply they will be unsure as to what their fellow team members are capable of or what their knowledge base is.

In an effective team the members also require commitment, but not just commitment to the project or the organization they work for. Team members need to be committed to each other's growth and success as well as achievement of team goals. In an effective team the members will encourage and motivate each other to grow. The more effective a team member is the more they can contribute to the team goals.

Team check: true or false

1   I have a dislike of other people and do all I can to avoid them. That shouldn't matter as long as I do my job well. As long as my skills are in demand I won't have any trouble getting work.

   TRUE ❏
   FALSE ❏

2 You have to be friends with your team members if the team is going to work.

TRUE ❑
FALSE ❑

3 The ability to get along with others is a key part of being a member of a successful team.

TRUE ❑
FALSE ❑

4 There always has to be a leader in any team.

TRUE ❑
FALSE ❑

5 Sometimes people are just naturally quiet. If a team member doesn't want to speak then let them be quiet. When they are ready they will talk.

TRUE ❑
FALSE ❑

The answers

1 False
In the modern working environment it is more important than ever to be able to work as part of a team. The days of the gloriously isolated 'expert' have long gone. Globalization and technological change has made teamworking essential. Maybe you do hate people but then maybe you had better learn to get along with them.

2 False
It is important to get along with your team members but you don't have to agree to be their best friend. Sometimes being overly friendly can have a negative impact on the effectiveness of a team. As part of a team you should strive to be professional but not necessarily become friends for life.

3 True
An effective team will be composed of members with a wide variety of personality types and from a range of backgrounds. You must be open to working with all of these people to achieve the team's goals.

4 False
Although it is common for teams to have leaders, in recent years we have seen the rise of the self-directed team. In such a team everyone is responsible for ensuring the team achieves its goals.

5 False
It may seem a kindness to let the quiet member contemplate and then come forth with their contribution when they are ready but it can be damaging. It may be that the team member is quiet not because they are considering but

simply because they lack confidence or feel they have not had permission to speak. In a team every member's contribution adds value.

Effective team members

So what makes an effective team member? What are the characteristics we need to look for or to develop? As I said earlier, communication is the key to good team-work and good communication skills are essential for an effective team member. An effective team member will be able to do the following.

Influence others by involving them

Effective team members seek to bring the other members of the team into the team activity. They will seek through clear communication to solidify the team. This is particularly important in the self-directed team.

Encourage the development of other team members

It isn't enough to simply involve people. An effective team member helps their fellow team members to develop and grow.

Consider and use new ideas and suggestions from others

Communication isn't a one way street. It isn't enough to be a good transmitter – you need to be a good listener too. Sharing of ideas is one of the core benefits of teamwork so you need to be open to the ideas of your fellow team members.

Understand and be committed to team objectives

While it may seem a terrible cliché it is simply a fact that to be effective in a team you need to be a team player and not a grandstander. While you may have your own objectives, and indeed your objectives may become part of team objectives, you must understand what the team is trying to achieve and not only focus on your part in the achievement.

Not engage in win/lose activities with other team members

Being part of a team is not about winning. Let me clarify that it is not about you winning or losing. For an effective team member it is what they can contribute, not what they can personally achieve. It isn't about saying 'I was right and you were wrong'. Rather it is about saying 'What do we need to do to work together and succeed. What can I do?'

The barriers to effective teams

So we've looked at what an effective team is and what an effective team member needs to do. Let's look now a little at some of the barriers to effective teams.

Assumptions of the way team members should think and work

Even the best of us tend to think 'if only everyone else in the world thought and acted like me there would be no problems'. We assume that our way of seeing the world is not only the best way but should be the only way any sensible person would see the world. This can create problems when working with others.

These perceptions of the world that we hold transform into rules governing responses to people and situations and this in turn becomes a source of ineffectiveness. When we are lured into thinking, 'There's a right way and a wrong way, mine is the right way', we are creating conflict and ruling out what could be excellent ideas from others because they conflict with our world view. Remember that an effective team is about opening possibilities and not excluding them because 'I wouldn't do it that way'.

Overbearing or dominating participants

While it is great to be engaged and enthusiastic, it is important not to let that become counterproductive. While you may have something to say and it may be important, so are the contributions of the other team members. Refusing or reducing the opportunities others have to contribute damages the team. Teams are more than the sum of their parts and if one part is starting to take over then that benefit will fall away.

Arguing team members

While I enjoy a good argument, a bit too much according to my wife, there is a time and a place for such things. While discussion is invaluable in teams, argument is not. Remember that an important aspect of teamwork is good communication. All too often argument is not that. Even reasoned academic argument can sometimes dissolve into near fisticuffs when passions are aroused and these are people trained to argue. Arguing members will result in disruption in the team. While team members should be encouraging input from others, it must be done in a manner that facilitates communication rather than closing it down.

Lack of contact between team members

While contact nowadays will not always be face to face (see virtual teams in particular) it is vital that it is maintained. This is kind of an obvious one: try to imagine a football team where the players never came in contact with each other (wait a minute, that sounds like the team I support – no seriously). It would be a pretty useless football team. Contact and communication go hand in hand. Teams who do not maintain high levels of contact aren't teams they are just loose confederations of individuals unaware of each other's aims.

Unwillingness to be involved

If you are not part of the solution then you are part of the problem. A little harsh but in the case of a team if you are not involved you are simply not in the team. Your name may be on the list but you are not playing. Teamwork demands involvement. Participants need to be committed to team objectives.

Overcoming the barriers

An excellent starting point is to facilitate effective communication. One of the best ways of beginning this process is encouraging the team members to start thinking about how they see the world and how it may differ from how others in the team see the world. This can be done with something as complex as psychometric testing or as simple as arranging some teambuilding exercises that help them look at the way they each deal with problems.

Psychometric tests

Tests such as MBTI (Myers-Briggs Type Indicator) can be very useful in getting you to think about how you prefer to view and experience the world while making you aware of the options that suggest how others may prefer to view and experience it. The only danger of these types of tests is the way that their results are used – as they are not intended for labelling. They can also be expensive but there are no real cheap options to produce a good team.

Designing team building

I am sure you are all aware of or have experienced team building exercises. They can be useful for bringing together a team or if some of the barriers above have reared themselves in your team. What you need to remember is that one size does not fit all. You need to consider what you want to achieve before embarking on one.

When designing a teambuilding exercise you need to ensure the following.

Sufficient time; protected time

Not only must you build in enough time for what you need to do, you must ensure that this is time that will be protected, that the team building will not be interrupted by other issues.

Preparation

Know your aims and be ready to meet them. Preparation is key. If you are running a team-building event and you don't appear ready then you have lost the confidence of the participants.

Legitimacy, authorization, support

Is the organization behind the event, do you have permission and support from those in authority. Never underestimate the power of legitimization by those at the top. If they believe in what is being done this sends a clear positive signal.

Materials

This is related to preparation. Make sure in advance you have all you require for all the participants.

Structured exercises and processing

The elements of your team building must be designed to develop the skills that are necessary. You must also ensure that the learning is being processed by the participants. This is where evaluation comes in.

Evaluation is an integral part of the team building exercise. It may be easy for some to simply drift, or socially loaf, through the process. Your evaluation strategy must look at these areas. What are the immediate, short- and long-term indications that team building was successful?

One way to approach this is by using the Kilpatrick model. The model was first published in a series of articles in 1959 in the *Journal of American Society of Training Directors* but was later collected into a book. The Kilpatrick model is a four-step model.

Step 1: *Reaction* – How well did the learners like the learning process?
Step 2: *Learning* – What did the participants learn? To what extent did the learners gain knowledge and skills?
Step 3: *Behaviour* – What changes were there in job performance resulting from the learning process?
Step 4: *Results* – What are the tangible results of the learning process in terms of reduced cost, improved quality, increased production, efficiency, etc.? (Kilpatrick and Kilpatrick, 2006).

The five stages of the team

Forming

- What is our understanding of the goals and objectives which this team was organized to achieve? How do we ensure that we are all heading in the same direction?

- What special skills, information, backgrounds and expertise do each of us bring to this team?
- What structure, format or style do we prefer for our meetings?

Storming

- What roles do each of us prefer on a team? What are our strong and weak roles? Which do we over/underuse?
- What are our preferred styles of working and relating? How can these differences be used to complement each other, and be sequenced for more effective problem solving?
- What stresses each of us? How might our styles change under pressure? What can we look for as signs of stress? How can we give useful and acceptable feedback and support at these times?
- About what are we most likely to disagree? What are our preferred modes of conflict and conflict resolution? How can we disagree constructively?

Norming

- What can we do to enhance the identity and cohesiveness of this team? How can we create our own team culture?
- What norms do we bring from other team experiences? What norms would we like to explicitly include or avoid?

Performing

- How can we ensure a team culture in which we can freely question and update restrictive norms?
- How can we best monitor and discuss our team processes so we can continue to develop and improve?

Adjourning

- (The break-up of the team.)
- What did everyone bring to the team? Are the team members feeling good about what they have achieved?
- Are the, now former, members feeling insecure with the break-up of the team?

A cooperation activity with cards

This is a brief activity to give you an idea of the importance of being able to work together. In this simple task, cooperation among the team members is necessary for the successful completion of the task.

- What do you need: a deck of playing cards for each team.

Preparation

- Divide the group into teams of around four to eight participants.
- Get the teams to sit on chairs in a line side by side (one line per team).
- Place a deck of cards on the floor next to the chair at the far end of each team's line.
- Once you give out the instructions allow the teams five minutes to plan their strategy.

Instructions

The participant nearest the deck should pick up a card and then pass the card from their left hand to the right hand of the participant to their left. The second participant passes that card to their left hand, then on to the right hand of the next participant. Play continues in this way until the last participant places the card in a pile on the floor next to them with their left hand.

No one may hold more than one card at a time.

Winning

The first team with all cards stacked at the end of their line wins.

Evaluation

- How did you determine your strategy?
- Was it successful?
- What emotions did you experience when a team member dropped a card?
- Which strategies worked best?
- What implications does this exercise have for our team back in our actual job?
- What will you take away from this?

Summary

Teamworking improves when those taking part are aware of their own and other members' contribution moment-to-moment. It requires self-discipline and a sensitivity towards others. The chairing role requires all of this and more in that the individual chairing the activities needs to consider the achievement of the team objectives and husband the available resources carefully (especially time). Getting people to contribute is one challenge, but an equally and sometimes more difficult task may be to get people to stop talking and allow others some airtime.

All the tips that we saw in the assertiveness exercise will come into their own while chairing team events. Practice makes perfect and managers should make a habit of passing the chairing role to other members of the group, so that everyone gets a chance to exercise those skills.

Tutor guidance

One exercise that you might like to try requires competing teams of four or five people in each team. It is based on putting together a *radio appeal for funds for a charity* (real or imagined) which must last for exactly 30 seconds and must include an address where donors can send their money.

The script must be assembled from words cut from a newspaper with scissors provided and stuck on the script board (A4 card) with a pritt stick provided.

Time allowed: 30 minutes.

You can use observers for each team or, if the number of teams is small, you can monitor their progress yourself. Few teams will complete on time without having to find quick ways of getting to the winning post and the point at which the team realizes that it will not complete on time is usually the defining moment for radical change and management of the group.

The task requires several stages, and timing the point at which each team reaches each stage will be important. These stages may include:

- discussion and plan of action;
- finding the words/writing the script;
- finding the words and sticking them on the script board;
- working out timings;
- having practice run-throughs with the speaker to achieve accurate timing final performance.

There are various ways that this may be approached and ingenuity and openness within the team will probably deliver the best outcome.

Watch out for Belbin roles applied or misapplied:

- a shaper takes over the running of the group, giving orders and directing operations;
- plants come up with ideas but are ignored or overruled;
- resource investigators get on with the tasks but without much coordination with others in the team;
- there is or is not a monitor evaluator who keeps track of time and makes announcements to the group;
- time slips away and two or three people get on with it while others sit back and watch;
- completer finishers bring the task to a conclusion or are too perfectionist and obstruct the team from getting to the winning post.

Observers may want to watch and note when team members make comments.

Team building comments:

- seeking ideas

- building/supporting
- seeking consensus
- summarizing.

Team demise comments:

- stating difficulty
- attacking/defending
- silence
- other behaviour (disengaging/walking out).

In most cases lack of coordination between team members will spell disaster in achieving the necessary goals to meet with success in the task. The opportunity for constructive feedback about team roles and individual styles will allow feedback, reflection and learning.

8

PERFORMANCE MANAGEMENT

Topics

- appraisal and the appraisal interview
- appraisal and the role of the appraiser(s)
- appraising performance and development
- supporting continued development and CPD.

Introduction

Appraisal interviews should be a crossroad between the past and the future: performance in the past, present position and future prospects. There are many imponderables surrounding the appraisal interview and in this chapter we will try to examine some of the more significant aspects which if missed out may cause the procedure to be just that – a process that the company expects to be completed every year, so that another HR process can be successfully concluded.

Such formality can lead to what some might describe as the bureaucratic approach to appraisal. There is a set of forms that need to be filled in and the manager and member of staff will do their best to achieve the outcomes the company wants without too much discussion or sidetracking from the task in hand.

The appraisal interview

How am I doing?

For some jobs the outcomes are self-evident and may be clearly stated in the employment contract. So, for example, in sales there will usually be a standard of performance that everyone must achieve to stay in the job, combined with personal targets that govern commission and that can vary according to the potential of the geographical area covered and the demonstrable experience of the individual who works in it.

This means that most salespeople know how they are doing, probably better than the appraiser (the sales manager) who rarely sees them in action and normally spends no more than one day a month with the salesperson in the field. There is an assurance that those who know what they doing and get on with it by themselves will yield the results the company expects. In this case, they could be forgiven for wondering why they are being called in for yet another meeting when they could be out on the road making more sales.

In contrast there are those who are struggling to achieve results, for whatever reason. Finding out what the problem is can be difficult, as they are in front of customers day to day unsupervised by the sales manager. They can be making lots of calls on prospective customers, but are these the right customers (do they have the money; the authority to spend it; and the need)?

So, the context in which the job is exercised may or may not give the manager/appraiser a clear overview of performance, or, alternatively, not very much useful information to act upon, apart from the results not indicating the standards and targets required. Unless the individual is perceptive and self-reflective, it is unlikely that he/she will be able to supply an accurate insight into the reasons why they are failing to achieve the required results.

How far is it just a subjective view of one manager?

It must be admitted that the personality of the appraiser/manager is crucial to the success of the appraisal. It would be nice to think that professionalism overcomes any personal feelings that may exist between people. However, we know that just as people buy from people they like, so people learn from people they like. And because the appraisal contains much that is learning, teaching and negotiation its success is largely governed by the rapport that exists between appraiser and apprai-see. That raises the question of whether individuals need a mentor who is not the manager/appraiser. It can be someone from their own peer group who is sympathetic and supportive, but also spends more time with them from day to day and so comes to know how they work and the problems they face (Clutterbuck, 2004).

Most people make choices about those they prefer to help them. They may have a favourite doctor in the health practice; a favourite priest in the parochial team; and certainly a favourite dentist. This suggests that most of us are more comfortable with a choice of coach or counsellor and that may not include the appraiser/line manager. If only it were possible to capture the benefits of successful informal interactions, the formal process of appraisal could be enhanced. For example, trainers often see individuals demonstrate potential that is truly impressive on the courses they run. But it is not always easy to get the trainees' line managers to accept that they have ability if the perceptions of previous performance at work did not include experience of a particular competence ('I've never heard John have a good idea').

BOX 8.1

A group of area and regional sales managers in the retail sector came on a training course run by a trainer who had had all of their store managers through various training events. The trainer began by asking these senior managers what they saw their role as in the company. The managers said that this was obvious as they all knew what they were doing and this was all a waste of time for them.

Eventually, tired of their truculence, the trainer put up a single slide on the overhead projector containing the names of all 106 store managers throughout the UK for whom the area and regional managers were responsible. They were listed in three columns: A – meaning the store managers were very competent; B – meaning they still had a way to go yet; C – meaning they were struggling. The group began to get very interested and the trainer said: 'I think our job is to get all your store managers into column A.' And then he turned off the projector.

The managers said, 'Put the light back on, we want to see which column our managers are in.' The trainer replied, 'So, you want to discuss what you now agree is the function of your job?'

The course continued in a more positive frame of mind.

So, all of this brings up the question of who knows what the real contribution and potential of the appraisee is. Having decided the answer to this we can then move on to the question of how we capture this information so that it is available to the appraiser, which brings us to the next question.

What evidence is produced to support the claims made by either side?

Some companies have in the past adopted the 360-degree appraisal approach as a way of including the views of those surrounding an individual member of staff – not just one manager, but colleagues and those working for them, too. Good idea though this was, most companies who tried to implement it found that it involved much preparation and paperwork/reports, which had to be collated and analysed, and often required a meeting at which issues arising were openly raised and discussed with the individual being appraised. Apart from time and effort required to make it work, some meetings degenerated into mutual blame sessions and offered an opportunity for open criticism from staff or teams working with the appraiser (Ward, 1997).

If we return to the question of evidence, then it is clear that it can be factual – like sales or production output figures. It is then objective, though there may be explanations that need to be explored further as to how performance is achieved. Not all high-performing members of staff have achieved success in the way that the company would want. What is more difficult to deal with are the perceptions that others may have and their relevance to the discussion about future action required. This is particularly the case for managers who have been called on to lead problem teams. Imposed change will rarely be welcome by team members and clearly the new manager may appear to have made these unwanted changes without the consent of the group. A 360-degree appraisal will probably raise concerns and objections about the manager's style without acknowledging that the brief from the company drove the changes that were implemented by him or her. So, the question of perception raises the issue of how individuals evaluate their own and other's performance (Fletcher, 1999).

Seventy-five per cent of employees consider that they are in the top 10 per cent of employees (Fletcher, 1993)

We raised the question of perceptions. This statistic may suggest that there can be a tendency for individuals to overestimate just how good they are at doing their job. It may be true that experienced operatives perform at an above-average level. However, the mismatch between perception and reality suggested by the statistic above begs the question of how that assessment has been made. It certainly makes it difficult for a manager to assess rewards for high performance, for, if we accept that no more than 10 per cent of staff can be rewarded for excellent work, then a lot of individuals are going to be disappointed, if not aggrieved. Fletcher is insistent that this a major reason for addressing the question of rewards on another occasion separate from the appraisal altogether. His view was, that once individuals realized they were not going to get the reward they anticipated, they tended to disengage from the appraisal interview completely.

Is it just about productivity factors?

There are those who believe that there is a trend apparent towards what is described as 'managerialism' that puts the emphasis on 'performativity'. By this is meant that the productivity factors of time, quality, quantity and costs become the major focus of the appraisal, especially in highly competitive sectors. Some people would describe this as 'you are only as good as your last sale' philosophy. Any downturn in performance (which may not be for lack of effort or ability, but only, as at present, due to a world depression) is alighted on and becomes the focus of the individual's effectiveness for the organization.

More insightful assessments might say that there are other factors that should be as relevant, such as a slow market, and yet this can often be overlooked or ignored by those focusing only on the comparative figures of performance. Sales managers may then fall back on the truism: 'when the going gets tough, the tough get going.' Performance can falter for many reasons, not always because of lack of effort on the part of the individual worker. A downturn in achievement can be an opportunity to readdress the core skills and their development – in other words coaching and development issues need to be addressed.

How far does attitude count?

In earlier times, school and work reports included personal comments from the report writer. 'This boy is lazy and needs to put more effort into his work' was regularly to be found on school reports. But are appraisers allowed to comment on attitude anymore? Is the statement, 'you've got the wrong sort of attitude' permitted as a comment, or not? Certainly, there may be some behaviours that are not appreciated within a company or culture. Most people have had experience of speaking up at management meetings to find that such frankness is not appreciated by the senior managers present. So, avoiding making negative comments at company meetings, for example, can become part of the culture, and the peer group may give warning to newcomers that such interventions will not be appreciated by managers. But for those who do feel that speaking the truth is important to their integrity at work there is a dilemma that may not be easy to resolve.

The main issue in all cultures is: how far can they assimilate or accommodate different behaviours from the norm? Deliberately screening out people whose views are uncongenial may not always be the best policy. Mavericks can have a prophetic voice. Their views may not be palatable to managers, who on the whole want to have an unobstructed run at meetings and in their decision making. However, there may be times when individuals have an insight into future prospects and will have the moral courage to speak up.

BOX 8.2

A foreign company in the UK whose emphasis was on performance and efficiency administered the A & B test to all employers before they were offered a job. The test identifies those workers who are likely to challenge (type As) and those who are quiescent, compliant and amenable to direction (type Bs). They chose type Bs in preference to type As.

The training manager saw a need for change and ideas from the workforce and saw no evidence that it was forthcoming from his current workforce. He contacted the training consultant and asked whether he could devise some training that would make his staff more innovative, creative and entrepreneurial.

The consultant came to the conclusion that their choice of Bs might make it difficult to transform compliant staff into the profile that he now required of his people. Only As would have provided that sort of base for creativity and interaction. Bs are more often compliant and wait to be told what to do by their managers.

The HR manager and trainer parted company. The training manager moved later to another company that was setting up in the UK. This time they looked to recruit As and Bs.

So attitude may be an important factor in recruitment decisions. Living with challenging people may also be the only way of encouraging innovation, new ideas and entrepreneurialism. Companies need to regenerate from time to time and sometimes individuals who make uncomfortable interventions in team discussions may be playing an important role which is ultimately to everybody's benefit (Ramamoorthey and Carroll, 1998).

Aims of appraisal

Communication

Communication is a two-way street, so it is said, which means that the appraisal should be a dialogue between the parties involved. Good interviewers are able to get their interviewees to talk 80 per cent of the time. It would be interesting to discover how many appraisers could boast a similar proportion of time allocation to the appraisee's opinions and views about their work experience and prospects with the company. Too often there is a focus on the paperwork which means that filling in the appropriate forms is more important than a frank discussion about the working experience of the previous year and the prospects that lie ahead. Perhaps a few open questions would be suitable to get into the evaluation of experience and review what the outcomes show about job, work, career and management of the individual within the organization.

Some analysis of the meaning of work outcomes should feature in this opening round of the appraisal interview. Fletcher himself advocates for professional staff a blank sheet of paper, rather than the stylized form so often used to guide the appraisal. This would certainly fit in with the knowledge workers in which appraising consultants makes more sense if it begins with an account from the appraisee. Finding out what interests individuals about their job may offer pointers to their future aspirations and potential. It may also indicate a specific interest in their career which could be the basis for further development.

As we remarked previously, Stewart's work (1991) indicates that few jobs remain static throughout the lifetime of the job holder. So, there will have been other job demands made that have had to be met by the appraisee that ought to be recorded in the paperwork, too. Being diverted by other demands, be they customer enquiries, complaints or problem solving, all takes time and effort. It could well mean a significant interference cost both to the individual and to the company. So, addressing such demands could be important to a discussion on whether the nature of the job is changing, and if so whether more support is needed to develop requisite competencies.

Discuss and clarify expectations, roles, aspirations and any issues affecting performance

Expectancy has always been critical to evaluating satisfaction or dissatisfaction with any job. Those with the highest expectations are therefore more likely to be disappointed by the actual job assessment than those whose expectancies are more modest. However, that apart, high expectancies may also be linked to higher aspirations. In which case, disappointment may mean a loss of motivation and a desire to move on and find personal and career development elsewhere. Frankness will be the basis of an open discussion and trust in the appraiser will be vital to bringing out such issues (Dries *et al.*, 2012).

Focus on how the individual with the support of the organization contributes to the aims of the business

Once again *strategic integration* is key here. Bringing day-to-day activities into the context of the bigger picture of organizational achievement may not be easy to achieve. For those whose efforts can demonstrably be seen to contribute to the top (and therefore bottom) line, the link is easy to establish. More effort may sometimes be needed to convince those doing functional or routine work that their efforts are equally important and appreciated.

For those who have been through several appraisal exercises there may be a feeling of 'what's in it for me?' High-stepping careers may not be everyone's aspiration. But it is encouraging to be asked where you want to be within a defined time frame. The answer to the question can often be quite surprising and also informative for appraisers to hear.

Training and development

Appraisal has always been a good opportunity for an organization to pull together a *Training Needs Analysis*. Sometimes a suite of courses is offered and managers are encouraged to propose any of their people who have not been through training courses necessary for development. Sometimes training courses are an important prerequisite for further promotion in the organization. So, from that point of view they are valued as an opportunity for the manager to encourage key members of staff and indicate that the company believes they have the potential to develop further in their career with the company.

Traditionally, less attention has been paid to development. And yet, as we have seen, individuals often have a *Personal Development Plan* and have already embarked on improving their knowledge or enhancing their skills in areas that they are interested in and committed to. Such self-learning initiatives can indicate an aptitude that might be useful to encourage in future career planning.

Identify opportunities for professional development linked to the employee's role and career aspirations

Preparing for new roles can be as simply supported as shadowing those who are already fulfilling those roles. But it needs the will to organize time and a suitable person to shadow, as well as finding a stand-in while the trainee is away shadowing the alternative role. We have already mentioned mentoring and how it can be used to help develop an understanding of other roles and their background – especially at a senior level in the organization. Finding suitable mentors who have time and a willingness to undertake this work is a major challenge in any organization but one that can pay dividends in staff retention.

Provide training, learning and development opportunities to enable employees to contribute to the performance of their organization and to enhance their career opportunities

We have already mentioned *knowledge workers* and their increasing importance to expertise in the organization. Those engaged in IT, sales and other value-added activities are more likely to leave organizations that fail to keep them at the leading edge of their occupation or profession. For this reason there can be a high turnover of such professionals which senior managers sometimes have difficulty understanding why this is.

Project work that keeps individuals ahead of their rivals will always command interest and commitment. There is the added benefit that such a project will provide knowledge workers with evidence that can be used to further their CPD with the lead body responsible for their discipline. This is a double bonus which can mean that knowledge workers are less likely to look for opportunities to develop elsewhere (Megginson and Whitaker, 2003).

Develop individuals in line with organizational succession planning

Succession planning has always been an activity that is difficult to arrange realistically. The movement of key staff is bedevilled by more frequent turnover than in times past, and when the time comes to make an appointment the chosen successor may no longer be with the organization. As we have observed, many workers spent all their working days in one industry, even in one organization. That has now ceased to be the norm for most individuals, whatever their skills base may be. There is an added challenge, which is that when the time comes for the changeover, either the candidate designated to take over is no longer available, or the circumstances pertaining to the role have changed substantially so that the designated successor is now no longer viewed as the ideal candidate to take over.

Perhaps the best outcome that can be hoped for from succession planning is that interested and committed individuals receive support and development appropriate to their job as it develops, thereby making them feel appreciated in the organization, and destined for career progression if they stay (Dries *et al.*, 2012).

Motivation

Influence motivation positively by providing feedback, recognition and praise

Motivation has for many years dominated the agenda of what the effective manager does: motivate his/her people. All of this made eminent good sense when jobs and organizations were stable and secure bases of employment. But, so effective has the strategy of flexibility been that there is much less that might make individuals feel committed to the organization that currently employs them.

Appreciation of individual effort and achievement therefore needs to have a shorter term pay-off while individuals are still with the organization, which is why CPD has much to commend it as a means of keeping knowledge workers committed to the organization for the duration of their work project.

Identify and provide opportunities for development including mentoring, shadowing and coaching

We have already looked at these activities as a positive opportunity to develop individuals on a one-to-one basis. They are only as good as the skills and commitment of those who are shadowed and those who act as mentors or coaches.

There is far more work yet to do to encourage older workers to stay on and fulfil those roles. At the moment the general mindset seems to be that either you work full time or you retire completely. As the age for retirement advances, there have to be opportunities for more flexible uses of those who have acquired knowledge, skill and experience and are prepared to stay on and help others who are taking their first tentative steps with the organization (Meyer and Smith, 2000).

Empower people by encouraging them to take responsibility for tasks and objectives, and to feel that they have the personal and organizational resources to achieve their objectives

Empowerment has always been a difficult topic to address. We might begin by asking what it means, exactly. Does it mean that individual staff can take the initiative for business decisions without reference to their manager? If so, then it invites a number of questions about budgetary responsibility and accountability in the organization.

The difference between mandatory and discretionary responsibilities needs to be clearly defined so that individuals know what it is that they can do, and what they need to refer upwards for permission. However, if we link it to the previous question, then it is clear that exploring developing roles and encouraging self-development on the job could well be linked to a mentoring or counselling role. Connecting with the line manager will be important, too, so that everyone is aware of the initiative and can take an interest in its developmental outcomes (Robertson and Swan, 2004).

Avoiding strategies

Don't have them

There are organizations whose lack of organization means that they do not conduct regular appraisals. It should be noted that members of staff can ask for an appraisal at any time – it is not necessary to wait until the next official appraisal date for everyone else. This may be important, for example, if a member of staff is considering applying for a promotion or a change of position.

Buy people off

Some managers are adept at using the appraisal either to offer training courses as a form of reward or as a means of deferring promotion applications (you need to have done the leadership course before applying for the next level). For knowledge workers that strategy is probably less effective, given that they may have their own aspirations for developing their career which do not include moving through traditional promotion levels in one organization.

Give everyone excellent gradings

Again, that is not unusual as a strategy and it does save the manager the trouble of addressing any difficult and contentious issues. It is a classic avoidance strategy, but it can misfire.

BOX 8.3

A group of 20 senior managers were all graded Box 1 (the highest marking) in a civil service department.

Later they heard that their managers were dissatisfied with the regular meeting they held with each other rather than spending time visiting clients.

Needless to say there was a significant feeling of grievance about this which was forcefully expressed by the group (Randall and Procter, 2008).

Talk about yourself

Some managers are good at relating their own experiences and development path. It is often meant kindly, but also frustrating for the appraisee, who wants to have time to talk about her/his own aspirations and achievements.

Make promises

This is a dangerous strategy, but one that was often used by managers who knew they would not be around to field questions the following year when the appraisee discovered that the promises had not been kept. The company's credibility lies in the hands of the manager conducting the appraisal and misleading staff can have long-term repercussions such as loss of trust in the organization.

Blame the last manager

Comments of any kind about previous managers should be avoided unless a promise to convey information upwards or to the HR department were made. In this case, checking what was said would be an important part of restoring trust between the individual and the organization.

Box marking system (1–5)

In some organizations in the public sector a box system of marking is used where Box 1 means fitted for promotion and Box 5 means an unsatisfactory performance. We have already mentioned the temptation to over-mark candidates to avoid confrontation or under-mark to keep them from applying for promotion and moving elsewhere. However, it might be advisable to use systems that require positive comment rather than a predictive marking system.

Preset comments; likert scales

A similar comment could be made about scales of 1–5 on all of the activities undertaken by a particular grade or job. Systems such as these are sometimes to be found in functional or routine jobs where the elements of a job description can be easily listed. If offered during an apprenticeship they can be helpful, though they need to be administered by the immediate supervisor responsible for the development of the trainee who has seen them in action.

Opportunity to criticize

Any temptation to introduce a hint of disciplinary procedures should be resisted. These should be addressed at the time when the incidents commented on actually took place and not sprung on the appraisee during the appraisal interview. It may be that reviewing competency development would be a more positive approach to addressing past problems.

Involving staff

Write your own report

We have already commented on Fletcher's (1993) suggestion that professionals can be given a blank sheet of paper and allowed to write their own account of what they have achieved and their aspirations for future development. Increasingly, knowledge workers are engaged by organizations whose managers have no knowledge of the expertise that they are required to demonstrate. So, only defined inputs (time, quality, quantity, cost) can be evaluated together with outputs (however these were defined). The process can only be defined and laid out by the individual performers themselves.

Gathering individual evidence of work demands

Filling in a time log for three typical weeks prior to an appraisal can be a useful exercise for individuals about to be appraised. As we have noted, most jobs change over a 12-month period and extra duties can have intruded on core responsibilities, requiring diversion to cover for unexpected eventualities or cover for absent colleagues. An accurate record of these types of interferences can be useful evidence of emergent change and alert the appraiser that missed deadlines or targets may be accounted for by diversion to other duties.

BOX 8.4

A salesperson employed to sell office equipment inherited from his predecessor many cold leads generated by marketing but never followed up. He embarked on a concentrated telephone canvass campaign.

It became apparent that his sales director who passed his desk every day was unhappy that he seemed to be spending all his time in the office instead of 'out on the road selling'. So he kept a time log listing all calls made and their outcome.

When the time for appraisal came round and the question about his staying in the office on the phone arose, he presented the time logs to the sales director. There was no further comment from the director. The evidence spoke for itself.

Speak to colleagues/senior staff/subordinates

Working with others across traditional disciplinary boundaries may provide useful references that are relevant to include in an appraisal. This particularly applies to those who are involved in short-lived interdisciplinary teamworking. For some these may last no more than a few weeks and this means that over the course of a year, several different teams will have been worked with. Some note of how each team project worked out could be useful to acquire before the formal appraisal.

Evaluation not just validation

Accounting for what individuals do is validation. There is every reason to do that as an employer to assess how efficient an individual is. Less often addressed is the evaluation of performance. Here there is a need to probe more deeply, and encourage reflectiveness in the individual. But, perhaps the end-users should be involved, too. Customer experiences can be important indicators of satisfaction, and, as we have said, in many professional relationships there are no other witnesses to what has been achieved out in the field (Fletcher, 2008).

Appraisal as a crossroads

To look at past achievement

Management control is based on monitoring performance factors; performativity; and productivity factors. But it also needs to reflect change, challenge and problems that have arisen, too. There will be two accounts: the appraiser's account, and the appraisee's account and both need to be considered by the other party. In some organizations an exchange of paperwork is arranged prior to the meeting so that each can see what the other has written. That means that at the beginning of the meeting the main focus can be what both parties are agreed on and where there are differences of fact or opinion.

To look to the future

It is tempting to look just at revised standards and targets at this stage of the appraisal. Flatter organizations mean less opportunity to climb through the levels of the organization. But preparing to develop aptitude and ability can be impor-tant to address, as we have seen, especially with knowledge workers. They will be looking for opportunities to develop their CPD, and embarking on projects that are current in their discipline will be important to support their future commit-ment to the organization.

The present is an opportunity

Pulling together the areas discussed is the final aspect of a good appraisal. Both parties should feel that they have had the chance to air their views and raise any concerns that they may have. The key skills are those we have seen before:

- P – probe
- L – listen
- O – observe
- D – decide.

If both parties are equally open to the other, then there is every chance that the appraisal will be both successful and worthwhile.

As far as paperwork is concerned then the advice on *correctly worded standards* applies:

- use behavioural words;
- include conditions where applicable (time, quality, quantity, cost);
- mention the standard underwriting the above (health and safety; employment law etc.).

Note that managers responsible for more than eight staff (in some cases now the span of control in some industries is 1:13) may struggle with time constraints. This may need to be thought about more fully. In some organizations, appraisals are delegated to other senior members of staff who do have available time and requisite knowledge of the job and person being appraised.

Any attempt to use bland and vague statements (on the whole has achieved well overall ...) should be resisted. The appraisal form is a part of the employment contract – and can in some circumstances alter the terms and conditions of the individual's job. Care should be taken that there is no possibility of a claim of constructive dismissal being brought by an appraisee (this would mean that the employment contract had been altered so radically that the job had become significantly different from that which the individual originally agreed to and proposed changes might make it impossible for them to continue working, for a specific reason).

The interview itself

Both sides should come prepared

This ought to go without saying. However, it could be that an open discussion, especially with knowledge workers, would make more sense before committing anything to official documents. This may be useful if a new manager has been appointed or a member of staff has been recruited from another section or from outside the organization. Informal meetings allow people to get to know each other and share ideas before there is a move to formalize both viewpoints.

Each should reveal to the other his/her comments

This may be better taking place prior to the formal meeting. Again, time to consider what has been written may be necessary so that reasonable agreement can be reached which satisfies both appraiser and appraisee. There may be other aspects that are triggered and that need to be included, in which case the final paperwork may need to be amended accordingly.

There is a balance to be struck between both party's views which should lead to a two-way discussion and equal time to listen and to learn. There should be a summary that includes:

- agreement about points that both parties agree on;
- factors that there is disagreement on;
- finally, summarize and read back (with action points, if appropriate).

If we look at the elements of the *psychological contract* then we can see that the detail of the discussion may focus on the *transactional* elements of the contract (time, duties, conditions of service). What is arguably more important is the *relational* part of the contract (trust, loyalty and honesty). Losing out on these long-term relationships could be more serious.

BOX 8.5

A member of staff, tired of seeing his contemporaries moving up the organization, decided to bring up an aspiration he had had for some years at his appraisal. He wanted to take up the position of training manager in the organization

He mentioned this to his manager at the appraisal and was told, 'Your name is in the frame'.

Later he learned that the job had already been offered to one of his friends and colleagues. He felt that he had been let down and misled.

He left shortly afterwards and secured a job in another organization.

Effective appraisals

Effective appraisals depend on the following.

Truth and frankness

There are some managers who hate to disappoint. This may lead them to be less than frank, and even sometimes misleading. They don't mean to be, but they want to be liked by everyone. If it is true that 'the truth will set you free' then temporary unpopularity may be a better strategy than the long-term disillusionment that can occur once the truth comes out.

Frankness and acceptance

Frankness also requires acceptance. Even if the comments are inaccurate, this means that there is a chance to put the record straight. Few of us appreciate hearing uncongenial facts about ourselves. But friendship depends on honesty. We owe that to each other if a good team is to flourish with no hidden agendas or reservations.

Absorbing and reflective

Perhaps we might ask: for whom? And then the answer should be 'for both parties'. For some managers that may mean making an effort to be interested in the other person, no matter what our own thoughts may be at the time. Certainly, setting a time, even notionally, would be inadvisable. Reflectiveness requires time to listen, reflect and learn.

Asking open questions

Getting people talking is an art rather than a science but there are some questions that may help to encourage fuller than one word answers:

- Tell me about …
- What do you think about …?
- What do you feel about …?

This may mean that using the appraisal as an opportunity to make announcements should be bypassed or put aside so that the opening part of the interview becomes a discussion in which the appraisee is encouraged to reflect on the previous period since their last appraisal. Such an informal start may trigger current concerns not reflected in the paperwork.

Listening

This should be obvious, but signals may suggest that the appraiser is not really listening too closely. Here are some suggestions for making attention more obvious to the other party to the discussion:

- engage eye contact when the other person is speaking;
- sit up straight and lean forward slightly;
- use nodding and assent to show you listen and understand;
- take notes, if appropriate;
- occasionally feed back what you have been told;
- probe signal words (people often use adjectives such as good/bad; difficult/easy, without giving a detailed indication of what these words mean exactly);
- summarize at the end of each section.

Responding not reacting

Don't show surprise, annoyance or anger. Be assertive, not aggressive or compliant. The three steps to assertiveness are:

1 show you listen and understand;
2 say what you think or feel;
3 say what you would like to happen.

Summarising for action

Finally, all agreed objectives should be recorded and some may have arisen as a result of the appraisal itself. This may mean redrafting the paperwork before signing it off.

All *standards should be correctly worded* as they could then be construed as modifying the employment contract of the individual concerned.

A clear distinction should be made between *standards* and *targets*. Standards are mandatory. Targets are usually discretionary (in the civil service they were sometimes referred to as 'stretch targets' – meaning that they were intended to give an individual something to aim for without being penalized if they were not achieved).

Aims of the appraisal

Developing cooperation between appraiser and appraisee

Working closely with others as a manager means building bridges and finding a rapport with others in the team. The appraisal is a prime example of an occasion when this needs to happen. The focus therefore needs to be as objective as it can be. Personal opinions need to be put to one side to avoid distraction from the subjects that matter.

Avoiding bureaucratic control

Paperwork is a means to an end, not an end in itself. It is there to record a constructive and encouraging encounter between two people who should respect each other, even if they do not like each other. It may best be completed when the best outcome has been achieved, when it becomes more likely that a negotiated agreement has been reached.

Focusing on the facts

It is worth remembering who has most of the facts about the job challenges faced and overcome (or not). This may only be available to the appraisee. Successfully surfacing those facts lie in the rapport which is built between the parties as they search to reach agreement and mutual understanding.

Engendering loyalty and initiative

This is an outcome that should emerge from a well-conducted appraisal interview. We are seeking to reinforce competence and commitment. So, the support offered and its relevance will be the gauge of whether we have been successful or not. People don't need to like each other to get on, but they probably need to respect each other's position in order to continue to trust each other.

Appraisee concerns

Moment of truth

Some appraisees have concerns that the appraisal will be used either to settle scores or to bring up unpalatable facts – such as a disciplinary interview, perhaps. No such surprises should be sprung on either party at an appraisal. Any issues not connected with performance overall should be kept for a more appropriate occasion.

Career progression?

The aspirations that individuals have are sometimes treated less than seriously by those more senior. Giving them due seriousness is important, just as discussing realistic staging posts or prerequisite training required. All sorts of people have done well in management and there is no one management profile that guarantees success.

Ongoing working relationship with the appraiser

All relationships suffer from strain from time to time. So, any concerns that may have arisen can be acknowledged as having been dealt with in the past. This is where they should stay unless there is unfinished business such as apology or explanation that needs to take place as a matter of closure.

Basic anxieties relating to self-esteem

Putting people at their ease is an art that needs to be practised. Counselling is an area that managers should only enter if trained and even then, the appraisal interview may not be the appropriate time for such personal interchanges.

Appraisees who feel overawed by the thought of their appraisal may need to prepare carefully using a mentor or coach to help them. A confident encounter does much to reinforce the belief that anxieties are often unjustified. Self-esteem benefits from positive experience (Aycan, 2005).

Coping with criticism

None of us deals well with criticism. However, there are times when truths have to be told and deficiencies come to terms with. Having got past the initial announcement, the most positive interviews focus on the future and how to overcome the deficiency. In this case, the support that the organization is prepared to give to rectify a situation is part of the correct process of dealing with matters that need to be addressed.

Dealing with poor performance

We will be dealing with disciplinaries and grievance interviews in the next chapter. But it may be worth going through the steps for dealing with poor performance at this point, in the rare cases, hopefully, that they arise during the appraisal interview.

Check the standard applying to the situation

Note that not everyone always knows what the standard is. It is worthwhile checking that the individual staff member can state what the standard is before embarking on further discussion about its application to different situations.

Check the current performance

Without firm evidence of performance to hand it might be advisable to defer dealing with the matter immediately. With firm evidence, it may then be possible to move to the next stage at a more appropriate time.

Measure the gap between performance and standard

Are we looking at occasional lapses or something more permanent? Is there a trend emerging or just the occasional tendency? Accurate assessment will make it easier to be realistic about the time needed to get performance back on track.

Investigate reasons for poor performance

Mitigating circumstances usually apply to medical conditions and these may need to be checked and validated by a medical practitioner. *Good cause* includes domestic upheaval or personal issues that have affected the individual and made it difficult for them to carry out their job.

Discuss options for addressing the situation

For some managers, offering individual members of staff options for future action may seem like a sign of weakness. They would, perhaps, have preferred to make a statement or state a position that the member of staff must observe. In fact, giving people options and then asking them which they would find most feasible gains commitment and is more likely to be adhered to in the future. A record of issues discussed and action to be taken should be made and circulated to both parties.

Agree support, if appropriate

Offering coaching, training or mentoring may be an appropriate suggestion and, if accepted, will give evidence that the organization has done all it can to assist and support its members of staff to overcome difficulties rather than be left to try and sort things out on their own.

Fix a review date

It is important to reinforce this and not just say that you will review it 'in the near future'. Be specific and make sure that it is a realistic and reasonable time period.

Make notes

The notes should include the three factors required by employment law:

1 Define what the individual needs to do (state it in behavioural terms).
2 Define the conditions clearly and make sure they are reasonable.
3 State what help the company will give.

Fix a review date.

Make sure the other person receives a written copy summarizing the above points

Remember that even a verbal warning should be documented and the member of staff has a right to a written copy of the outcomes agreed in any interview held.

Different options for performance management

How organizations and their managers attempt to manage performance may be a function of custom and practice – 'the way we do things round here'. Such procedural approaches have about them a uniformity that can be introduced during induction training and thereafter reinforced by managers, supervisors and the peer group. Thus new recruits find that a consistent message is reinforced and once they have adapted to and adopted the required behaviours, it all comes as second nature.

There is, of course, an inherent problem that may lurk here: how do managers or change agents bring about change in the face of basic assumptions, sometimes deeply embedded, of the way we do things round here? We can consider here some of the alternative approaches.

Management by objectives

This approach has been around for many years and has about it a simplicity in concept that most businesses should be able to adopt. The levels to address, as we have seen, are as follows:

- organizational objectives (often stated in turnover or profit-related target increases);
- departmental goals (how the organizational objectives will impact on each department);
- individual key tasks (applying the departmental goals to its individual staff members).

Today we might recognize this breakdown of objectives into goals and key tasks as being in accord with *strategic integration*. It should then underwrite all the stages of the HRD list and particularly annual appraisals, when changes may need to be made to the employment contract in accord with revised key tasks and targets.

Self-appraisal

We have already commented on the popularity of self-appraisals, especially for professionals and knowledge workers. The discretion that such workers have could be considerable, and finding out how they exercise that discretion an important insight for the manager and company to grasp fully. As we have seen, such accounts can be accompanied by time logs to give a better idea of how the balance of a professional's time is apportioned across the duties required of them.

Team appraisal

This is about the 360-degree approach while confining the numbers to the working team rather than a wider body of workers. Among the practices that can be enlightening are the questions:

- What do I do that helps you?
- What do I do that hinders you?

The appraiser and the appraisee should ask these questions of each other. Everyone in the team should then receive feedback of the results, having given answers to everyone in the team, too.

BOX 8.6

This personal touch can be approached in another way. Some trainers use it at the end of courses. It is sometimes referred to as *Notes of Happiness*.

Each participant, including the trainer(s), fills in a paper for every individual stating: I like you because: and then listing three things that they liked about each individual.

At the end of the course individuals can take away the notes written for them – though as they were anonymized, the identity of the senders was not revealed.

Balanced scorecard

The important standards applying to stakeholders, customers and fellow members of staff are published and used to compare performance between periods and between teams performing in a sector. How often teams/individuals exceed these targets is also noted. It must be said that in a time of development and high stepping economic performance, it can be a motivating factor to those involved in the business at whatever level. However, in times of economic downturn or obsolescence it can be less helpful, as it alerts individuals to the risks and losses that the company may now face.

Individuals may work exceptionally hard and still find themselves made redundant and without a job.

Upward appraisal

We have already seen this approach in the 360-degree approach to appraisals. Frank feedback can have its downsides, too. Managers sent in with a brief to implement change may not find those on their staff affected by this change necessarily appreciate the efforts made to increase efficiency or impose greater performativity.

Scores may be held longer term against those who have registered dissatisfaction against the agents of change. Given that appraisals are meant to engender goodwill, it is questionable whether this exercise is always appropriate.

Evaluative appraisal

We have already mentioned *evaluation* and distinguished it from *validation*. It is worth emphasizing again that evaluation means assessing how an individual or group have contributed to the company's *effectiveness* (rather than its *efficiency*). That means both customer satisfaction and our inroads against the competition. These factors are not often addressed as thoroughly as they could be and often the competition is less well known than they should be.

BOX 8.7

A company selling printing machines found that the foreign competition gave away their machines in return for an exclusive contract for supplies and servicing over five years. The 40 UK salespeople for the UK firm asked for the same concession at a meeting with senior managers.

The sales director replied, 'I don't want to hear any more of this negative mental attitude. Anyone can sell what we haven't got. I want people who can sell what we have got.'

Needless to say, several of the salespeople left and joined the competition

---

Development appraisal

We have already remarked on the importance of CPD to knowledge workers. It is significant that the principles that underwrite CPD are spreading to other jobs and occupations, too. Drivers of public service vehicles are being required to demonstrate their continued development, citing their experiences and the learning they have derived from it. Ongoing assessment of workers in this way is intended to encourage them to be committed to their own learning and encourages a continued interest in learning through experience and in-service training.

There is nothing new about this. In the days of steam trains, for example, drivers were expected to attend what were called Mutual Improvement Classes, and older more experienced drivers exchanged tips for improving engine management and driving with younger, up-and-coming colleagues.

Performance measurement

There are some companies and cultures that seem to specialize in measuring what are sometimes referred to as profitability metrics. Certainly, senior managers are furnished with key information for each accounting period. We list some examples below.

Financial

- sales turnover per employee (£)
- pre-tax profit per employee (£)
- return on capital employed (£K)
- return on investment (£K)
- return on net assets (£K).

It is worth noting that the first two factors focus on the employee. So, for example, we might ask whether all employees in the company are equally responsible for sales. It is a rough and ready way of making comparisons year on year. But it should be noted that new CEOs have on occasion reduced the headcount, knowing that the sales or pre-tax profits per employee would automatically go up without anything much changing in the processes of the company.

The final three factors are indicators of the overall running of a company. Managers should be able to manage negotiations on the margin of the goods they buy in. This will affect the gross profit. Thereafter, their ability to operate flexibly with the workforce costs will influence the net profit. How that affects the capital employed, the investment or the return on net assets may be less a function of the day-to-day operating decisions they make and more to do with decisions made about inward investment and the assumptions on which those decisions were made. So, assumptions made that there would be a continued upward trend in sales may not be realized during a downturn or recession (Gilmore and Williams, 2009).

People

- value-added per employee ($£$)
- total leavers/total employees (%)
- early leavers/total employees (%)
- days lost to absenteeism per employee
- employees completing annual appraisal/total employees (%).

It should be noted that value-added is a difficult calculation to assess accurately. In monetary terms value-added could refer, like the tax of the same name, to the amount of value (price) enhanced by the operative. So, wood bought in at $£100$ is made into a chest of drawers and sold for $£500$. The carpenter's value-added is $£400$. Not all jobs can be easily quantified in this way. What are the ministrations of a good nurse worth? Probably far more than he or she is paid for.

The figures on leavers and absenteeism relate closely to Guest's organizational outcomes and we have illustrated the calculation of interference costs that these incidents involve. Certainly, they should be monitored closely and the costs calculated.

Customer

- complaints per customer (%)
- orders not delivered on time (%)
- satisfied customers (%)
- new customer revenue/total customer revenue (%)
- marketing expenditure/turnover (%).

As we reflected, the gauge of *effectiveness* has to be the end-user or customer. So, the calculations associated with customer complaints and missed deliveries are particularly germane. Satisfied customers are more difficult to assess and constant requests for online feedback on every transaction become tiresome to customers unless there is a problem.

The two final factors are more significant and are not unconnected with marketing expected to yield attention in the marketplace. Comparative figures within the sector can be used to compare how much more is being invested than the average spend on marketing overall.

Innovation, learning and development

- R&D expenditure/turnover (%)
- training expenditure/turnover (%)
- training expenditure per employee ($£$)
- employees attending courses/total employees (%)
- revenue from new products/total revenue ($£$K).

Not dissimilar from the previous list is the question of investment against innovation and in this sense the first and last factors may very well correlate. Of the three other factors, the findings of the Handy Report in 1987 suggested that UK expenditure on training was significantly less than our competitors.

Validation and evaluation of training are important calculations to be made. Of the two, validation is more accessible in the sense that testing of knowledge and skills at the end of training is usually self-evident. More difficult is evaluation, and once again it is the end-user or customer who has the final say, but is not always asked what they think. For the individual involved in a training course, more than the usual 'happy sheets' put out by the trainer should be undertaken. Skills such as interviewing should be used soon after the end of the training, otherwise the skills are lost. Much therefore depends on the communication between the trainer and the manager of the trainee. What has been observed as potential on a training course is rarely picked up and used fully by the line manager, which often means that the opportunity to consolidate newly learned skills is overlooked.

Finally

- keep all promises;
- fix review dates;
- have appraisals at other times, too;
- you can ask for an appraisal any time;
- there is no law that says every year only;
- humour is allowed;
- friendship can come into this as appraisal properly done helps cement respect.

Our future at work depends on continuing development, now more than ever.

References and further reading

Aguinis, H. (2009) *Performance Management* (2nd edn). Prentice Hall, NJ: Pearson.

Anderson, G.C. (1993) *Managing Peformance Appraisal Systems*. Oxford: Blackwell.

Aycan, Z. (2005) The interplay between cultural and institutional/structural contingencies in human resource practices. *International Journal of Human Resource Management*, 16(7): 1083–1119.

Clutterbuck, D. (2004) *Everyone Needs a Mentor: Fostering talent in your organization*. London: CIPD.

Dries, N., Vantilborgh, T. and Papermans, R. (2012) The role of learning agility and career variety in the identification and development of high potential employees. *Personnel Review*, 41(3): 330–358.

Fletcher, C. (1993) Appraisal: An idea whose time has gone? *Personnel Management*, 25(9): 34–38.

Fletcher, C. (1999) *Appraisal: Routes to improved performance*. London: CIPD.

Fletcher, C. (2008) *Appraisal, Feedback and Development: Making performance review work*. London: Routledge.

Gilmore, S. and Williams, S. (2009) *Human Resource Management*. Oxford: Oxford University Press.

Handy, C. (1995) *Gods of Management: The changing work of organizations*. Oxford: Oxford University Press.

Handy, C. (1987) *The Making of Managers: A report on management education, training and development in the USA, West Germany, France, Japan, and the UK*. National Economic Development Office. London: NED/MSC.

Megginson, D. and Whitaker, V. (2003) *Continuing Professional Development*. London: CIPD.

Meyer, J.P. and Smith, C.A. (2000) HRM practices and organizational commitment: Test of a mediation model. *Canadian Journal of Administrative Sciences*, 17(4): 319–331.

Ramamoorthy, N. and Carroll, S.J. (1998) Individualism/collectivism orientations and reactions toward alternative human resource practices. *Human Relations*, 51(5): 571–588.

Randall, J.A. and Procter, S. (2008) Ambiguity and ambivalence: Senior managers' accounts of organizational change in a restructured government department. *Journal of Organizational Change Management*, 21(6): 686–700.

Robertson, M. and Swan, J. (2004) Going public: The emergence and effects of soft bureaucracy within a knowledge-intensive firm. *Organization*, 11(1): 123–148.

Stewart, R. (1991) *Managing Today and Tomorrow*. Basingstoke: Macmillan.

Torrington, D., Hall, L., Taylor, S. and Atkinson, C. (2011) *Human Resource Management*. Harlow: FT Pearson.

Ward, P. (1997) *360-Degree Feedback*. London: IPM.

GRADUATE ATTRIBUTES

During this exercise you will address the following graduate attributes:

- a capacity for problem identification, the collection of evidence, synthesis and dispassionate analysis;
- a capacity for attentive exchange, informed argument and reasoning;
- an awareness and appreciation of ethical and moral issues.

Performance management: appraisal

Appraisal for senior staff

Let's look at an imaginary case and consider how we would deal with it. The issue of appraisal for senior staff can be an extremely tricky one. If we think about it, the hierarchical structure of many organizations makes downward appraisal far simpler.

Look now at the situation described below and think about how you would deal with it.

You have been asked to come in and advise the managing director of Randim Futures, a small software company located in the Kingdom of Fife in Scotland. The company consists of 20 people, mostly knowledge workers but with a few manual staff.

James Randim, the managing director, started the business with a group of friends and enthusiasts who are still with him after five years. Each of these three friends has a directorship in the company. The four directors (the managing director is one of this group) have adapted to the role that suits him (yes, they are all male) best – from research and development to marketing and sales and HRM.

For all of its five year history the firm has operated very informally. It is not at all uncommon to see people wandering around the office in shorts and t-shirts. The company has no fixed hours and those who work for Randim Futures are free to work from home if they so choose.

Recently the managing director has come to be concerned about the state of the company. He considers that there appears to be a lack of progression for most of the staff. He knows that they are good at what they do, but is deeply concerned that there is no progression or career development for the staff. This is why he has called you in.

What you need to do

As a consultant to Randim Futures you are expected to produce an account making clear to the managing director what the options for training and development would be for these key senior managers. He also wants you to produce a suggested programme for developing all staff, one that might reinforce training and development for the whole company and encourage a culture of commitment and innovation.

Things you need to think about

- What is the content programme that will support this change?
- How much will it cost?
- Who will be involved?
- How will they know whether the programme has been successful, how will you evaluate?

So how are you going to tackle this?

Let's start with the basics. There are three levels to a well-written piece of work:

1 narrative
2 explanation
3 analysis.

You will need to make an effort to explain how what you are suggesting will work; why it works that way; and what are the likely outcomes of doing things in the way you suggest.

It is important that you make your reader aware that there is a world of understanding based on theories that have been tried and tested by professionals over the years, supported by sound theory and good practice.

Finally it is important when giving this kind of advice that you apply your theories clearly to the context in which the company is operating. Most CEOs like to know how much something is going to cost. So you will need to justify your suggestions with supporting evidence of the costs and benefits of following your suggestions.

We know that losing high-tech and professional staff can cost up to £10,000 each time one leaves. The problem with owner/friend founding groups is that the route to directorship looks closed off. So we need to put an appraisal system in place that will offer not just training but development, and CPD, too.

Let's look at the problem

The first thing that you need to be aware of are the constraints of a family firm or, in this case, a closely knit tight group of founders who are still in positions of senior management.

Family businesses frequently assume the legal form of private businesses that can be generally classified as micro-, small- and medium-sized enterprises. It would be usual to see family members represented in senior management. Further, because of this situation, the senior management may not be solely profit maximizers. It is likely to be the case that they will also pursue other important objectives such as maintaining or enhancing the lifestyle of the owners, and providing employment for family members in the management team.

The strengths of the family firm would include a strong culture, shared identity, very low senior management turnover, long-term perspective, increased responsibility, faster decision making and a clear and defined history. But its weaknesses will include elements such as favouritism, a lack of succession planning, a lack of strategic planning, family conflicts may spill into the business, reluctance to recruit the best person if they are outside of the family, less incentive for transparency and reluctance to change.

While Randim Futures may not be an actual family firm, it does have many elements in common with the family firm. It has a tightly knit senior management group composed of friends and they have fallen into the roles that best suit them. All that we know about Randim Futures suggests that there will be a reluctance to change. We cannot even assume that the managing director is that committed to change. After all, he is part of the group of friends.

What you are going to suggest is very much a cultural change for this organization. It is changing a culture from the Zeus to the Athena organization (Handy, 1995). Zeus culture, Handy says, is like a spider's web: 'lines radiating out from the centre' represent 'divisions of work based on functions or products' (Handy, 1995: 14). Handy saw the most important lines in such an organization being those that encircle the spider because these are the lines of power and influence, losing importance as they go farther from the centre (Handy, 1995). What is important here for Randim Futures is Handy's idea that the relationship with the spider matters more in this culture than does any formal title or position. He maintains that the speed of decision in this kind of culture is dependent on Zeus and his circle (Handy, 1995).

They need to structure themselves for a future that can encourage growth and allow promotional opportunities to those who are not part of the 'founding father' group, while getting the founding group members to encourage development of those around them. They may need to become an Athena organization.

The Athena culture is based on the approach that views management as being basically concerned with the continuous and successful solution of problems (Handy, 1995: 70). The management accomplishes this by first locating or finding the problem, then utilizing appropriate resources to solve the problem and then await the results. In this type of organization, performance is judged by the results or problems solved. These types of organizations draw resources from around the organization in order to solve a problem (Handy, 1995: 72).

Getting there from here

So we know, roughly, what Randim Futures needs to do but how do they get there? I think what is needed here is appraisal and coaching. What we have is a situation in which the organization is unlikely to change and adapt due to its Zeus culture, an organization where the possibility for development and progression is almost nil. The top slots are full so the only way to progress is through dead men's shoes. Such an organization may be losing talent because they have no chance to develop beyond their current position. We need to demonstrate the need for CPD to the senior management and the best path to this is appraisal.

Aguinis described performance management as a 'continuous process of identifying, measuring, and developing the performance of individuals and teams and aligning performance with the strategic goals of the organization' (2009: 3). Probably the most important thing here is the concept that it is continuous. Appraisal without clear considerations of the extent to which an individual is contributing to organizational performance and about how performance will improve in the future would not be fruitful performance management.

To 360 or not to 360?

One of the questions here is how do we get appraisal that will take in all levels of the organization? After all, senior managers may seek development even if they have nowhere to progress to. Of course they may need progression; perhaps they are not being best served by simply maintaining the status quo, perhaps they need to move on beyond Randim Futures.

A 360-degree feedback input component can be very valuable in evaluating performance and in ensuring that an organization's limited human resources generate a return on investment. It also ensures that these valuable resources are taken care of and remain actively engaged in their tasks; 360-degree feedback can play an important investment in the development of employees.

The advantage of 360-degree feedback is that rather than relying on the perceptions of one individual it takes into account multiple perspectives. It can provide a more comprehensive picture of behaviour or performance which can be especially critical when it is difficult to observe all areas of performance. As the name suggests, it provides far more than top-down evaluation. So, senior management is also being appraised both by those at their level and by those beneath them. This has the potential to reveal their strengths and weaknesses as well as those of their employees. It opens up the discussion of their needs for development (CPD) and progression. It could help to show whether the rigidity of the senior management structure is holding back the company.

There are possible problems – 360-degree feedback may seem wonderful but it is not without issues and you must be prepared to demonstrate an awareness of these issues. There are some significant disadvantages to using 360-degree feedback.

It is likely that Randim Futures is a poor feedback environment (common in close-knit small-scale organizations) and so the first exposure to 360-degree feedback may be accompanied by some degree of trepidation on the part of both the organization and its employees. It is vital to the process that employees understand that the feedback they receive will be used purely for their own developmental benefit or else resistance to the process may well render it useless.

Executive coaching

In executive coaching, senior managers work with professional behavioural coaches to assist them to see clearly things they do that are effective as well as those that are ineffective. The coach will help them to analyse why some things they do work and why others don't. It is designed to open doors for the managers and allows them to see what they need to do to move forward.

The usual model would be that senior managers would be offered regular one-on-one confidential coaching meetings with the behavioural coaches where they would receive feedback on their progress.

In the case of Randim Futures senior management, such coaching may be expensive but it could be extremely beneficial. The company may be in very real danger. At present there is no sense that the senior management are getting any form of CPD.

Thinking points

Can Randim Futures afford not to pursue some form of appraisal that will reinforce the need for CPD? It is a small software company in a small country but it is certain that its competition is worldwide. Without CPD they are going to lose software developers and the employees that stay will increasingly be behind the curve as far as their skills go. Although the expense of pursuing appraisal and coaching may be high, it is unlikely to be higher than the cost of losing professional staff (£10,000).

Randim Futures may wish to maintain some of its old culture, casual attire perhaps, but it clearly needs to move beyond its current structure if it wishes to remain competitive and an appraisal system that involves everyone would be the ideal vehicle to mobilize that future.

Bibliography

Aguinis, H. (2009) *Performance Management* (2nd edn). Prentice Hall, NJ: Pearson.
Handy, C. (1995) *Gods of Management: The changing work of organizations*. Oxford: Oxford University Press.

Tutor guidance

Once again this case study can be used as a discussion vehicle or as another opportunity to make a presentation or write a report. Convincing those who feel that they do not have a need for something is the most difficult task of all for trainers or consultants and small groups can be more resistant than most, particularly if they are responsible for founding the company.

Imagining the future growth of a company and the problems that can attend it can be difficult for the founders. So, presenting benefits will be an important part of any presentation or report.

The issues that need to be addressed include:

- development issues for the managing group;
- strategy for growing a company culture in the knowledge sector;
- appraisal options as a crossroads for training and development at a specific point in a company's history;
- career paths and staff retention;
- training for appraisers;
- training for appraisees;
- evaluation issues;
- likely costs.

Once again *interference costs* can be an important lever to gain commitment from managers. Losing professional staff can be an expense that costs the company significant amounts of time and therefore money. An IT company may find that keeping their people long term can be a challenge – one that needs to be addressed proactively.

9

REWARDING PEOPLE AT WORK

Topics

- strategic approach to reward
- reward and competitive advantage
- reward packages; internal and external considerations
- job evaluation and regular reward reviews.

Introduction

One enduringly popular view of reward would probably be defined as pay. It would be fair to say that attempts to recruit people without pay would be difficult unless the work was voluntary or vocational and the individuals had other means of financial support. That means that for most people there will be a level of pay that they will consider reasonable enough to engage with the job on offer. This may often be based on the going rate for the job to be found in most companies operating in a particular sector.

Knowledge of what others are paid is most often embedded in the peer group. Those who have left a company and end up working for a competitor are quick to pass on information about comparative pay rates and conditions of work to their friends and erstwhile colleagues. Though it must be said that pay rates alone do not always indicate what exactly must be done for the amount of reward paid for any job and whether there are other benefits that come with the job.

BOX 9.1

In this respect, the higher education sector offers a case in point. Although there are stated pay bands for particular academic jobs, the amount of work to be undertaken can vary both within and between universities. What for some staff members might seem a light teaching load can be offset by heavier demands for published research or greater management and administration duties.

Universities vary in the amount of contact time staff are required to have with students and such responsibilities as student advising and marking is rarely taken into account in the workload model.

There is a term that some academics use called 'cognitive calculus' which means that individuals have their own way of assessing what is a fair reward for a particular job. This may depend on how much effort they have to expend in doing the job – and is often a personal assessment based on previous experience. It can also depend on how much time is needed to complete the job satisfactorily (Farrell and Rusbult, 1981), as not all job responsibilities can be completed within core hours. Those who carry large classes, also carry larger marking loads than their colleagues with fewer students. As with any inherent or acquired ability, those who find a job easy to accomplish may feel that the reward is worthwhile. Whereas those who struggle to accomplish it within the time allocated may have to expend extra time and effort and may therefore find the reward less acceptable. At this point we may be looking at *aptitude*. Those who have a natural aptitude for any job may consider the reward offered more than adequate. They may, indeed, finish earlier than their colleagues and so have the discretion to do other things that interest them within the time allowed.

BOX 9.2

A management training company allowed its training consultants ten hours to design a company training course. One of the consultants discovered that he could complete the work on average in four hours on the train to and from work.

He overheard a colleague complaining that it took him on average 20 hours to complete the design of a training course. He realized then that he had an aptitude to complete set work faster than his colleagues. The comparative benefit of this was not lost on him.

He set up in business on his own, confident that he could fulfil the work at the going rate faster than his average competitor.

In a sense what we have discussed applies to all business sectors. High-fliers usually do better than their colleagues at achieving the job objectives. They may be faster, more accurate and achieve more in the time without feeling that their energies have been overtaxed. So, for them the job is well within their comfort zone and the demands made on them are less than onerous.

For the organization, finding competent and experienced workers is always a challenge. Most people want to be part of an organization in which staff are proud to work and willing to give their commitment. Money is important as a comparative factor and payment below the going rate will always be resented and will very likely lead to the search for more equitable rewards elsewhere. However, there are other factors that may make staff feel more or less committed to staying, and though money is important there may be other considerations that rank highly, such as working with colleagues you find congenial, or the convenience of being close to home (Armstrong and Brown, 2009).

All of this suggests that paying the going rate for the job is important to attract suitably competent and committed workers in the first place. However, retaining them may require more effort to keep them happy in the workplace. So, in this chapter we will be considering the different elements that may go towards making up a package that is competitive with other organizations in the sector but distinctive enough to make individuals want to stay on.

Strategic approach to reward

- business direction
- culture
- reward values
- reward strategy
- required competence.

The above list includes the elements that are linked to each other in a logical sequence, suggesting that the strategy of the business leads on to the strategy of reward. It would be gratifying if the process worked as seamlessly as the list suggests. What we observe here are all the elements that connect in some way to the final outcome of satisfaction with reward. However, it would be difficult to say in which order they can be addressed. If we accept that business direction is what Guest refers to as *strategic integration*, then we might accept that this is a useful place to start. But we might then find that radical change is needed to acquire the competencies to achieve the business objectives. That might mean a change of culture, if by culture we accept Deal and Kennedy's definition of 'the way we do things round here' (1982). And, that, as we have seen, may be easy to state but more difficult to achieve.

So, decisions made could well mean a required change in the culture and a different set of reward strategies and values to attract and keep the people we want. Whether current workers will respond to such changes positively is always open to question. If by culture we mean perceptions or attitudes, then the change process could take time to achieve.

BOX 9.3

In the days of British Rail the organization spent £3 million training guards in customer care. Most guards had been employed and trained to guard the train in the event of an emergency but were unused to relating to passengers directly and certainly would not have expected to check tickets or give advice and information to passengers.

At the end of the training BR chose the 10 per cent who showed aptitude for the new role and appointed them to a new role of senior conductor with a different uniform and pay and conditions.

Over the following 20 years into privatization of the railways that new role has now become standard practice throughout all railway companies.

We will be considering these different but related factors throughout this chapter. The employment market does not get any easier to operate in. *Flexibility*, which has been the hallmark of the modern organization, brings with it complexity which traditional approaches to reward had tried to rationalize. Similarly, *commitment* becomes more difficult to achieve when consultancy contracts, interim managers and subcontractors are added to the mix of people working within an organization.

So, we will refer to traditional ways of rewarding workers, always aware that job security in the organization may no longer be assumed by either workers or managers. This means that there are other factors apart from monetary rewards that become important to those working in the organization.

Payment systems

HR as a practice has usually sought to deliver reward to people on two levels:

1   a connection between employee pay and employee performance as a variable incentive linked to corporate objectives through a performance management process;
2   a market-related approach to pay and benefits to reflect the commercial worth and value of what people are asked to do.

How is the balance between the two aspects achieved? First, the connection between pay and performance needs to be clarified. Variable incentives suggest that flat levels of pay need to be linked to targets, and these targets need to be linked to the incentives. As we have seen already, the productivity factors of time, quality, quantity and cost do not always support each other directly. Sometimes it may be assumed that quality will remain constant while the other three elements can be altered to increase output, for example, reducing time and cost. Constantly searching for ways of getting more for less may eventually impact on quality of service, if only because those staff who are expected to deliver increased productivity do not always feel that the changes to their terms and conditions are either equitable or fair (Armstrong and Brown, 2001).

The second aspect makes perfect sense as long as it is possible to estimate accurately the value and worth of what people are asked to do. But who makes that judgement? How accurately can that be assessed by managers working within an industry? As we shall see, the use of external assessors skilled in such evaluative work may be the only reasonable answer (Fletcher, 1993).

What we can say is that modern social media make it more difficult for a company to keep its pay and conditions a secret. Change can be and is instantly commented on through personal communications systems. Countries that seek to suppress access to such media may be doing their ultimate ability to compete globally no favours at all, as once their citizens do find out what the facts are elsewhere there may be a measure of resentment that that truth was suppressed and an increased determination to seek the rewards that are on offer elsewhere.

Reward and competitive advantage

Stredwick (2000) offers a list of aspects that can be considered by strategic planners and we will comment on each of them in turn.

Reward for achieving required results

What first springs to mind here is a basic link between production and incentives. There are some working environments where this would be readily accepted, and sales is one obvious environment where that would be accepted as normal. But whether that can be applied to other service industries is something that is in current debate among both unions and politicians. Most people do not want to be operated on by surgeons who have productivity targets. Policing and targets for arrests and charging suspects would be viewed with equal disquiet by most reasonable citizens. Similarly, payment by results for teachers could be a slippery slope to careful deselection and exclusion of slow learners or those with learning disabilities so that only the best will yield the excellent results required to achieve the rewards. So, here we can see that the undesirable outcomes that incentives might have on *quality of service* needs to be carefully monitored and reviewed.

Pay for performance, skill and competence

This ought to be self-evident. But interestingly, it does not always cover customer care, patient care, spending extra time, for example, with those who are grieving or traumatized. Who assesses that good-will element, and are they in a position to see it when it happens and reward it? Caring about others is a function of commitment as well as competence and the neglect suffered by those in care homes, hospitals or other institutions is not always evident, and commitment is sometimes completely lacking. That continues to be a problem both in the public sector and privately run facilities. So who owns the homes and how clients pay may make little difference to care outcomes that are essentially voluntary and go largely unrewarded in monetary terms (Armstrong and Mirlis, 2004).

Flexibility with a broadband structure

For years, employers have sought to move away from *collective bargaining* by unions. They have preferred instead flexibility of reward according to experience and application to the job and commitment to the organization. They have been frustrated by predictive pay rates applying to all within a grade and sought the discretion to award differently for different people. The danger is that such discretion can be used in ways that may appear discriminatory to those who feel that their efforts have been overlooked.

BOX 9.4

Not long ago a group of academics were engaged by a university. They were all appointed to Lecturer grade. In those days the grade was distinguished between Lecturer A (lower pay band) and Lecturer B (higher pay band).

It was only after they became friendly and compared notes that they discovered that all the females had been graded Lecturer A and their male colleagues Lecturer B (the distinction has now been scrapped).

Flexible benefits to promote diversity of choice

In a sense this follows on from the previous point discussed. Flexible benefits can extend to many different options. But how they are valued depends on the individual rewarded by them. The offer of a variety of rewards included in a package would seem to be important here and we examine the cafeteria approach to reward later in this chapter. Such a variety of options has to be paid for, and sometimes individuals would prefer money, which enables them to make choices in their lives for themselves.

Pay determined to meet local conditions

The London weighting allowance is a case in point. Traditionally, it costs more to live in or travel to and from a capital city, so wages were adjusted upwards to take account of the extra costs involved. Interestingly, that has been outstripped by the price of housing and the cost of rail fares, so for many occupations the option to live locally to their work became less feasible to fund even with the weighting allowance. So, for example, at one time bus drivers were driven into the capital from well outside London and taken back home at the end of their shift, thereby significantly extending their working days, nights and weekends.

Paying for employee's ideas, initiative and innovation

Certainly, this is a useful idea but one rarely used with anything more than a token payment. Compared with banking where per cent bonuses on deals done produce exceptional rewards, the rewards offered for ideas in industry are small by comparison, so the incentive to respond them is equally small. Staff with ideas to offer contribute because, like those who enjoy customer care, they get a personal satisfaction from making that contribution. A share in the per cent yield of innovation, however, would be appreciated much more.

Incentives based on broad measures of organizational success

The name John Lewis may spring to mind here. One fair way of rewarding everyone is to make sure that that reward is linked to shares in the company. In that way the efforts of all are rewarded equally and their share issue gives them a feeling of investment in their own company. Few organizations set out to emulate this approach to rewarding their employees perhaps because the owners and shareholders do not want to see their equity diluted. However, companies that recognize the value of gaining *organizational commitment* will consider this a strategic benefit worth introducing.

Summary

Reward as a term extends much more broadly than just the financial package arranged between employer and employee. We have only to ask individual staff members whether they find their job rewarding or not to find out that the term applies to a general feeling of well-being and satisfaction that transcends just the money side of the transactional contract.

So, reward can also include: holidays; cars; time off in lieu; houses; training support; private health provision; share options and so on. The critical factor is how it rewards effort at work in both the mandatory and discretionary parts of the employment contract.

But even as we say this, there are other factors that might suggest that individual workers also enjoy working with others and that the manager is key in their feeling that they are accepted and progressing in the organization. These are personal judgements that are not part of the contract but yet play an important part in whether staff want to stay or are considering move on. This means that there will be a mix of influences that affect the decision to stay or go, and finding out what these are may not be discovered either quickly or easily.

Total reward

The Chartered Institute of Personnel Development (CIPD) suggests that 35 per cent of organizations are adopting this approach (Armstrong and Murlis, 2004), and this may include the following.

Redesigning work

There is nothing new in using *flexibility* more strategically within the workplace. Not all work needs to be done under the eye of a supervisor nor on the company's premises. Working at home and telecommuting are appreciated by the increasing number of people who look after dependents and would otherwise have to embark on expensive and tiring commuting journeys. It means they can do their work when it fits in with their family responsibilities while meeting their work deadlines in the usual way.

BOX 9.5

For one university professor this meant working between 10pm and 4am in the morning – usually in his office but also elsewhere.

As a colleague and collaborator, out of hours mobile phone calls received his undivided attention during those hours.

There are also the questions of *job rotation* and *work rotation*. As we have seen, these were originally introduced in the car manufacturing industry and intended both to relieve the boredom of traditional car production lines and also to ensure that each member of the quality circle was capable of covering for colleagues in the team should they be absent from work for any reason.

From manufacturing this practice has spread to other industries, so that work rotation is extremely useful for exposing *graduate management trainees* to every part of the company before deciding with them which section or department they would be best allocated to. For *accelerated promotion path* candidates it is likewise helpful to enable them to experience the aspects of the senior post that they are expected to occupy at the end of their training (Hendry *et al.*, 2000).

Symbolic rewards

Certainly there are some companies that have adopted schemes that highlight particular members of the team both with colleagues and customers. Awards of all kinds such as cups or medals can add a competitive element to inter-team rivalry. However, if the same team wins all the time, it can become demoralizing for those who feel they never get a chance to excel and be acknowledged publicly.

Investing in people

The award *Investors in People* was introduced in the early 1990s to attempt to get companies to link their training needs to the investment needed and apportion it to all individuals within the organization. For core members of staff this is best practice, of course. But it is worth asking whether staff that are on consultancy contracts or are subcontractors are offered support, too. It would be easy to overlook them and believe that they are well provided for themselves. However, unless the company can contribute to their efforts at CPD in some way, it may be more difficult to retain their continued commitment. Involvement in projects that enhance their professional development will usually be appreciated and encourage staff to stay.

Personal development plans

Work is not just about work, it is also about people's welfare, health and development outside work. Companies such as Marks & Spencer had an enviable reputation for taking care of their staff. Gym membership, fitness classes, health initiatives are all a part of taking an interest in people and making it easy for them to avail themselves of activities outside work. Managers tend to focus on work responsibilities and targets at appraisal, but much less on what interests people have outside work. An interesting job engages people at all levels of their interests, both personal and professional (Pilbeam, 1998).

Reward strategy

Employee objectives

Purchasing power

Keeping good people requires a constant assessment of what costs are locally. The principal outlay of a domestic household is housing, whether owned or rented. So, how far people's disposable income is absorbed by this cost will be relevant in their decision to stay or move. Those who moved out of London in the past, for example, found that their living costs went down on average and they could afford to invest in a bigger property. Employees trying to move in the opposite direction would find that the same factors usually work to their disadvantage. We have already referred to weighting allowances as one way of addressing this. Assistance with a loan to cover the outgoings of an annual season ticket is also a way of showing appreciation of the major costs that can be incurred when moving to a life of daily commuting.

Equity

People are aware of what they earn in comparison with others doing a similar job elsewhere or in the same organization. This means that should they feel less well rewarded for doing similar work, they are likely to feel aggrieved. This has traditionally been the case for females in the workforce. On average they are likely to be earning 75 per cent of what men earn in similar occupations. Though this is against the law, putting together a case in an Employment Appeal Tribunal is nowhere near as easy as it sounds. There are all sorts of excuses that can and are used to suggest that men are more experienced or better qualified than their female colleagues. And staff know that such cases do not improve their popularity with the company and that such action could affect their promotion prospects.

Rights

And, we should add here, responsibilities. This ought to be self-evident – it is part of the employment contract both expressed and implied. In other words, not everything is included in the written part of the employment contract, but a reasonable employee would do it anyway; for example, observance of health and safety at work. However, custom and practice can still be a potent force in some workforces and sometimes the law will acknowledge and support this. An obvious example would be drinking at work. In some breweries production workers were able to enjoy free beer at lunch time. In some transport companies office staff (not drivers) were able to go to the pub at lunch time. Increasingly, such anomalies have mostly been reduced and no members of staff are allowed to drink alcohol during the working day.

Unions are usually quite protective of members' rights. Payment for all sorts of extra duties is jealously guarded. It took years for the railway industry to negotiate one-man-only operations on the front of trains when steam traction was replaced by diesel locomotives and there was a similar resistance to abandoning a guard's van at the rear of every goods train and allowing the guard to ride on the rear footplate of the locomotive. However, the industry now accepts the concept of train crew whereby those working as conductors can be admitted for training for driving duties – something that was jealously guarded by the drivers' unions in the past.

Relativities

Traditionally, what were called differentials between grades were also protected during annual pay negotiations. Workers and their unions were acutely aware of the differentials to be maintained between skilled, semi-skilled and unskilled workers. In traditional car companies, for example, there could be as many as 120 different levels and within those many different grades, all of which made for complex and contested negotiations absorbing significant time and effort on the part of the personnel department who were often tasked with the negotiations.

It could be said that automation has encroached upon such distinctions. Spot-welding machines took over from manual welding many years ago and computerization has made even skilled work replicable by machines. Traditional crafts and trades have therefore contracted or disappeared, or are dealt with by subcontractors or outsourcing. The large organization with many levels has therefore been delayered with no more than five or six levels between the top executive and the functional workers.

However, pay differentials for the core workers that remain will be as keenly monitored by staff as they ever were and managers need to review pay and rewards regularly, using an outside agency whose expertise and integrity is accepted by all parties.

Recognition

Traditionally, promotion and pay rises have been the most acceptable means of recognizing excellence at work. However, with the delayering of organizations the opportunities for rising up the promotion ladder may be somewhat curtailed. On the other side, unbundling businesses may be able to offer more responsibility early on in a career with an organization.

We have already spoken of more traditional ways of acknowledging employee of the month and rewarding people who come up with innovation or new ideas, which is another way of recognizing merit and achievement. Most people find that a word of appreciation and thanks is also rewarding. It does depend, though, on a manager who is both observant and in a position to notice when extraordinary efforts have been expended on behalf of the organization.

Composition

How reward is made up is important to most workers. At the level of monetary recompensation the breakdown between basic and commission is a vital balance to achieve for salespeople and negotiators. One rule of thumb was that the basic should cover the normal domestic outgoings with commission providing the extras that an individual needs. This ensures that salespeople have reasonable security together with a need to generate more sales to enhance their discretionary income. However, some salespeople are commission only, which means that they will expect a higher percentage of the sale. This has traditionally been more prevalent in the financial sector, though as we have seen, it can give rise to dissention when monies paid are outlandish or out of proportion to the effort required. So, per cent rates on large financial transactions may appear unjustified if the transaction was routine and required no exercise of expertise (Locke and Latham, 1990).

For those keen on progressing in an organization, the chance to experience other, related jobs may be appreciated. Work rotation can be an enervating experience for accelerated promotion path candidates. It can also provide those interested with a taste of what a posting elsewhere could entail – particularly if service abroad has not been experienced previously, shadowing someone else can be a useful introduction.

Employer objectives

Prestige

Most employees want to feel they work for a well-respected organization. In the UK people are less likely to talk about their work organization than in the US. However, they are as likely to recommend it to a friend or warn off possible recruits if they feel disaffected. Organizations that work to engage their staff are more likely to gain their *organizational commitment*.

Competition

Most employees talk to their friends and acquaintances and exchange views about employers. They are particularly likely to speak to those who work in the same sector. Such networks are active in exchanging information about terms and conditions. Indeed, it is quite likely that when one person finds a better employer they contact others in the sector to let them know just how good things are in the hope of encouraging them to join as well.

Control

We might construe this as access: access to resources; access to opportunity; access to congenial colleagues. Rosemary Stewart (1991) reflected that it was most likely that the job will increase in scope over the first few months with more opportunities and work becoming available. She found that most people were happy with this situation. Much less happy were those who were constrained to do only what the job description laid down.

Autonomy is another variant of this control that people like to feel they have over their job. Indeed, most people who prefer working on their own value this more highly than anything else – a boss or a job that allows a choice of exactly how and when to do the job (provided that the targets and deadlines are met).

All of this suggests that *strategic integration*, when properly extended to embrace the job, informs people of how their work fits into the strategic plan and enables them to explain this to others – particularly prospective colleagues or customers. If it is true that knowledge is power, then being knowledgeable in front of significant others is both highly gratifying and a gauge of trust from the organization.

Motivation and performance

This follows on from the point made previously that people whose skills fit in with both the job content and the preferred style of working will usually be most satisfied with their job and their work. Workers' enthusiasm can be infectious and encourages new recruits to want to stay on during the first few months of getting used to a new position. Such workers make good supervisors, mentors and trainers, because good practice is caught not taught and commitment is demonstrable to those who are learning about the organization early on.

Cost

We could consider this in two ways: what are the costs to the individual of doing the job and working for the organization? Is there a price to be paid in terms of health, for example? There have been many examples of working environments that were virtually certain to put an individual's health at risk just by working there. If we think of mining, for example, many miners died of silicosis. Similarly, workers in the construction and ship building industries found that later in life they had contracted asbestosis and the most dangerous working environments tended to be in the construction industry. In other areas living near nuclear facilities can increase the likelihood of contracting serious illness. All of this suggests that disregarding health and safety issues damages not just the health of individuals but the reputation of businesses that have profited, wittingly or unwittingly, from practices deleterious to fellow human beings.

The other issue is realistic investment levels. Working with substandard equipment in poor working conditions does not improve motivation or a willingness to stay on. Cost cutting and economies only work for a short time, provided that all are making an effort to achieve the same end – the preservation of the business and investment in the future. But working for an organization whose motto is 'as long as people keep applying for our jobs, we will keep offering the lowest rate' means high staff turnover and low quality outputs which soon communicates to the wider markets and prospective employees.

Change management

Most people now accept change as normal in the workplace. Continuing in gainful employment in any sector means grasping new ideas and concepts as well as becoming familiar with new equipment and computer software. However, what people resent is the way change is managed, or in some cases, mismanaged. Most important is involvement in the change process. Being consulted, or at least properly informed, ought to be obvious to change agents, whether external or internal, as the right thing to do.

Feeling consulted about how change could best be implemented is a matter of respect for staff and often assures their *commitment* to the final outcome. Finally, training should be properly funded and be adequate to support the training need that exists within the company and all those affected by the change.

A significant number of key people leave their company within the first few years following a merger. That suggests either that companies are not good at managing change or that they embarked on something that pleased their financial backers but left the workforce unconvinced of the need for personal disruption during the change. Once again, consultation early on might have been the opportunity to reinforce the message of why change is needed through consulting people on how it might best be achieved (Bullock and Batten, 1985). The second factor is time to become accustomed to the changes decreed and adequate support during the transition, though against this we might also see the demands of global trading continue to drive a 24/7, 365-day trading year. This does not make it easy to find time to adapt and assimilate new methods before the demands of the market become pressing.

Market mechanisms

External markets

External relativities

How many potential employees are there in any sector? A shortage of available candidates will mean there is a problem recruiting and retaining skilled and professional staff. Recent figures suggested that of the academics involved in teaching in business schools, 2,000 are shortly to retire. Behind them there are 594 appropriately qualified PhDs. However, 90 per cent of them are non-EU citizens, which means that they are unlikely to stay for more than a few years before returning home to settle down. On top of that government restrictions on work visas make it difficult to secure even those who do want to stay. Perhaps age discrimination legislation and the need to work longer will conspire to defer these demographic challenges that await us in the future and sustain the businesses on which we depend.

Over market/market rates

Can paying more than the going rate make it easier to attract staff of the desired quality? Well, in any free market it may be that this will work temporarily. However, once the competition is alerted to this strategy it will not take long before everyone is offering better or more favourable terms and conditions. On average people attracted in that way may also be on the look-out for better options and therefore be more likely to move should another and better offer be made to them.

Independent comparators

This is probably more apparent in the public sector where rigidity of roles and ranking are still an issue that continues to apply. It is certain that those within the public sector note comparators most closely between their own and other public sector departments. Senior executive officers in the civil service were used to comparing their earnings levels with superintendents of police. Under the Thatcher government the police were favoured with above-inflation pay rises – to the consternation of the senior executive officers in other parts of the civil service.

However, the erosion of TUPE (Transfer of Undertakings (Protection of Employment) Regulations, 2006) rights during periods of privatization makes the continued existence of inflexible working practices less defensible. Pressures will continue to be put on publicly funded bureaucracies to adapt to more flexible working practices and the trend to amalgamate small units into larger bodies will be irresistible. One example is the creation of a single Scottish police force from the seven local forces that prevailed in the past. The cull of officers will begin at the top, with six fewer chief constables and a cull of deputy and assistant chief constables throughout the country.

Specialist reward consultancies

Official bodies whose business is devoted to analysing and comparing the going rate for jobs and work in most sectors are likely to be a consistent and reliable guide on pay and rewards within any industry. Certainly, as we saw in the last chapter, the advice given by the experts is that money and rewards should be put in the hands of such experts, if the appropriate rate for the job is to be offered to competent and experienced people (Fletcher, 1993).

The attempt to be objective is always worth the effort. Social media make access to data in any field immediate for individuals, so a company's transparency is not just the best policy but also avoids the suspicion that the company is not interested in fair rates of pay for its staff or is seeking to avoid addressing adequate rewards.

Word on the street

In any small and local market it may be that this is still a viable option for a company to rely upon. However, increasingly, knowledge workers pass freely across borders and, particularly if they are international consultants, they will know what the reward comparators are. Most at risk are those who put salary as negotiable, in the hope of getting someone to under-pitch in order to get the job. It will not take long before such recruits discover what their peer group is getting by way of rewards. Such knowledge may lead to serious demotivation and a desire to move on.

Job ads

It seems increasingly that jobs recruiters and job applicants find one another using modern social media. Sites such as LinkedIn enable potential job applicants to make their profile available online. It may even encourage prospective employers to make a direct approach to a prospective employee. Such modern media must be a headhunter's dream come true. By the same token, job seekers can find out much that they need to know about a prospective employer before they make an application. Tweeters and bloggers everywhere are now the modern word on the street.

Internal markets

Enterprise

One approach can be using and developing those who already work for the company in contingent areas to the work required to be done. For example, those who work in a sales office are often well placed to know the customers, speak to them every day, answer their problems and facilitate order progress. It might be possible to train and support such staff in negotiation skills and territory management, thereby offering staff a path of career development to another level of expertise within the company.

By comparison, it would take a seasoned salesperson coming in from outside several months to learn product ranges and customer contact patterns, and start to become effective at selling the company's lines.

Collective bargaining

This is still predominant in unionized environments, the majority of whose members are in the public sector. It provides a natural justice that those doing the same job should be equally fairly rewarded. We know that what it cannot do is be flexible to the needs of a local market. We can see governments attempting to change this by offering local agreements or by privatizing, which may well deprive union members of their trade union, pension and earnings rights and consign them to the subcontract segment of Handy's Shamrock organization.

The erosion of previously held workers' rights has been a constant focus of political initiatives as parties seek to reduce the tax burden and increase competitiveness. The debate about making profit from public services such as the National Health Service in the UK is one that will continue to be hotly contested, though it is clear that the enthusiasm for private finance initiatives has not diminished as the search for economies in public services continues.

FIGURE 9.1 Elements in reward assessment.

Source: Adapted from Gilmore and Williams (2009: 176).

Figure 9.1 suggests a balance between the different factors that are apparent in reward management. In some ways they are likely to give rise to conflicting objectives, especially where the ability to compete is made on the basis of the lowest tender being accepted regardless of its quality. A recent example of the private sector's provision of support services was at the London Olympics in 2012 where a private contractor failed to produce the requisite number of security officers. This is an obvious example in which the government retained the duty to supply the need and had to bring in 18,000 military personnel to cover the gap and pay again in order to fulfil their legal obligations.

The problem with privatization comes for governments when there are no further contractors willing to undertake the work being outsourced. Indeed, with the privatized railways in the UK, two private providers withdrew from their operation in the middle of their contract. The government had to intervene and take over the running of the services through the Department for Transport.

As to fairness and equity of rewards, it has to be said that workers with rare skills are more likely to be able to maintain reasonable recompense. Those whose skills are easily replicable are more likely to slide down in the relative pay scales. In comparative terms this outlined the three questions that all workers need to ask themselves as an indicator that they can remain in continued employment:

- What do I cost?
- What do I yield?
- How does that compare with others doing similar work throughout the world?

The third circle linking pay to organizational objectives we will examine in more detail. Where job elements are measurable and testable, it would seem quite feasible. However, it may be the case that not all jobs offer that option. Innovation and creativity are much more difficult to measure and reward, as is risk taking in business.

Banding schemes

For many organizations reducing the levels within the organization has been a continuing objective. Combining that objective with the need to keep differentials between jobs and promotion prospects alive has been addressed though banding pay within the organization. So in some universities there are certain levels that run across academic, academic-related and the administration functions. Within each level not only are the competencies designated clearly, but the reward band allows an individual to start at the bottom end of the pay band and advance through incremental payments year on year until the top of the band is reached. Promotion to the next grade would enable the progressive pay increases to continue in the next band above.

Potential benefits

One of the benefits of a banded reward system is that it clearly applies to the appropriate level of competencies required within the band. It also gives managers the discretion to reward individuals within their band as they demonstrate continued experience within the job.

It can also cope with changes in function across the constituent disciplines, allowing comparison to be made between those functions. As with work rotation, it offers workers the chance of development in different functions, demonstrating comparative knowledge and skill levels which may then be transferable across the organization.

In this way it can respond to the changing nature of work while satisfying employee expectations within an industry and encouraging the retention of employees who are interested in developing their career in different roles while continuing to work in the same organization.

The make-up of reward packages

Basic rate

This part of the package relates to the regular payment of a stated amount which will be paid regularly throughout the term of employment. It is usually related to a standard of performance – in sales, for example, a minimum input of sales over a stated period.

Plussage

As the term suggests, this is added payment for duties undertaken over and above what the original employment contract laid down. It applies only during the time during which these additional duties are performed, so it is not permanent payment and may not necessarily contribute to the individual's pension. So, someone who takes up the role of acting supervisor might be rewarded in this way during tenure and then either confirmed in post or resume her or his former position. If confirmed in post then the employment contract would be redrawn to reflect the relevant increased payment for the job of supervisor.

Benefits

These can come in many guises. They can include assistance with travel to and from work; luncheon vouchers; accommodation (free or subsidized); opportunities to purchase products at a subsidized rate. For those involved in travel for the company of more than 18,000 miles a year, a car may be provided and all expenses paid.

Premia

For some companies there are certain activities that they will reward more highly. It may be that particularly difficult or complex operations require more from those who undertake them. So a premium may be offered while these duties are undertaken.

Overtime

This again speaks for itself. But it is also sometimes linked to time-and-a-half or double-time payments for unsocial hours such as night work or weekend working.

Incentives

Most salespeople will be well aware of incentives – sometimes referred to as commission. It is usually a percentage payment over and above a certain level of sales and can vary from product to product. Thus it rewards those who sell particularly expensive or complex products.

Bonus

It has become popular practice to offer bonuses for hitting particular targets. These targets can be personal ones, or for those at a senior level they may be for organizational achievement. There is some controversy surrounding such payments. Like payment-by-results they can cause individuals or groups to skew their results or hold back on contracts until they can be attributed to the period in which the bonus applies. They can also have more serious consequences as when directors were offered bonuses for reducing deaths and injuries in the industry. Managers lower down were then leant on to reduce the reporting of incidents so that their senior managers would be paid their bonuses.

Fairness of distribution

It must be said that equity is a subjective judgement. Often custom and practice has endured and reinforced in the minds of staff that this is 'the way we do things round here'. Inequity occurs when staff become aware that the effort required to achieve the reward is higher for people lower down the organization than for those at the top. As we remarked earlier, comparison with what applies among the competitors may alert staff to the fact that there are fairer opportunities elsewhere.

Job evaluation and regular reward reviews

As we have remarked earlier, Rosemary Stewart (1991) commented on the propensity for work demands to expand over the course of the job. Her research suggested that within three months most jobs increase as the boss delegates more to the subordinate, colleagues and staff ask for help, and customers make contact for help and advice.

It is rare for jobs to remain the same in terms of their demands and responsibilities, and Stewart suggests that those that are thus constrained are likely to be less satisfied with their jobs than those who take on more.

Structural changes within organizations likewise involve change in what people are asked to do and who they are asked to work with. Downsizing can often involve the need to take on more work as others leave and are not replaced. All of this suggests that regular reviews of what people do and how they are rewarded could avoid grievance, or staff looking to move elsewhere (Coates, 1994).

We have already said that this should not be dealt with at appraisal, but should be entrusted to an outside body with expertise in job evaluation. The following are points that may be useful to bear in mind:

- Job evaluation is concerned with the job elements themselves moving down to the specifics of task analysis, if necessary – particularly in a new working environment where technology or process is new and for which there are no precedents. It is not about the performance of individuals themselves, so it should not be regarded as an opportunity to use an external assessor as an appraiser.
- The technique is systematic rather than scientific. It is still a judgement made by the assessor but it should enable comparability to be made on a more objective basis.
- Job evaluation does not eliminate collective bargaining. It may indeed require further negotiation to determine whether certain jobs now merit being included in a different level in the pay banding offered. So, it determines differentials but not pay levels – that is still to be determined within the organization itself.
- Only a structure of pay rates is produced so other payments or benefits have still to be determined by the organization itself.

Some organizations have tried using a points system, so particular parts of a job are weighted with a certain number of points. So, the head of department was determined at 20 points; course leaders 10 points. In all 60 points was required as demonstrating a reasonable workload.

Discussions then centred on whether the course leaders were comparable in the workload that they carried. Some courses might contain 200+ students, where in other subjects a big class might be considered to be 25. The same debate was to be conducted for heads of departments. How many people/sections were they responsible for and were those sections comparable in terms of the workload that they carried? This brings us back to fairness and equity: comparability will be closely examined by those who know what the workload involves. Preparation time, for example, and marking and supervision loads are hotly disputed topics when points systems are mooted (Brown and Heywood, 2005).

In short, there are no easy ways of evaluating the comparators that lie between jobs in a similar role and function. For knowledge workers and those who employ them, this can be a matter of serious consequence if it does not deliver.

PRP – Explain What You Mean

If PRP is intended to mean *performance related pay* then it can be admitted that it works well in jobs that have traditionally been rewarded by payment for performance (sales would be a case in point).

The problems arise when employers attempt to impose it on sectors that have not traditionally been paid in that way. This is not to say that no attempt should be made to examine whether payment by performance would not be feasible, and indeed, perhaps welcomed by the best performers. However, there are other considerations that may need to be taken into account.

First of all, quality. It would be fair to say that when time is reduced and quantity increased or costs reduced, the temptation to cut corners on quality may be overwhelming. That means that perhaps health and safety becomes more inconsistent or even disregarded. For teachers paid by results there will be temptations to make sure that as many students pass as possible, regardless of how good their work really is.

The second point to make is that most people believe that they are above-average performers (Fletcher, 1993). That means that a system that rewards the best performers may find others whose aptitude is not so pronounced feeling aggrieved that it is always the same few who end up with higher rewards. In teamworking, members' feelings can run high and a sense of resentment develop that pervades the goodwill within the group.

So, in short, the system needs to be transparent and not contain any of the traps that we have described above (Newton and Findlay, 1996).

If PRP means *profit related pay* then it can be said that this works well in teams where everyone shares in whatever is generated at the end of the year. The John Lewis Partnership would be a good example of this approach to reward sharing. However, it has to be said that most companies have not rushed to emulate their example.

If we look at the indicators suggested for assessing *performance related pay* they are sometimes referred to as follows.

Performance indicators

We have already commented on the need to define standards with care and accuracy. But we have also mentioned that there are some jobs where it is difficult to measure the outcome. Internalized functions such as thinking and planning may appear to be periods of inactivity to the observer. Sometimes knowledge workers themselves do not know how much time will be required to accomplish an innovative or creative task.

The phrase itself can do no other than indicate. It cannot predict unless there is no discretion left to the operator except perform to the standard laid down. For those in counselling or caring roles this can present difficulties. Often patients need longer to explain their needs and longer to recover from medical procedures. Some of the targets imposed on the Health Service have led to patients being discharged before they were ready to cope with leaving hospital because the bed was needed and bed occupation is severely constrained by imposed targets.

Acquisition or utilization of competencies

The emphasis now made on management competences should be the focus of developing and managing people. It encourages managers and assessors to move away from commenting on 'attitudes'. But it should also be acknowledged that much that knowledge workers achieve is governed by tacit knowledge, which means that sometimes the workers themselves are unaware of just why they are successful at what they do. That makes it difficult to analyse how they are successful, and so difficult to pass on their aptitude to other colleagues through structured training.

A related and important point is the ability and potential of people at work. Much store was set by the learning organization in the early 1990s (Senge, 1990). But the attempt to mobilize the potential that lies within any workforce is usually marginal at best. If employers were serious about growing their own talent, they would spend much more time, effort, and investment in engaging that potential in achieving the future which they espouse in their strategic plans.

Achievement of job objectives

This ought to go without saying; however, job objectives do not remain static and interference in achieving objectives is frequent in a global economy. We return to the challenge that this gives to workers, those who manage them, and those who try to evaluate their efforts.

Appraisal ratings

Appraisal ratings are only one attempt to evaluate what people do and to capture their aspirations and support them. Particularly to be avoided are tick box systems that seek to put workers into different categories. One such system was used in the civil service. It was a five-box system whose categories were as follows:

- Box 1: Fitted for promotion (money was usually awarded for this grade)
- Box 2: Above average performer
- Box 3: Average performer
- Box 4: Below average performer
- Box 5: Unsatisfactory.

In one particular year no money was available for pay rises, so managers were advised not to give Box 1 markings. This, as can be imagined, led to some puzzlement for those who had been marked as Box 1 in previous years suddenly being marked Box 2 (Barlow, 1989).

Fletcher's (1993) suggestion that professional/knowledge workers should be given a blank piece of paper to fill in all that they perceive they do should be the basis of any dialogue about future performance and development aspirations.

Summary of PRP provision

Integration of PRP with holistic performance management by effective manager

This is the counsel of perfection. Given that all three conditions are in place the system ought to work well.

High level of trust between manager and staff

Of course, but it is often absent, particularly during periods of change. People do not always tell each other what they think and feel about change. The price of such frankness could be career limiting and most people know and avoid sharing their views with significant others in the workforce. Involving staff in their own development and training preferences may redress the balance between management directiveness and staff quiescence (Burton et al., 2004).

Work activity measures are both valid and reliable

As we have seen, once again a counsel of perfection. No one wants to use an invalid or unreliable measure of performance. But once again in times of change, performance can be variable and therefore not a reliable indicator of what people can do under more stable conditions. Working in any promotional capacity during an economic downturn will always be difficult and expected results may not be forthcoming. It depresses everyone involved and is not a fair measure of what would normally be achieved.

Assessment of performance is fair in practice and perceived to be fair by those involved in it

This relates to the second factor in this list. Trust is vital in any acceptable exercise of assessment. But it is most often lost when the perception of management decisions is found wanting in equity and fairness. Without this balance, the exercise will largely be meaningless and may even engender further mistrust. As we have seen, for professional workers their own assessment of their contribution to the business can be vital for generating trust between managers and staff.

PRP amounts that are meaningful

This aspect is only to be measured against what is perceived as fair and comparable to what others in the sector would expect.

BOX 9.6

A salesperson worked for a company selling weighing equipment. His terms of commission were: 5 per cent for sales up to £500; 2½ per cent for sales between £500 and £1,500; ¼ per cent for anything over £1,500.

He had the opportunity of selling a weighbridge which earned the company £50,000.

He received just over £50 commission.

He and his colleagues concluded that the extensive six months work to achieve that sale was not worth making in the future. He left the company shortly afterwards.

Overall reward structures are competitive, so that PRP is genuinely in addition to normal pay

The above example more or less makes that point quite eloquently.

Cafeteria/flexible benefits

The following is a list of benefits which can offer choices to those who want to be part of a more flexible system. However, some of the benefits which used to be offered are becoming rarer now.

- bars and drinks cabinets have disappeared from most, if not all organizations;
- luncheon vouchers are rarely heard of now;
- subsidized canteens are less often available;
- benefits must be declared for taxation purposes more so than in the past;
- cars cannot be given as tax-free perks unless the driver is doing more than 18,000 miles for business purposes;
- directors' dining rooms and managers' restaurants are becoming extinct;
- company holidays as an excuse for free drinks at company expense is not thought to be good practice;
- parties on company premises are not permitted.

So, emoluments of all kinds are rarer in most workplaces today than they once were. Presents of all kinds must be declared or better still refused. The days when companies could claim tax on these benefits are largely past.

We are left with a fair day's wage for a fair day's work, with incentives for people whose job involves risk taking in return for incentive, commission or reward.

Summary

A changing and flexible job market requires a flexible and responsive appraisal system. In many organizations the traditional exercise has some way to go before it succeeds in responding to that evolving need. The appraisal process continues to labour under the guise of a bureaucratic duty that all give their best efforts to but that does not often either capture the individual's aspiration nor satisfy the need of the organization to capture the information it needs to understand the developing needs of its people.

Organizations have adopted the change paradigm in order to benefit from the flexibility offered and the economies that that may bring with it. However, they have not always acknowledged that the people who make them successful now have a different focus of work and career. The portfolio career is a reality for most workers: the current job must enhance knowledge, extend skill and consolidate around experience in a way that makes the individual more employable. Organizational commitment is on hold until such times as mutual trust begins to generate and sustain loyalty between worker, manager and organization (Cook and Macaulay, 1997).

References and further reading

Armstrong, M. and Brown, D. (2001) *New Dimensions in Pay Management*. London: CIPD.

Armstrong, M. and Brown, D. (2009) *Strategic Reward: Implementing more effective reward management*. London: Kogan Page.

Armstrong, M. and Mirlis, H. (2004) *Reward Management: A handbook of remuneration strategy and practice*. London: Kogan Page.

Barlow, G. (1989) Deficiencies and the perpetuation of power: Latent functions in management appraisal. *Journal of Management Studies*, 26(5): 499–518.

Brown, M. and Heywood, J. (2005) Performance appraisal systems: Determinants and change. *British Journal of Industrial Relations*, 43(4): 659–679.

Bullock, R.J. and Batten, D. (1985) It's just a phase we're going through: A review and synthesis of OD phase analysis. *Group and Organization Studies*, 10(4): 383–412.

Burton, R.M., Lauridsen, J. and Obel, B. (2004) The impact of organizational climate and strategic fit on firm performance. *Human Resource Management*, 43(1): 67–82.

Coates, G. (1994) Performance appraisal as an icon: Oscar-winning performance or dressing to impress. *International Journal of Human Resource Management*, 5(1): 167–191.

Cook, S. and Macaulay, S. (1997) How colleagues and customers can help improve team performance. *Team Performance Management*, 3(1): 12–17.

Deal, T.E. and Kennedy, A. (1982) *Corporate Cultures*. Reading, MA: Addison-Wesley.

Dries, N., Vantilborgh, T. and Pepermans, R. (2012) The role of learning agility and career variety in the identification and development of high potential employees. *Personnel Review*, 41(3): 340–358.

Farrell, D. and Rusbult, C.E. (1981) Exchange variables as predictors of job satisfaction, job commitment, and turnover: The impact of rewards, costs, alternatives, and investments. *Organizational Behavior and Human Performance*, 27: 78–95.

Fletcher, C. (1993) *Appraisal*. London: IPM.

Fletcher, C. and Williams, R. (1992) *Performance Management in the UK: Organizational experience*. London: IPM.

Gilmore, S. and Williams, S. (2009) *Human Resource Management*. Oxford: Oxford University Press.

Grint, K. (1993) What's wrong with performance appraisals? A critique and a suggestion. *Human Resource Management Journal*, 3(3): 61–77.

Hendry, C., Woodward, S., Bradley, P. and Perkins, P. (2000) Performance and rewards: Cleaning out the stables. *Human Resource Management Journal*, 10(3): 46–62.

Locke, E. and Latham, G. (1990) *A Theory of Goal Setting and Task Performance*. Englewood Cliffs, NJ: Prentice Hall.

Morgan, A. and Cannan, K. (2005) 360 degree feedback: A critical enquiry. *Personnel Review*, 34(6): 663–680.

Newton, T. and Findlay, P. (1996) Playing God? The performance of appraisal. *Human Resource Management Journal*, 6(3): 42–58.

Pilbeam, S. (1998) Individual performance related pay: Believers and sceptics. *Employee Relations Review*, 5: 9–16.

Senge, P. (1990) *The Fifth Discipline*. New York: Doubleday.

Stewart, R. (1991) *Managing Today and Tomorrow*. Basingstoke: Macmillan.

Stredwick, J. (2000) Aligning rewards to organizational goals: A multinational's experience. *European Business Review*, 12(1): 9–18.

Townley, B. (1989) Selection and appraisal: Reconstituting social relations, in J. Storey (ed.) *New Perspectives on Human Resource Management*. London: Routledge, 92–108.

Townley, B. (1993) Performance appraisal and the emergence of management. *Journal of Management Studies*, 30(2): 27–44.

GRADUATE ATTRIBUTES

During this exercise you will address the following graduate attributes:

- a breadth of knowledge, understanding and skills beyond their chosen discipline(s);
- a capacity for attentive exchange, informed argument and reasoning;
- an appreciation of the concepts of enterprise and leadership in all aspects of life;
- an ability to communicate effectively for different purposes and in different contexts.

What is negotiation?

Negotiation is finding a way for all parties to gain something they value from the resolution of a position of conflict. It is generally used in circumstances where each party has a similar power level. You enter into a negotiation when you wish to reach a resolution and both parties have something to gain from the interaction and exchange. It means finding a way to solve a problem that enables both parties to work together in the future. If you wish to have a long-term relationship with the other party you need to negotiate.

What skills do you need?

Observation skills

The ability to listen, observe and record activities of others, dealing with a number of individuals at once. The use of *active listening skills* is vital to a good negotiator.

Organize and plan

You need to be able to set out in detail what you expect from the negotiations and have a knowledge of your own limitations.

Empathy and rapport

It is vital that a negotiator has the skill to establish quickly and maintain a rapport with the other side of the negotiation. This is where empathy enters in as a valuable skill. To create and maintain a rapport you need the ability to see the others' points of view and appreciate their feelings on the issues while at the same time holding on to your own view and desired outcome. While you need to see the broader picture you must never lose sight of your goal.

Creativity

Negotiators must be creative. You need the ability to think round or through a problem and to try something different to help solve the issue. I am hesitant to use the cliché 'outside the box' since it is horribly overused but a good negotiator must be prepared to see potential solutions that may elude those following traditional routes.

Moving blockages

As a negotiator you need to be able to move blockages. It can be very easy for negotiations to bog down in details that are not necessarily relevant to a solution. You must avoid this. A good negotiator will have the skill to choose the appropriate tool or statement to move on from a block. You also need to notice when arguments are going round in circles and work systematically through this by suggesting new paths out of the circle.

The six stages

- preparation
- discussion
- regroup
- negotiating
- consensus
- closure.

Preparation

Questions to ask:

- What's the problem?
- Who is concerned with it?
- What would happen if it did not exist?
- What happens now that it does exist?
- Who currently gains from it?
- Who currently loses from it?
- Get we get a very precise statement of the issues?
- Can we set best and realistic outcomes?
- What is the best we can hope for?
- What is the worst?
- At what point do we back off?
- Can we phase any of our outcomes?
- What about the other party?
- Can we set a range of negotiation?
- Can we establish your BATNA (best alternative to a negotiated agreement)?
- Can we verify your levels of negotiating authority?

Thinking about outcomes

Before you begin negotiation it is always worth spending time working out the answers to all the points below. It is useful to define outcomes precisely so that you can recognize when a negotiation is taking you along the path you want and when it is veering towards the cliff.

- What do you want?
- What do you wish to avoid?
- How do you want it?
- How don't you want it?
- Where do you want it?
- Where do you not want it?
- When do you want it?
- When don't you want it?
- What will it be like?
- What will it be unlike?
- How will you know when you have got it?
- How will you know if you haven't got it?

Asking these questions, or ones like them, will help you establish your *negotiation range*. And what, you may ask, is a negotiation range? Very simply it is this: the difference between the minimum that you will accept and the maximum you want.

If you have two groups negotiating, Group 1 and Group 2, we would hope that they could come to an agreement and where there is an overlap in the negotiation range then agreement is far more likely. In essence, your negotiation range is about give and take, what you can afford to give to the other side to reach a negotiated agreement and what you need to have from them.

Very much linked to your negotiation range is your BATNA. Essentially your BATNA is your answer to the question 'suppose we can't agree a negotiated settlement?' This is always an important question to ask. In any negotiation you need to know at what point you are going to walk away. In most circumstances there is an option you can take if agreement simply cannot be reached. If you ask your boss for vital training and they say no then you may look at leaving the organization. Your BATNA isn't always a pleasant option, but it is an option. So, set a BATNA and get agreement from your organization on the BATNA so that you can negotiate with the knowledge of a fallback position.

Communication skills

The effects of body language or nonverbal communication can be high. This means that as a negotiator you need to be able to interpret body language and understand what the individual is actually saying with their eyes and posture. Be careful not to over-interpret gestures – look for patterns rather than single gestures. I may be sitting with my arms folded because it's comfortable not because I am withdrawn, as some books on body language may say.

The importance of listening as a conversational act is clear from the quantity of time spent on it (estimated at between 50 and 60 per cent of speech interaction), and also on the work it does in contributing to the success of the event. An important skill for you as the negotiator is *active listening*.

Active listening is a technique designed to increase the likelihood of clear communication. It is about listening with the eyes as well as the ears. In active listening you are trying to understand what the speaker is really saying. For instance, if I yell at you with my face contorted in red rage that 'I am happy!!!', the actual message I am trying to communicate may not really be that I am a happy person. While this is a gross simplification it does get over the purpose of active listening. In this case the active listener would feed back to the speaker, or yeller in this case, that what they were hearing was that they were not happy but rather quite angry. You must listen for meaning.

Information is at the very core of negotiation, and communication is about the flow of information. As a negotiator you are seeking to gather information from the other side while controlling the information you give to them very carefully. Each side will be testing the other, trying to gather information about their negotiation range, looking for ways to advance their outcomes and seeing whether they can agree to some outcomes of the other side that they don't care too much about. It is a game of move and counter move where each side seeks to maximize its outcomes while arriving at an agreement that will not preclude working together again in the future.

Negotiation is about winning but not about destroying the other side. Both should walk away from the negotiation feeling that they have gained from the process and that they can live with the agreement.

Time for a quick self-assessment task

In the questions in Table 9.1, rank yourself from 1 (low) to 10 (high) in terms of your current negotiating ability. Then, thinking about the sort of negotiations you may be involved in, rank yourself how you wish to be and start to think about how you are going to get there.

Discussion

- meet to discover
- use your active listening skill
- avoid commitment
- establish rapport
- identify interests and needs
- separate people from the problem
- focus on interests not positions
- identify language patterns.

Meet to discover

Negotiation can be a long process. Your first meeting with the other side is to discover what the other party wants and needs and to express your wants and needs. It is an opportunity to share information and to start to create rapport. If you make it clear that this is what you want from the first meeting then neither side will feel deceived later on in the negotiations.

TABLE 9.1 Skills self-assessment questionnaire

Skill statement	*Current level*	*Desired level*
I find it easy to put myself in the role of others		
I find it easy to observe interactions		
I find it easy to listen without interruption		
I find it easy to give feedback		
I find it easy to determine the other party's negotiation limits		
I find it easy to help a discussion progress when it is blocked		
I find it easy to know when to walk away		

Active listening

Here is where the skill will start to become useful in discovering what the other side actually wants and needs and what they may be willing to be flexible over.

Avoid commitment

The first meeting is just that, a first meeting. What you are doing here is discovery; be careful not to get sucked into commitment at this point. The negotiation process has just begun; there is time for commitment later.

Establishing a rapport

Identifying interests and needs – simply about learning what the other part wants and making sure that they understand what you want.

Separate people from the problem – there is an unfortunate tendency in all of us to judge people. It is important to remember in negotiations that you don't need to like the people you are negotiating with – you only need to be willing to communicate with them and not base your decisions on their personality.

Focus on interests not positions – there is no point in denying that both sides will approach a negotiation with a position on the problem but what is important is that those involved don't allow those positions to obscure common interests.

Identifying language patterns – adherents of neuro-linguistic programming (NLP) suggest that there are certain patterns of language that individuals prefer and ways they like to understand the world. Some are visual, some auditory and some prefer feeling.[1] The important point here is to learn how those you are negotiating with like to communicate.

Regroup

Evaluation

Effective meetings occur when negotiators work to find better ways to reach solutions. Participants come to a meeting with ideas, skills, knowledge and experience. The negotiator's task is to produce an environment where evaluation is a normal part of the process.

The benefits of an evaluation will be clearly demonstrated in the improvement of future meetings. Ideally the product of the evaluation will be feedback into the improvement of future meetings.

Revisit outcomes

What can you give the other side in the negotiation that adds value to them but involves negligible cost or expense to you? What else would you like from the other parties that are outside the current scope of negotiation? Would your extra demand be easy to fulfil? Is what you will give the other side easy to fulfil?

When deciding on a value-add you must think of something that would benefit the other party, that is in your gift to offer and that will not impact you greatly in terms of resources. The benefit of the value-add is that it can open up the negotiation process.

Negotiating

Always negotiate the Big Picture first. What does this mean? It means look at the broad principles that inform the negotiation. Consider the intention of the negotiation and divide it into large-scale chunks. Once you have those you can start to work on the details.

Concessions

Here each side starts to move further along their negotiation range towards the other party. Concessions tend not to be made without something comparable from the other side. It is a case of if we ..., then will you ...?

Compromise

In this part of the negotiation process each party is flexible to the needs of the other party. It can result in neither party getting exactly what they want but it can produce a solution. Both parties gain something but, generally speaking, compromise is not a satisfactory outcome from the negotiation.

Consensus

The negotiation is over and now it is vital that you ensure consensus. This is done by following these guidelines.

Restate final agreements

It is important to restate all the stages of the agreement thoroughly and to get everyone to agree on them. There is a danger that participants will forget details or will only remember the final points of the discussion. Try to construct the final agreement in a manner that is readily comprehensible by all.

Ensure that those who made the deal have the authority to do so

This is vital: if they don't you don't have an agreement and you've wasted all that time and effort.

Check with each party individually that they agree

Again this is vital. What you are doing is ensuring everyone understands and agrees. This should prevent people returning later and claiming that this was not what they understood by the agreement.

A negotiation exercise

Three groups are involved in negotiation with many points of contention. You will be asked to take a role in one of the groups. This can be done as individuals or as teams of negotiators.

Peach Technologies

You are a board member of Peach Technologies and the president of the company has asked you all to come here today to discuss a very important issue. The company has identified the town of Rufus in Fredonia, as the prime spot to build its new factory. There is a vacant lot next to the river called the Spalding lot which your company wishes to use as the factory site.

As a business your main concern is profit. It is your aim to build the factory on the least expensive land available and to spend the least amount of money on the running of the factory.

The Spalding lot is the best location for the factory because:

- it is the least expensive land in town of a size adequate for your needs;
- the lot already has good road access;
- the lot is well placed as it is adjacent to the river which can be used for your factory's waste requirements;
- the location of the lot, near the town, will enable people to come to work more easily;
- wages are currently low in Rufus due to a poor industrial base and high unemployment.

Oddly, the people of Rufus seem to object to Peach Industries building the factory on the Spalding lot. You don't understand why there is such a fuss about this. Peach Industries will bring much-needed jobs to the town of Rufus which is short on industry. There seems to be some concern about possible pollution.

If the town of Rufus is going to make a real fuss about this you may be willing to spend a little money to make sure that you control potential pollution. If you find some people hard to convince of the benefits of having the factory in Rufus you could sweeten things with some donations to the town or sponsoring one of the local sports teams. However, this is all you are willing to do.

The Rufus Environmental Protection Committee (REPC)

You are a member of a group that supports the environment. You are committed to ensuring that people are not allowed to pollute the air, land or water of the community. The river is a special source of concern because:

- it is the source of the drinking water for the people of Rufus;
- a rare group of amphibians make the river their home. The rare Flywheel amphibians are already breeding poorly and you are very concerned that pollution in the river could wipe them out completely.

You want to make sure that businesses cannot pollute without consequence. The REPC are very much against the idea of the Peach Industries factory being built on the Spalding lot. You are convinced that Peach Industries uses dangerous chemicals in the production of its tablet computers and you are very concerned that the company will dump these chemicals into the river. You are absolutely not open to bribery. You are not without sympathy for the employment needs of Rufus – after all, you live there. You would consider Peach Industries building their factory on the Spalding Lot if they agreed not to pollute the river and to your group being allowed regular inspections of their factory.

The combined workers of Rufus

You are part of the union that represents the workers of Rufus. The majority of the working age population of Rufus belongs to the CWR (Combined Workers of Rufus). You are very concerned by the lack of employment opportunities in Rufus. Your main concerns are:

- that everyone in the town should have access to employment;
- that such employment should involve reasonable wages in line with living expenses;
- that the employers treat the workforce with respect;
- that the employers provide a safe working environment.

You are undecided about whether you support Peach Industries' factory coming to town. While the factory will provide nearly 500 badly needed new jobs and you really want the jobs to come to Rufus, you are concerned that a big company such as Peach Industries will exploit its workers. The CWR wants to ensure that Peach Industries pays workers good wages, provides reasonable paid holiday time and ensures that they work in a safe workplace.

While you do care about the environment it is not your main concern but you may be able to get Peach Industries to offer higher wages to workers if you side with the environmentalists. But, on the other hand, you don't want to frighten off Peach Industries and risk the new jobs.

The negotiation

The three groups are being brought together by Mayor Hackenbush in the hopes that they can come up with an agreement.

Things to consider:

- What is your desired outcome?
- What value-added may you have to offer?
- What are you willing to give and for what?
- What is your BATNA?

Summary

Negotiation is crucial to all human relations and especially to those involved in business. A business that is inflexible is one that will easily lose good will. No one wants to feel that they have had to yield without gaining any benefit for themselves of the causes they believe in strongly. Confrontation rarely achieves anything positive either in the long or short term.

For those involved in successful negotiation, knowledge of the other side's position is as important and sometimes more important than a full appreciation of their own position. Time spent in reconnaissance is seldom wasted.

Tutor guidance

You can develop your own negotiation scenarios and put together teams of negotiators based on the three roles of leader, observer and summarizer.

Both teams need a written brief about their negotiation position as illustrated above.

Each side will need information about the range of negotiation and the limits beyond which each side would not be authorized to go.

Both sides would also need to be briefed on what they would be prepared to compromise on and what they would perceive as a benefit were it offered to them.

Once again the roles need to be clarified (for example the observer, sitting between the leader and the summarizer, is in a good position to take notes that are visible to her/his colleagues sitting either side of her/him).

The tutor will be in a good position to note and give feedback on the following points:

- ability to explore the other side's position;
- ability to pick up on and probe signals ('we could not negotiate on core time', 'so, what could you negotiate on, then?');
- packaging points of agreement (summarizer role);
- proposing alternatives (leader role);
- seeking commitment;
- handling concerns and objections.

Further comment can be made on the team roles and how they interfaced with each other:

- having a system of signals (such as moving an object on the table in front of you) that indicates a desire to intervene in the discussion or ask a question;
- noticing what the observer writes;
- seeking an adjournment for further consultation;
- using sharp-angled questions to probe and gain commitment from the other team.

There are no preset ways for staging a negotiation. Whatever our agreed position may be, our ability to discover the position of the other party is paramount in achieving a successful outcome.

Note

1 For more on NLP I would recommend Thorson's work: O'Connor, J. and Seymour, J. (2003) *Introduction to NLP Neuro-linguistic Programming*, London: Thorsons. It will give you a good basis for pursuing this route.

10

EMPLOYEE RELATIONS

Equality and diversity

Topics

- traditional worker representation and erosion of union membership
- high performance management and organizational outcomes
- equality and diversity
- discrimination, harassment and bullying
- action learning and self-development.

Introduction

At the heart of HRM theory there is a preference for a direct relationship between the worker and her/his manager. There should be no intermediaries to come between them. There should be no need for any representation of workers as a group to the members of management. This belief is sometimes referred to as a *Unitarist* approach to management. So, this philosophy towards the management of people would ideally preclude the existence of unions in the workplace. After all, if workers have something to say, they should feel free to share it with their managers. Managers and staff are all working for the same organizational objectives, anyway. So, why should there be any need for any other bodies intervening in that relationship?

Unions sprang up during the Industrial Revolution, as we know, when often workers found themselves working in intolerable conditions, lucky to get a reward and often uncertain what that reward might be. Managers were not always fair-minded or just to their workers. Sometimes children and women were employed in appalling conditions, as is still the case in some emergent economies in the world today. Such workers needed to get together to express their views and ideally that alliance needed an institutional base separate from and therefore independent of the managers. This is sometimes referred to as the *Pluralist* approach to management. It means that workers have the right to be members of the union and to withdraw their labour should they feel that their rights are threatened by decisions or actions the management take without proper consultation and agreement.

Sometimes this is referred to as *joint regulation*: its main elements include a recognition that there is a conflict of interest in the employment relationship.

For some commentators the point is made even more strongly: that the employer–employee relationship is inherently exploitative (Warhurst and Thompson, 2006). Those who espouse this view would say that even though there may now be equitable rewards and better working conditions for most workers than was the case in the past, the employer always has more instrumental power than the employees do. In other words, they would say that the employer has the right to recruit, to make redundant, to sack, to put workers on short time and so on. Employees have duties towards the employer that include loyalty and trust as well as adherence to the terms and conditions that lie within their employment contract.

Trade unions have a legitimate role representing the collective interests of the workforce

So, this all suggests that trade unions have a duty to represent the workers' interests, to put up objections to management when those interests are put at risk, and, if appropriate, advise their members on appropriate action should managers not respond to their reasonable requests. Of course, the term 'reasonable requests' does bring up the question of what is reasonable, and often there will be divergent views of what that answer is. This suggests that there are areas of negotiation that need to be explored, and unions play a major role in such negotiations on behalf of their members.

Collective bargaining

One of the principal roles that unions play lies within the variance that employers can impose on their members in different parts of the sector. So, to avoid such disparity between individual pay and conditions, unions have traditionally negotiated the pay and conditions of all their members. In this way conflict can be avoided and differences can be negotiated and contained within reasonable boundaries, making it less likely to be disruptive to the business, while ensuring the equality of treatment for all its members wherever they may be working in the sector.

Of course, managers may find this irksome and in some countries union organizers have faced threats and even death for becoming active in standing up for their members' rights. But in a democratic society the right of individuals to have a say in their working lives is accepted – largely because they spend much of their lives at work and also because a workforce satisfied that its rights have been properly addressed is likely to work more satisfactorily than one in which its staff feel aggrieved or treated without respect by managers and the company in general.

Union membership

TABLE 10.1 Trade union membership UK, 1990–2011

Year	Union membership (1,000s)	Density (%)
1990	8,577	37.8
1995	6,904	32.2
2000	6,892	29.5
2005	6,803	28.3
2010	6,306	26.3
2011	6,163	25.7

Source: Labour Force Survey, Office for National Statistics.

If we take economically active figures for the population in the UK, it is rising towards 29 million people. So, Table 10.1 gives an indication of the fall-off in membership. We will examine the reasons why this reduction in membership has occurred. Suffice it to say here that the year 1980 has often been seen as the high-water mark of union membership, when more than 12 million workers were members, and it was believed that the Thatcher government which came into power in 1979 engineered this downturn in union support . As we shall see, political strategies to curb unions, which was definitely on the government's agenda in the 1980s, was not solely responsible for the figures that we see (Johnson, 1991). Technologies and their application to skilled and craft-based jobs played an equal part in the fall-off in membership that we can see continuing here.

Thatcherism included a belief that *privatization* was better for service provision than the inflexible, inefficient and slow public sector that always seemed to cost more for doing a similar job. Thus far evidence that this is true has not usually supported this belief if the question of quality of service is included in the assessment of the outcomes of privatization.

The public sector has remained much more closely wedded to union membership, accounting for 5.7 million of the current active union members, leaving fewer union members in the private sector. Indeed, while the private sector lost nearly 70 per cent of its membership between 1980 and 2004, the public sector has remained steady and, latterly, recorded a modest increase since the Labour government took over in 1997. It is, however, the case that the militancy that was seen in the 1970s has not been so apparent even with the coalition government's austerity provisions, which have focused on cutting down the numbers of public sector workers.

Before we leave the statistics entirely, it is worthwhile considering the question of days lost in strikes and the numbers of people involved in them over the years 1946 to 2003. So, whereas in 1946 1.8 million days were lost in strikes, which

312 Employee relations: equality and diversity

increased in the 1970s to 12 million days lost, this number fell in the early part of the twenty-first century to just over half-a-million days lost in strikes.

This suggests that strikes are far fewer than they were just after the end of the Second World War and are usually of shorter duration. This may suggest that arbitration services are more effective than they were then and that legislation against what was once referred to as 'wild-cat strikes' has now been replaced by the need for unions to ballot their members before strikes can be called. It may also be the fact that most workers are disinclined to risk their jobs in an era of insecurity in all employment sectors.

Reasons for reducing union membership

Automation has done away with semi-skilled jobs

The gap between skilled and unskilled jobs has been eroded by technology. Gone are the days when welding is done in car factories by welders. Spot-welding machines now undertake the same task. Increasingly, even skilled work is being taken over by technology and tasks that once required highly knowledgeable and skilled people are now possible to complete with computerized machinery. We have only to consider drone technology to recognize that the days of human beings piloting aircraft for any purpose may be beginning to be less likely in the future, too.

The implication for unions

One of the best remembered moves against intransigent unionists was perhaps the print unions who plagued the newspaper industry for decades. Membership was held by the members themselves and was closely guarded to ensure that only relatives of members and favoured friends were admitted. Strikes were routine and power lay in the hands of the heads of the print 'chapels', as they were called.

The advent of technology which enabled journalists to input their own material directly to print format meant that the need for hot-metal print setters was no longer required. All that was then needed was one newspaper proprietor to put up premises that were defensible and away from the traditional venue of Fleet Street in London. Rupert Murdoch was that proprietor and the company was resited at Wapping – a lot easier for the security authorities to keep away unwanted attention or interference from demonstrators looking to blockade the premises.

Similarly, militancy has been the approach of union leader, Bob Crowe, whose National Union of Rail, Maritime and Transport workers has been active in bringing London Underground to a halt with frequent stoppages and strikes. The response of the London Mayor, Boris Johnson, has been to bring forward the technology to support driverless trains by 2020. It seems that few jobs are indispensable where technology is concerned and confrontation hastens the automation of human functions at work.

Legislation requiring ballot of members before strikes

As we have seen, wild-cat strikes were frequently called by union leaders and often the only balloting was a show of hands at mass meetings of the workers, thus making it difficult for those not in agreement to express their views. Legislation brought in during the 1980s required unions to ballot their members and more recent court actions have sometimes successfully challenged the validity of the ballots taken and overturned the union's right to call out its members on strike.

It has even become the practice in some companies for employers to contact union members individually, warning them that strike action could put their contract of employment at risk, thereby seeking to temper any action there might be for members to withdraw their labour.

Restrictions on secondary picketing during strikes

In 1977 a company called Grunwick in North London refused to recognize union membership. As a result, the union movement mobilized hundreds of their members to obstruct the passage of traffic into the company. The feud ran on for two years with nightly updates and filming of the clashes between union supporters and the police; 550 union members were arrested and the violence led to injuries and charges by the police. The vote of confidence that the Labour government lost in early 1979 led to the election of a Conservative government with a mandate to introduce legislation controlling what was then known as secondary picketing. Effectively, while traffic or visitors have to listen to a reasoned argument from two union representatives of the strikers, no longer can a mass body of people wilfully obstruct traffic or the entrance to company premises.

Increase in knowledge workers/consultants

It would be fair to say that the demise of traditional crafts and trades once represented by traditional unions has seen an increasing number of knowledge workers to which we have referred throughout this book. Such workers, as we have seen, are often either self-employed or operating under a consultancy contract.

However, it should not be thought that such workers are completely without representation. There is certainly evidence that the Law Society and the British Medical Association are equally powerful at protecting the position of lawyers and doctors respectively as is any other form of union that was founded to protect the status of its members.

Collective bargaining

Even collective bargaining has sometimes been circumvented by employers – by the simple ploy of paying more than the union rate to its workers. As we have noted, in the days of the publicly owned railway in the UK, train drivers frequently went on strike for more money as their wages amounted to not much more than other transport drivers. Privatized railway companies such as Virgin offered more than double the going rate so that now drivers routinely earn around £30,000 per annum. Strikes on the railways by drivers are now comparatively rare compared with the days of public ownership.

Reduced membership

As with any other industry, unions have found themselves beset by lowering income as they have lost members. This has meant amalgamation of unions so that there are fewer bodies representing reducing numbers across a wider range of jobs. In service industries unions have traditionally been weaker than their colleagues in manufacturing industries, which has meant that their hold on these sectors is necessarily more tenuous. One example, USDAW, the shop workers' union, has always found it difficult to recruit members. Some companies make it clear to recruits informally that joining the union could preclude their progression to management positions.

Government legislation was introduced to allow any group of workers with 40 per cent in favour of setting up union representation at their place of work should be allowed to do so (The Trade Union and Labour Relations (Consolidation) Act 1992).

Public sector

As we have already seen, the public sector dominates the figures for the concentration of union membership and it would be fair to say there is good reason for members to seek protection. Politicians have always seen the civil service as a drain on its funding. Public servants have been perceived as inflexible and because it has not followed the lead of the private sector to delayer its levels of hierarchy it costs more to run with a heavy on-cost of senior managers to pay for. Proponents would point out that a public service does not have the choice of cutting out uneconomical or marginal services.

Strong resistance to privatization because of loss of TUPE rights

Members know that privatization will mean the erosion or even loss of trade union, pensions and earning rights under new management (Transfer of Undertakings (Protection of Employment) Regulations Act, 2006 (TUPE)). So, civil servants have much to lose when their jobs are outsourced to the private sector. If we look at the case of the police forces throughout the UK, not only are they carrying a heavy on-cost of senior managers in relatively small forces, but officers can retire after 30 years' service and draw their pension. So large is this debt that the police authorities have had to ask central government to help cover the considerable deficit that is now carried by the police services UK-wide. However, it is true that private companies such as British Airways carry a similarly heavy pension debt; but, their ability to generate revenue is arguably an advantage in covering this liability long term, provided they can keep up in terms of their revenues. Significantly, the current drive for reductions in public spending have led in Scotland to the forma-tion of one police force from the current seven local forces, and England and Wales are seeking a similar reduction to their 43 forces.

The question of pensions requires radical thinking by governments that seek to encourage individuals to defer taking them and work longer (Snape and Redman, 2003). Employment Equality (Age) regulations in employment was introduced in 2006 by the government in the UK but thought still needs to be given to how to allow pensioners to reduce their hours and draw a commensurate part of their pension without becoming liable for tax. This applies for societies everywhere that have grown accustomed to having a welfare state available to provide for essential services, including pensions. However, our major competitors in the East and Asia do not cover this for their citizens, which can make our goods and services pro-portionately more expensive and therefore potentially less competitive. This is a position that will need to be carefully and thoughtfully addressed as more people pass what used to be termed the age of retirement.

Unitarist approach to managing

As we have seen, the unitarist approach would envisage no union representation at all, but a direct line between management and staff with no intervention from third parties such as unions. Nissan in the UK recruited 2,000 workers out of 20,000 applicants (Wickens, 1987). They chose workers with no union affiliations, and their factory in Sunderland thereafter went on to break worldwide company production records.

British Rail's new HR manager, recruited from outside the industry in the late 1980s, wrote to all drivers at their homes reminding them that an intended strike could put their employment contract in jeopardy (the strike collapsed). It is now much more likely that management will contact staff individually to gain the sup-port of members to vote against taking strike action.

Jaguar (John Egan) could not get more than 45 per cent of workers to adapt to quality circles (Storey, 1992). Jaguar is now foreign owned and producing more cars than ever before worldwide. Opportunity resisted does not revisit those who reject its invitation to change.

New technology college

The new head teacher at a newly opening academy inherited 48 staff from what was previously a run-down, inner-city school. He offered the staff a contract based on exam performance of their students in public exams. Four out of 48 teaching staff accepted the contract and returned to their jobs.

Close a brownfield site – open a greenfield site?

This is the classic dilemma for management in organizations. Comparative costs will always work against companies that fail to respond to competitive pressures. Dyson has always maintained that his company can design innovative products that can capture a worldwide market, but that after three months of production in the UK it will be necessary to move production offshore where labour is cheaper and more flexible.

High performance management

Set up formal teamworking initiatives

If we go back to TQM then it is clear that *quality circles* and devolvement of work processes to the working team are crucial to this initiative. There are many other industries that have sought to emulate this outside the car manufacturing industry.

Allowing *autonomy* within working groups makes them respond to the need to compete and take responsibility for what they produce. This means that possessing knowledge and skill in any role or function needs to be complemented by the ability to work well in a team and be self-reflective about working with others. It also means shared responsibility and not looking for 'the management' to tell us what to do. This introduces challenge and also risk into the job situation though how this works in practice is not always as straightforward as it sounds (Procter and Mueller, 2000).

HRM theory also supports and encourages *functional flexibility* (job/work rotation) so that individuals can cover for one another and the on-cost of hiring many different specialists can be reduced within a more integrated workforce capable of covering more than one core competence.

The key to success is innovation and creativity. Teams use brainstorming activities to develop ideas and solve problems and they operate flexibly so that the right person with the necessary expertise is deployed in a facilitating role when required for the success of the group. Not everyone is open to this kind of interaction with work colleagues and negotiational skills are at a premium for all involved in such teamworking situations (Storey, 1992).

Finally, there is the need for flexible rewards and incentives. Calculating these equitably and fairly will always be challenging. However, profit-related pay always rewards groups that have been successful, while continuing to invest in bringing others to the same level of skill, performance and commitment (Manning, 2006).

Organizational outcomes

As we remember from Guest's diagram, the organizational outcomes of getting the HR outcomes right should be positive in terms of the organizational outcomes: *innovation and creativity*. So the benefits of working flexibly should yield results that demonstrate continuous learning. Such proactive approaches to managing people offer the following.

Employees focused on quality

They are more effective in their jobs because they are involved through *strategic integration*, and so committed to the organizational objectives. They know where their job fits into the targets required and therefore are self-motivated and do not need continuous supervision.

High commitment management approach

Increases discretionary effort at work (Huselid, 1995) because it offers more opportunity of *flexibility* at work. This is not just functional flexibility, but the flexibility that allows genuine choice of when, where and how individuals and groups carry out the tasks they are responsible for. In this way an emerging connection between sophisticated HRM, organizational commitment and business performance can be demonstrated and supported by individuals in teams, although proponents did not always take into account what effect economic downturn would have on workers' rewards.

Managers capable of leading such initiatives (Purcell et al., 2003)

In this scenario the manager's role ceases to be command and control, but becomes *facilitational*. The manager is there to make it easier for people to achieve their objectives. Originally, in the quality circle the central focus of attention, the team leader, was responsible for the training input for team members in the circle. Newcomers are integrated into the work environment and given the support they need to acquire the necessary knowledge and skills to become a competent member of the team through job rotation and training support.

The model derived from manufacturing has been introduced in different ways in different industries. Interdisciplinary teams can contain core workers, consultants and subcontractors. Finding common ground, reaching consensus about agreed objectives; allocating tasks fairly; all of this needs to become part of the management process and requires people who are responsive and flexible in their dealings with others. Not everyone can cope with these demands and choosing those that can is not as simple as it seems, either (Kirsley *et al.*, 2006).

The public sector is noted for its attempts to stay in touch with its people. It may be that the more permanent employment and traditional job security in the public sector has built up traditional and new ways of keeping people in touch with managers and their thinking. Certainly the opportunity for feedback is more likely to be attempted by the public sector (Doyle *et al.*, 2000).

In contrast, the more transitory nature of working in the private sector means that managers feel less need to update their staff as project work may be of a limited duration.

Managing conflict in organizations

It is certainly true that conflict resolution is a priority in any well-run business. Problems that are ignored in the hope that they will resolve themselves usually end up getting worse if not addressed quickly and effectively before they get out of hand. Failure to take effective action early on can lead to some of the negative consequences that Guest shows as part of the organizational outcomes of HRM theory: *it is not only strikes that affect work, but also other forms of protest action.*

Working to rule

This is a tactic that is used in industries where, for example, time spent in relation to the vehicle and its load is part of the duties of the driver or pilot. For much of the time that can be done without loss of time or overmuch effort. However, working to rule could mean that more time and effort are spent than usual which may affect the running of the service to the scheduled time.

Intermittent absence

Guest makes a similar point here, that intermittent absence can be a sign that people who might once have put themselves out to get work, now feel that relations with management have got to a point where it is not worth going to the extra effort of booking on at work. One good example of that was the dispute between cabin staff and British Airways 2010–2011. On one occasion the cabin crew voted for a strike and received warning letters from the company that such action could jeopardize their employment contract. On the day of the strike there was a mass sick absence affecting 2,000 BA cabin crew, all of whom were supported by medical certificates.

Loss of good will

This often affects customers, wittingly or unwittingly. Phones may not be answered as promptly and replies to questions can be curt to the point of off-handedness. Dispirited workforces are easy for the customer to spot and difficult for managers to recover from. It is not a disciplinary offence but the impact on the customer may mean that they are unwilling to return or move their custom elsewhere.

Industrial sabotage

This is much more difficult to spot once it takes hold in a company. However, the old adage of 'throwing a spanner in the works' is apt to describe what takes place. Giving the company the benefit of the doubt and continuing on with faulty equipment is no longer an option. Indeed, faults can be an ideal opportunity to refuse to continue while using health and safety considerations as a suitable excuse for delay or cancellation of the service.

High labour turnover

We have already seen how the interference costs of high staff turnover can escalate easily if it remains unchecked. And yet how does a company turn this around?

BOX 10.1

A DIY company had a problem in one of its London stores in an affluent area where staff were difficult to attract and keep. Every manager who went there was defeated by what they saw as low quality staff often drawn necessarily from outside the catchment area of the store. One manager described it as, 'if they're warm and breathing we have to have them in the door'.

The company solved its problem by sending in their best manager in spite of his living 50 miles away and being unable to relocate to London. Within three months his policy of talking to people, listening to their problems and taking an interest in developing them paid off. High staff turnover was no longer a problem in the store.

Increase in grievances

This is yet another sign of unhappiness with the work environment. Staff become more aware of things they are not happy about. Popular causes of grievance can be the allocation of working patterns; the allocation of shift patterns; the allocation of time off; the same rewards for variable workload schedules; poor management; lack of support and training; promises made by management but not kept. As we said, in good times people may be inclined to give the company the benefit of the doubt. But once perceptions are dominated by the belief that nobody cares, the effects can take hold very quickly.

Conflict resolution – other routes

Union negotiation/agreed procedures

Unions offer training to their officials in negotiation skills so that their intervention in matters under dispute can be positive and helpful. Gone are the days when once the union officials had decided on a course of action members were expected to go along with their decision. Local and national action is always balloted among the members, and national expertise draws on experience that could be relevant in local disputes.

ACAS (Advisory, Conciliation and Arbitration Service)

A body set up by government in the turbulent 1970s, it has provided its services in difficult and complex cases or those situations where impasse has been reached between the parties. A recent example was the tanker drivers' dispute in the UK in 2012 in which drivers working under different contracts for different providers used the union to raise concerns about disparities in pay and health and safety concerns over driving conditions.

ACAS was called in and agreement was reached after several days of intensive negotiations. Once agreement is reached it is binding on both sides to adhere to the outcomes of the findings.

Employment appeal tribunals

Cases that are disputed in spite of attempts at internal company procedures can be referred to the Employment Appeals Tribunal. However, success rates traditionally have not necessarily been over successful. A look at the figures suggests:

- in 30 per cent of cases there was not enough evidence to proceed
- 30 per cent of cases are settled before any hearing takes place
- 30 per cent of cases go to a hearing
- only 3 per cent of cases heard are followed by job reinstatement (though more complainants will be awarded compensation).

The biggest risk for individual employees appealing to the Tribunal is that of publicity which could affect their future employment prospects in the sector. Those pursuing organizations on grounds of discrimination have often found it hard to secure employment within the sector, and it is almost impossible to prove that failure to shortlist or appoint for another job was influenced by awareness of contention with a previous employer in a tribunal case. For Nicola Horlick, a successful fund manager, winning a legal action against her employer for discrimination led to her having to set up her own organization (Kellaway, 2012). Few cases lead to job reinstatement.

Equality

This concept requires a *standard* against which the position of different groups can be measured. That can be difficult to define accurately, especially if there is a suspicion of disparity in pay levels between different groups all ostensibly doing the same job. Unless people volunteer what they earn then there is a duty of confidentiality on HR not to divulge information about what others earn (Miller, 1996). Excuses can readily be made that the conditions of work or qualifications between two workers are not comparable.

It would be impossible to check whether people are treated in exactly the same way as everybody else because how people feel about the way they are treated is likely to differ between individuals. Favouritism may be easier to identify provided that objective measures can be put in place for comparative purposes (how many weekends off have others had compared with any other individual, for example, ought to be calculable).

Interestingly, European law has accepted that where people feel harassed or bullied there is a prima facie case to answer. This at least is supportive of a hearing without the need to establish that a detriment had taken place.

A more sophisticated approach might be treating people differently in ways that are fair and tailored to their specific needs. That means that not everyone has the same needs and therefore differences in support for different individuals will be possible, and indeed, likely.

In other words, equality needs to be balanced by diversity (Ellis and Sonnenfield, 1994).

Diversity

The concept of diversity offers acceptance that there will always be differences between people and the way they are treated. Things you might get away with saying to a group of friends might well be considered inappropriate among work colleagues or in public places. So, context governs how an incident is interpreted by others (Frank, 2006).

Coming to terms with such differences should create a productive environment in which everybody feels valued, where their talents are being fully utilized at the same time as organizational goals are being met (Blaine, 2007).

In order to compete in a global market, employers need to be drawing from the widest possible talent pool to ensure they have access to the breadth and depth of skills available to meet their business need and satisfy their clients. Most health practices would take it for granted that a female patient may wish to consult a female doctor. Patients value diversity and the ability to choose from among a group of professionals to find the one that suits them best.

Chartered Institute of Personnel and Development

The lead body for HR is the CIPD. This body monitors the progress made in the important areas affecting the working environment through its 135,000 members. It summarizes its approach as follows: people make the difference at work – but everyone is different.

People issues: people want to work for employers with good employment practices and to feel valued at work. This also creates a climate of productivity and *commitment*, an HR outcome, which in turn offers links to *creativity and innovation* – one of the organizational outcomes of HRM (Guest, 1987).

Market competitiveness: a diverse workforce can help to inform the development of new or enhanced products or services, open up new market opportunities, improve market share, and broaden the customer base through shared identity which different cultures can bring to their members (Kandola and Fullerton, 1998).

Corporate reputation: increasingly, corporate image is being linked to the concept of *corporate social responsibility* in which ethical behaviour plays a key part. Every member of staff plays a part in this, as can be seen by the global banking crisis at the moment. If custom and practice is 'the way we do things round here' then it may be difficult for an individual to stand up for what is right. Once the peer group accepts illegal or immoral practices, the chance of lone individuals blowing the whistle on such practices requires moral courage of the highest order. Some whistle blowers have had to sacrifice their career and family in order to stand up for the principles of justice, freedom and right.

Social learning theory

This includes all that governs social interaction from our early years. Parental guidance, schooling, early social groups, all these play a role in the way we see the world and the way we interpret events that go on around as and derive meaning and ascribe value to them.

It entails identifying situations; interpreting information about those situations; making a judgement on how to respond to situations appropriately. It means learning schemas and scripts (Schank and Abelson, 1977) where we learn what to do when we go into a social situation; and how to respond appropriately. We learn how to frame and give a context to what we see.

So, an organization that wants to develop its people through the stages of personal growth needs to embark on mentoring, shadowing and role modelling which are ways to initiate new members into a company's way of doing things but also of evaluating events and making sense of them (Schein, 1985). The staff handbook tells us what we should not be doing. Good role models show us how to do the right things and do things right. Mentors are good at opening minds to possibilities rather than closing them to alternative prospects (Clutterbuck, 1992).

Discrimination

In a sense the closed-mindedness we referred to in the previous paragraph lies at the heart of much that would be described today as discrimination. It is related closely to equality and diversity, for it is in short a denial of both aimed at individuals or groups, causing them to be treated differently.

A short definition of discrimination includes patterns of behaviour whereby particular groups of people are stereotyped, victimized and discriminated against on the presumption that they possess certain characteristics not acceptable to our own group. This may cause them to be treated differently from those not included in their group.

For example, adverse perceptions of women's childcare responsibilities are a considerable obstacle to the attainment of promotion, career progression and equal pay. We have all heard the remark from a manager after interviewing female applicants: 'She will only leave and have a baby.' But structures also need to change to enable those with responsibilities as a carer to work without the constraint of inflexible shift patterns, for example.

As far as the law is concerned what people do and say are the criteria that govern whether behaviour can be construed as discriminatory. We cannot legislate for what people think. But we can monitor how often they hire people from ethnic minorities, for example. In London, 25 per cent of the population come from such mixed ethnic groups. But when we come to analyse the number of such people in the Metropolitan Police we find that the figure stands at around 7 per cent. That disparity may have been one of the critical factors in the McPherson Report declaring the Metropolitan Police Force to be 'institutionally racist'. Putting it right, however, is a more difficult challenge which requires senior managers to be proactive in promoting ethnic-friendly approaches to integration and development in the organization (Kirton and Greene, 2010).

The law protects both actual and potential employees and distinguishes between direct and indirect discrimination.

Direct discrimination: usually fairly obvious on grounds of age, gender, race, religion etc. which causes a difference of treatment to take place compared with other groups in the workplace.

Indirect discrimination: occurs when a rule is invoked that automatically excludes some individuals from applying for a position (requirement that females wear skirts may exclude those whose religion forbids them to display their legs; applying a test to one group not asked of another: asking females to lift a heavy piece of equipment while not asking male applicants to do the same).

Positive discrimination

Some organizations set about putting right disparity by choosing only members of a minority group until the gap was closed. However, this is reverse discrimination and is now deemed illegal, too. So, selection must be based strictly on competence to do the job.

BOX 10.2

A few years ago a Springboard Course was arranged for females in a department of the civil service. It was intended to bring on more females into management positions.

Needless to say it has since had to be opened up to any staff who feel they need more support in order to advance through the ranks of the organization.

Principal legislation on discrimination in the UK

Sex Discrimination Act (1975)

It is unlawful to discriminate in employment on the basis of gender, pregnancy or marital status. Indeed, discrimination on grounds of pregnancy will usually incur the highest award that can be given under the Act.

Race Relations Act (1976)

This is straightforward and usually obvious. Companies now are required to keep records of the ethnic composition of those applying for jobs; candidates must provide this information before any decisions are made about shortlisting and interviews take place. The purpose of this is to enable monitoring to take place where an accusation of discrimination is made about an organization.

Employment equality (2003)

This applies to discrimination on grounds of sexual orientation and is unlawful. The law also applies to gender reassignment so that those who undergo this procedure should not find that their employment is put at risk.

Employment equality (religion or belief) (2003)

These issues often arise over religious dress issues or worship requirements.

BOX 10.3

In the 1950s bus crews were required to wear uniforms with caps and badges.
    The first Sikh driver was allowed to wear the badge on his turban.
    The other drivers then came to work wearing different hats (beach hats, straw hats etc. but with the badge on).
    Today integrating religious dress into uniforms is not an issue, though as we saw in a case at British Airways more recently, wearing a religious symbol as jewellery might be challenged.

Disability (1995)

It is said that 11 per cent of economically active people have a disability of one kind or another. It may be defective sight or vision – but without making adjustments such as glasses, hearing aids, etc. it would be difficult or impossible for them to do their jobs effectively. The law expects employers to make reasonable adjustment to allow disabled persons to work and this has been reinforced by access legislation which came into force in 2004 and requires public buildings to be accessible to those who need lifts or ramps to access the workplace (Woodhams and Corby, 2007).

Employment Equality (Age) Regulations (2006)

At one time job adverts were allowed to feature age requirements and often such phrases as 'under 45' were to be found quite commonly. This legislation enshrined the right of people to apply for jobs regardless of their age (with the exception of statutory age restrictions or licensing requirements).

This was overtaken in 2010 by the banning of compulsory retirement ages altogether so that employees can only be dismissed due to lack of competence.

Interestingly, one of the UK's foremost universities recently voted to impose a compulsory retirement age of 67 to allow younger members of faculty to take over posts in the university. However, those already in a post cannot be affected retrospectively. So, only those who join after the vote is taken (assuming that it is passed) and sign that employment contract will be accepting retirement at 67.

More recently, the provision of the Equality Act (2010) has come into force. The primary purpose of the Act is to bring together the different Acts and Regulations that have traditionally underwritten anti-discrimination laws in Great Britain. This included the Equal Pay Act 1970, the Sex Discrimination Act 1975, the Race Relations Act 1976, the Disability Discrimination Act 1995 and the major statutory instruments protecting discrimination in employment on grounds of religion or belief, sexual orientation and age. This now requires equal treatment in access to employment as well as private and public services, regardless of the protected characteristics of age, disability, gender reassignment, marriage and civil partnership, race, religion or belief, sex and sexual orientation. In the case of gender, there are special protections for pregnant women. In the case of disability, employers and service providers are under a duty to make reasonable adjustments in the workplace to overcome constraints to working experienced by disabled people. In this regard, the Equality Act 2010 did not change the law but does clarify how the legal principles apply in the many different contexts that are now included in the Act.

Harassment

This is usually described as unwanted conduct that violates people's dignity, or creates an intimidating, hostile, degrading, humiliating or offensive environment. The behaviour is interpersonal and may be focused on individuals or groups

It can be any direction in the hierarchy

It can be directed upwards as well as downwards. So, it may not be a manager harassing staff. It can also be aggressive behaviour from a member of staff to a manager. In fact in many environments the custom and practice can be that of a macho approach that encourages confrontation.

It can take many forms:

- exclusion from information required to do your job and perhaps then being blamed for not knowing;
- undermining others, particularly shouting in front of others or in a public place;

- unrealistic deadlines: 'I want it done now' approach to management;
- malicious gossip – this is much more difficult to get to the bottom of as often the perpetrator will deny vehemently having said anything of the sort;
- name calling and also 'joking'. References to 'paddies' aimed at Irish people can be equally offensive. But when asked about it afterwards the perpetrator will say that it was only meant as a joke.

Bullying

Bullying is more difficult to define. Often 'unacceptable behaviour' is used to cover this – and this needs to be discussed with everybody in the organization, especially during induction training so that clarity is achieved at the outset and people are under no illusion that the company will take accusations of bullying seriously (Rayner, 1997).

Work climate

This often has a lot to do with bullying. In the oil industry some managers were referred to as screaming skulls used to screaming directions on oil platforms to be heard against the wind and weather. The problems arose when they were transferred to an onshore job. Staff in offices resent being addressed in the same way.

Some working environments encourage 'rough and tumble'. There are, for example, initiation rites in the armed services which, while they may be tolerated in a single gender environment, become improper in a mixed gender environment. Senior officers need to be aware of such 'rites' and clamp down on them early and consistently.

High levels of long-term sickness can be a consequence of bullying at work (25 per cent of targets of bullying leave to get away from it). This suggests that spotting who goes off and why may be the first indication that something is amiss in a department or section. Another point to watch is places rarely visited by members of management. There should be no such areas in any organization. Senior managers should be able to turn up anywhere, anytime. They are much more likely to catch offenders in the act if they do (MBWA = management by walking about) (Ishmael, 2000).

Disabled people

Disabled people appear to be more likely victims of bullying. Perhaps cowards prefer victims whose ability to respond is perceived to be curtailed in some way. Managers have a particular duty to take care of those less able to take care of themselves (Woodhams and Corby, 2007).

Measures the organization should take

Check company policy and procedures

Staff handbooks need to make it clear what the definition of harassment and bullying are, mentioning examples of behaviours that might be construed as offensive to others.

All employees need training

Everyone needs to understand their rights and obligations under these laws. As we have noted, it is not just managers who are likely to turn to bullying or harassment as a tool to control others or gratify their own need to dominate others.

Managers need the confidence and skills to identify and act

Situations arising at work need prompt attention from a manager. Management by walking about (MBWA) is an important activity in this regard. Catching someone in the act is not likely to occur if managers remain rooted to their office or work space. Regular absences can sometimes encourage people to use the opportunity to commit acts that they would not do if they knew they were likely to be observed.

Procedures for dealing with offences

Make sure a good formal complaints system exists. This should be available to those who are likely to have to deal with offenders and training should include role-play and comments on performance by tutors and trainers. Knowledge of personnel procedures needs to be complemented by practised skill and consolidated experience.

Asking about incidents

Feedback should be sought from all employees on a regular basis, both formally and informally. Of particular value are *exit interviews* in which those who have left the company are revisited three months after they have moved on. Often where high staff turnover occurs in just one part of the organization there may be an underlying problem that needs to be addressed. Manager problems are a major reason for people seeking to leave the organization and may be more easily divulged once staff have left.

Finally, HR is responsible for keeping track on changes in the law or its application. The CIPD magazine *People Management* features regular examples of situations that have gone to Tribunals reporting the outcome of the findings and the effect that this may have on future practices.

Dignity at work

Dignity and respect are difficult to define but easy to identify. Thoughtfulness for others can be as simple as holding open a door and letting someone come through first; asking after people; showing interest; listening well; giving eye contact; showing support; giving encouragement. It happens in the small things that govern our everyday lives – not just our working lives.

This emphasis on positive behaviours should start at the top and percolate throughout the organization. Managers lead by example. So there should be no shouting at individuals or groups. There are better and more reasonable ways of showing disapproval – if that is appropriate.

Generate a positive code of conduct

Behaviours do not always happen on their own, so promote training on *assertive* behaviours for everyone. Once again role-playing is an important part of developing skill and receiving feedback (good as well as corrective). The best training is good example.

Discouraging temper tantrums

People fear moodiness at work in others often because it makes them feel insecure and uncertain how to approach those who show variable behaviour at work. How do you cope when you are not sure what you are dealing with?

Assertiveness training can help (say what it is you don't like; say what it does to you; say what you would prefer the other person to do).

Giving feedback to staff

Managers should be able to comment assertively on behaviours at work, if it is an issue for other people. Pay attention to reinforcing the positive (through training) as well as moving quickly to act on negative situations.

Management by walking about

Good teachers practice this and so do good managers. Managers who are found only on the management floors of the organization are less likely to know what is going on in the business. First-hand knowledge can only be acquired by regular contact with those who are carrying the front end of the business.

Keep your ears open

Sometimes a word comes informally – which is why informal contact with others is worth encouraging (though not gossip). Rumours are usually worth following up, if only to discover whether they are justified or not. Early informal interventions are more likely to achieve success than waiting for matters to become formal and more advanced. Offenders are often put off from reoffending once they know their behaviour has been noted.

The Learning Organization

In the 1990s much time was given to the idea of the learning organization (Senge, 1990). Its popularity as an idea paralleled the growing interest in knowledge workers. The idea behind this was that increasing change initiatives followed so fast upon one another that organizations were in a time of continuous change. What followed from this was that people working in all sectors should be ready to learn from change and become more deliberate in the ways that they do this.

Behind this lie two concepts. The first is self-reflection and the second is evaluation. In a fast-paced workplace finding time for either of these might be easy. But, if we go back to classical approaches to learning then the reflectiveness required to learn always was part of the learning cycle (Figure 10.1).

At work, time constraints can force people into a pragmatist–activist role much of the time. We learn from working, but the time to find out more about why we were successful is not always available to us.

BOX 10.4

Charles Handy tells the story of his time as head of a business school. He was approached by a young millionaire who asked to be admitted as a student to one of the university's business degree courses. Handy expostulated with him that he already knew how to be successful as a businessman, so what need had he of studying further.

The young millionaire answered, 'I want to discover why I was successful – otherwise I shall not be able to repeat it.'

Handy accepted him on the course.

So, reflectiveness allows us time to ask why and then to do something about it so that we are not trapped into a continuous cycle of activity that does not progress or develop. What this means is that there are different contexts for learning, both of which need to be addressed. The first is the achievement of business objectives which we might illustrate as shown in Figure 10.2.

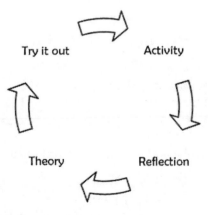

Try it out   Activity

Theory   Reflection

FIGURE 10.1 Learning cycle.

Source: Adapted from Kolb *et al.* (1974).

The second is the reflectiveness required of a manager which is again a cyclical process and can be illustrated as shown in Figure 10.3.

The review process leads on occasion to a replanning that takes into account that during any business period, sales projections are not always realized in the way expected. Continuing on in the same way can only lead to disaster. Change on the run requires reflection and review followed by action. *Strategic integration* is not a one-off activity. It requires constant revision and therefore constant communication so that everyone knows that changes have had to be made and what the implications are for their own job objectives.

There are two aspects of this that we might consider. First, action learning and, second, self-development. We will consider them in turn.

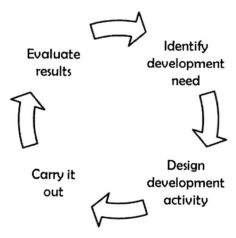

FIGURE 10.2 Evaluational cycle.

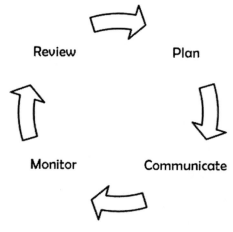

FIGURE 10.3 Management cycle.

Action learning

Reg Revans will always be associated with this movement and it is no coincidence that the Human Relations School began at around the same time in the early 1950s using similar approaches. The idea behind both movements was that workers if consulted are often better at diagnosing problems and putting them right than their managers. Hands-on experience derived by direct involvement in the work gives people a chance to consider how they could improve what they do and even overcome problems to which no solution has been apparent to managers.

The work included mining and nursing and supported the view that, given a facilitator to mobilize the process, and time to consider the problem, staff were quite willing and able to spend time applying themselves to solving quite major problems and improving what they do in the workplace. The serious implementation of such principles can be found in the movement towards TQM in the 1980s when kaizen was introduced into car manufacturing. These weekly team meetings were intended to extend the consultation of workers in improving their work processes. Though it would be fair to say that this would usually count as incremental change rather than the more radical change undertaken in the original *action learning* projects.

The function of the facilitator is not just to offer support and guidance where needed, but to make sure the political blocks are removed once workers do come up with a feasible solution.

Self-development

Ten per cent of staff are probably doing something developmental on their own in their free time. Interests and hobbies usually require knowledge and skill and are consolidated by experience and training. The challenge for managers is to find out what those activities are. Individuals themselves are sometimes modest in what they see as extra-curricular activities and are sometimes surprised when it is pointed out to them they have had to develop and demonstrate knowledge and skills of a significant order to achieve what they have done. The fact that they have not been paid sometimes blinds people to the competence that they have developed and that they could be applying to their work.

There are so many different activities that might be applicable to the job environment:

- courses (OU; Open College)
- learning (do-it-yourself books; languages; skills)
- study (guided reading; iPod; CDs)
- literature (group reading circles; discussions; debates)
- art (collecting; exhibiting; trading; e-commerce)
- hobbies (all sorts ...).

It is all worthwhile work – and yet few get paid for it. But they do all get a reward (self-satisfaction, fulfilment, proving a point) and this may indicate an aptitude that could make it easy for them to avail themselves of job opportunities that they had not considered they were trained for.

Recruitment and appraisal interviews are both opportunities to find out what people do in their spare time, which may become the foundation for developing their management and work-based competencies. As important are informal conversations with staff during off-duty moments. What they have learned and their continuing interest in it can indicate aptitudes that may have been dormant or unnoticed at work.

Learning contracts

We have already mentioned CPD as important in the lives of most knowledge workers. We could also mention that supporting individuals who are undertaking further studies or courses is often also appreciated and makes people feel that the company is equally committed to their *personal development plan*.

Learning agreements can be informal and reviewed between learner and mentor/manager on a regular basis. They can be supported by time made available or payment towards any costs.

Company-sponsored formal support for a course such as an MBA degree can be arranged so that the candidate agrees to stay for a stated time after achieving the award or qualification or, if they leave early, has to pay back what the company paid towards the degree.

The Handy and Constable Reports

In 1987 these reports came out with some comparative figures indicating how much the UK invested in training and qualifications compared with our competitors. The differences are significant. We compared unfavourable with Japan, Germany and the USA – our major competitors at the time. Our numbers of qualified managers was lower; our number of graduate managers was lower; and many of our young people left full-time education two years before our competitors. Money spent on training was significantly less than our competitors, too. With a little more investment the productivity of workers can be transformed. It could also make us more effective.

The Labour Government's commitment to putting 50 per cent of young people through university has been a laudable objective. But that is only a beginning of providing a learning platform for individuals to build upon. Turning work experience into development and learning opportunities will be a lifelong occupation for most people in active work and will last throughout their careers. Companies that support that work are more likely to be rewarded by the loyalty and commitment of their staff. In such value-added businesses, continuity among the staff will be important for retaining customer goodwill.

Summary

Equality and diversity will continue to be the guarantee of success in global businesses. Employing people from different backgrounds, nationalities and cultures will continue and companies that are good at integrating and absorbing people from different backgrounds will always have a better chance of excelling in their field through their people. Change is normal but can only be overcome through people, and the wider the source from which they are drawn, the more likely they are to achieve success through working for commonly held objectives.

References and further reading

Atkinson, C. and Hall, L. (2009) The role of gender in varying forms of flexible working. *Gender, Work and Organization*, 16(6): 650–666.

Blaine, B. (2007) *Understanding the Psychology of Diversity*. London: Sage.

Buchanan, D. and Badham, R. (2008) *Power, Politics and Organizational Change*. London: Sage.

Clegg, A. (2012) On my agenda: The diversity/creativity link. *People Management*, April: 45–47.

Clutterbuck, D. (1992) *Everyone Needs a Mentor: How to foster talent within the organization*, 2nd edn. London: Institute of Personnel Management.

Doyle, M., Claydon, T. and Buchanan, D. (2000) Mixed results, lousy process: The management experience of organizational change. *British Journal of Management*, 1(1) (Special Issue): 59–80.

Ellis, C. and Sonnenfield, J.A. (1994) Diverse approaches to managing diversity. *Human Resource Management*, 33(1): 79–109.

Frank, J. (2006) Gay glass ceilings. *Economica*, 73(291): 485–508.

Grainger, H. and Holt, H. (2005) *Trade Union Membership 2004*. London: DTI.

Guest, D.E. (1987) Human resource management and industrial relations. *Journal of Management Studies*, 24(5): 503–521.

Hakim, C. (2004) *Key Issues in Women's Work*. London: Glasshouse Press.

Handy, C. (1987) *The Making of Managers: A report on management education, training and development in the USA, Germany, France, Japan and the UK*. London: National Economic Development Office.

Huselid, M. (1995) The impact of human resource management on turnover, productivity and corporate financial performance. *Academy of Management Journal*, 38: 635–672.

Ishmael, A. with Bunmi Alemoru (2000) *Harassment, Bullying and Violence at Work*. London: The Industrial Society.

Johnson, C. (1991) *The Economy under Mrs Thatcher*. London: Penguin.

Kandola, R. and Fullerton, J. (1998) *The Dynamics of Managing Diversity*. London: IPD publications

Kellaway, L. (2012) Nicola Horlick now. *Financial Times*, 12 May.

Kirsley, B., Alpin, C., Forth, J., Bryson, A., Bewley, H., Dix, G. and Oxenbridge, S. (2006) *Inside the Workplace: Findings from the 2004 Workplace Employment Relations Survey*. London: Routledge.

Kirton, G. and Greene, A. (2010) *The Dynamics of Managing Diversity: A critical approach*. London: Butterworth Heinemann.

Kolb, D.A., Rubin, I.M. and McIntyre, J.M. (1974) *Organizational Psychology: A book of readings*, 2nd edn. New York: Englewood Cliffs.

Manning, A. (2006) *The Gender Pay Gap*. London: EOC.

Miller, D. (1996) Equality management: Towards a materialist approach. *Gender, Work and Organization*, 3(4): 202–214.

Procter, S. and Mueller, F. (2000) Teamworking: strategy, structure, systems and culture, in S. Procter and F. Mueller (eds.) *Teamworking*. Houndmills/London: Macmillan.

Purcell, J., Kinnie, N., Hutchinson, S., Rayton, B. and Swart, J. (2003) *Understanding the People and Performance Link: Unlocking the black box*. London: CIPD.

Rayner, C. (1997) Incidence of workplace bullying. *Journal of Community and Applied Social Psychology*, 7(3): 199–208.

Revans, R. (1980) *Action Learning: New techniques for management*. London: Blond and Briggs.

Schank, R. and Abelson, R. (1977) *Scripts, Plans and Knowledge*. Mahwah, NJ: Lawrence Erlbaum.

Schein, E.H. (1985) *Organizational Culture and Leadership*. San Francisco, CA: Jossey Bass.

Senge, P. (1990) *The Fifth Discipline: The art & practice of the learning organization*. New York: Currency Doubleday.

Snape, E. and Redman, T. (2003) Too old or too young? The impact of perceived age discrimination. *Human Resource Management Journal*, 13(1): 78–89.

Storey, J. (1992) *Development in the Management of Human Resources: An analytical review*. Oxford: Blackwell.

Warhurst, C. and Thompson, P. (2006) Mapping knowledge in work: Proxies or practices? *Work, Employment and Society*, 20: 787–800.

Wickens, P. (1987) *The Road to Nissan: Flexibility quality teamwork*. London: Macmillan.

Woodhams, C. and Corby, S. (2007) Then and now: Disability legislation and employers' practices in the UK. *British Journal of Industrial Relations*, 45(3): 556–580.

GRADUATE ATTRIBUTES

The diversity/creativity link

During this exercise you will address the following graduate attributes:

- an intellectual curiosity and a willingness to question accepted wisdom and to be open to new ideas;
- an openness to, and an interest in, lifelong learning through directed and self-directed study.

Read through the following article. At different points in the narrative you will be asked to stop and answer questions. Please make notes so that you can contribute to a discussion. How far can HR engage with its staff from day to day? Is there a foolproof way of raising issues of importance that might start people talking to others about their experience or even contacting HR directly? Perhaps more modern methods would help HR stay in touch with its clients.

Questions:

- **Why does HR need to raise a discussion among a working team?**
- **Comment on the skills required to capitalize on responses from the working team.**

For bigger companies this is a challenge. For there is nothing worse than being stuck in a faraway place feeling isolated and with no one to talk to about challenges that can happen at work. HR sinks or swims by its ability to reinvent itself periodically and to innovate continually. This suggests the need to employ creative people and build a work environment that is accepting of difference in all its various guises. HR often works hard to put together and support diverse teams because in the international marketplace they perform best. But creativity can come at a price: as when there is a wide diversity of thought, evaluation and practice. What works well for one group may not work as well for another and individuals as managers tend to do what they know has worked in the past.

For example, it may be that diversity is more often honoured in the breech than in the observance. Most well-established companies have a track record that predates equality legislation and stretches back to early attempts to integrate staff from different backgrounds. For the current generation of HR departments the challenge is to develop the legacy – and then be on the lookout to extend its brief to include social media too. Who would have thought that people would use text messaging to bully others at work, in school or in domestic life?

Questions:

- **Is diversity dependent on a variety of employment backgrounds contributing to future strategic goals of the organization or just people getting on together?**
- **What part can HR play in encouraging equality in the organization?**

One good example of the cost of non-communication is the situation of many mergers and acquisitions. Some years ago one of the authors worked in the financial sector in a bank that was taken over by another. Coffee times were an opportunity to overhear what people actually thought about day-to-day decisions made by managers. Promotions were closely watched to see which of the previous organization's managers were promoted in the newly merged organization. The organization was totally silent about promotion prospects and criteria for promotion.

So, for HR and line managers, communication is the top priority. HR despair that their efforts are overlooked or even not known about. For, in most large organizations, a profusion of material lies on its intranets and websites. But staff do not know about it or have little time to familiarize themselves with it.

We could take one example of discrimination: staff with disabilities. The HR team need to look at the performance management process to make sure, for example, that the way the company assesses people does not prejudice employees with disabilities. Here the contact with line managers is essential to ensure that individuals are monitored and supported in their work. All concerned have to accept that for an individual tasks may take a little bit longer, and make allowances for this. But why would any firm employ people whose disabilities handicap them in the performance of their jobs? Once again the answer links back to a company's need to tap a diverse pool of talent that is inclusive and supportive.

Questions:

- **What view should HR have about diversity in the workforce?**
- **How should they engage line managers in this work?**

Although collecting statistics is important for tracking progress in any HR activity, numbers alone do not tell the whole story. It is important to know, for example, what proportion of the company leadership team is female. But as well as focusing on the numbers, HR and line managers should be as concerned with making sure that people who may be reluctant to present themselves as managers are treated with respect and supported in their quest to further their career in the company.

It should be the same with declaring a personal health problem. Knowledge is power not just for the sufferer but for the organization, too. For example, some companies have introduced reversed mentoring, where managers are briefed by those who have a personal condition to cope with in order to help them understand what that condition can mean for their member of staff in their day-to-day coping with their job. Similarly, talks from members of such bodies as Alcoholics Anonymous can also be a good investment for making sure that everybody has a greater understanding and awareness of the dangers of addiction and the ways that may be open to overcome it.

By giving people who want to speak out a platform to talk about their challenges, whether personal or in groups, information becomes more widely available to the working team and managers are as much in need of such learning opportunities as anyone else.

Questions:

- **How effective could 'reverse mentoring' be at changing a culture to appreciate diversity?**
- **What indicators might there be to show that such an HR strategy had been effective?**

Connecting people to strategy

There are few companies for whom radical change has not been necessary to remain in touch with their market. But as we have seen, *strategic integration* is one of the most difficult things to put across within the organization. It ought to be easy but how does it apply to individuals – that is what each person wants to know.

To help staff to identify with a new strategic agenda, the HR team may consider running a series of company-wide events. At one level the gatherings can be an exercise in communication. The aim is to make the strategy real for people. They also have the practical purpose of giving participants, working in groups, opportunities to try their hand at some problem solving. First the groups are asked to think up a technical solution to an everyday problem that they see, perhaps unaddressed. Then they are asked to think about the various interest groups that would need to come together, in the real world, to put a change plan into action.

Although most HR and line managers are committed to the power of face-to-face events to put across strategic integration, there is an extended role for social media technologies in bringing people together to make them feel part of the wider group. We notice how news sites allow for comments following lead articles. Following discussion programmes on television or Twitter can be equally involving. What others think can be a great stimulus. To change Weick's famous saying, 'How do I know what I think till I hear what I say' we could say, 'How do I know what I think till I tweet what I say?' It is a form of democratic debate that is worth investing in.

Questions:

- **How far could online discussion facilitate strategic integration?**
- **Are there any constraints to online brainstorming?**

Engaging with the future

Most change consultants are aware of the value of the question focused on imagining what the world of work would look like in five years' time. Out of all the creative ideas that surface – some may be outlandish but some could be prophetic. Perhaps there is even the option of giving opinions on how past performance has placed us and what our potential for growth now is.

Another innovative idea might envisage virtual skills bases replacing local HR teams, making it possible for business managers to call upon specialist skills, located anywhere in the world, as and when they were needed. You might, for example, draw on a particular compensation package from an Asian partner or a case study skill from the Middle East.

Could online performance management catch on? It might overcome the problem of frequently reforming interdisciplinary teams that turn over three or four times a year, leaving appraisers with little idea of the different impacts that have been made. Perhaps restricted access accounts of how the team members performed and their feedback on the work could be useful to include through social media.

Questions:

* How beneficial would access to HR skills from other parts of the organization be?
* What are the risks of embarking on such a strategy?
* How comfortable would you be with online comments about your performance?

Summary

Using technology for wider learning can facilitate openness and development at the grassroots of the organization. Organizations that fail to adapt in the face of a mobile workforce constantly on the move need to use all available platforms for mobilizing opinion, thought and learning among their people. *Strategic integration* could be the main beneficiary and HR then becomes a crossroads of communication throughout the organization.

Tutor guidance

Innovation and social media would seem at first sight to complement each other well in the fragmented employment experience that most workers face today. Access to information is more immediate and easy to obtain, especially if individuals are willing agents. This would seem to suggest that current information about what individuals feel and think about their work life can be more readily obtained using modern methods, thereby reducing the loss of contact that sporadic working patterns may bring about.

However, there is an issue about how far individuals might feel comfortable about instant evaluation by their peers, encouraged by the company. The constant surveillance that is sometimes mentioned as the outcome of computerization and cameras makes people feel they are more observed, particularly where it takes place without their prior knowledge and consent.

So there is a worthwhile debate to be had here about how far freedom of information needs to be balanced with the right of the individual to confidentiality. There is a growing suspicion that surveillance is extending its reach within and outside organizations and HR needs to safeguard its own neutrality if it is to play the role of honest broker to all sides in the company.

11

DISCIPLINARY, GRIEVANCE AND SICK ABSENCE

Topics

- performance, disciplinaries and grievance
- targets and correctly worded standards
- interviews, mitigating circumstances and good cause
- handling concerns and objections
- sick and intermittent absence
- experience of change at work and future challenges.

Introduction

Employee relations is a comprehensive term that can mean many things to different people and organizations. Its meaning can range from a general, all-embracing approach to building a rapport with staff to the more specific elements of managing the employment contract. How people feel about the organization depends on the series of management interventions that take place at work and on how individuals and groups feel about the way they have been treated. This is more than just having clearly written policies and procedures in the company. It also depends on how these measures are implemented and whether people feel they were fairly handled (Blyton and Turnbull, 1992).

In this respect, lack of consistency is a complaint that, if justified, is most likely to give rise to grievance among staff. Similarly, for the company and its managers, implementing standards at work can be difficult, not necessarily because the standards are complex, but because the memory of how others were dealt with in the past will be closely monitored and compared with what takes place in the present day. Tribunal cases are often pursued for reasons of feeling aggrieved based on different practices in different parts of the company and what appears to be different outcomes for similar offences. Lawyers called upon to represent such cases will thoroughly search all the company's HR records to uncover such inconsistencies.

BOX 11.1

A case heard at tribunal involving accusations of improper conduct towards members of a manager's staff found the respondent cross-examined for over an hour.

The HR manager was cross-examined for over five hours as similar cases were examined to discover whether there had been inconsistencies in the way that similar accusations had been dealt with and resolved by the organization in the past.

In this sense then, there is a clear connection between employee relations as a general aspiration of fairness towards employees, the way in which company policy is implemented and the procedures followed in each case. Such events are closely monitored by everyone in the company to see whether past practice has been followed or perhaps exceptions have been made that suggest that the policy was inconsistently applied.

Company procedures for dealing with variance of performance are often expressed in terms such as *disciplinary* and *grievance* procedures. There is an unfortunate connotation that attaches to these words that can imply a punitive system that seeks to lay blame and identify responsibility and guilt for events that took place in the past. It might be better to speak of *standards and targets* which may better express the aspiration of restoring good practice and clarifying uncertainty about what is the right thing to do or what is to be avoided in the future.

The *employment contract* is a legally binding agreement reached between two parties: the company and the individual. But, as Guest (1998) points out, a contract is normally between two people. So, in the place of the company there are managers who represent the organization and are responsible for implementing procedures where the contract is thought to be at risk or breached in some way. In the same way the employee may be uncertain whether the goodwill, loyalty and trust they have invested in the organization through their efforts have been rightly acknowledged or not.

But, Guest is right to raise the point that organizations cannot by themselves rise to the challenge of administering fairness and justice for all. Their managers are responsible for mobilizing the spirit and letter of the law that underlies the employment contract. If we go back to the *psychological contract* we can allow that the *transactional elements* of the contract are often easier to raise as issues because the factors underlying behaviours are usually measurable and testable, and therefore evidence can be adduced in their support or lack of it. But what is more difficult is the *relational elements* that Rousseau (1990) speaks of. Managers owe it to themselves and their colleagues to undertake formal procedures with members of their staff without putting at risk the trust and goodwill that underpins all good working relationships. This is a difficult balance to strike.

BOX 11.2

A checkout operator in a DIY store was suspected of shoplifting and on searching her flat the police discovered £1,500's worth of expensive domestic drilling equipment. The member of staff had not sought to sell or give the items away. They were all found under the bed.

Further enquiries uncovered that the member of staff resented the way in which the manager shouted at her in front of customers and thought that the best way to get her own back was to steal the most expensive items in the store. That way when it came to stock taking, she thought, the manager would be in trouble for losing so much expensive equipment (drills at that time were highly priced and easier to remove than they are today).

Responsibilities made clear

A more positive term to use about employee relations might be mutual *responsibilities* and duties.

The company has responsibilities towards the members of staff. These are laid out under various laws and these should be found in the *staff handbook, company policy, procedures and practices, operations directory, personnel and training manuals* and any other formal company documents where working conditions and required behaviours are defined. Correctly worded and consistent standards lie at the heart of any reasonably managed working environment. Where they are not clearly defined it invites the accusation that a reasonable member of staff could not be expected to adhere to what was not clearly stated or was inconsistently stated in company documents.

The member of staff has *duties* balanced by *responsibilities* and exercising those rights in a reasonable way will be part of an ongoing partnership between the individual and the organization. There will always be areas of discretion that are given to staff that will need to be exercised with care for others and awareness of risk to the work and wider environment. However, the balance to be struck between the exercise of complementary responsibilities is not always clear and needs to be defined as accurately as possible because context can alter circumstances and guidelines and training rarely covers all eventualities.

So what has changed in the context of work during more recent times?

We have a less quiescent workforce than once was the case. If Handy was correct that by 1995 75 per cent of jobs would be held by knowledge workers, then it becomes clear that the traditional supervision of workers is not as feasible as might once have been the case. For example, IT workers are likely to know more about computers than those they work for. So, it is difficult for managers to supervise and correct staff who exercise a specialist skill when they are not familiar with the working of computer hardware and software themselves. All that managers can focus on are the *defined inputs* (productivity factors) and the *required outputs* (effectiveness factors) that surround the process of an operation and in which the expert exercises problem-solving abilities.

The *Shamrock organization* (Handy, 1989) also indicates the fragmentation of employment experience for those working in the different areas as core staff, self-employed consultants or subcontractors. At very least we need to ask what the implications are for commitment and motivation, particularly *organizational commitment* which was stated as one of the principal HR outcomes of HRM theory. The focus of workers' commitment on short-term contracts may be with the company, their manager or perhaps their own career and their employability after the contract has finished. It may be that they have job, work and career commitment, but that organizational commitment is more difficult for them to define and feel committed to, owing to the temporary nature of the contract under whose terms they work.

More employees are likely to be *university graduates*. And those in receipt of higher and further education are schooled to be critical and questioning in their approach to their work. In this respect *instructional technique* (single loop learning) works only for those who need to know little or nothing about the business they work in. For them, just learning what to do will occupy their attention without worrying about why we do it that way and what it means in business terms. For those schooled to find out why and its significance, more will be expected in induction training, for example.

All of this suggests that the world of work is much less predictable for individuals and for organizations than might once have been the case. If core workers can be required to keep to a dress code, does this apply to the consultants who come in and work for them? Similarly, working for another company can hardly be held against self-employed consultants because if they work for more than 75 per cent of their time for one company, they may put at risk their self-employed status. But, then, are they bound by the same conditions of confidentiality as their core staff colleagues? They might also find themselves speaking to customers on the company's behalf. So, what can the company require of them in this respect? Can they be truthful about their reservations about what the company is offering and are they free to speak their mind and advise on the options that the customer has, or must they abide by the company's sales and marketing policy? Fragmented working has made some aspects easier for core staff managers, but for those in the other segments of the organization the requirements may not be as clear-cut as might first appear.

Disciplinaries: poor performance

Poor performance often begins sporadically – a missed deadline here, a forgotten meeting there – and therefore is often overlooked initially by the manager. Only when others comment – sometimes other colleagues – does it come to the manager's attention. Managers may rightly try to speak informally to staff that are not fulfilling their obligations and sometimes temporary efforts to improve may result. All of this is good practice. However, managers do not always make a note that they have spoken to staff informally nor do they always keep accurate records of what they observed and the occasions when it took place. This means that if challenged in more formal interviews or hearings managers will not always have clear and explicit evidence of past poor behaviour over an extended period. The first issue of importance for managers, then, is to keep a note of what they have observed at the time they observe it. That way they have begun to put in place an audit trail that can be called on later should the matter be tested in a more formal setting.

Second, preparation to speak to staff whether formally or informally should begin with a review of the *standard* that applies. Is it clearly stated in the staff handbook or other company documents? Is it part of the employment contract? The fact that it isn't should not be a cause of not acting, however, as there are both *expressed* and *implied* parts of an employment contract and a tribunal will usually take account of what a reasonable person would have done in the circumstances where less explicit guidance has been available. But assuming that there is a standard clearly expressed, it may be worth checking on the wording to see whether it is correctly worded and will stand up to scrutiny outside the company.

As we have seen, there are three parts to a correctly worded standard:

- behaviour
- condition
- standard.

We will comment on them in turn.

Behaviour

The behaviour should be described in testable, measurable terms. So, such words as 'understand', 'appreciate', know', 'have a firm grasp of' are not testable because the verb defines an internalized activity. We cannot see other people's knowledge or understanding unless it is demonstrated in a way that we can see or hear something that gives us evidence that they know or understand what they need to know. Standards often fail at this first step. So, as a senior manager or consultant, an initial scan of official company documents should enable us to see whether the actions described do satisfy this important requirement which makes us secure in terms of a legally secure definition. So, statements that read as follows would need to be reviewed:

- appreciate the principles of banking;
- have a firm grasp of the powers of an arresting officer;
- understand the Highway Code;
- know the steps for repairing a type A engine.

These are not testable as they currently stand. So, they might be better expressed as:

- state the principles of banking;
- explain the powers of an arresting officer;
- explain the Highway Code;
- assemble a type A engine.

Conditions

The relevant conditions under which the behaviour is to be exercised should be stated and here we revert to the efficiency or productivity factors:

- time
- quantity
- quality
- cost.

How long does someone have to fulfil the standards; are there quantity targets required; are there quality outputs; and is cost a factor? If they are then they should be stated in specific terms. If all four conditions are stated then there is a tightly worded standard that defines the behaviour required in specific terms.

Standards

The context in which actions take place is also relevant. So, for example, the pressure to produce more can find those pressurized taking short cuts. For production workers that may mean, for example, removing safety guards from machinery to enable them to operate more quickly and achieve the increased targets. The question of violation of health and safety then becomes a serious issue. So, the final clause might be worded:

- adhering to all health and safety requirements.

The interview

Once the standard is clarified and the evidence of the behaviour assembled it may be opportune to interview the member of staff whose performance has been below standard. There are three aspects that need to be addressed within the interview that may help in achieving a logical sequence and make sense to those involved in the process:

- *Test the standard*: does the member of staff know what the standard is? One possibility might be to start by asking whether the member of staff can state what the appropriate standard is.
- *Identify the behaviour*: lay out clearly the evidence as it has arisen over the period observed. Vague statements about 'late coming' are less convincing than a clearly drawn up schedule of times and dates observed and noted by the manager.
- *Measure the gap*: between the standard and the behaviour. Not everyone realizes that the employment contract is legally binding and can sometimes be invariable unless prior agreement to change it is obtained.

BOX 11.3

A sales director noted that one of his area managers was taking to leaving the office at 4pm so that he had a head-start to get onto the M25 before others on the industrial estate who left work at 5pm. The secretaries began to comment that there was one rule for managers and another for staff.

The sales director spoke to his area manager and said that his employment contract clearly stated that the core hours were 9am–5pm. So, in future he should not leave the office until 5pm or after.

What the director didn't know was that the area manager used to get in at 7am, clear up and put the coffee on and start work early. He did point this out to his boss, but his boss was adamant that we 'have to set a good example to the girls'.

He thereafter kept to core hours and his goodwill and flexibility diminished as a result.

Perhaps his contracted hours could have been changed?

At this stage the interviewer may want to ask whether there are any reasons why this drop in performance has come about. And basically there are two headings that might be relevant here:

- *mitigating circumstances*: usually health factors that can have affected the performance of the individual concerned;
- *good cause*: other personal factors that may have had a material effect on the behaviour at work. This might be a situation at home, financial worries and, increasingly for people with older relations and children, looking after dependents etc.

The explanations may contain within them the beginnings of a discussion about how to progress the situation in the future. Good practice would suggest that staff should agree to clearly defined steps for proceeding when they return to work. So staff should be told clearly:

- *the behaviour* that is expected of them in the future (again in specific, testable terms which we discussed above);
- *the conditions* under which that behaviour should be exercised (time, quantity, quality, cost);
- *the support* that the company will give them (training, coaching, time off to seek medical advice, etc.).

Finally: fix a *review date*.

We should be able to offer these steps in writing to the individual once the interview has been concluded. This applies both to formal and informal warnings. The fact that a warning is considered to be 'verbal' does not mean that nothing is written down or that the member of staff does not need a copy in writing of what was agreed between them. Good practice requires that they are provided with clear guidance in writing.

Concerns and objections

There are several traps that the unsuspecting manager may fall into while running a formal or informal interview about poor performance. First, there are extenuating circumstances. *Custom and practice* has long been a phrase that is acknowledged in UK law, though it is becoming less significant as European law plays a more central part in our courts. What this means is that sometimes the question of what people got used to doing in the past would be seen as influencing what they would consider reasonable. It should certainly raise the question of whether a loophole needs to be closed or not. Similarly, the excuse that a previous manager allowed exceptions to a rule may suggest that a clearer extension of the law needs to be made by the manager. Clarifying a standard and its application for everyone could be a better way for a new manager to assert his or her authority than alighting only on one offender.

BOX 11.4

A newly appointed manager came across a member of staff making phone calls abroad during working time and raised this with her as being a violation of the company's rules on two counts: personal phone calls during working time and unauthorized phone calls abroad.

The member of staff pointed out that her mother-in-law was seriously ill with a terminal disease and the previous manager had said that she could ring once a day if she needed to find out how her mother-in-law was.

Clearly, time to clarify the situation for the whole team, not just the person immediately affected.

More serious would be the claim that *no training* had been given – hence the problems that arose on the job. Certainly, companies are usually far more careful in ensuring that induction trainees sign off on their training log to avoid such claims. But those further on in their career progression might have been put in the situation of promotion with an offer of training later. Supervisors in the retail sector were often promoted and told that they would be sent on a training course later. Sometimes this could be up to two years later. During that time they could reasonably claim that they had not been properly trained – hence the problem which they were unable to deal with effectively.

Reference to *other members of staff* who appear to have got away with similar behaviour but have not been picked up about it becomes a difficult claim – especially for a new manager. It may be that other people have been warned or that they have extenuating circumstances. However, it may not be possible to enlighten others about this for reasons of confidentiality. Managers usually learn to say: 'We are not talking about X, we are talking about you.' However, if the claim is accurate managers would do well to examine all other cases that have occurred, as this is just the action that would be taken to satisfy a tribunal that the company had been consistent in its treatment of some similar cases.

Setting the record straight

There are other issues that arise when setting up the terms of future behaviour. One will be the accuracy of defining the behaviours required of the individual. But another that often raises its head is the time allowed for improvement. In general, tribunals look closely at *how reasonable the time scale* was and will reflect whether poor performance over a long period not followed up promptly would suggest that more time should be allowed to the individual to bring themselves back up to standard. Requiring immediate adherence to a rule, while necessary in health and safety issues, for example, may be unreasonable where a new level of competence is being attempted.

One last factor remains: *fixing a review date*. Any vagueness about future review could be construed as lack of commitment by the manager and risks the appearance of leaving a problem unresolved. This also allows the manager to demonstrate that a continued interest was taken to ensure that any support promised has been successfully delivered.

Gross misconduct

It is usual for these items to be listed separately in the staff handbook, so that people are aware from the outset what constitutes gross misconduct. Violence against another person and theft are usually included. But there are other issues that are less clear-cut whose implications are emerging as new opportunities emerge for betraying trust – for example, using social media.

Principal among these will be using company resources such as computers for personal purposes during working time. More serious will be cases of accessing illegal sites or downloading illegal material. Most serious is divulging company information or data to third parties, particularly competitors. The law is still being tested by cases arising from claims made that an individual has breached company security or divulged sensitive information. So, perhaps, more warning needs to be given to induction trainees and core staff about texting, emailing or talking to others about company business and conveying, wittingly or unwittingly, sensitive information. Employees owe their employer a duty of trust in this regard. But what is sensitive may be a matter of opinion unless clarified beforehand.

It may seem at first that gross misconduct is an open and shut case. However, managers are advised that they should investigate the circumstances surrounding such events. It is not unknown that those who have struck out at another person have done so under duress or threat. And there has always been an acknowledgement that 'bad blood' between individuals can affect the context in which an event occurred. Insulting behaviour aimed at family members or friends, for example, may well trigger an instant response which will be regretted later.

Clearly the offender will be suspended while the event is investigated so that witnesses can be interviewed without feeling threatened or at risk of intimidation. But ultimately the full circumstances surrounding a case may mean that there is more than one offender and that others' behaviour will also need to be addressed.

Offences away from work

The question of what may be relevant to an employee's contract with regard to conduct away from the workplace is certainly important to clarify within a company. For those working in retail, for example, shoplifting in another store would be deemed as gross misconduct even if it takes place off-site in another store. Similarly, for those in positions of trust, there could be offences that are deemed relevant to their office or job. It would be important to consider whether they have violated a position of trust and whether that would affect their ability to discharge their work responsibilities. Such matters should be included in the staff handbook to ensure that everyone is aware of the implications of such offences.

Good practice

Most people complain that lack of communication bedevils their life at work. Sometimes, therefore, being picked up for poor performance will come as a complete surprise to the individual concerned. Similarly, being called to a meeting with no knowledge of what is to be discussed and unaware of the evidence collected may be perceived as a lack of consideration or an attempt to gain an advantage by taking the individual unawares.

Keeping notes of all events that have been seen or noticed, or mentioned by other staff, should be a regular practice for managers with responsibility for staff.

Such notes are valid in a tribunal. But if they are not kept it will be difficult for a manager to substantiate claims that are later made about the details of a case.

There are two other matters that are important to consider, too. First, there is the matter of the representative or friend that the individual brings with them and the role they play in the interview and the role of HR. Some organizations like to have a member of HR sitting in with the manager on crucial interviews, particularly when interviews are done infrequently or a matter may be contentious. The member of staff should be alerted to their right to be accompanied, too. All that then remains is to clarify the role that any representative can play before the interview begins: are they allowed to speak; are they allowed to ask questions or make statements on behalf of their colleague or friend, or not?

It remains to say that early intervention when things are observed to be going wrong is the best policy for any manager to pursue. The relationship that the manager has will be crucial to their ability to resolve matters quickly. Informal contacts may encourage members of staff to mention concerns that they have so that the manager learns about individual situations informally and early notice of a problem or situation will allow action to be taken informally before matters become too far advanced.

Grievance

What concerns individuals about their working conditions or colleagues is a subjective interpretation of events and it is fortunate that the emphasis of the law on, for example, harassment is action deemed to be threatening by the person who complains about it. This means that there are fewer objective situations that need to be supported by requisite evidence before action can be taken. It is therefore tempting for managers to seek to defuse situations informally, taking into account that a formal intervention by the manager with the alleged offender might make things worse.

Making a formal complaint requires for most people a great deal of moral courage. They know that what they are about to do is likely to be unpopular. So, not to be taken seriously or to be talked out of it by the manager is frustrating. For the manager there are similar constraints, particularly if the complaint is about senior or influential members of staff. For both parties, then, there is always a fear that making a complaint could have career-limiting consequences. This can be countered by the thought that not to take action could be considered as being remiss in failing to discharge a clear responsibility.

The grievance interview

This is the one interview that the manager is unlikely to be prepared for and so no preparation is possible. It may also be the case that there are some managers who will be better at handling a grievance interview than others – as success is often a function of listening skills, a sympathetic approach and a willingness to suspend judgement.

In most interviews managers are advised to ask *open questions* to ensure that both parties share the time available and one person does not dominate the interview to the detriment of the other. Such opening statements can be:

- Tell me about ...
- What do you think about ...?
- What do you feel about ...?

In the case of the grievance interview, however, the narrative will usually be initiated by the individual who brings the complaint and often there will be a strongly held feeling that accompanies the account or narrative as it unfolds. Clarifying what is being said can be an important way of probing the objectivity of what is being offered. It is referred to by negotiators as *probing skill*. The usual open questions are replaced by *closed questions*, which seek information or clarification:

- When exactly did this happen?
- How often did this occur?
- Who else was there at the time?

The skills of the negotiator are equally applicable to the grievance interview. As we have seen in previous chapters they are fourfold:

- *P* – probe
- *L* – listen
- *O* – observe
- *D* – decide.

The mnemonic offers a useful prompt: it can be a detailed process of unearthing exactly what is being alleged. Once those details have been fully divulged then the interviewer can *summarize* what they have been told to reassure the interviewee that they have been listened to accurately and to check that there is nothing that has been left out.

For some managers the temptation to explain to the individual what should happen next will be strong – if only to regain control of the interview. Perhaps better is the question:

- What would you like to happen next?

Satisfying those with a grievance that they have been heard also includes exploring the options that may be available to bring about a satisfactory conclusion to the situation – and, just as important – what are the implications or consequences of proceeding with a certain course of action. Care will need to be taken not to appear to dissuade individuals from taking action. On the other hand, careful consideration of consequences, witting and unwitting, will be important to explore as hasty interventions can sometimes have unwanted and long-term consequences.

Once this stage has been exhausted a summary of action points for both the manager and the individual should be made and a date for a future meeting should be fixed, if feasible.

It would be gratifying to think that exercising the skills we have described would bring about a satisfactory solution. Sadly, that may not always be possible. But, overall, the impression made by the manager should be positive, supportive and sincere. Stories drawn from one's own experience are to be avoided, and oblique or specific references to third parties avoided at all costs. Margaret Wallace, a marriage advisory counsellor, used to tell trainee counsellors: 'The success of the counsellor may be gauged by the impression he or she made on the couple, after they forgot everything that was said.' And the overriding impression afterwards should be that the manager listened, asked insightful questions, made notes (if relevant), was fair-minded, explored all feasible options and was supportive throughout the interview.

Sick absence

One of the big interference costs in companies, along with staff turnover, which Guest includes in his negative organizational outcomes of HR, is sick absence. No organization keeps account of the costs that this may involve, but it could be significantly higher than many managers give it credit for. It is not a new phenomenon and has bedevilled organizations as long as work procedures have necessitated groups and teams working together to achieve objectives.

BOX 11.5

In earlier times the British Motor Corporation and many other British industries were renowned for absences, particularly on Mondays and Fridays.

This meant that workers who were absent had to be covered for by colleagues on the production line to cover the work that they would have been doing had they been there to do their job. Those filling in were not always as familiar with the task as they should have been to accomplish it effectively.

BMC cars were notorious for breaking down a short time after being released to the customers. People were frequently heard to comment, on hearing this, that 'it must have been a Friday or Monday car'.

On top of that there is what is sometimes referred to as 'hostile environments'. The police and nursing are two such working environments in which injury is often caused in the course of their work and therefore time off is needed to recover and be fit for work again. So, not surprisingly we find that the average annual number of days off sick can be as high as nine in the police. This is considerably higher than the national average of around four days.

In other workplaces a number of days allowance is made for being off sick. In the civil service, for example, it was often usual for staff to be asked at the end of the year whether they had 'taken their sickies yet?' So, the convention within the service of taking the relevant sick days became a right that people were actively encouraged to make full use of.

There is a classic distinction between sick absence and intermittent absence. The former is related to sickness supported by a doctor's note or can sometimes be long-term sickness that requires a different approach. Intermittent absence is an accumulation of a day here or two days there which, when added up, may come to a significant amount of time off in the course of a year.

Some companies have a number of days over a period which will then trigger an investigation into intermittent absence. An example would be that anyone whose absence in a 12-week period totals 20 days off sick in all will trigger such a formal investigation into the causes of the absences. This prevents objections that others have had several days off too, and nothing appears to have been done about them. The inquiry will examine the reasons for absence and can include offering the individual an opportunity to see the company's medical professionals for a second opinion about their condition. Individuals must give their consent to this and allow access to their medical records from their general practitioner. They do not have to agree to this, but refusal might later be construed as being unreasonable if they do not. The purpose that underlies such procedures is to ensure that the individual is able to fulfil their working contract and it may be useful to introduce it in those terms.

Long-term sick absence

There are medical conditions that mean that an individual is off on long-term absence owing to being unable to come into work and do the job. These conditions do not necessarily involve sickness in the traditional way in which we use the word. They can include accidents that involve long-term healing processes (compound fractures, for example). Most companies cover a full-time salary for six months and thereafter it falls to half salary for the subsequent six months. At that point a review of the individual's health prospects becomes important. And the criterion used is: will the individual be able to return to fulfil their job contract (and if so, when)? In the event that the medical condition will not allow the individual to return to their job then the contract may be deemed to be impossible to fulfil.

In all cases the advice to managers is to stay in touch with members of staff who are off sick. Not only does that indicate that the company and its managers and HR are concerned for the welfare of their people, it also allows the company to have updated information on how the person concerned is progressing from week to week.

More proactive ways of dealing with sick absence

There are other approaches that have been tried in some companies. One is seeking to incentivize people to come to work by rewarding individuals or teams that have no sick absence record. In some companies a material reward is offered to winning teams (cash or a prize of some kind). It must be said that there may be more luck involved in actually winning such contests. The downside has to be that people will come to work when they should really be at home, thereby putting colleagues at risk by coming in and spreading their condition to others. There is also the possibility of peer pressure, when teams find themselves near to winning the prize. Any member who goes off sick at that point puts the whole team's achievement at risk. This puts added pressure on those who really are ill and need to be off work but struggle in regardless of how they are feeling. In some cases, that may put at risk health and safety, and make mistakes or accidents more likely.

Dealing with sick absence as a disciplinary matter may be equally counterproductive. Most people do not want to be ill. And it could be argued that even those who do 'enjoy ill health' need as much sympathetic handling as those who are genuinely unwell. An objective investigation is to be preferred in which concern for the person's condition precludes hasty personal judgements made by managers that their staff are malingerers who need to be dealt with harshly (the short, sharp shock approach).

Proactive approaches to health

More positive are well-woman and well-man groups run to encourage individuals to pursue their own investigation into a regime that addresses ongoing good health in their lives. That could include exercise and free or subsidized gym facilities. It could also include dieticians and personal counselling to seek to support individuals in a healthy lifestyle in which they can learn about themselves and respond to changing personal situations proactively with help and support.

For the future there are still the major problems that society shies away from: smoking and drinking (both drugs). An Australian medical academic recently suggested that there may come a time when smokers need a licence to smoke and that they would be confined to a ration of no more than 50 cigarettes a day. Interestingly, most organizations have a robust policy for dealing with those who use drugs or attend work under the influence of drink. Professional drivers and pilots are rightly subject to random checks. All staff in transport companies are banned from drinking during working hours, including breaks and lunch time. But few companies take as proactive an approach to the stress that may cause individuals to turn to drugs to alleviate their condition at work. The same applies to smokers. The huddle of smokers around doorways or bus shelters is always depressing, not just because others have to walk through the smoke, but because of the interference cost of smoke breaks to the business. Smoking increases the risk of respiratory diseases and cancer of the lungs. Non-smokers are quite justified in believing that extra breaks for smokers during the working day amount to a significant amount of time off work over the course of a working year. But apart from inveighing against smoking and smokers in general, it may be worthwhile instituting programmes that encourage and support those who want to give up smoking. Such voluntary schemes are usually appreciated by those who are addicted to smoking and keen to receive support in their effort to try and give up.

Reviewing employee relations

As we come to the final chapter of this book it is appropriate that we review the concept and practice of *employee relations*. Writers offer a range of approaches to the topic from the general overview of what companies may strive to achieve to specific activities that organizations may embark upon in managing their people. We have focused on the list of management interventions that staff can expect during the course of their career, sometimes referred to as the HRD list:

- recruitment
- induction training
- supervision
- management review
- appraisal
- reward
- development
- structure
- *communication.*

We emphasize communication as a summary of the impressions that are derived from staff experience gained at every stage of their career. One unsuitable or inappropriate intervention by a manager may convert someone whose goodwill could previously have been relied upon to someone who is disaffected and uncooperative.

Every company strives to be the best that it can be in every one of the stages involved in working life and HR seeks to give support to good outcomes, too. But, there is a wider context that might be worth exploring as we bring this chapter on employee relations to a close.

We introduced two illustrations early on that offered an overview of what HRM theory sought to offer organizations (Guest, 1987). The first is shown in Table 11.1.

TABLE 11.1 Overview of links in human resource management theory

HRM policies	Human resource outcomes	Organizational outcomes
Organization objectives Management of change	Strategic integration	High problem solving/change
Recruitment/selection/ socialization	Commitment	Innovation and creativity
Appraisal, training and development	Flexibility/ adaptability	High cost-effectiveness
Communication of standards and targets	Quality	Fewer customer complaints Low turnover/absence/grievance

Source: Adapted from Guest (1989) in Blyton and Turnbull (1992: 21).

FIGURE 11.1 Segments of the Shamrock organization.

Source: Adapted from Handy (1989).

The search for connections between HRM policies, HR outcomes and organizational outcomes remains to be supported by the evidence and each company owes
it to themselves to continue to try and validate that search for the value-added
that well-run procedures and committed and well-trained managers can bring to
the organization. In this book we have sought to examine where best practice
has established itself and how its refinement depends on adapting to the context
in which we find ourselves. Finding out how people feel about the organization
they work in is a worthwhile continuing exercise that managers need to invest
in. Failure to do that may leave managers exposed to events that they had not
expected and did not foresee.

The other diagram is Handy's Shamrock organization (Figure 11.1).

As we have noted, even Handy himself was surprised at the speed with which this
model seems to have been implemented in organizations. In his first book outlining
the model in 1989 he suggested the age of core workers might realistically be 27 to
45. But less than five years later in 1993 he was suggesting that the upper age for
being retained as core staff might well have dropped to 35. So, when we consider the
implications of these diagrams and what they mean for one another we can see that
there are anomalies that arise between the theory of best practice and the fragmentation that now pervades the world of work for those who experience it.

At the simple level of applying the steps in the original list of management interventions we might ask which of the steps applies to which parts of the Shamrock
organization? Consultants are usually hired for their expertise and knowledge
which they bring to the company on a temporary basis. So, induction training
does not apply to them – or does it? Do they get an appraisal along with everybody
else, and if so, who does it? If we look at those offering subcontracted services
then similar questions arise. They are recruited and trained by the subcontracting

company and complaints about any lack of proper outcomes are monitored by their own supervisors. The only comeback for the core company would normally be to revoke the contract at the end of the term. This means that the all-embracing nature of HRM theory is less likely to apply in the way envisaged for those servicing the work on a consultancy or subcontract basis.

The implication for Guest's diagram is that the HR outcomes may well be affected in the sense that the organization appears to gain *flexibility* in all four senses of the word:

- time
- number
- cost
- functional.

No one now is employed for longer than is necessary to secure the necessary knowledge and expertise to achieve the business objectives. Numbers therefore vary according to staff needing to be on-site or applying their efforts to achieve the organization's objectives at a distance. *Functional flexibility* is achieved by this means and the costs kept to the minimum required by the company at the time. We might describe this as a just-in-time approach to people.

But the implications for *commitment* now become apparent. There are different types of commitment described by academics:

- job
- work
- career
- organizational.

(Porter *et al.*, 1974)

So, we can see that for both consultants and subcontractors there may well be job and work commitment while they are working for the organization. But for consultants there will be several organizations that they serve and for subcontractors there can be no guarantee that the contract will be renewed at the end of the term. As for career, all workers will want their work experience to make them more employable so that when they do leave they can be assured that their enhanced skills and improved knowledge will improve their prospects of employability once their present contract is ended. But where is the *organizational commitment*? HRM theory made great play for this outcome of organizational commitment. But under the fragmented and temporary working conditions that apply in the Shamrock organization, organizational commitment may be less apparent and certainly more fleeting as individuals focus on their future prospects outside the organization. Even the core workers will be considering which direction their career will take when their time as permanent staff is finished with the organization.

So, in the following paragraphs we will consider the historical issues that have arisen since HRM theory first emerged in 1984; the current issues that are still with us; and some of the future challenges that await people and organizations in the future. At each stage we will consider what the implications are for the HR outcomes of *strategic integration, commitment, flexibility* and *quality*.

New public management

At about the same time as increased change took place to traditional organizations there was a political movement to privatize some of the functions traditionally held within the public sector. Governments around the world introduced such exercises as market testing: a check to see what functions could be subcontracted to outside private organizations more cheaply and flexibly. Civil servants responded vigorously to this initiative and in 80 per cent of the cases put up good arguments and evidence for keeping services in the public sector (Hood, 1995). Undaunted by this finding, Compulsory Competitive Tendering of services was launched both at a national and local government level. The original idea behind this initiative lay in an American article by Osborne and Gaebler (1992) which asserted that the private sector was much more responsive to the customer than the public sector was. Bound by red tape and regulation, public sector employees had no discretion to delight the customer, whereas private sector employees had more discretion to respond to customer need.

This alleged inflexibility of public servants was linked to an assertion that because they were aware of the bottom line, private sector workers were more committed to flexible working and commitment to the company's and customers' needs. This made them inherently more efficient since they could vary what was offered at the point of service rather than apply the same rules and regulations invariably to all situations.

As we shall see, there are some inherent and often unchallenged flaws in the arguments in favour of privatizing public services. At very least, public servants have traditionally been well trained and supervised in their jobs. They may have been constrained by the procedures that they were required to administer, but they were not as inflexible as some proponents of privatization sometimes allege. Privatized contractors have not always served the customer better whether in care homes or in supplying the Olympic games in London with security officers. The drive for profits can lead to a reduction in service and employing staff at the lowest rates possible.

Another point that we might make is that there is no necessary correlation between privatized services and efficiency. Indeed, we can point out that the profit motive will usually seek to avoid marginal services: every bus operator wants to run commuter services. But marginal services, unless subsidized, are usually quickly cut out or discontinued; so the customer is not served at all. Public service acknowledged a need for marginal services and sought to balance out the costs of the service between peak time and off-peak periods. Private profit will seek to avoid such disparities, creaming off what is profitable and avoiding running what is not.

So, once again, privatization seeks to achieve *flexibility* in all its aspects. However, the quality of service and value-added to the customer depends on whether it is profitable to the company or not. So commitment to the customer may be variable, whereas the public sector has a statutory obligation to provide the service. Some might argue that this is not a level playing field.

The learning organization

In a sense we could say that the idea of the learning organization was intended to encourage continuous learning at work. An alternative approach has been to suggest that *organizational learning* is going on all the time at work. Individuals and groups certainly learn and teach each other many different things at work. The problem lies in capturing that learning and teaching successfully so that others can benefit from it (Easterby-Smith *et al.*, 1999). Some organizations have instituted learning groups, or cafeteria-style informal interchange among key workers. However, evidence suggests that these are used but patchily in organizations (McKinlay, 2002). Similarly, pilots were encouraged to phone a reporting line to report near misses so that air traffic control would be alerted to regular occurrences of infractions of airspace and review procedures for spacing aircraft in critical areas.

But overall, there are constraints on experts divulging what it is they do and how exactly they do it. Consultants are aware that there is a risk that if the client were to know what they know, then their access to business might be more restricted. Most professional boundaries are well defended by their members and action is taken to defend their knowledge and skills from outsider influence or interference (Nicolini *et al.*, 2008).

Opportunities for workers to share their knowledge became part of the TQM approach to developing knowledge and skill based on encouraging the exchange of experience between working teams. In Japanese practice such events became known as kaizen – the working teams meeting each week to exchange knowledge and information on ways that working procedures could be improved. Sharing knowledge in this way would allow other teams to benefit from the experience and knowledge of those who had learned more efficient ways of doing things. However, not all sectors are willing or able to share their knowledge in this way.

Knowledge management

Knowledge workers have been an elite part of any workforce dependent on specialist skill and knowledge. They have often organized themselves and become responsible for training and inducting new members, developing their professional body of knowledge, and defending their professional boundaries from those who might otherwise seek to replicate what they do without their authorization.

More difficult to manage are those who have specific knowledge of the company and then leave for another organization or to set up in business on their own.

In sales it used to be the custom to require salespeople to sign an agreement that they would not approach customers on their territory for a period of two years after they had left the company. It has to be said that these agreements were never possible to enforce in law as companies and individuals are free to approach whom they wish in a free society. As knowledge becomes more available on the internet it becomes more difficult to keep data secret from those who want to find out what the competition is doing.

So, 'managing' knowledge is probably the wrong term to use with regard to internalized processes or finding out tacit knowledge derived from experience, if by managing we mean directing or controlling the actions of other people. Individuals manage and develop their own knowledge and do so without necessarily heeding what their managers or teachers tell them.

In their defence we should say that knowledge workers are often required to exercise that knowledge and skill only when needed. So, organizations are but a temporary home for those experts who work in them. Whatever they learn from the experience enhances their profile and employability and, they might argue, is fair recompense for their lack of job security and for working hard at getting work as well as fulfilling the contracts made.

For the core organization there is a dilemma. As far as *strategic integration* is concerned, how far can consultants and subcontractors be involved in the process of defining organizational objectives? If they are not, then their commitment can only exist at the level of the function that they play. They are part of the implemented strategy of *flexibility* and their *commitment* will usually only be temporary.

The employee experience of change

There was an early debate in the 1990s (Blyton and Turnbull, 1992) which made the distinction between HRM as human resource – management (the managerial approach to people and change); and human – resource management (appealing to the softer side of managing people). It coincides with another phrase common at the time describing some organizations as having a 'strong culture', which suggested a deterministic approach to management (Legge, 1995), which was part of the deterministic approach to change. Leaders of change needed to have a clear vision of the new way ahead (Kanter, 1995), and an ability to project this so that their followers would be assured that the future was supported and that the temporary pain of disruption would eventually be rewarded by the arrival of everyone at the new envisioned future.

This would today be seen as a top-down or imposed change model, in which the management decide what has to happen and then decree how change will take place. There is an alternate possibility in theory: emergent or bottom-up change. Lewin (1947), as the father of the step approach to change, embarked on unfreezing people's attitudes by holding sensitivity or T-groups with groups of workers affected by change. Later writers suggested that this open approach could be regarded as a phase of *exploration* (Bullock and Batten, 1985), which they suggested top-down approaches to change usually left out.

An alternative argument might suggest that there is not always time for such consultation and that someone has to take decisions for the good of the organization and to secure its future.

Furthermore, for many individuals and groups at work, change initiatives have neither stopped nor slowed down. Often each one has been succeeded by another initiative before the results of the preceding change programme have been evaluated. For core workers this may be a fact of life, but that does not make it any easier for individuals affected to cope with it.

Prospective challenges

We know that the quest for automation will continue. It has already eroded traditional skilled and semi-skilled jobs and will continue to assail the holders of specialist skills and knowledge. The search for staff who are constant learners continues, but its proponents do not always acknowledge that aptitude governs the boundaries of the possible for individuals and the comfort zone within which they feel able to be successful.

The pressure on organizations to work smarter and harder will not diminish either. So the *zero hours contract* begins to permeate not just routine, functional jobs, but the professional knowledge worker, too. A recent advert for someone to provide 'doctoral supervision' in a university indicated a zero hours contract. While on the subject of that sector we might ask how soon it will be before tenured staff become an exception rather than the rule in universities. At that point students will not know who exactly will turn up to take their classes. It could be anyone on a temporary contract, paid by the hour. The gap between researchers and teachers would then get wider, with a few research-led institutions and the rest as teaching academies.

For many professionals the search for economies is still current. So, for example, the traditional support given to professional flyers has been eroded by low-end operators. At one time the airline would pay for its pilots' medicals and relicensing costs. For many pilots that is no longer the case – they must pay their own costs. Similarly, during the takeover of another aircraft company the aircraft and uniforms were changed to that of the acquiring company but the terms and conditions of work were not adjusted to accord with colleagues already in the organization (which meant lower pay). It may not be long before pilots are offered a zero hours contract. We could even conceive surgeons may find that under privatized medicine they will be called on when needed on an hourly rate.

Such questions do raise the fear of variable *quality* and that is the one HR outcome that it is assumed will not change during radical change. Yet, quality depends on *commitment* and commitment sits uneasily with *flexibility* and a strategy that is constantly changing. Ironically, such conditions of service make *strategic integration* much less, not more, feasible.

References and further reading

Barham, C. and Begum, N. (2005) Sickness absence from work in the UK. *Labour Market Trends*, April: 149–158.

Blyton, P. and Turnbull, P. (1992) *Reassessing Human Resource Management*. London: Sage.

Bullock, R.J. and Batten, D. (1985) It's just a phase we're going through: A review and synthesis of OD phase analysis. *Group and Organization Studies*, 10(4): 383–412.

Burgoyne, M.J., Araujo, L. and Easterby-Smith, M. (eds) (1999) *Organization Learning and the Learning Organization*. London: Sage.

Easterby-Smith, M., Burgoyne, J. and Araujo, L. (1999) *Organizational Learning and the Learning Organization: Developments in theory and practice*. London: Sage.

Fevre, R. and Lewis, D. (2012) Why ill-treatment at work is hard to change. *People Management*, June: 31–35.

Guest, D.E. (1987) Human resource management and industrial relations. *Journal of Management Studies*, 24(5): 503–521.

Guest, D.E. (1989) Personnel and HRM: Can you tell the difference? *Personnel Management*, 21(1): 48–51.

Guest, D.E. (1998) Is the psychological contract worth taking seriously? *Journal of Organizational Behavior*, 19(S1): 649–664.

Handy, C. (1989) *The Age of Unreason*. London: Business Books Ltd.

Hood, C. (1995) *The Art of the State: Culture, rhetoric and public management*. Oxford: Clarendon Press.

Kanter, R.M. (1995) *World Class: Thriving locally in the global economy*. New York: Simon Schuster.

Legge, K. (1995) *Human Resource Management: Rhetorics and realities*. Basingstoke: Macmillan.

Lewin, K. (1947) Frontiers in group dynamics. *Human Relations*, 1(2): 150–151.

McKinlay, A. (2002) The limits of knowledge management. *New Technology, Work and Employment*, 17(2): 76–88.

Nicolini, D.J., Powell, J., Conville, P. and Martinez-Solano, L. (2008) Managing knowledge in the healthcare sector: A review. *International Journal of Management Reviews*, 10(3): 245–263.

Osborne, D. and Gaebler, T. (1992) *Reinventing Government*. Reading, MA: Addison-Wesley.

Porter, L.W., Steers, R.M., Mowday, R.T. and Boulian, P.V. (1974) Organizational commitment, job satisfaction, and turnover among psychiatric technicians. *Journal of Applied Psychology*, 59(5): 603–609.

Rousseau, D.M. (1990) New hire perceptions of their own and their employer's obligations: A study of psychological contracts. *Journal of Organizational Behavior*, 11(5): 389–400.

GRADUATE ATTRIBUTES

During this exercise you will address the following graduate attributes:

- an awareness and appreciation of ethical and moral issues;
- an understanding of social and civic responsibilities, and the rights of individuals and groups;
- a readiness for citizenship in an inclusive society.

Please read the following case study. At different points in the narrative you will be asked to stop and answer questions. Please make notes so that you can contribute to a discussion.

In 2007 a pilot survey of more than 1,000 British employees and 60 in-depth cognitive interviews with members of the public was conducted by Fevre and Lewis (2012). The results of the survey revealed that British employees understood the term 'bullying' in different ways. Despite a number of attempts by policy makers to define bullying, the concept remains elusive. Some groups of employees found it easier to apply the label 'bullying' to their work experiences than others. Thus, it is perhaps better not to try to measure bullying but rather to explore the ill-treatment that people are trying to make sense of when they apply labels such as bullying or harassment to incidents in their working lives.

This change in terminology has also helped to get a more accurate picture of what is regarded as ill-treatment in British workplaces. A variety of studies have shown that people are more likely to admit to being ill-treated than to being victims of bullying. Research carried out through face-to-face surveys could be seriously underestimating the experience of ill-treatment, simply by labelling it as 'bullying'.

At the extreme end of the spectrum few of the survey respondents had experienced violence in the workplace over the previous two years. This suggests that the majority of incidents that people find threatening are more likely to come under the headings: unreasonable treatment and/or incivility/disrespect.

Questions:

- **What incidents might the term 'experienced violence' include at work?**
- **What is the value in moving away from 'bullying' as a concept?**
- **In what way is 'ill-treatment' a more helpful phrase to use?**

So what constitutes 'unreasonable treatment'? Well, some of the examples cited included events such as coping with unreasonable workloads, unfair decisions, continual checking of work and having their expressed opinions ignored by others around them at work. The majority of the offenders in just over two-thirds of the incidents were, unsurprisingly, the manager or immediate supervisor.

Unreasonable treatment was found to be more common among full-time, well-paid professional and technical jobs in larger organizations. These are the sort of workplaces where you might expect to see an emphasis on professional HR, clear policies, good training of managers and trade union monitoring.

Employees with disabilities – wherever they worked – were at greater risk of unreasonable treatment and were put at risk because of the manner in which employees dealt with sick leave, the management of ongoing conditions and making reasonable adjustments. Younger workers and higher earners were also at (slightly) greater risk of unreasonable treatment, as has been found in the financial sector where females have sometimes been seriously disadvantaged by their male colleagues. However, the most common reason for ill-treatment lay not in individual behaviours, but in the characteristics of the workplace.

The biggest risk factor, however, was working in a place where the fairness and respect score was low. The key issues boiled down to: whether the staff felt the needs of the organization were put before the needs of individual staff members; whether staff had to do what they considered unreasonable; and whether people's individual views were respected.

Questions:

- **Why would well-paid professionals in larger companies be more likely to experience unfair treatment?**
- **Why would people with disabilities be more likely to report unreasonable treatment?**
- **What comment would you make about the three factors cited in the final paragraph?**

Incivility and disrespect

In one company the author worked in, the expats tended to shout at individuals with whom they were annoyed in public. Furthermore, there was an unwritten rule that staff did not attempt to leave work before their immediate boss had left to go home. This was sometimes referred to as a 'career-limiting thing to do'. Similarly, in two companies in different sectors, on joining the company they were advised by their line manager not to join the union 'if they wanted to get on in management'. Managers and supervisors accounted for four out of ten of these incidents, with co-workers accounting for one in five and clients and customers most of the remainder. In one industry connected with the oil sector such managers were referred to as 'screaming skulls'.

Again, no matter where they worked, minority groups were more at risk of incivility and disrespect. Interestingly, it was often put across as 'humour'. Specific minority groups were also more likely to be on the receiving end; not necessarily ethnic groups, with the risk for lesbian, gay or bisexual employees being almost as great as the risk for employees with disabilities.

Apart from the particular risks of providing a service to the public (such as hostile environments faced by medical staff or police and verbal abuse to call centre workers) the other workplace characteristics that lay behind ill-treatment concerned patterns of organizational structure, including loss of job control and increased pace of work. Recent reports of large organizations moving in from abroad indicated that the work is unremitting hard labour, closely monitored by supervisors, with the risk that a day off sick could mean that you have no job when you return.

The present government was even about to embark on a deal consisting of shares in the company in return for renouncing your labour/human rights at work. HRM as we understood it at its inception is being systematically destroyed.

Questions:

- Why would 'incivility and disrespect be more likely to affect minority groups?
- Why might change give rise to more complaints about unreasonable treatment?
- Why might politicians want to destroy human rights legislation as it applies to work?

What now for HR and leaders?

The workplace culture of fairness and respect has implications for the conduct of HR professionals and the division of responsibilities with line managers – and this lay at the heart of HRM theory. For example, much ill-treatment might be avoided by HR reclaiming the management of sickness absence or providing proper support to managers to take into account the circumstances of individual employees. Outsourcing HR functions might also exacerbate the feeling of alienation that some workers feel.

Organizational leaders must also accept that pressurizing managers to increase production leads to shortcuts and management styles that truncate human rights in the interests of productivity increases. MBWA remains the most potent weapon in the armoury of senior managers. If you turn up unexpectedly it is amazing what you will find out.

Questions:

- Should senior managers be tasked with MBWA in their employment contract?
- Should abuse and loss of temper be addressed as gross misconduct?
- What role should HR play in upholding human rights at work?

Tutor guidance

We return to the moral dilemma that faces HR: how to balance fairness between the company, its managers and its staff. Well drawn-up policies and procedures are the necessary prerequisites of a well-run organization. But there is more to do and moral values need to be discerned, defined and defended to ensure that fairness and respect are supported for everyone who feels disadvantaged.

Students are often experienced in working in jobs in less than ideal conditions. It would be worthwhile drawing on these experiences to explore how far the HR theories are fulfilled in their day-to-day experience.

One point that is worth addressing in the growing awareness of rights and duties that are expected at work and a growing confidence and willingness to speak about it, is to be found in routine jobs in retail, bar work and the leisure industries. This is where most students often have to work to support themselves through their studies, and the experience that they exchange within the peer group or through social media. Recent events surrounding the abuse of vulnerable people in the Health Service and the abuse of children in care highlight the growing disenchantment that people experience with institutional collusion or inaction in the face of unacceptable behaviour at work.

Once again the role of HR as a prophetic voice in the company merits discussion. In this sense HR can fulfil an educative function that can challenge the outer reaches of the organization where less than acceptable practices may still be apparent. In this respect there is a need not just for proactive training events to increase awareness for groups and individuals, but also for moral courage to stand up for what is right, sometimes in the face of embedded poor practice that has for too long been tolerated or ignored by managers at work.

12

IHRM, REVIEW, CRITIQUE AND DEVELOPMENTS

Topics

- HRM convergence and divergence
- national cultures and difference
- the challenges of service abroad
- outsourcing HR provision.

Introduction

The world is more easily accessible to outsiders than it has ever been and the interconnectedness of working and personal life is daily more apparent. National boundaries are often easier to pass across than was possible in the past and organizations want to do business around the world not just in their local market. One of the traditional vehicles for getting established abroad has traditionally been the MNC.

If we look at activity in any of the major sectors such as oil then it becomes apparent that the large organizations will have a track record of knowledge and expertise and access to capital that make it possible for them to set up collaboration with countries who have oil reserves and they are therefore the most likely first entrants into new opportunities for business growth abroad.

They will also have policies, procedures and practices that go with them wherever they establish themselves. Once they have set up a presence in another country then 'the way we do things round here' can be exported to the new environment. Locals may be recruited to help operate the new office. But they will be expected to do things according to the company's policy, procedure and practice. This being the case, it is fair to ask how internationally consistent the practice of HRM has become around the world (Sparrow *et al.*, 2004).

Globalization

If an agreed definition can be found for this frequently used term then we need to be clear about the similarities and differences between national cultures for in a sense this phenomenon is not new. Colonization has always presented interesting examples from history where the local situation asked for different practices that would fit in with local expectations. This presents the head office with a problem: can we afford to be seen to make changes to what we regard as being important to accommodate the custom and practice of the home company or should we insist on our way of doing things at home on people serving abroad?

BOX 12.1

Missionaries in foreign counties have often been faced with this dilemma. In Western Christianity, for example, the traditional colour for funerals has been black.

However, when Christian missionaries went to China they discovered that the custom and practice in China was to wear white for funerals.

The missionaries asked the Church authorities whether they could adapt to fit in with local convention and wear white. The authorities in Europe said no.

Allowing people to make sense of their experience sometimes requires significant adaptation.

Traditionally brides in China wore red. They still do today, though many change into white for the reception, as they have seen and sought to emulate what Western brides wear.

Sometimes emulation gives rise to voluntary adoption.

The production comparators may well be widely shared criteria that are developed and supported as technology drives new opportunities for growth and development. But at a local level the interpretation of newly imposed practices may give rise to different meaning and value depending on the basic assumptions held within the local culture.

So while it may be the case that MNCs diffuse best practice across borders, there is always the context of the receiving culture to be considered. Supranational organizations may have exercised more influence on the development of employment law, for example, in a way that suggests that best practice in HR has been consolidated around those companies and their practices uncritically imposed. However, that would suggest that culture is affected by edict or imposed practice and discounts the effect of divergent influences on imported practices from the home countries (Adler, 1991).

Convergence

It is often noted that HRM itself was born in the USA and adopted and adapted by other countries in the West. Europe has a strongly held belief about social welfare and support for employees. So the legislation that supports HR practice has developed there embracing beliefs about the rights of the individual workers and the duties and responsibilities of managers to safeguard and uphold those rights in day-to-day practice. It would be reasonable to assume that such norms and beliefs will travel with companies whose bases and ownership lie in the home country.

This might suggest that we can expect that there will be a trend towards closer HRM practices around the world. As firms expand and extend their operations abroad, the practices that lie at the heart of the organization are transferred to the countries in which they operate, thus giving rise to a convergence of operations that is imposed on the local national culture. We might see this as an imposed change that makes the practices of HR consistent and predictable wherever the company goes around the world. IBM would be a good example of this and Hofstede (1980) based his research into the variance between national cultures on the many employees the company had employed throughout the world.

At the level of Guest's HR outcomes we might therefore ask how *strategic integration* is extended to the outlying parts of the company and how *quality, flexibility* and *commitment* are developed in different cultural contexts. It would be easy to believe that the traditional management /HR interventions are easy to identify:

- recruitment and selection
- induction
- supervision
- management
- review
- appraisal
- reward
- development
- structure
- communication.

These activities are all open to regulation and procedure laid down for conducting any of the important activities such as recruitment and training when new staff are taken on. In respect of measuring and validating that is done elsewhere abroad it might be expected that HRM would be able to offer a predictive set of personnel practices internationally. But there are other factors that may influence how far such a simple model could be expected to remain intact and be a perfect reflection of the practices that have been laid down by head office (Brewster *et al.*, 2005).

Technology

At first glance technology may be seen as a driver of convergence. It is clear that certain providers of computer services have offered the same facility to users everywhere. So the use of common computer programmes should allow workers around the world to operate at a similar level of performance. In theory, then, the functional levels of the business can be assured wherever that company chooses to go by the systems that support them.

On the other hand, not all countries can offer the same infrastructure to support new technology and in some countries access to social media can be deliberately obstructed by the state. Broadband provision and wireless masts need to be installed to a similar level of sophistication as the home country if operations elsewhere are genuinely to live up to the standards that apply in other parts of the world.

Minimum economic plant size

How many units need to be produced in order to be competitive in a world market is more clearly calculated by economists and financial analysts today. Managers in an industry are expected to demonstrate economies of scale wherever their outputs are produced. However, if we look at the traditional *productivity factors* it is clear that there will be variation between countries and their populations:

- *time*: how long does it take to produce specific targeted units crucial to a business?
- *quantity*: how much is produced in that time?
- *quality*: what sort of standard is feasible in the specific context and are there particular challenges such as climate that make quality outcomes more difficult to achieve?
- *cost*: this is often the decider for offshoring. Can the company pay less to a local workforce than they would have to pay at home?

These considerations suggest that uniform HR practices might have to be adapted to fit in with the local situation in which the company finds itself or even that the variation in comparative costs, say, is an economic benefit to manufacturing abroad. The expectancies of a local workforce may be very different from expectancies of workers in the home country. That may mean that adaptation of the policy, procedure and practice of HR may need to be made to bring it in line with the expectancies of people working abroad (Perlmutter, 1969).

Divergence

Family

What makes us different from others may be found from early experiences of socialization. The family provides an early base of experience in which norms, beliefs and customs are assimilated by imitation, influence and training. Schein's *basic assumptions* may be absorbed at an early age and therefore are, as he suggests, taken for granted as part of interpreting the outside world and deciding what is right and wrong or good and bad. Manners, acceptable behaviour and relations with significant others are usually learned locally.

Education and training

Socialization continues for those who go through a system of formal education and training. This may set up ambiguities for those encountering something different from their home environment. But success depends on getting on with the peer group and adopting and adapting to 'the way we do things round here', both formally and informally. Coping with and becoming assimilated to different standards and expectations will be the gauge of success in the eyes of significant others, such as fellow workers and influential colleagues. Few will wish or seek to stand out from commonly accepted practice, and acceptance by others becomes for most people a prime social objective.

Law and conventions

DiMaggio and Powell (1983) refer to law as part of *coercive isomorphism*. This means that the same requirement is required of everyone. It may be in the national context or a different context but the essential factor will be a legal or cultural requirement. DiMaggio and Powell also mention *normative isomorphism*, by which they mean professional or other conventions that govern specific occupations. This can include such professions as medicine or law where a separate body is responsible for training, certificating and monitoring its members (Nicolini *et al.*, 2008). These may override local conventions and reinforce convergence in professional practice. Alternatively they may be interpreted and enforced by a local convention which then reinforces divergence.

State, industry and public policy

Not all conventions are necessarily reinforced by the law. There are customs and practices that may go back to early founding periods in an industry or sector. All those in the sector adhere to those practices. DiMaggio and Powell refer to these as *mimetic isomorphism* in that competitors tend to adopt similar practices adopted within the industry by their competitors.

IR systems

Industrial relations tend to have grown up within a national context. So, the relations between companies and unions and their members, for example, are likely to differ both within and between industrial sectors. What has been agreed between unions and the companies they work with will therefore differ, too. So, companies coming in from abroad may decide that they want to readdress such agreements before they decide to set up and do business there. Certainly, both Japanese and American companies have been less welcoming of union interference (as they see it) than traditional UK companies. Indeed, some in-coming companies have negotiated non-union agreements on greenfield sites to avoid the need for dealing with unions at all (Wickens, 1987).

Tax systems

Multinational companies have a freedom denied other organizations to offshore their profits and minimize their tax liability. Taking advantage of offshore tax havens appears to be a thriving business for consultants specializing in tax avoidance. Governments who need the jobs that MNCs provide may be disinclined to lean too heavily on those who provide employment for their workers. However, taxpayers may take a less generous view and the brand of offending companies may suffer a detriment in the perception of their local customer base.

Financial systems

How companies finance their operations can be less than self-evident. For governments seeking inward investment there can be incentives such as a moderated tax regime or prior investment in necessary infrastructure to support the operation. Experience suggests that once the benefits of the temporary arrangement have been absorbed the company may relocate itself away from the local scene and seek the benefits of offshoring more cheaply elsewhere in the world.

Cultural differences between societies

National conventions are necessarily diverse and require scrutiny before investment is made. How and who is managed and what is expected of incoming managers can be a matter of diverse perceptions. Local laws and customs can impose restrictions that do not apply in the home country. Failure to take account of these conventions could give rise to differences of opinion about what is acceptable and what is not. So, for example, local religious observance can give rise to differences of custom and practice that is not open to negotiation and needs to be observed if the company is to settle successfully and attract local workers (Edwards and Rees, 2006).

The point to make about divergence is that the differences between individuals and groups may lie in the conventions that each has been brought up with. It is not just differences in behaviour, which can be trained and is measurable and testable, and so can be monitored to prove that change has taken place. The issue at the heart of differences lies in interpretation. The basic assumptions that we all have allow us to experience events in the world around us and derive meaning and ascribe value to what we see.

> **BOX 12.2**
>
> A mother disciplines her child in a public place by giving the child a smack.
>
> A number of onlookers witness this event. Some approve and others disapprove.
>
> It is likely that those who approve might hold the assumption that proper discipline is good for the child (spare the rod and spoil the child). The action was right and good.
>
> Those who disapprove might well believe that it always wrong to hit a child (or anyone else, for that matter). So they will interpret the smack as both wrong and bad.

So, what we can conclude is that *basic assumptions* lie at the heart of a culture and that those who hold those assumptions are likely to draw similar conclusions about events they see going on around them. As far as HR practices are concerned, therefore, the company's procedures may well be enforced as a practice. But their meaning and value will be interpreted according to the receiving culture and may be amended informally accordingly. This means that matters that would be challenged in the home country go unattended elsewhere. Similarly, matters that would go unremarked in the home country may give rise to offence when they take place elsewhere.

Hofstede

Geert Hofstede is perhaps the most well-known researcher to devise what was to become part of the staple content of most courses on national cultures. His research into subjects in IBM, a company that at the time was spread throughout most countries in the world, enabled him to come up with his four basic dimensions of cultural difference between nations:

- power distance
- individualism vs collectivism
- masculinity vs femininity
- uncertainty avoidance.

He came up with a fifth dimension that he initially called 'Confucion dynamism' but that he later changed to 'time orientation' (meaning long-term vs short-term approach to life and work).

These categories allowed Hofstede to identify a profile of national identity based on his findings and went on to suggest that this profile might influence the kind of organizational grouping that would be favoured within that culture. He referred to different forms of local organizing:

- a pyramid of people
- a well-oiled machine
- a village market
- the family.

Other researchers have questioned some of the assumptions on which Hofstede relies (McSweeney, 2002). One of the principal reservations is that his research subjects were all employees of IBM, which at that time had its own strictly applied recruitment profile for selecting employees. We could also say that most of the observations of his research subjects are derived from behaviours observed. That is a common form of research and is perfectly valid in that respect. However, it does not reveal how individuals and groups interpret behaviours – the basic assumptions from which they derive meaning and ascribe value to what they observe around them. We might also note that within any national culture there is a range of variation between individuals and groups. So, not all members of the national culture can be assumed to interpret events in a similar way.

We can agree that there may be different conventions that are associated with national culture: how people greet each other; whether it is customary to get close to another person during conversations in public; whether it is acceptable to speak to other people across the gender divide about particular subjects and so on. But most of this can be learned through exposure to a culture or by training, so that the correct behaviours can be adopted and others are not discomforted by unexpected or unacceptable behaviour (Trompenaars, 1993).

Like everything else that governs human experience and cross-cultural interactions, it is always possible that change may modify expected behaviours so that gradually different ways of doing things become acceptable rather than remarkable. One example may offer evidence of such change: Hofstede's concept of *masculinity*. To suggest that a national culture is masculine presupposes that there are a number of behaviours that indicate that, for example, role typing is occurring. That typing might be related to roles within the family or jobs allocated to men rather than women – and the reverse. But over the course of years it is possible that attitudes to such roles change. So, over time men do take more part in child rearing; women are allowed to drive trains, take their full part in the armed services, and fulfil their civic responsibilities in society. Attitudes do change over time and acceptance of different behaviours is always possible. So, cultures do move on and the challenge for the researcher is identifying when basic assumptions shift and what has triggered those shifts.

All of this may seem an extended review of one commentator on national cultures. However, Geertz Hofstede is as often quoted in schools, colleges and universities as is Mazlow when motivation is discussed. It is worth pointing out that the context in which a researcher derived their insights is equally liable to change, which means that what was once relied on as valid may no longer apply in quite the same way as a context changes.

So, reviewing DiMaggio and Powell's three factors of institutionalization we might consider that *coercive* factors depend on the law in force at the time. For some countries in Europe the imposition of European law has not been welcomed when it affects taken-for-granted custom and practice at the local or national level. But more interesting is the behaviour of local courts and the response of law enforcement officers on the ground. Within Europe there is much variation with regard both to health and safety and to such simple things as wearing car seatbelts or motor cyclists wearing crash helmets. Those who holiday elsewhere in Europe other than the UK will notice immediately differences of enforcement policy by the police and the comparative seriousness with which such infringements are perceived and dealt with by local courts.

As far as *mimetic* influences are concerned, these are more likely to apply to sectors or industries where competitors are closely monitored and their decisions emulated to avoid loss of market share by implementing different or new practices. Appearances are important in assuring customers that the service is as good if not better than others can offer. Constant incremental change becomes the usual way forward for those emulating other operators in the same sector. There is no guarantee that the change in behaviour will bring about a change in attitudes, but the thought of losing market share can sometimes be a potent and effective driver of change.

Finally, there is the *normative* influence of professional or occupational groups within institutions. Doctors, lawyers, nurses and professionals of all kinds can call upon their expertise as a barrier or boundary that non-members are not allowed to cross. However, we have seen that technology can erode the stranglehold that an occupational group has on its sector. At one time the print unions had a stranglehold over the publication of newspapers. That was no longer the case once their skills were superseded by automation, making their expertise redundant. The same has been true of many semi-skilled jobs in factories where, for example, machines now perform what would once have been done by trained operatives. Braverman (1974) foresaw this and described it as the deskilling of traditional workers. In manufacturing it has made the stranglehold of occupational unions much more difficult to maintain and as a result manufacturing industries have been able to reduce the on-cost of their staffing well below their colleagues in the service sector.

Even in the service sector the search for economies has continued unabated. The traditional on-cost of staff in service industries has continued to run as high as 75 per cent. So, banks and financial institutions are keen to encourage access to accounts online or by telephone banking, and cash dispensing through ATMs. Their most expensive investment is high street branches where costs are high for a lower yield than automatic transactions would give them. Call centres have likewise become an industry within some sectors. It reduces the cost of handling customers face to face, though its effectiveness for the clients is sometimes questionable. Efficiency factors may be offered to the company by organizing in this way, but effectiveness factors may mean a less than satisfactory service to the clients and customers. The trusted and well-known bank manager is a thing of the past and the industry has suffered for replacing this personal focus of trust and loyalty for bank customers.

So, thinking global while acting local is often quoted as the watchword in glo-
balized industries. But the reality of bringing about compatibility between local
and global is still something that needs to be worked on constantly. If we consider
that globalization is a confluence of factors brought about by convergence of practices, we need to accept that divergence is alive and well at the local level. So,
the tension that may exist between global opportunity and local constraint is something that will always be present. As has been seen in Europe, imposing a common
currency has not eliminated the variance between borrowing and taxation rate
differences between the constituent countries that joined the union. The same
applies to HR systems adopted by organizations that move round the world. We
can export policy, procedure and good practice. But, whether everyone adheres to
the letter of the law depends on the interpretation that is given to decisions made
about people and how those people respond to the organization at the local level.

On the evidence of European integration, Brewster (1995) conducted 16,000
questionnaires in 14 countries and found that there was little correlation between
countries within the EU on HR practices. He concluded that the variance between
countries on such conventions as union membership, pay and security of tenure offered many different approaches; for example, both the UK and Ireland
were closer to some American practices than they were to mainstream European
countries. He noted particularly that it was most difficult to establish consistent
linkage between *strategic integration* and *HR practices* and that it was difficult to get
agreement on strategy and its formulation, again because of variance in practices
between companies. He points out that this has caused some British authors to
suggest that American texts on HRM need to be read, therefore, 'as indictments of
what American industry largely was not' (Hendry and Pettigrew, 1990: 19).

International HRM

There are now few countries that do not have experience of incoming investment and development from MNCs. Some have been Japanese, some American
and some European but in future it seems likely that there will be other emerging
nations who seek to expand elsewhere in the world away from their home market.
For all of them, the quality of managers serving abroad is more critical than in
domestic operations because mistakes made abroad are more difficult to monitor
and review.

The Japanese expansion after the Second World War will always be associated with manufacturing industries that pioneered and implemented the tenets of
TQM, and whose work had been pioneered by writers and gurus in the USA. In
local markets such as the UK their manufactured goods, including cars and motor
bikes, had a refreshing consistency of quality about them in comparison with the
variable quality of locally produced products. Unsurprisingly, that gave them the
edge in the market that eventually saw the demise of the local organizations that
failed to adapt to more demanding regimes of quality assurance in production. As
we have seen, their approach to organizing their factories meant strong direction

from the centre with expat managers at senior level running their units abroad. The model was unitarist and excluded active involvement by the traditional unions. In some of the literature this is sometimes referred to as *greenfield sites* – the opportunity to open up as a new production unit and choose the people best suited to the Japanese way of production and quality.

In comparison, attempts to introduce quality circles on *brownfield sites* in the UK met with resistance and even good managers seeking to implement the new approaches to production met with limited success. As we have seen, John Egan as managing director attempted such a conversion at the Jaguar Motor Company in the early 1980s but never managed to persuade more than 45 per cent of the workforce to take part in reorganizing around quality circles (Storey, 1992).

In contrast, the American approach placed more emphasis on the operational determinism of fixed standards and processes in production which can be implemented anywhere and managed either by expats or local managers. The focus on management metrics coupled with computerization gave managers the immediate access they needed to the comparative figures of production, margin, profit, wastage rates, all of which could be attributed to the level of the individual, with appropriate action being taken against anyone who fell below the determined utilization levels.

These different ways of dealing with their operations abroad were sometimes distinguished between polycentric, geocentric and ethnocentric approaches (Perlmutter, 1969). This gave rise to a different approach to the staffing of different MNCs. So, the *ethnocentric approach* would lead to a reliance on *parent country nationals* (PCNs) – individual managers chosen from the home country to spend a stated time in different foreign units interspersed with periods back at head office.

A *polycentric approach* would suggest a greater dependence on *home country nationals* (HCNs) – those recruited from the local workforce of the host country and chosen for their ability to manage local affairs with a knowledge of the local marketplace for staffing needs. HCNs rarely, if ever, served at head office, more often remaining in post locally for the organization.

For MNCs operating an ethnocentric approach, the use of *third country nationals* (TCNs) was more common. These members of a global, transient workforce could be drawn from countries other than the home or host countries and in general offer a greater flexibility of time, number and cost which enabled their terms and conditions to be adjusted to suit the needs of the business at any particular time or place.

Not all MNCs are as rigid in their practices as suggested by these distinctions. There are companies that employ a combination of all three types of manager, which allows them the greatest flexibility in using PCNs when necessary, with a network of HCNs who are locally permanent and experienced in the local market, together with TCNs complementing the workforce as and when necessary, mostly at the functional level. In HR terms this allowed for a similar distinction as we observed in the Shamrock organization with PCNs being core staff, HCNs a local network of management expertise and TCNs in the subcontract fringe. The duties and responsibility for each sector of workers is similarly variable with PCNs enjoying the full array of HR support, HCNs enjoying support limited to their staying in post in the host country, and TCNs used as and when needed with little HR support and certainly not the full array of services expected by expats.

Shortages of international managers

The prospect of moving abroad with all expenses paid will be attractive to many executives working to develop an international profile in their career. Such experience ought to be the basis for an international career and promotion to the highest level of the organization. However, it would be more accurate to say that the experience of those who do go abroad can be less than positive. Mature and experienced staff will often have family responsibilities so the question of what happens to the spouse and children becomes a crucial question. Will children join the family wherever the expat is sent? Will they be educated in the home country and sent out to be with their parents during the school vacation? And what about the spouse? There are some countries where there is not much to do if you do not speak the local language and there is little or no social network to join. Travel and career opportunities may well be restricted and shopping may be a choice between very expensive international stores and the local market. Increasingly, there is a trend for partners and spouses to keep their own career which they do not choose to give up so therefore going abroad is not an option for them. In short, the number of non-returners to service abroad or leaving early is in 30 per cent of cases a function of family problems that have not been resolved successfully.

Cost of failure in this respect is more critical to international business. The marginal costs of travel and accommodation abroad is a considerable on-cost, while the going rate for those serving abroad is often higher than for those doing the same job in the home country. Furthermore, it is usual for terms abroad to be confined to three years after which there will be a move, either home or to another country altogether – again meaning uprooting the family and perhaps different schools once again for their dependent children.

Preparation for service abroad

There are several suggested areas that can be useful to address when considering suitability for an overseas posting, such as culture. Does the culture resemble anything previously experienced by colleagues and can this experience be readily drawn on? Does the situation itself provide support systems that can pick up on an induction programme on arrival at the destination? Two points of contact might be relevant here: first, the host country manager who will probably have seen many other PCNs arrive for a first time posting. There may be a briefing session set up to include partners and spouses. Two areas need to be addressed: getting into the job itself, which may require briefing on the contacts to be worked during the posting, and setting up home in a new and foreign environment. A point of contact is vital in both respects and a useful network of contacts needs to be readily available in case of emergencies.

Second, there are colleagues who have served in the country previously. This can be a two-edged sword, as experience is individual and comparisons are sometimes not valid as what appeals to one expat may not be attractive to another. However, problem awareness is useful, and the assurance of contacts to call on for advice even more reassuring.

Expectancy theory suggests that those with the highest hopes may have greater disappointment if these are not realized. So, a realistic appraisal of the local facilities would be important to anyone going without prior knowledge or experience. Can the local food be eaten; can the water be drunk; is it safe to swim off the local coast – all are relevant questions especially if going with the family. Local religious customs about what is considered respectable to wear in public will be equally important and whether public transport is considered safe at all times and in different places. Climate change affects most people moving abroad so being prepared for outbreaks of prickly heat or the onslaught of local insect life will be important.

Then, there is the job itself. Is this a new venture for the expatriate or have they had previous experience? Sometimes it is assumed that professionals will be able to cope with anything and quickly learn on the run. However, even where there is previous skill and threshold knowledge in a necessary business expertise, the context can make a difference as to how those skills are exercised. Many are the accounts of blunders unwittingly committed by the unwary visiting managers as to how locals deal with initial introduction, negotiation, social invitations and how to develop a good business relationship with customers and suppliers.

And then there is one topic that is rarely dealt with in the HR handbooks: *business ethics*. What is the company's policy about entertaining prior to an order being obtained or advantage given? How do we deal with offers of bribes, emoluments or similar incentives? Custom and practice abroad can be a minefield for the unwary. But often such matters are assumed to be within the knowledge of whoever goes out to represent the organization abroad. That would be an unwise assumption to make, and one that could potentially be disastrous for future business, should it go wrong. There needs to be a clear policy and guidance about how to negotiate and exclude unsafe or unethical practices without giving offence to others for whom it may have become custom and practice.

HR support

It is likely that the HR support available at home is not so apparent to those who are serving abroad. So, apart from prior language training and cultural briefings, what other support can HR arrange for expatriates and their families? High on the agenda would be mentoring and coaching. Staff who have been away previously are ideally placed to help others assimilate foreign cultural experiences and fit into a new or different way of life. Being supported by someone more experienced is a useful way of assimilating a different culture prior to arrival.

The partner or spouse can feel left out of this process of preparation and should be included in cultural briefing sessions. It may be that previous partners or spouses of those who have been out before would be useful to lead discussions or question and answer sessions for those who are going to accompany their spouses abroad.

Passports and luggage can get lost or stolen during journeys abroad. A contact who can be used to speak to locals in an emergency can be a lifeline for times when arrangements do not go according to plan.

BOX 12.3

A visit to an Asian country included several department representatives and nationalities arriving at the airport together. Individuals queued in different lines according to their passport status and the party only reassembled on the landside of the airport.

One member of the party, a national of the country visited, did not emerge on the other side but, knowing that she spoke the language, her colleagues moved off to the hotel provided for their first stop.

After two hours the foreign visitors began to worry about their colleague and rang the airport. The message that came back was that their colleague had been detained because of 'passport irregularities'.

A brief phone call back to head office briefed a director who spoke the local language, who rang and discovered exactly what the problem was. Through contacts with the British Consulate he was able to arrange for another visa and passport to be issued and the colleague was released without further problem.

It transpired that the passport that had triggered suspicion had an identical number with another passport. It took a while to establish that it was the other passport that was a forgery.

There is just one other consideration: repatriation support.

Returning from overseas service can be equally as difficult to adjust to as the journey out and settling in can be. Offering mentoring and counselling may assist those returning to come to terms with what can be another stressful experience. Whatever is offered by way of a new job may take a while to settle down to. Those who have made that adjustment in the past may well be in a good position to offer a listening ear and reassurance that problems of reintegration in the company can be overcome (Sparrow *et al.*, 2004).

Benefits and challenges of IHRM

Common centralized data

It ought to be possible for the central HR function to monitor the performance of the different parts of the organization around the world. But data is not information and turning data into information requires interpretation based on knowledge of local conditions applying to each part of the organization. A good rapport between line manager and HR department has always been important for securing consistent results and achieving *strategic integration*. For many managers, the HR implications of what they do is not always apparent to them so regular briefing between managers and HR is an essential part of closing the loop between actions at the local level and outcomes for the organization more generally.

Consistent strategy across MNC

Here we come to the fault line that runs through all organizations: the global strategy and the local tactics. Consistent strategy means a coordinated plan that must be applied at the local level by local managers. HCNs are not always privy to the development of strategy at the centre of the organization. It might be thought that the PCNs would have a part to play in promulgating centrally developed strategy. However, for many PCNs the job in hand may be project-led and not specifically concerned with supporting more general strategic plans at the local level.

BOX 12.4

A consultant working with an MNC was presented by the managing director with a copy of the strategic plan for the organization.

On taking it away and reading it the consultant discovered that the target for increased growth was the same per cent for all parts of the organization.

On seeing the MD again the consultant raised this point as being unusual – most discrete areas of a multiple business have their own growth rate.

The MD replied that not too much notice should be taken of the figures as they were intended for the taxman.

The consultant wondered whether managers in the field were aware of this and how they worked round this.

Disseminating good practice

Monitoring what people are doing at a distance is a common problem for managers running businesses that are geographically dispersed. But for HR working in an MNC it is crucial. Induction training is offered when people arrive at the company for the first time. But what happens as they move from position to position in different venues? Effective appraisal can be difficult to organize unless colleagues were involved in the set-up of projects and can evaluate their outcome.

In some organizations return to head office for specific training courses has been a common practice. In one organization running such a system, 80 per cent of the training manager's budget was absorbed in travel costs getting staff back to the UK for training courses. Staff did not object to this as it gave them a chance to visit family and friends back home. But more training could have been done had more remote means been available to communicate with and update staff on the latest good practice. More recently some companies have adopted the practice of 'flocking', in which staff gather locally and use modern methods of communication to take in training messages and discuss revised good practice.

Common HR practices makes it easier to compare staff between locations

Managers in remote locations know that they are unlikely to receive visits from senior managers from head office unannounced. Monitoring the standard indicators from the organizational outcomes should indicate unusually high staff turnover, sick absence and grievances, and would trigger a warning that something was seriously amiss, requiring outside intervention.

Legal requirements of host countries

Working in some countries may be refreshingly free of constraints to employment strategies from abroad. Employment of local workers is considered a priority by local employers and so company requirements will be adhered to. It is more likely, however, that employment legislation is different from what pertains in the home country. Hours that people work and holiday entitlements alone can be diverse and so is much else that is taken for granted as good practice and enshrined in operations directories, HR and training handbooks, and any of the other traditional guidelines that govern good HR practice in the home country.

An experienced HCN will be able to modify and adapt most prescriptive policies to allow local custom and practice to flourish and work for the goodwill of the local staff. However, that does raise issues of standards and targets – and, more importantly, when they are not delivered, how and when to intervene and handle disciplinary and grievance procedures.

Different labour markets

The accepted standards for working hours and holidays vary from country to country and it is easy to assume that parent country regulations will be accepted as part of the employment contract. In America, as in the UK, a long hours culture is accepted among managers, and in Japanese companies leaving work before your manager would be perceived as a career-limiting thing to do. Religious practices such as midday prayers can spill over into the workplace, too, and become part of custom and practice.

BOX 12.5

A management trainer tasked with running courses arrived on time at
7.30am to find the training room empty. Course attendees began arriving
about 8.15am and servants appeared to ply them with coffee and sweets.

Half of the course arrived and once settled the course began. At 12pm the
assembled group got up and left for prayers (12–1pm). After lunch the other
half of the group appeared.

The only time the whole group was in place was when a senior manager
came to pay a visit.

Different worker expectancies and values

The local culture and practice will probably govern the expectancies of those who
apply locally for jobs in an international company. Expectancy plays an important
part in governing how individuals and groups evaluate their experience at work.
Western values are unlikely to be accepted uncritically by those who hold different
values. Most managers find that working with people to achieve more satisfactory
results in the long term is preferable to insisting on strict adherence to company
regulations. Of course, in respect of health and safety no compromise should be
sought, though it should be said that TCNs are often left to work as they would
do it in their own country.

Critical differences

Here is a list of some of the key points that can give rise to misunderstanding
between managers and staff from different cultural backgrounds:

- The definition of what it is to be an *effective manager.*
  Formal and informal styles are part of a local culture. Historical relations between
  countries can have bedevilled relations in the past and therefore there are fears
  that, say, a dominant attitude to local workers can be expected from managers
  coming from the home country. Hofstede's work reinforces the differences that
  can emerge between different nationalities that have to work together.
- Giving *face-to-face* feedback.
  Once again what others are comfortable with will be the gauge of their
  acceptance of a manager. Conventions about raising family or personal issues,
  especially in mixed gender relationships, will be important to observe to avoid
  resentment or embarrassment. What individuals deem fair can be a function of
  group beliefs and past practice. Deviation from this, however well intentioned,
  may not be appreciated. Hofstede's uncertainty avoidance may indicate how
  different cultures expect to be addressed on matters pertaining to personal
  performance.

- *Readiness* to accept international assignments.
  What is accepted in one society may present difficulties to members of another group. Such simple things as discussions or brainstorming can present problems for those who are taught to believe that they should not speak unless spoken to or that to initiate a conversation could be deemed inappropriate or unacceptable. Serving abroad may raise all the issues of behaving differently elsewhere and being separated from the support of friends and family on which individuals normally rely.
- *Expectations* of manager–staff relationships.
  Informal socializing is considered an advantage in some cultures. In the UK going to the pub is an acceptable way of getting to know others off duty. Some training courses are designed to bring about reliance on one another in an active team environment and involve interaction with others who have previously been strangers. This can be difficult or impossible for some cultures to accept as being the normal or right thing to do.

BOX 12.6

A manager who was popular with his team, leading them from the front both formally and informally, was moved to take over another team. He regularly took the team out after work and encouraged a more informal approach at work.

He was moved to head up another team where his approach did not elicit the same response at all. His results there were catastrophic and the team withdrew their goodwill.

On further enquiry the new team divulged that they resented going out with him socially. As far as they were concerned, work was work and at 5pm they all expected to go their separate ways.

- Pay systems and differential concepts of *social justice*.
  Reward and discipline often mean taking a view of individual behaviour within the group. Who stands out and who is an average/below-average performer. This means exercising careful judgement mindful of the subjective judgements that are likely to be made by those affected by the decision. Pay and promotion always involve making a judgement that will advantage one group or individual and not another. Whether the peer group will accept the manager's decision depends on what they think is fair. For PCNs this can be a difficult decision as they have no previous experience of what their predecessors did and why they did it. Charles Handy relates a story of working for Shell as a graduate management trainee and deciding on changes that went disastrously wrong. On being summoned to giving his account of why he had decided to make the change, his manager said: 'When you want to know what

works round here, ask the ****natives.' The HCM is the person most likely to know the local background and give advice accordingly.

- Approaches to *organizational structuring* and *strategic dynamics*.
  This brings us to the final point that structuring the way people work and implementing new strategies need to take account of past practice and what people are comfortable with themselves. *Aptitude* is the basis of potential and ability and though risks must occasionally be taken when making appointments to new positions, people need to work within their limits and be provided with support and training (preferably before they undertake new work). What sort of training will be considered best depends on the perceptions of local sensitivities and the peer group.

Measuring HR's strategic influence

Clearly define business strategy

This needs to be related to strategic integration. And that means the links between the three levels within an organization should be addressed:

- organizational objectives
- departmental goals
- individual key tasks.

Strategic plans that do not drive down the implications of broad organizational objectives to the detail of individual job descriptions are liable to be disregarded as irrelevant by those further down at the functional level of the organization. Leaving it to the discretion of others to work it out is not always a recipe for clarification and could cause confusion and disagreement.

What should be added here is that HR has a role to play in helping to define and clarify strategic objectives, though the number of HR managers who make it to a place on the board has always been a small minority. It may be argued that their lack of involvement at least gives them protection from the accusation that they have been complicit in supporting downsizing, say, when they have to implement a redundancy policy. However, some advisory role to the Board would be a useful contribution. At least they can then implement policy changes with a clear understanding of the thinking behind decisions made about future action.

Develop a business case for HR as a strategic asset

We now return to the original diagram adapted from Guest that summarizes the claims of HRM and note that the connections between the strategic level and the connections with HR outcomes and organizational outcomes can be difficult to establish in comparative terms (Table 12.1). For one thing, high problem solving and innovation are difficult to measure and difficult to stimulate by such traditional training routes. So, establishing that *strategic integration* has made these outcomes possible is not always easy.

Similarly, *innovation* is difficult to measure and difficult to attribute to its original sources. It may well be that recruitment can identify individuals who will enhance the reputation of the company for innovation and creativity. But there is no guarantee that such inspired individuals will be able to succeed within their new environment without the support of a team who share the viewpoint of change and development.

No one would deny that *flexibility* ought to give the company the best chance of achieving high cost-effectiveness. But, HR on its own cannot guarantee that its activities can reinforce this, as day-to-day decision making in any business lies with the line managers.

More measurable are the negative aspects of *staff turnover, staff absence* and the incidence of *grievance* in the company. However, even if that is accurately monitored, there is no guarantee that the source of the problems can be identified, still less rectified by HR activity on its own. Monitoring and reviewing where the company stands is difficult for an expertise manager to do as the line manager is responsible for day-to-day activities in the team.

Create a strategy map (objectives/goals/key tasks)

This enables HR to identify *key deliverables* from the strategy map. A simple manpower planning inventory should then be able to pinpoint where in the organization support and training in the requisite competencies have been identified.

The next step will be to draw up a training plan to ensure that the appraisal system and those who administer it address the right people to engage their commitment to the development plan for people in the business.

TABLE 12.1 Overview of links in human resource management theory

HRM policies	Human resource outcomes	Organizational outcomes
Organization objectives Management of change	Strategic integration	High problem solving/change
Recruitment/selection/ socialization	Commitment	Innovation and creativity
Appraisal, training and development	Flexibility/adaptability	High cost-effectiveness
Communication of standards and targets	Quality	Fewer customer complaints Low turnover/absence/grievance

Source: Guest (1989) in Blyton and Turnbull (1992: 21).

Design a strategic HR measurement system

Validation is a key word in training and development practice. It requires assembling the evidence that competencies have been mastered at the end of the training and are being adhered to in the workplace afterwards. Line managers therefore have a key part to play in furnishing this evidence and will often claim that they are far too busy to undertake it. Much closer liaison between trainers and line managers would help identify those who have demonstrated potential during training courses. Such information can help to make appraisal interviews more relevant to those who undertake them. Targeted training is a much better use of resources than the scatter-gun approach or what was referred to in some organizations as 'sheep-dip training' (giving everybody in the organization 'awareness training').

Learn fast how to interpret the results accurately

One other element that can enhance the search for meaning is *Evaluation*. This is a word that managers pay lip service to but rarely have time to address. How people felt about change and training programmes they attended becomes important to discover not just in initial comments at the end of the training (sometimes known as 'happy sheets') but further along the employment experience. In this respect, the question of mentors and coaches can play a part. Those whom we want to develop will need ongoing support if they are to fulfil their potential in demanding roles and having someone on hand who can support and sustain that quest for self-development is an important role to support.

Bring up the results at regular management meetings

Managers are frequently as much in the dark about organizational goals and their achievement as anyone else in the company. HR can therefore be a proven asset if it engages in monitoring and reviewing the evidence of progress throughout the organization. As we said, the learning organization is difficult to envisage in realistic terms. However, organizational learning is going on all the time – mostly unbeknown to managers. So, any organizational achievements should be celebrated in the organization. And as the agent of training and development, HR can play that role much more fully if it wants to.

Present to the Board before the annual general meeting

There will always be laggards among managers in any organization. Some of them play that role in a senior position. Figures of comparative performance of the different divisions whose managers are represented round the Boardroom table can be just the incentive needed to encourage some of the less enthusiastic members to take a more active part in developing the company's day-to-day objectives. Healthy competition alerts managers of the need to highlight and encourage achievement among their teams. The non-executive directors will take note of those who support such initiatives and their opinions could be vital in future Board meetings.

Outsourcing HR provision

There are several activities that can be outsourced to other organizations that specialize in specific HR operations. We list some of them here:

* pay and pensions
* training
* HR call centre
* data and records
* information and advice
* legal support and services.

None of the above has to be undertaken by in-house staff, and there need be no conflict of interest in respect of confidentiality about staff work or personal issues.

A good example is the recruitment procedure. The interference cost involved in continuous recruitment rounds is significant to any organization. But there are functions within the process that can be confidently handled by an outside organization:

* placing adverts;
* issuing application forms;
* receiving application forms;
* dealing with candidate management;
* providing information for shortlisting and interviewing;
* arranging interviews and assessment dates;
* preparing and sending offer and reject letters;
* drawing up and sending out contracts;
* requesting references;
* sending out starter packs;
* entering new starters on records system;
* monitoring equal opportunities.

The important functions that managers will want to keep within their own remit would be:

* determining the need for the vacancy;
* confirming/drawing up job and person specifications;
* defining selection and assessment processes;
* shortlisting;
* carrying out interviews;
* making final selection decision;
* co-determining salary package.

So, in short, managers should be reassured that there is no risk of:

- loss of control
- loss of the personal touch
- doubts about quality and commitment of external staff
- fragmentation of HR integrity.

Instead, the important aspect of the *psychological contract*, its relational element, can be reinforced by strategies that involve managers when they are needed rather than taking up their time in routine, functional tasks that could be fulfilled by others. The organization reinforces trust and loyalty among its members, demonstrating a readiness to use its staff effectively only when their input is necessary (Adler, 1991).

Trends and tendencies for the future

It is clear that HR practices do not stand still and practices that are found to work in one country will be quickly adopted elsewhere if efficiency and profit warrant it. That will always place HR under the company spotlight and under pressure to continue to find new ways of finding efficiencies to support competitiveness and the company's survival.

There are some trends that are clearly here to stay:

- individual working hours being decoupled from operating hours;
- working from home;
- interim management contracts;
- virtual organizations (remote working);
- individual expectancy to achieve more family quality time.

HR can and should question how far these initiatives reinforce value-added for the staff and therefore value-added for the customers, too. The search for value-added will continue at work and HR will be a principal agent in supporting this quest in all that is done in the company by its people.

Disturbingly, there are more menacing trends that are being espoused by some politicians and some managers such as *zero hours contracts*. The effectiveness of such initiatives has to be the clients or customers and the evidence emerging from some privatized organizations is that the experience for the customer has not been improved. Removing workers' rights may be espoused under the guise of improving efficiency and therefore profitability. But this can put effectiveness at risk and impact on the customer. Some of the outcomes of reducing supervision in order to reduce costs have given rise to lack of care in nursing homes; care for the vulnerable; and safety for users of services. Drucker's maxim that 'if you think training's expensive, try ignorance' remains relevant in the continued quest to reduce taxes and reduce the size of the state. There are some services that remain the responsibility of society even if contractors are tasked with undertaking the work. There should have been a statutory supervisory agency overseeing the financial sector. There was not and the banking system collapsed. Management and supervision remain the responsibility of the manager. Walking away from that responsibility should not be an option. The consequences can be global.

Liberalizing markets and privatizing services will continue to be offered as ways of stream-lining business and making 'the bottom line look healthier'. However, there are considerations of natural justice. So, a recent foray by politicians in the UK into personnel practices suggested that workers could be offered shares in the company in return for surrendering their rights under employment law (unfair dismissal; appeal to tribunals etc.). HR is in a good position to monitor and warn against such measures and to act as the conscience of the organization. Natural justice is not an option, it is a human right.

The days of fulfilling the dreams that HRM theory offered at its inception are unlikely ever to be realized. *Flexibility* has been achieved as its proponents wanted, but it has been at the expense of *organizational commitment* and sometimes, sadly, of *quality*. Fragmentation of the experience of employment can never fulfil the realization of the original theory of HRM. But the quest for *strategic integration* requires that the search for balance, fairness and justice can never be taken for granted. HR will always have a key part to play in that search.

References and further reading

Adler, N.J. (1991) *International Dimensions of Organizational Behaviour*. Boston, MA: PWS-Kent.

Blyton, P. and Turnbull, P. (1992) *Reassessing Human Resource Management*. London: Sage.

Braverman, H. (1974) *Labor and Monopoly Capital: The degradation of work in the twentieth century*. New York: Monthly Review Press.

Brewster, C. (1995) Towards a European model of human resource management. *Journal of International Business Studies*, 26(1): 1–21.

Brewster, C., Sparrow, P. and Harris, H. (2005) Towards a new model of globalizing HRM. *International Journal of Human Resource Management*, 16(6): 949–970.

DiMaggio, P.J. and Powell, W.W. (1983) The iron cage revisited: Institutional isomorphism and collective rationality in organizational fields. *American Sociological Review*, 48: 147–160.

Edwards, T. and Rees, C. (2006) *International Human Resource Management: Globalisation, national systems and multi-national companies*. London: FT Prentice Hall.

Guest, D.E. (1989) Personnel and HRM: Can you tell the difference? *Personnel Management*, 21(1): 48–51.

Hendry, C. and Pettigrew, A. (1990) Human Resource Management: An agenda for the 1990s. *International Journal of Human Resource Management*, 1(1): 17–44.

Hofstede, G. (1980) *Culture's Consequences: International differences in work-related values*. Beverley Hills, CA: Sage Publications.

Hofstede, G. (1991) *Culture and Organizations: Software of the mind*. London: McGraw Hill.

Hofstede, G. (2001) *Culture's Consequences: Comparing values, behaviours, institutions, and organizations across nations*. Thousand Oaks, CA: Sage Publications.

McSweeney, B. (2002) Hofstede's model of national cultural differences and their consequences: A triumph of faith – a failure of analysis. *Human Relations*, 55(1): 89–117.

Nicolini, D.J., Powell, J., Conville, P. and Martinez-Solano, L. (2008) Managing knowledge in the healthcare sector: A review. *International Journal of Management Reviews*, 10(3): 245–263.

Perlmutter, H.V. (1969) The tortuous evolution of the multinational corporation. *Columbia Journal of World Business*, 4(1): 9–18.

Schein, E.H. (1985) *Organizational Culture and Leadership*. San Francisco, CA: Jossey Bass.

Sparrow, P., Brewster, C. and Harris, H. (2004) *Globalizing Human Resource Management*. London: Routledge.

Storey, J. (1992) *Development in the Management of Human Resources: An analytical review*. Oxford: Blackwell.

Trompenaars, F. (1993) *Riding the Waves of Culture: Understanding cultural diversity in global business*. London: McGraw-Hill.

Wickens, P. (1987) *The Road to Nissan: Flexibility quality teamwork*. London: Macmillan.

GRADUATE ATTRIBUTES

During this exercise you will address the following graduate attributes:

- an ability to communicate effectively for different purposes and in different contexts;
- an ability to work independently and as part of a team;
- a diverse set of transferable and generic skills sensitive to cultural differences.

Presentation skills

When I think of presentation skills and the impact having to give a presentation has, I think of the US comedian Jerry Seinfeld:

> Surveys show that the #1 fear of Americans is public speaking. #2 is death. Death is #2. That means that at a funeral, the average American would rather be in the casket than doing the eulogy.
>
> (Jerry Seinfeld)

I would suggest that Americans are not alone in this hierarchy of fears. What I hope to do here is make it less of a horrifying experience because if you are reading this book it is certain that you will be doing a presentation at some point in your near future. Presentations are part of academic life, part of the interview process for jobs and certainly part of the tasks for those in a management role.

So let's begin with some basics, let us look at what Aristotle had to say about presentation skills.

Aristotle taught about the essentialness of three presentation components:

1 Ethos

The ability of the presenter to establish credibility with the audience.

2 Pathos

The ability of the presenter to display and arouse passion with the audience.

3 Logos

The ability of the presenter to exemplify the stature of an expert with the audience.

Looking at these very brief statements they raise some very interesting issues. Let's look at them one at a time. First is *ethos* and it is really quite simple: why should I waste my time listening to you if you don't appear to be a credible person? In other words if you don't seem secure in what you are saying why should I listen. Second, we must look at *pathos*, why would we want to display and arouse passion? Aren't we meant to be being professional here? Well the answer is really simple, if you don't care about the topic why should the audience? One of the hardest parts of presenting is keeping the audience interested. Third, we have *Logos*, once again it is about why I should spend my precious time listening to you. If you don't appear to be expert in the field that you are presenting on then exactly why should I listen to you? So Aristotle's essentials may be old but they are relevant today.

Here are my three favourite quotes that I like to relate to presenting:

> To be persuasive we must be believable; to be believable we must be credible; to be credible we must be truthful.
>
> (Edward R. Murrow)

> [I]n a society whose communication component is becoming more prominent day by day, both as a reality and as an issue, it is clear that language assumes a new importance.
>
> (Jean-Francois Lyotard)

> Before I speak, I have something important to say.
>
> (Groucho Marx)

Of these three I think Mr Marx's is the most important. While all three can be easily related to Aristotle's essentials, Groucho sums it up beautifully. If you don't consider what you have to say as important that will be clear to your audience and if it isn't important to you I'd rather catch up on my sleep.

The elements of presentation

There are essentially five elements to presentation:

- purpose
- audience
- planning
- design
- implementation.

Purpose

What do you want to achieve through your presentation? A simple but vital question that will shape your presentation. Do you want to inform? Do you want to persuade? Do you want to entertain? Do you need a synthesis of all three? What are the key points that you must get across and how will you ensure that they get across?

Audience

Who are they? What is their knowledge level on the subject area you will be presenting on – is it high or low? You don't want to talk down to an audience but neither do you want to talk over their heads.

How motivated is your audience? Do they want to be there or do they have to be there? This can make a big difference, how are you going to motivate an audience that don't want to be there?

What is your audience's fatigue level? How long can the presentation be without causing them to pass out from exhaustion or at least lose interest? When in the day will your presentation be? This can make a real difference. If it is at the end of the day perhaps all your audience really want to do is go home. That means you really have to develop pathos.

Planning

What is your subject? Where are you presenting? What is your audience expecting from the presentation? What is your time limit? These are all questions you need to address when planning your presentation.

Many presenters fail to consider two of these elements, place and time. The physical limitations of the space you have can greatly influence your presentation style but perhaps time is the more important of the two. I don't clearly know how many times I've had to truncate a presentation because those before me have gone over their time but it's a lot. The discipline of time management must absolutely be applied to presentations. You don't want to fail to use the opportunity the time-frame gives you but you also don't want to abuse it.

Good words to consider during planning are these:

- aim – what do you want to achieve;
- content – what needs to be in your presentation to achieve that;
- structure – what needs to be where to achieve your aims;
- signposts – how will you make sure people walk away with the key points;
- timing – how long do I have;
- outcome – what do I want to achieve.

Design

What do I need to include to ensure my presentation is effective? We hear a lot nowadays about 'Death by PowerPoint', as if PowerPoint itself is somehow responsible. It isn't, it is a tool like any other that can be used correctly or abused. Yes, I have had to sit through presentations where the presenter had 200 slides for an hour-long presentation or slides with so much on them that they are unreadable, but PowerPoint didn't do that, the user did that. Thinking about how many slides in your timeframe and what needs to be on them is essential.

Implementation

Time to actually give the presentation but how are you going to do it? What is your presentation style?

More on all of these later. Now it is time for a little exercise.

Exercise 1

Think about the worst university lecture or business presentation you have ever been at … Okay, thought about it, then answer these questions:

- What was wrong with it? Was it dull? Was that because you didn't like the topic or because the lecturer/presenter couldn't communicate it? (These are very different things. We don't always like all of everything but that doesn't make the lecture/presentation bad.)
- Was it because the lecturer/presenter didn't know their subject?
- Was it too long?
- Were the slides unclear?
- Was there no clear relation between what was on the slides and what was being said?
- How would you do it differently?

Creating the presentation

Let's look now at some general tips on creating a presentation.

It's called what?

Titles are very important things; they are there to inform and to appeal. The title may be the first, or only, thing your potential audience knows about your presentation. Imagine that you are at a conference and you are going to be presenting. You are one of many competing presentations. Now, unless you are the star of the field you are presenting in, why would I come to your presentation rather than someone else's? Often all I see are a list of titles.

Here is one of my all time favourites:

Sequence±structure±function studies of tRNA:m5C methyltransferase Trm4p and its relationship to DNA:m5C and RNA:m5U methyltransferases.

I'd go and see that. Well to be fair maybe I would if I was in the field but I have spoken to some who are in the field and they suggested that they might avoid that one. Your title should be appropriate and appealing to your audience. It needs to inform them of what the presentation is about without being too verbose.

In the beginning

'Begin at the beginning,' the King said, very gravely, 'and go on till you come to the end: then stop.'

(Lewis Carroll)

Sage advice from the Reverend Dodgson and so often ignored. Introduce yourself to your audience. Make it clear to your audience your aims and objectives. Let them know why they need to know what you are about to tell them.

Content

What you need to tell them. It is important that you think carefully about what you need here. You need to consider what your key points are. That is to say what points must your audience come away with even if they forget everything else, and how are you going to signpost these key points.

This is the end

If you want a happy ending, that depends, of course, on where you stop your story.

(Orson Welles)

- Know when to stop.
- Bring all your points together.
- Repeat them for the audience (repetition brings remembrance).
- Remind them what they mean.

It has been suggested that roughly 24 hours after hearing a presentation, the listener will forget at least 50 per cent of all the information presented. In 24 more hours, another 50 per cent will be forgotten. So if you want people to remember your key points then emphasize and repeat.

Handling the questions

At the end you will face the inevitable questions. Here are some suggestions of what you need to do:

- Try to anticipate and to encourage questions from your audience and PREPARE for them or possibly for the lack of them.
- Listen to the question; think about it; TAKE YOUR TIME and give a good response.
- Make notes if required.
- If you don't have an answer say so.
- Don't see questions as criticism (even if they clearly are) – respond positively.

Presentation nerves

These symptoms are the reasons Mr Seinfeld says death is number 2:

- nausea
- butterflies in the stomach
- dry mouth
- shaking
- sweaty palms
- palpitations
- talking too fast
- speaking too quietly
- stammering
- forgetting what you were going to say
- an overwhelming feeling of impending doom.

So how do you overcome them? Well, there is really only one answer and that is practice. No matter what anyone tells you, the only way to overcome these issues is to become confident in your skills and the only way to do that is to practise.

The technical stuff

Approximately 80 per cent of what we learn is learned visually and only 20 per cent is learned aurally. That makes visual tools such as PowerPoint very useful in presentations. However, don't overload your audience's brains. Keep the information on each visual aid to a minimum and remember your time limit. You must give your audience time to look at and absorb the information. If every slide is up for five seconds they aren't going to be able to do that.

Successful communication involves clarity not confusion. Be clear in your language as well as your visuals. They need to work in harmony.

Remember language is about how you say it as well as what you say. Remember pathos? You need to be invested in what you have to say. You also need to look at your body language. Are you stiff as a board or do you look too relaxed? You need to be comfortable but professional.

You need to practise. I suggest practising on your friends, you can always make new ones, or in front of a mirror. The best thing, if you have no friends or they are not available, is to video yourself and watch what you do. I am willing to bet you will be surprised by your body language and the 'umms'.

Practice means that when you actually have to deliver the presentation you are ready. It isn't new to you, though it will be to the audience, and you have done your timing so you know when you have to end.

In conclusion

- tell them what you are going to tell them;
- tell them it;
- tell them what you told them (repetition brings remembrance);
- answer the questions (it will be easy because you are prepared).

Exercise 2

The elevator pitch, think about your subject. How would you reduce what you have to say into a two-minute pitch?

This is a great way to bring out the key points. It really makes you think of what is essential and can help to reduce padding and superfluous slides. Give it a try.

Summary

For your final activity choose a subject from your course material and prepare a group or individual presentation of 20 minutes with 10 minutes for questions. Indicate to your audience who you want them to be (a group of directors; a group of first-line managers; a group of new recruits).

- Video your efforts and then play them back.
- Seek constructive advice on how you can improve your style and content.
- Practice makes perfect.
- Enjoy your audience.

Tutor guidance

Most students have a presentation component to their final work, sometimes addressed to clients with whom they worked outside the university. A final piece of work can be a good preparation for job interviews which frequently require prospective applicants to speak for a stated time and then answer questions.

It may be that a final presentation relating to a topic considered on the course could be presented to a group of managers (tutor and colleagues playing that role). The purpose of the presentation will be to give an overview of the topic with recommendations for good practice and future challenges at work, with questions then taken from the audience.

Preparation will be important to ensure that when presented with the challenge, presenters will be prepared not just to communicate well but also to answer questions at the end of the session and perhaps get involved in a discussion. This can usefully focus on:

- preparation: notes; equipment; PowerPoints;
- delivery: open gestures; eye contact; managing the audience;
- pace, pitch and audibility;
- position, movement and stance;
- question handling; answering difficult questions;
- handling concerns and objections;
- humour and handling the unexpected.

Question handling offers three possible strategies:

Honesty: if you don't know say so.

Deferral: 'at the moment it is impossible to answer that question. Once we have the information we will of course tell you.'

Avoidance: a good strategy for dealing with leading questions ('what I think doesn't matter. It's what the group thinks that counts').

The best example for those embarking on *graduate attributes* is the role model offered by the tutor or manager. Good performance is caught, not taught, and all of us value from the example of different ways of approaching the more challenging moments in both our business and our personal lives. We hope that this book will have encouraged those who use it to take the risk of exercising what they know in the interactive exercises that offer the opportunity to enhance knowledge and develop skill.

Skill without knowledge is vacuous. Knowledge without skill is powerless. A combination of the two may well combine the benefits of both and encourage managers to continue in their search for best practice in managing their people at work more effectively.

INDEX

absences 385; as employee action 318; health approaches 353; long-term sickness 352; performance measurement 265; use of sick days 351–3
accidents 18; standards 227
Action Learning 2
Advisory, Conciliation and Arbitration Service (ACAS) 319–20
age: changing social trends 78; legal regulations for work 324–5
The Age of Unreason (Handy) 18, 140, 141
air traffic controllers' strike 149–50
airlines, outsourcing jobs 142–3
Alvesson, M. 19
appraisals *see* performance appraisals
The Apprentice: Karren Brady and 79
Arab Spring 68
Argyris, Chris 106; Lewin and 2, 110; loop learning 13, 212
Aristotle 390–1
armed forces 10
assertiveness: concept and value of 124–5; development of 127–31; and passive or aggressive style 125–7; tutor guidance 131–3
authority 71, 72
autonomy 284; within groups 84, 316; Peters and Waterman 4
Avery (W & T) 85

Batten, D. 106–7, 110; exploration and planning 112; partnership and 112; phases of change 212

Beckhard, R. 138–9
Belbin, Meredith 240; roles in teamwork 223; team building for change 110
best fit approach 43–8
best practice, model of 48–50
Birmingham City Football Club 80–1, 82
Blyton, P.: *Reassessing Human Resource Management* (with Turnbull) 6
body language 128
Bourneville 1
Bowden, J. 24
Brady, Karren 79–83
brainstorming 175–6
Branson, Richard 34, 37
Brewster, C. 375
Britain: Civil Service assessments 98; labour market 381; poor training investment 170
British Airways: changing mindsets 8; pensions 315; strike against 318
British Broadcasting Corporation (BBC) 48
British Foundry Association 170
British Medical Association 70
British Motor Corporation 16, 351
British Rail 55, 276, 315
British Standard 5750 148
Bullock, R. J. 106–7, 110; exploration and planning 112; partnership and 112; phases of change 212
bullying 326; graduate exercise 362–3
bureaucracy: changing customer needs 85; machine/Fordism 74; professional 74; Weber on characteristics of 71

business process re-engineering 109,
149–51
businesses *see* organizations

call centres: outsourced 387; surveillance
150–1
careers: appraisals and progress 259;
assertiveness 130; commitment to 7,
118, 142; providing opportunities 219–
20; secure employment 45; succession
planning 249
Carroll, Lewis 394
Champy, J. 43, 150
change: challenge to beliefs/values
103; commitment and 140–4;
continuity and 96; culture and 38,
137–9; delayering 15–16; employee
experience of 359–60; evaluation
process of 115; force-field model
105–6; graduate attributes 156–66;
HR and 11, 57; identifying need
113; impacts on organizations 100–5;
insecurity about competency 103–4;
intervention techniques 113; for leaner
production 86–7; management support
113; market-led 173–4; Nadler's action
steps 101; organizational development
107–15; organizational restructuring
99; pay and rewards for 285–6;
planning 114; process re-engineering
149–51; processual 51; psychological
approach 105–7; resistance to 114;
routines and 102–3; symbolic 15;
training for 109–12; unbundling 16
Chartered Institute of Personnel and
Development: total reward 280; work
and approach of 321–2
citizenship: graduate attributes 24–5, 30
Civil Servants: outsourced jobs 314, 357;
pay structures 286–7
coercion, organizational contexts of 67–9
cognitive calculus 274
commitment: career 142; in change 285;
consultants/subcontractors 18, 356; HR
role 59; HRM theory and 140–1; job
141; levels of 7; organizational 21–2,
142–4; work 141–2
communication: change and 106–7,
156; cultural differences 382;
employee relations 354; grievance
and 350–1; leadership qualities 136;
matrix organization 73; Michigan
model 5; negotiation exercise 301–8;
performance appraisals 247; team
members and 231, 235–6

competencies 170–1; change and 139;
management 206; monitoring 56;
rewarding acquisition of 294; selection
practices 48; skills training 204–6
competition 277–8; competitive advantage
models 57–8; diverse workforce and
321; implications for organizations
83–4; pay and rewards 284
conflict: bullying and harassment 325–6;
company policies 326–7; discrimination
322–5; within organizations 318–19;
routes to resolution 319–20; in
work climate 326 *see also* discipline;
negotiation
Confucian dynamism 151, 372
Constable Report 332
consultants: commitment 356; HR
involvement with 87–8; strategic
integration of 52–3; subcontracted
143; unions and 313; work for HR
departments 18–19
continuing professional development
(CPD) 46, 53; appraisals and
264; change and 169; knowledge
workers 221; learning contracts
332; loop learning 214; motivation
250; personal development plan
220; professional performance 217;
requirements 88; rewards 281 *see also*
learning
contracts: discipline 340; failures of 18;
zero hours 360, 388
control: change and 100; pay and rewards
284
convergence 368–9
cost: pay 8; quality and 9; reducing 146;
resource-based model 50
critical thinking: analysis 26–7;
argumentation 27–9; general guidelines
25–6; graduate attributes and 24–5
Crowe, Bob 312
culture: change and 137–9; concept
in organizations 134–6; divergence
369–72; masculinity/femininity 372–3;
nations/societies 368, 371–5; normative
influences 374; pay and rewards 275;
Schein's layers of 135, 138; stereotypes
151–2
customer relations: defining needs of 145,
146–7; delighting the customer 119;
employees conduct and 98; Peters and
Waterman 3–4

De Wit, B. 32
Deal, T. 38, 53, 104, 175, 275

decision making: changing traditional bureaucracy 14–15; executives 14; HR managers and 186–7; for leaner production 86; objective assessment for 98; participation 118; Peters and Waterman 3

Defeat into Victory (Slim) 50

delayering 14, 15–16

delegation 72

Department of Agriculture: Learning and Development exercise 89–94

development: employee relations 354; Michigan model 4, 5

dignity and respect 327–8

DiMaggio, P. J. 67, 370, 373–4

disability 324, 325, 326

Disability Discrimination Act 324, 325

discipline: appraisals and 252; employees' explanations 345–6; equal treatment and 347; evidence 348–9; grievance 349–51; gross misconduct 347–8; the interview 345–6; objections and loopholes 346–7; observing poor performance 343–4; offences away from work 348; poor performance 343–4; procedures 340–1; representation 349; responsibility 341; time scales 347

discrimination 18; definitions of 322–3; graduate exercise 363–4; legislation concerning 323–5; positive 323

diversity: concept of 321; graduate exercise 334–8

Doyle, M. 149

Drucker, Peter 161; organizational objectives 6–7, 39, 224–5; pyramid of pay 15; on training 10, 200, 388

Dyson 316

economics: leaner production 86; political factors and 68–9

Edinburgh trams 52

education: for changing occupations 76; global divergence 370

effectiveness: evaluation for 225; training 208

efficiency, marketing 34–5

Egan, John 16; management of Jaguar 42; quality circles 100, 137; unitarist approach 315

employee relations: concept and practice of 354–7; trends and challenges 360; unitarist management 309 *see also* trade unions

employee resourcing *see* recruitment

employees: appraisals 220–1, 259–61; assertiveness in workplace 130–1; attitude 246–7; autonomy 222–3, 284; change and 359–60; changing behaviours and attitudes 42; collective bargaining 288–9, 313–14; commitment 7; consistency in treatment 339–40; consultancy workers 87–8; core 17; dignity and respect 327–8; empowerment 99–100; evaluations 76; exit interviews 115, 184–6; expanding responsibilities 168–9; expectations and aspirations 247–8, 248–9; functional 12–13; graduates 342; high turnover 319; historical perspectives 1–3; HR as advocate for 57, 216; insecurity about competency 103–4; job and work rotation 118–19, 179; job in/security 45, 49, 104, 219; manpower inventories 170–1, 183; normative power of professionals 120–1; organizational threats to 84; peers and 38, 104, 120; psychological contract 53–4; quality and 99, 317; responsibilities 341; revenge of 341–2; rights of 282; rivalry 195; self-perception of performance 245; Shamrock organization 87–8; sharing the success 279; skilled and semi-skilled 360, 374; status differentials 47; subcontracted 17, 53, 87, 142–3, 167; supervision of 215–16; surveillance 150–1; survival rates 184; in takeovers 99; traditional pyramid and 12–14; transactional/relational elements 53; trust 101; work studies of 182–3; zero hours contract 360, 388 *see also* pay and rewards; recruitment; teamwork

employment: age and 78; shifting occupations 76–7, 78; skills and migration 79; social and demographic trends 77–8

Employment Appeal Tribunals 216, 320

Employment Equality Acts 315, 324

employment law 216; standards 227

empowerment: appraisals and motivation 250

The Empty Raincoat (Handy) 18, 140

entrepreneurship 4

environmental issues: people and technical systems 84; water management 66–7

Equal Pay Act 325

equality: complicated aspects of 320–1; legislation concerning 323–5 *see also* discrimination; diversity

error rate, standards and 227

executives: asking and listening 84–5; authority 71, 72; traditional pyramid top 14
experience: competency factor 44–5
expertise: power of 121; professionals and change 139

face-to-face contact 22
family life and work: Karren Brady and 82–3
feedback and evaluation: organizational learning and 37
Fineman, S. 152
Fleet Street journalists 312
Fletcher, Carl 49, 220–1; appraisals 245, 247, 252; describing jobs 295
flexibility: change and 115–16; consultants and 18; cost 144; four factors of 8; functional 144, 204, 356; handling challenges 84; HR role in 59; job/work rotation 316; matrix organization 73–5; number 144; organizational commitment and 117; pay and rewards 276, 278; recruitment 171; team work 47; time 144
Ford, Henry 3
Fordism 74

Gaebler, T. 357
GEC 35
gender issues: cultural differences 151; legislation and work 325; national cultures and 372; Sex Discrimination Act 323
Georgiades, N. 8
globalization: convergence 368–9; divergence 369–72; technology of 215 see also multinational companies (MNCs)
goals/objectives: communicating to employees 224; formal reviews of progress 225; management by 39–41, 261–2; performance targets 224–5; standards and 226
Gold, David 81
graduate attributes: academic excellence 24–5; active citizenship 24–5; appraisal exercise 267–72; assertiveness 124–33; bullying exercise 362–3; change 156–66; communication 29, 61–3; critical thinking 24–9, 61–3; DALD exercise 89–94; development of 24; diversity/creativity exercise 334–8; ethical problems 192–3; identifying problems 61–3; learning and personal

development 24–5; negotiation exercise 298–308; presentation skills 390–7; protégés 194–5; rivalry 195; skills monopolies 193–4; teamworking exercise 229–41; tutor guidance 30
grievances 18, 319, 349–51, 385
Grunwick 313
Guest, David: commitment 140; conflict in organizations 318; on contracts 340; flexibility 144; HRM outcomes 21, 356; interventions 368; negative outcomes 110; organizational outcomes 9, 41–2, 115; overview of HRM 354; psychological contract 53; quality 53; recruitment 171; strategic integration 31–2, 97; testing HRM 6; training/learning 209, 214

Hamel, G. 149–50
Handy, Charles 100; *The Age of Unreason* 18, 140, 141; doing business with laughter 22; *The Empty Raincoat* 18, 140; knowledge workers 205, 342; learning success 329; organizational spider's web 269–70; Shamrock organization 16–18, 355; *Understanding Organizations* 16 see also Shamrock organizations
Handy Report (1987): result of 332; on training 266
harassment 325–6
Harvard model 5, 11
Hassard, J. 138–9
Hawthorne experiments 2
health care 78–9
health and safety 18; costs and 285; organizational coercion 67; stakeholders 85; standards 227
Health and Safety and Work Act 3
higher education sector 274, 278
Hofstede, Geert: cultural stereotypes 151–2; managing change 109; national cultures 368, 372–5; uncertainty avoidance 382
Honda 47
Horlick, Nicola 320
Human Relations movement 2
Human Resource Development 41
Human Resource Management (HRM): assessing outcomes 6–10; as business partners 55–7; business strategy 384–5; CIPD approach 321–2; compared to Personnel 10–11; consistency in treatment 339–40; consultants 18–19; delivery of theory 21–2;

effectiveness 55–6; employee relations 354–7; executive positions for 186, 216; fairness and respect 363–4; flexibility of organizations 122; four key roles as partners 57; future prospects 21–2, 388–9; Guest's model of 31–2; hard and soft 9–10; hard and soft planning 43, 171–2; historical background to 1–3; international perspective 366; involving approach 187; job specializations 97–8; Karren Brady case study 79–83; for leaner production 86; management *versus* managing people 359–60; objectives/goals/key tasks 385; origins of 3–5; outsourcing 387–8; policies and outcomes 6–7; presentations at AGMs 386–7 *see also* recruitment

Human Resource Management, International (IHRM): centralized data 379–80; consistent strategy 380; different labour markets 381; good practices 380–1; multinational companies and 375–7; national legal requirements 381; possible cultural misunderstandings 382–4; support from home 378–9; worker expectancies and values 382

IBM 151–2, 373

immigration: availability for recruitment 173; employment skills 79; visa restrictions 286

In Search of Excellence (Peters and Waterman) 3–4, 98, 119

individualism/collectivism 151, 372

industrial relations: global divergence 370–1 *see also* trade unions

industrial sabotage 318

information technology: global businesses 215; telecommuting jobs 78

innovation and creativity 385; mimetic factors 69; performance measurement 265

Institute of Personnel Management 2

International Business School 87

International Standards Organization (ISO) 9000 146, 148

Investors in People 206, 281

Jaguar Motors 16; quality circles 42, 100, 137; unitarist approach 315

Japan: car industry structure 14, 15; labour market 381; multinational companies and 375–7 *see also* Nissan; Toyota

jobs *see* careers; employees; work

Jobs, Steve 9, 34

John Lewis Partnership 218; employee rewards 293; pay and rewards 279; team efforts 47

Johnson, Boris 312

Jones, L. 152

kaizen *see under* knowledge

Kennedy, A. 38, 53, 104; on culture 175, 275

knowledge: competency factor 44–5; kaizen/sharing 46, 49, 55; tacit 49

knowledge workers 19–20; continuing professional development 221; controlling knowledge of 358–9; experience of 69; growth of jobs 342; tacit knowledge 20–1; transfer of knowledge 214; unions and 313; the virtual organization 21

Kotter, J. P. 108

labour *see* work

Lansley, Andrew 70

law and conventions: coercive isomorphism 370; coercive power of 120, 121

leadership: HR theory and practice 56; prophetic 67; quality of 135–6 *see also* executives

learning: action learning 331; active fostering 46; contracts 332; fostering 49; graduate attributes 24–5, 30; kaizen 331, 358; loop 12–14; market strategies 37–8; objectives 207–8; organizational 49, 214–15; self-development 331–2 *see also* Learning Organizations; training

Learning Organizations 211–12, 328–30, 358; managing change 109

legal services, outsourced 387

Legge, K. 137

Lewin, Kurt 2; force-field analysis 105–6, 108; organizational intervention 107; T-groups 359

Lilirank, P. 147

line managers: personnel responsibilities 11; traditional organization pyramid 13

LinkedIn 287

London Heathrow Airport 98

London Olympics 289, 357

London Underground: driverless trains 312

loop learning 12–14; mnemonics 213; single and double loop 212–13; triple loop 213–14

loyalty: appraisals and 258; psychological contract 22

Lyotard, Jean-Francois 391

McGregor, Douglas 2, 58, 106, 110
McNulty Report 38
McPherson Report 323
McSweeney, B. 151–2
management by objectives 39–41, 261–2
managers: 'back to the floor' 217; business processes re-engineering 149–51; command and control 117; cultural styles and expectations 382–3; dealing with conflict 318–19, 327; expectations/ disappointment 378; facilitational 317; good leaders 135–6; high performance 316–18; incivility 363; international 377; Michigan model 4; panopticon strategies 116; pragmatism over planning 174–5; span of control 72; supervising performance 215–16; traditional pyramid of 13–14; unitarist approach 315; walking about 328
Managing Today and Tomorrow (Stewart) 168, 169
manpower inventories 170–1, 183
market strategies: competition 36, 41; effectiveness and efficiency 34–5; fit in environment 33–4; fit of organization 33–4; learning 37–8; management by objectives 39; market- vs resource-led 32; organizational culture 38; power groups 38; quality initiatives and 146–7; strategic integration 31; supplier/ customer power 36; traditional planning steps 35–6; vision 36–7
Marks & Spencer: 'employer of choice' 57; management/staff ratio 72; personnel/ HRM 10; supervisors 13
Marx, Groucho 391
Maslow, A. 373
mentoring/shadowing 250
Mercedes 57
Meyer, R. 32
Michigan model 4–5
motivation: appraisals and 250; pay and rewards 284–5
Mueller, F. 111
multinational companies (MNCs): advantages of IHRM 379–81; HRM and 375–7; international managers 377
Murdoch, Rupert 312
Murrow, Edward R. 391
Myers-Brigg Type Indicator (MBTI) 236

Nadler, D. A. 100–1, 103
National Health Service (NHS): forecasting availability of people 173; NHS Direct worker presence 21; performance and

targets 294; profit and 288
National Union of Rail, Maritime and Transport workers 312
National Vocational Qualifications (NVQs) 206
negotiation: change and 107; conflict resolution 319–20; graduate exercise 298–308
neo-institutionalism 67–70
Nissan cars 8, 137

Oakland, J. 112, 145
objectives *see* goals/objectives; management by objectives
oil industry: change exercise 156–7; scenario planning 181
O'Leary, Michael 17, 181
organizational development (OD): application of 113–15; interventionist strategy 107–12; time and motion studies 182
organizations: achievements of individuals 248; board control and 72; centralization/decentralization 72; changing contexts 70–1; coercive factors 67–9; commitment of 21–2, 174; commitment to 7, 142–4; competition 83–4; concept of 95–7; conflict within 318–19; culture of 64–7, 384; delayering 14, 15–16; design of 97–8; discipline and grievances 339–41; employee share of success 279; financial systems 371; flexibility and matrix 73–5; forecasting budget 182; global convergence 369; high expectations for employees 169; high performance management 316–18; historical principles of 71–2; HR managers and decision making 186–7; in-house professionals 117; industrial policies 370; interpersonal life in 84; job security 219; job specializations 97–8; Karren Brady case study 79–83; learning 214–15, 358; mimetic factors 69; neo-institutionalism 67–70; normative pressures 69–70; objectives 39–41; outside influences 83; pay and rewards objectives 284–6; performance management systems 224–6; PESTLE model 65; power and control 75–6; quality initiatives 145–9; restructuring initiatives 99; rewards and changes 292; secure employment 49; shifting policy and strategy 174; strategic

integration 6–7; structure of 12–16, 40, 70–1, 97; tall/flat 75, 116; trends 84–5; unbundling 14, 16; using objective assessment 98; virtual sphere 21–2, 388 *see also* Shamrock organizations
Osborne, D. 357

partnership 112
pay and rewards: aspects of 273–5; banding schemes 289–90; benefits 290; cafeteria/flexible benefits 296; changing roles with 276; cognitive calculus 274; competitive aspects 277–8; confidentiality 277; cultural differences 383–4; employee objectives 281–3; employee relations 354; employer objectives 284–6; equity and rights 278, 281–3, 291; evaluations and regular reviews 291–4; external markets and 286–7; flexibility 8, 278–9; internal markets and 288–9; managing change with 285–6; Michigan model 4, 5; outsourced pensions 387; overtime 291; packages 290–1; part of Personnel work 3; performance related 46–7, 49, 218, 277–8, 293–6; as power 121; profit sharing 217–18; pyramid of 15; recognition 283; reviewing outcomes 225; satisfaction with 221; strategic approaches 275–6; symbolic 280; systems of 276–9
peer groups 38, 104, 120
pensions: changing social trends 78; NHS doctors 70; outsourcing 387; public sector 315
People Management magazine 327
performance appraisals 220–1; 360-degree approach 244–5, 263, 270–1; aims of 247–9, 258; attitude 246–7; avoidance strategies 251–2; CPD and 264; as crossroads 254–5; effective features 256–8; employee concerns 259–61; employee relations 354; evaluation *versus* validation 263; evidence for 244; graduate exercise in 267–72; influencing motivation 250; the interview 255–6; involving staff in 252–3; measurement of performance 264–6; Michigan model 4, 5; pay and rewards 291–6; productivity and 245; self-appraisal 244, 245, 252–3, 262; subjectivity and 243–4; succession planning 249; of teams 262–3; value of 242–3

performance management: features of 224–6; by objectives 261–2; poor 343–9
personal development: analysis in appraisal 248–9; loop learning 214; rewards and 281
personnel departments 1
Peschisolido, Paul 82
PESTLE model 65
Peters, Tom: *In Search of Excellence* (with Waterman) 3–4, 98, 119
Pfeffer, J. 44–5, 48
Piderit, S.K. 103
pilots 45, 103
planning 174–6
police: bureaucracy and change 85; discrimination 323; pay structures 286–7; Sheehy Report on structure 15
political organizations 67–9
Porter, Lyman 356
Porter, R. 141
Powell, W. W. 67, 370, 373–4
power: change and 100; cultural differences 151; dealing with power groups 38; organizations 75–6; types of 120–1
Prahaled, C. K. 149–50
presentation skills 390–7
Prichard, W. 138–9
Private Eye 66
private sector, unions and 311
problem solving: learning 37; Peters and Waterman 3
Process Consultation (Schein) 109
Procter, S.J. 111
production, lean 86–7
productivity: factors in appraisal 245; Peters and Waterman 4; quality and 8, 146
profit sharing 217–18
project management 116–17
public sector: pay structures 286–7; privatizing services 357–8; unions and 311–12, 314–15

quality: concept of 144–5; consultants and 18; employee focus on 317; factors of 8–9; HR role in 59; organizational standards 56; recruitment 171; resource-based model 50; senior managers and 112; staff responsibility and 99 *see also* Total Quality Management (TQM)
quality circles 8, 42; changing organizational structure 14; kaizen 45; learning and 46, 55; setting up initiatives 316

Race Relations Act 324, 325
railways 38
rarity 51
Reassessing Human Resource Management
    (Blyton and Turnbull) 6
recruitment: aptitudes 188; assessing
    professionals 177–8; best fit approach
    219; best performance approach 219;
    candidate in working conditions
    189; core and consultant workers
    179; within culture 190–1; employee
    relations 354; existing resources 179;
    experience requirements 190; future
    needs 172, 173, 179, 183; handovers
    196–8; HR at decision making level
    186–7; in-house 169–70, 176–7; labour
    turnover index 183; market-led trends
    173–4; Michigan model 4; outside
    resources 180; outsourcing functions of
    387; scenario planning 180–1; supply
    and demand 173; testing 188–9; trends
    analysis 182; uncertain employment
    167–8
resources: people 56; resource-based model
    50–1
retirement: legal matters 325 *see also*
    pensions
Revans, Reg 2, 331
rewards *see* pay and rewards
rights traded for shares 363
risk assessment 67
The Road to Nissan (Wickens) 43–4, 100
Robertson, M. 17
role models 322
Romme, A. Georges 14
Rousseau, Denise M. 53, 104, 341
Rowntree Foundation 1
Ryanair 181

Schein, Edgar H. 96, 106; basic
    assumptions 370; layers of culture
    135, 138; Lewin and 2, 110; *Process
    Consultation* 109, 110
Schon, D.: loop learning 12, 212
Scottish Police College 212
Seinfeld, Jerry 390
Senge, Peter 37; learning organization 46,
    211–12
service sector 374
Sex Discrimination Act 323, 325
sexual harassment 151
sexual orientation 324
Shamrock organizations: change and
    109, 342; concept of 16–18, 95; core
    workers and commitment 140–1;

decentralization 116; expertise 51;
    flexibility 144; focus of HR 87–8;
    HRM policies 355; online contact
    21; pay and rewards 288; secure
    employment 45; subcontract workers 53
Sharifi, S. 138–9
Sheehy Report 15, 85
skills: competency factor 44–5; expertise
    management 120
Slim, General Bill: *Defeat into Victory* 50
Smith, Adam 71–2
social contexts: trends for employment 77–8
social justice, cultural notions of 383–4
social learning theory 322
staffing: flexibility and 8; line managers and
    11; minimal 4; online contact 21–2;
    span of management control 72
stakeholders: defining 85; Harvard model
    5; outside the organization 11; power in
    organizations 76
standards: definition and wording of
    226–7; discipline and 340, 344; poor
    performance and 343; *versus* target 258
status: bureaucracy 71; differentials among
    workers 47; hierarchies 116
Stewart, Rosemary 66; job expansion
    222–3, 247, 284, 291–2; *Managing
    Today and Tomorrow* 168, 169
Storey, J. 16
strategic integration 6–7; achievements
    of individuals 248; best fit approach
    43–8; the big picture 40; consultants
    and 18–19; HR and 10, 42, 57, 59,
    216; human resource development 41;
    learning and 330; objectives, goals and
    tasks 40–2; organizational design 97;
    pay and rewards 275, 284; planning
    and 175–6; recruitment and 171, 174;
    relocation 42; technology and 74
Stredwick, J. 277
Sugar, Lord Alan 79
Sullivan, David 80–1
supervisors: employee relations 354;
    Michigan model 4; traditional
    organization pyramid 13–14; training
    and 13
Swan, J. 17
SWOT analysis 35, 66

T-/sensitivity groups 105–6, 110, 359
tasks in management by objectives 39–41
tax systems 371
Taylor, F. W. 2
teachers 315
teamwork: across boundaries 85–6;

benefits of 230–1; best fit approach 47–8; creation of team 236–9; DALD exercise 89–94; definitions of 229–30; effectiveness 232–6; empowerment initiatives 118–20; formal initiatives 316; graduate exercise 229–41; HR theory and practice 56; participation in decisions 118; recruitment candidates and 189; roles within 223–4; status differentials 47; supporting change 110–11; types of teams 231–2; unitarist model and 100

technology: adapting to change 103; feedback on problems 76; flexible working 47; global convergence 369; matrix organization 73; for presentations 395–6; requires constant change 168–9; technical systems 84; types of 74–5 *see also* information technology

telecommuting 216; pay and rewards 280; trend towards 388

testing: A & B types 246; affective 189; cognitive 188–9; psychometric 236; psychomotor 48, 188

Thatcher, Margaret 311

time: flexibility and 8; quality 9; resource-based model 50

Torrington, D. 59

Total Quality Management (TQM) 8; best practices 49, 50; empowerment and teamworking 100; job rotation 118; kaizen 331, 358; quality initiatives 14, 145–9; resource-based model 50–1; Wilson's model 145, 146

Toyota cars 145

trade unions: air traffic controllers 149–50; collective bargaining 288–9, 310, 313–14; dealing with power groups 38; effect of automation 312; global divergence 370–1; membership trends 311–12, 314; negotiation/agreed procedures 319; Nissan and 100; protecting rights 282; relations with management 309–10; representing collective interest 310; strike restrictions 313; unitarist approach 315

training 211–14; 'Acommodare' exercise 61–3; appraisals and 248–9; attitude and others 207; for change 109–12, 148; development activities 221; discipline and 347; Drucker on 10, 200, 388; evaluation 209–11, 386; experience of 201–2; fostering development 49; global divergence 370; hard HRM 9; induction 4, 354; insecurity about 103–4; as investment 170, 200–1;

Investors in People 206; loop learning 212–14; mentoring/shadowing/coaching 250; methods and validation 208–9; organizational needs 203–4; outsourced 387; professional performance 217; reviewing outcomes 225; skills 204–6; supervisors 13; trainee existing skills 204; trainer's skills 202–3; validation 386 *see also* learning

Transfer of Undertakings Regulation Act (TUPE) 287, 314

trust: employers–employees 101; psychological contract 22

Turnbull, P.: *Reassessing Human Resource Management* (with Blyton) 6

unbundling 14, 16

Understanding Organizations (Handy) 18

Union Carbide, Bophal disaster 85

unions *see* trade unions

United States: labour market 381; multinational companies and 375–7

USDAW 314

values and beliefs: challenge of change and 103; leadership and 136; Peters and Waterman 4; resource-based model 51

Van Witteloostuijn, Arjen 14

Virgin Trains 34; driver pay 314; industry strikes and 38; vision 37

Wallace, Margaret 350–1

Waterman Jr, Robert H.: *In Search of Excellence* (with Peters) 3–4, 98, 119

Weber, Max 71

Weick, Karl 30

Weinstock, Lord 35, 85

Welles, Orson 394

Welsh, Jack 52

West Ham Football Club 79, 81–3

Wickens, P.: *The Road to Nissan* 43–4, 100

Wilson, D. C. 145, 146

Witteloostuijn, Arjen van 14

work: changing context of 342–3; division of labour 71–2; function flexibility 8; redesigning 280; rotation 219–20, 280, 283, 316; semi-skilled jobs and automation 312

work–life balance 9–10, 221–2

workers *see* employees

working hours: decoupled from operating hours 388

working to rule 318

zero hours contract 360, 388